Generational Wealth Management:

A Guide for Fostering
Global Family Wealth

Generational Wealth Management:
A Guide for Fostering
Global Family Wealth

Lisa Gray

To Scott —
who deals with the perspectives,
cultured and group biases &
juniors — both in practice and
the prose.
challenging amities —

[signature]

E
U
R
O
M
O
N
E
Y

B
O
O
K
S

Published by
Euromoney Institutional Investor PLC
Nestor House, Playhouse Yard
London EC4V 5EX
United Kingdom

Tel: +44 (0)20 7779 8999 or USA 11 800 437 9997
Fax: +44 (0)20 7779 8300
www.euromoneybooks.com
E-mail: hotline@euromoneyplc.com

ISBN 978 1 84374 280 7

Typeset by Phoenix Photosetting, Chatham, Kent

To my Nomad children, Adrianne and Tripp, and my Artist grandchildren,
Davis and the little girl who is on her way to us

Other books by Lisa Gray

The New Family Office: Innovative Strategies for Consulting to the Affluent
also published by Euromoney Books, 2004

Contents

Contents

Part 3 – B. Prioritisation, risk level assessment, and investment policy

Part 4 – Ongoing monitoring and review

Contents

Prologue

As recently as 25 years ago, wealth management did not really exist. Several professions shared the responsibility of advising the wealthy. They did so with respect to one or another facet of the challenge which wealthy families faced, but hardly ever wondered as to whether there might be interactions between the solution they offered and those which might be suggested by other professionals. Further, many of these specialists were still quite early in the journey which eventually took them to discovering that certain aspects of their own trade needed to be enhanced, either because they had failed to recognise the essential difference between the wealthy and the rest – be they individuals or institutions – or because the results of the application of their expertise were significantly affected by what others might be doing alongside them with the families they served.

These discoveries were at the forefront of two 'evolutionary revolutions' which allowed the wealth management industry to start to address the needs of the wealthy – needs, which in all honesty, the wealthy themselves often had some difficulty articulating in a rapidly changing world. Yet, as the needs of the wealthy evolved along with changes in the world in which they lived, so evolved the responsibilities of their advisors. It might thus make sense to chronicle the developments which this industry experienced in the last 10 to 20 years or so, in order better to position the contribution of this book within that evolutionary process. In so doing, we hope to clarify the book's usefulness to the reader – whether a family of wealth or a professional who serves them.

To begin our brief examination of these industry revolutions, consider the 'simple' world of asset managers 20 years ago or so. They thought their responsibility simply involved earning the highest possible investment return subject to some risk tolerance. They were avid students of Modern Portfolio Theory (MPT); many really believed that optimality, as defined within the MPT context was some sort of holy grail. How many of them understood that it was not what their clients got that mattered, but rather what they got to keep? For the large bulk of the asset management profession, taxes were indeed something that could not readily be handled through the processes they used. A vocal majority often professed that one should not let the tax tail wag the investment dog; a quiet minority might occasionally focus on taxes, but usually only did so late in the year, when it might make sense to realise a few hitherto unrealised capital losses. Whether the lack of focus was a conceptual oversight or an understandable and laudable focus on delivering somewhat uniform performance to all the clients of the same firm, the story really does not tell! Yet, whether averse to tax-efficiency or simply too narrowly focused on it, our asset managers both really missed the point that eventually became accepted wisdom: taxes matter and every day is tax day! An unrealised capital loss has an option value that must be incorporated into the management of any portfolio.

A single-minded focus on investment returns within some 'reasonable' risk tolerance was, however, not the only oversight! Consider the various estate managers who did not necessarily appreciate that there also was some interaction between the potentially numerous structures they created to facilitate wealth transfers and the management of the assets which resided in these structures. Just as tax-efficiency involves recognising the interaction between tax and asset management, 'estate tax or trust efficiency' involves the recognition that there are important interactions that one ignores only at one's client's peril. The notion originally conceived by Jay Hughes that one should work to minimise the share of the pie of the tax authorities who, though not always visible, were always present around the family conference table was not routinely accepted, at least early on. Intergenerational loans were one of the early potential solutions – effectively recognising some form of 'generational location'; but Bill Reichenstein and William Jennings had not yet demonstrated the importance of thinking of asset location, although John Shoven and Clemens Sialm had conducted pioneering work on this issue.

We can take this much further. Consider the crucial challenge associated with the formulation of an acceptable investment policy. In some ways, the industry may have been lulled into some form of complacency by the fact that wealth, back then, was still principally inherited. Thus, according to the proverbial – but hardly generous, or even nice – label of 'trust babies', many wealth holders were either schooled in the need to think in a long-term manner, or, admittedly more frequently, really saw their fates solely the responsibility of the managers of their trusts. Yet, as more and more assets accumulated in personal accounts, which the beneficiaries duly controlled in some manner or form, it was becoming painfully obvious that the traditional efficient frontier construct which applied to institutional clients was not really appropriate in the private wealth environment. A technician might point to the fact that it is easier to grasp the notion of a liability stream meant to be defeased by the assets in the portfolio when these assets were intended to benefit pensioners, charitable organisations or endowment pools.

Behavioural finance had been born from the work of Amos Tversky and Daniel Kahneman – the latter earning a Nobel Economics Prize for their joint work on prospect theory and soon captured the imagination of a few finance or investment professionals. Traditional finance might be great at prescribing how individuals *should* behave, but this did not seem to fit too well with anyone's practical experience with the wealthy; by contrast, behavioural finance was quite good – and believable – at describing how individuals *actually behaved*. Thus, a body of academic and practical literature began to appear, with Meir Statman deserving a particular mention for having thought of and proposed the notion of a 'behavioural portfolio'. His contribution involved recognising and was based on the novel notion that individuals not only had multiple goals, but also that each goal had its own risk profile. This gave birth to the concept of goal-based asset allocation, which was recently substantially 'boosted' by the publication of an article which effectively concludes that a group of optimal sub-portfolios can be viewed as optimal as well; the authors of this article are notable in that they include Meir Statman, whom we have already met, and Harry Markowitz, who, with Bill Sharpe, were the fathers of Modern Portfolio Theory and together also earned a Nobel Economic Prize for their findings on this topic.

The first really conclusive evidence of some revolution is the notion that a term which no one really used 20 years ago is now a part of common speech: integrated wealth management was born out of the recognition that there are multiple dimensions to the notion of managing wealth and that these needed to be coordinated in order for any solution to be really optimal for each family.

Arguably, we are now at the dawn of a second industry revolution, one to which Lisa Gray, with this book, is greatly contributing. To a large extent, it is fair to posit that the first revolution involved two facets. The first was the recognition by most of the specialists that serve wealthy families that they needed to sharpen their own skills. This was a direct outcome of the notion that wealthy individuals have special traits and special needs; serving them effectively could only be done if one developed customised tools which were potentially very different from those used previously: these had typically been mere variations on themes which had been sourced from a different sub-segment of the industry and successfully applied to different clienteles. The second was the recognition that no area of expertise could pretend it was operating in a vacuum. Each and every discipline had some connection to many of the others; failing to identify this connection had the potential to lead to a disastrous solution, as, in an extreme case, the two specialists might be working at cross purposes.

This second revolution is both much more subtle, but also potentially much more complex. It involves the integration of a wide variety of soft issues into a framework which hitherto only paid lip service to them. What makes it subtle is that many observers believe, wrongly as this humble commentator thinks, that 'we have made all the progress that we need to make'. They believe that all the soft issues that matter are already in the picture; going further involves nit-picking! Admittedly, several of the issues which Lisa and others tackle can be viewed as somewhat esoteric. Yet, I can testify to the fact that they are crucially important, as I will mention a little later. What makes it more complex is the fact that it deals with issues for which most people are not ready.

Many specialties are, almost by definition, caught in the bind of not having a natural solution to the problem. Consider a multi-national family; consider the legal profession, focused here on either income or estate tax issues. How does one operate across legal systems which might not only not be compatible, but in fact be actually incompatible? The likely solution probably involves looking at third-party jurisdictions which are compatible with both original locations. Yet, this will need to be studied in much more depth.

Other categories of soft issues bring us more directly into the work of Lisa and thus into this book.

Lisa Gray is one of the distinguished followers of Jay Hughes and has taken pains over the last several years to add to the integrated wealth management body of knowledge. Her original contribution was focused on the formulation of models geared to integrate family dimensions into the governance and policy elaboration processes. Lisa and I co-authored an article where we illustrated the importance of understanding that individual family members play different roles; we also showed that helping each member understand both the role that he or she should play and the roles that other family members should be expected to play can go a long way to addressing the needs of family which might otherwise appear somewhat dysfunctional.

This book takes this notion quite a bit further. Lisa is in fact working to show that family and cultural dynamics are not only useful, but in fact crucial. The book uses a wonderful balance of theoretical discourse and case studies to help the reader. Theoretical discourse is needed to provide both an understanding of the principles which are at play and the credibility they need by being placed into some literature continuum. Case studies are equally essential in that they show practical applications of these principles. They also very importantly help the reader appreciate the roles that different cultural frameworks can play in the integration of these principles into practical solutions.

An important, in effect indispensible, element of Lisa's work also incorporates, and then expands upon, another aspect of Jay Hughes's work: families should not solely focus on their financial capital; authentic wealth has multiple dimensions. In many ways, just as Meir Statman led all of us to understand that individuals have multiple financial goals, each with a distinct risk profile, Lisa is teaching us that the authentic capital of any family is multi-dimensional. Obviously, there is a financial dimension to this problem; but the fact that it may be the facet that one encounters first does not make it the only one or the most important. What about the social dimension? What about the emotional dimension? Again, why should we exclude the artistic dimension or the intellectual dimension? Though initially constrained, this list can literally be expanded ad infinitum, if one simply accepts the idea that any given adjective may not adequately capture the essence of what some family will see as crucially important.

Why is it important to think of more than one dimension? Well, in many ways, Lisa provides the answer within the chapters of this book. Yet, a simple example makes the best story. Last winter, Lisa and I were with the representative of the second generation of a very wealthy Middle-Eastern and European family. The individual with whom we were meeting told us that he and his siblings originally only focused on financial or business issues, probably impressed by the need to build on the family's fortune. Is this not the natural reaction to the proverbial fear of the 'shirtsleeves to shirtsleeves in three generations?' How better not fall into the trap of dissipating the wealth than by committing to add to it? Yet, this led the individual to underestimate the importance of a child's artistic leanings. That the child was serious enough to pursue the dream despite a less than supportive initial family environment is proof that a real passion is hard to contain. The child proved particularly successful in this endeavour and the family proved particularly enlightened in recognising this success. The story thus has a happy ending: the child is charged with expanding the artistic dimension of the family's wealth, while others are naturally working on other dimensions.

I think that Lisa's work can honestly be argued to offer an important next step in the multi-stage revolution through which the wealth management industry has been proceeding. Lisa's appreciation of the role of family and cultural dynamics, together with her strong advocacy of the multi-dimensional nature of a family's wealth, will probably in due course be viewed as the foundation on which solutions to one of our industry's most vexing current challenges can be built: how do we deal with multi-national, multi-cultural and multi-religion families which are gradually gaining in importance? Years ago, marrying outside of one's country, culture or religion, though not unheard of, was still somewhat rare. There was thus some unintended but quite useful homogeneity in the needs and emotional frameworks of the various agents at work within individual families. If these multi-dimensional marriages were rare but not taboo then, they have effectively almost become somewhat of a norm in several countries, in part in line with the proverbial notion of the world becoming more global. This will require that the wealth management industry works to develop a number of new approaches which will most likely integrate the work which Lisa develops in this book. Look around you and ask yourselves whether you know a couple where some measure of multi-dimensionality exists. I would be willing to bet that almost everyone will find at least one such couple, be it multi-religious, multi-ethnic or multi-national to name just three of these multiple axes.

I know that Lisa worked very hard on this book and asked many people for their help and comments. This, combined with her fluent writing style, makes the book a must-read for anyone who wishes to capture both the current essence of the family wealth management challenge and to be able to confront future issues successfully.

Happy reading!

Jean L.P. Brunel, CFA
Managing Principal, Brunel Associates, L.L.C.
Editor, *The Journal of Wealth Management*
August 2010

Foreword

Lisa Gray has studied generational wealth management in a thoughtful and rigorous manner for more than a decade. It has been a pleasure to watch her challenge all assumptions and create her own foundations and approaches.

The book is divided into four parts. In part one, Gray begins with a focus on the different generations. Her premise is that it is the generational differences that cause the most misunderstandings in families. Her unspoken message is that if families could appreciate each other's generational perspectives better, that appreciation would go a long way in resolving disagreements. Of course, with the goal of transferring wealth to the next generation, those generational perspectives are vitally important.

Her explanations of generational differences, and their impact on assumptions about wealth, are thorough. She gives several actual family cases, then explores the maze within each family of their generational misunderstandings of each other. Next, she compares the generational issues in the United States with those in Europe, Latin America, Asia and the Middle East. She ends that first division with a separate explanation of generational differences among women.

Part two of the book addresses governance issues. Gray has developed over the years a 'three forms' approach to family governance, which she summarises. Then she moves on to address governance in the context of the family, in the family business, and in the family office. She ends this part with a case study of the successfully continuing family of Laird Norton in the United States.

In the third part of the book, the previous building blocks lead to an analysis of how investment goals are affected – by the generational views and the governance roles. Finally, in part four, Gray includes a number of practical tools she has developed to help families assess their progress.

In sum, this is an insightful argument for understanding the causes that make generational wealth transitions so difficult, and then applying practical tools to increase the success by families.

Barbara R Hauser

Introduction

For the entire 22 years I have spent in the wealth management industry, I have pondered how families might be better served by their advisors and by the wealth they have been so fortunate to accumulate. I am not sure we often think of our wealth as serving us. Most often, it seems, we end up serving our wealth. I believe that is the result of not realising the true definition of wealth or the roles it is intended to occupy within our lives.

Wealth is a gift. This book tells the story of wealth as a gift. It also tells the story of wealth in a role it was never intended to occupy – that of divider of family, destroyer of relationships. It is a story told from the heart of the author – my heart. It is in our stories – particularly our family stories – that we find meaning in our lives. Wealth can be part of that meaning, or it can destroy any family story even before it has been written. So many elements of my own experience with money, its management, and the relationships which surround it, were woven into this book as it was written. I have seen material and financial wealth practically destroy family relationships, regardless of asset level – whether multiple billions or only a few million. Net worth has nothing to do with it.

I have also seen wealth bring families together to enrich each other's life experience and to express the joy of being family together – a family with the gift of wealth. These families do not confuse wealth with love; they also do not mistake the family business for wealth. They use wealth as a tool to nurture their care for each other's happiness and fulfilment.

It is the mission of this book to help significantly more families set themselves upon a path toward such joy and enrichment through a process of wealth management that more directly addresses family goals and better fits the family's needs.

In our global society today, families often lose sight of the wealth sitting right in front of them – their family members, the intellectual, human, and social capacities each possesses, and the relationships that enable those capacities to flourish and their potential to be reached. This wealth is less readily visible than the material and financial assets we usually associate with the concept. These assets are not manmade; they are innate. The gift that material and financial wealth can offer is the opportunity to nurture that innate wealth – each family member's authentic wealth – so that it provides fulfilment for its possessor, celebration of life, and joy of spirit which binds a family together in a way that is different than any other family.

Not every family experiences wealth as a gift. These families experience wealth as a divider, as a source of dysfunction which ultimately tears the family apart and diminishes all forms of the family's assets. Six of their stories are told in the Preamble which sets the stage for Chapter 1. Happier stories of wealth may be found in Chapters 14 and 20 and scattered throughout in the form of case studies. It is for both kinds of families that this book is written. It is hoped that the stories found within this book will inspire the gift of wealth for those families who own it. That hope is accompanied by well researched, time-tested philosophies and is supported by tools which have been proven in their use. Neither the philosophies nor the tests of time are entirely mine. I have been the beneficiary of the wisdom and experiences graciously shared with me by many others, including family clients and advisors to families of wealth.

Significant portions of other people's work – specifically that of James E. Hughes Jr., Jean L.P. Brunel, Neil Howe and William Strauss – have been used with their permission as a basis for the philosophies and processes outlined in this book and to create the tools described and used in my work with families and their advisors. I am extremely grateful for their generosity and hope that I have honoured their gift and their trust. To quote a dear friend, 'no one has a monopoly on brains', and I claim no exception.

A new approach to family wealth management

By redefining wealth and, in the process, discovering new assets within the family wealth portfolio to be managed, this book introduces concepts which, when applied consistently over time, will equip families to thrive in the face of the well known proverb, 'shirtsleeves to shirtsleeves in three generations' and all its translations around the world, from culture to culture.

My hope is to create awareness among families that they have a choice; they may sit by and allow the law of entropy Hughes so appropriately applies to have its way, effectively falling prey to the edicts of the Proverb or they may choose to work with the tools nature has given them to navigate a more optimal path. All families have these tools at their disposal, regardless of cultural background and regardless of asset level.

Sometimes, the clearest way to discovering a better way of doing things is to examine situations which did not yield wealth flourishing results. The stories in the Preamble offer stark examples of this. Although each family's story is different, they share many common elements. I believe this is why families of wealth seek out other families of wealth with which to share experiences, possible solutions to similar issues, and to offer each other advice. Sometimes, however, it is pragmatic to look through a lens that is broader than the spectrum of families sharing similar experiences.

That is why it is extremely important to address these issues with family advisors as well as with the families they serve. In the effort to raise the level of relationship between the two, it is essential for both to do the work. Therefore, I hope members on both sides of the spectrum will find new pathways in their relationships with each other as they turn the following pages.

How this book is organised

The book has been divided into four Parts, each of which serves a specific purpose and each of which is aligned with the components of the new approach to family wealth management that is introduced in Chapter 1.

Chapter 1 lays out the sequence of generational influence as follows.

1 Generational perspectives assign roles to family members.
2 These roles determine how the family interacts – what is more commonly known as the dynamics of the family.
3 These dynamics are reflected in the family governance system.
4 The family governance system sets the goals of the family.
5 These goals are then translated into a financial language which facilitates a goal-based asset allocation.

6 Trust-level communication provides the oil for this translation.

7 New risks are discovered which simultaneously illuminate the need for new types of protection.

8 The entire process is monitored and flows back through the generations of family as the family transitions through its multi-generational lifetime.

The Preamble contains the well-publicised stories of six wealthy families whose names have been left out, not for purposes of confidentiality, but so that you may grasp the weight of the stories more vividly without the distraction of the famous names attached in the media sources in which they were reported.

Part 1 delves deeply into the family system – what are its origins, how is it created, what factors determine its nature, what elements emanate from it. The focus here is on generational perspectives in American, European, Latin American, Asian, and Middle Eastern cultures and the influence those perspectives have on the decisions families make about the management of their wealth. As I have worked with families of wealth and their advisors over the past 22 years, I have observed the infiltration of generational perspectives within the family system. These are foundational elements, of which families are almost entirely unaware, working behind the scenes to wield their influence in ways families never suspect.

Part 1 is the largest section of the book. Chapter 2 positions generational perspectives as the primary influences on wealth management decisions in families. It shows the stealth with which these influences infiltrate the family system, setting up biases which form the dynamics of family and which start the process of wealth dissipation over three generations. Chapter 3 is an important precursor to our discussion of generations across the globe because it sets the framework for the formation of the systems of family governance. Generations are defined by their location in time. This is why an understanding of the way humans measure time is so integral to our ability to understand ourselves and our family members and their view of the world.

Part 1 then spends a great deal of time examining the perspectives of generations in the major cultures of the world and offers a lens through which families of all levels of wealth, in all parts of the globe may learn lessons of value. It also places the generations of family within the cyclical forces of nature and offers families of wealth the choice to either work with those cycles or to fight against them through the imposition of linear time measurement.

I find the generational perspectives of the cultures of the world to be fascinating. What is even more fascinating is the connectivity among them. Although each generation speaks its own 'language', the language indigenous to each generation has similarities across cultures. The various cultures of the world simply add different shadings to the generational language. So, even though this book uses American generational perspectives as a reference point, generational elements span across time, across cultural societies, across gender, across the globe. The generational sea change spanning the globe as I write has been called, 'the next Great Generation' by generational experts William Strauss and Neil Howe. Its influence is also examined across cultures and across the lines of gender roles.

The last chapter in Part 1 addresses the generational perspectives of women and their influence on this small society called 'family'. Interest in the roles of women flows through the cycles of time, reinterpreted by the cycles of generations that ebb and flow throughout history. The gender overlay adds dimension to the family's generational maze and adds perspective to the generational experience.

As with every section of the book, Part 1 closes with a summary of the most important points to be gleaned from the chapters which went before it. It also lays the groundwork necessary to prepare us for Part 2.

After this extensive exploration of the historical relevance of generational perspectives, an even more important exploration awaits in Part 2. Surely it is a good and useful exercise to examine issues of relationship, generational perspectives, and definitions of wealth that exceed our linear comfort zone. But what relevance does such an exercise truly hold for families? What do we do with the information gained once these issues have been fully examined and understood? How does this knowledge help families make better wealth management decisions and reach their goals more efficiently and effectively? How does it help advisors rise to a higher level of service for families? And ultimately, how does this process help shatter the proverb's fulfilment rate?

These are the questions Part 2 begins to answer.

Part 2 focuses on the family governance system, offering a different approach to governance that more directly matches the needs of families and the utility of the governance concept. It begins by examining the roles that family members occupy and the impact those roles have on the family wealth, particularly in setting up the governing bodies of the family. It closes with the case study of a seventh generation family in which all the principles laid out in the governance discussion may be found to have been practised.

The Part 2 summary brings the governance component all together, showing families of wealth and their advisors how governance may be better utilised through an understanding of its authentic role within the family system and its connection to the family business and the management of the family wealth.

Part 3 serves to segue into the more traditional elements of private wealth management, yet with a new perspective. It begins by closing the bookend discussion of family roles begun in the first chapter of Part 2 (Chapter 9) and continues by showing how the goals of family wealth become lost in translation on the way to the investment management piece. It then offers an introduction to a set of tools which, when implemented appropriately, helps families more successfully navigate that translation to a goal-based asset allocation which is directly aligned with the family governance system. Part 3 closes with a different type of discussion about risk management and asset protection which addresses all assets of the consummate family wealth portfolio©.

Part 4 brings advisors into the mix, showing how families may select a team of advisors which may optimally serve them. It tells the stories of two families to show how the book's philosophies function in real life, in real families. The last chapter of the book launches us on to further exploration through experience. The Epilogue leaves us with a different perspective on the three generations Proverb.

How to use this book

The book is designed to be read from start to finish, front to back. However, there are points of interest scattered throughout which may offer a more appealing sequence based on the level of need and the interest of the reader. Rather than ask you to avoid the impulse to skip around, I would like to issue the invitation to do so. The hope is that wherever you start, sufficient interest will be built, urging the exploration into other areas of the book so that, eventually, there will be a cohesive, continuous, flow of beneficial guidance which applies to whatever needs have inspired you to open these pages.

Choosing to skip around also reflects the nature of the work advocated in this book. Families' lives do not always flow in sequence – at least, not according to any preconceived sequence we might imagine! Therefore, any process which attempts to place families of wealth on a different track must be flexible enough to accommodate the family's current needs while the process is being implemented. Families just don't 'stop' so that they can do the work with consultant and family to improve the way they relate to each other, how they relate to their advisors, and how their wealth is managed. Life goes on and so must the functioning of the family.

Wherever you start, I urge you to read the book in its entirety – including all the chapters on generational perspectives and on generational perspectives of women – and to take note of how the various components build upon each other. This is an important aspect of the new approach in an attempt to show the influential momentum which builds from one side of the process to the other. The structure is designed around a new approach to wealth management housed within a construct called the Generational Wealth Management Continuum[SM].[1] Within that construct, you will find a cohesive process within what I hope will be enlightening information that will lead to the flourishing of your family's wealth in all its forms.

Although this book is meant to be a guide and does provide a general description of processes and tools, its authentic role is to bring awareness rather than instruction. In working with families across the globe, I have found it is quite difficult for families to truly take an objective step away so they can see the generational forces at work among their dynamics in a way which would sufficiently alter their paths toward fulfilment of the Proverb. Most often, they are too close to their own dynamics to be able to see and work through these issues clearly. Understanding generational perspectives may be compared to learning another language; a language that shapes the way we think early on and in a permanent way.

Language implies a frame of reference. This is easily seen by considering the different perceptions and interpretations of the various cultures around the world. Learning another language – whether cultural or generational – broadens the scope of perception and can alter interpretation.[2]

The generational perspectives of each culture are, therefore, interpreted through a particular culture's language. Interpretation of the 'languages' of perceptions differs within the generational maze of family. Therefore, the most objective and utilisable interpretation of this book is greatly facilitated by the broader view of a third party to prevent the perception of family roles as competitive rather than illuminating.

What this book hopes to accomplish

The most important point in the entire book is the fact that everything that happens within the family system and family governance determines what happens on the private wealth management side. If the book can effectively get that point across and create awareness of the stealth influence of generational perspectives, the biases they create, and the roles they play within the management of the consummate family wealth portfolio[©], I will have accomplished what I set out to do. That realisation will lead you to the rest of the book.

Throughout the book, family case studies from all cultures have been used as illustrations. In all the cases where family names have not been mentioned, the stories are conglomerations of the stories of multiple families in which every family who reads this book will find familiarity. These are family situations which are common to families of all levels of wealth, in every culture, and of almost every asset level. All aspects of the stories used as case studies have been taken either from multiple, conglomerate, real life examples who have shared complexities and experiences which are common to families all over the world, or they have been completely fabricated based on these common experiences. No names are actual names of people unless they are part of the family stories in Chapters 14 and 20. Although many families will be able to identify with certain aspects of these stories, no single family's situation has been the inspiration for them.

With that, I invite you to turn the page and join me on a journey to discover a new approach to family wealth management that more closely matches the needs of families wherever they live in their relationship with their wealth.

---

[1] 'Generational Wealth Management Continuum' is the service marked property of graymatter Strategies LLC.

[2] Boroditsky, L., 'Lost in Translation', *The Wall Street Journal,* July 24, 2010: http://online.wsj.com/article/SB1000142405 27487034673045753831315927678868.html?mod=WSJ_hp_mostpop_read.

Preamble: six global family stories

'If you look deeply into the palm of your hand, you will see your parents and all generations of your ancestors. All of them are alive in this moment. Each is present in your body. You are the continuation of each of these people.'

Thich Nhat Hanh[1]

Family story 1: if only his father would listen. The company stock had languished over recent years and the founder had turned down yet another of the son's ideas, this one about expanding the product line, saying only, according to the son's recollection, 'We know gum'. The stock continued to languish. After the founder's unexpected death, the son inadvertently had the opportunity to implement some of the ideas for which he previously had failed to receive his father's support. The result was a significant refuelling for the company and a more robust equity market performance for the shareholders.[2]

Family story 2: another very private family had a century-old legacy of keeping the wealth intact for the benefit of the family as a whole. The founder's grandson had specifically charged the next generations with maintaining this legacy but two years after his death, 11 fourth-generation cousins threatened to sue, claiming according to reports, 'breaches of fiduciary duties, self-dealing, conflicts of interest and other improprieties'.[3] A document was drawn up which split the wealth into 11 pieces, shattering the family legacy. A few years later, two younger cousins, step-siblings to their father's older children, sued the family because they felt they had been left out of the agreement and, thus, did not receive an appropriate share. Family leadership stated that the family had decided, based on the step-siblings' youth, to view them as part of the fifth generation rather than the fourth generation of which they were genealogically a part. The 11 cousins participated equally in settling the matter.[4]

Family story 3: grandchildren of another founder of family wealth had appointed a trustee to oversee the family's holdings. This trustee gained the complete confidence of the grandchildren and basically took control of the family meetings, so much so that, over time, his activities were not well monitored. It became an unspoken rule that future generations did not question his authority, even to other family members. But as unwise management decisions began to dissipate the family fortune, a couple of younger-generation cousins did raise questions – publicly. Although their complaints were eventually considered, the cousins were essentially ostracised by the family. It took years for these cousins to regain the family's favour.[5]

These are well-publicised stories of family owners of large public American companies – their names can be guessed without looking at the footnotes. The poignancy of the tales recounted above lies not in the media hype but in the common threads of family dysfunction around wealth. What breeds such dysfunction? Is it a condition that only plagues American families? Is it limited to families with lofty levels of wealth?

Family story 4: an Asian family's patriarch privately awarded a grandson, whom he felt possessed the greatest entrepreneurial potential of the family, a five-year stock option to potentially gain control of the family business. This move supposedly had been taken to bypass control by the patriarch's two sons. However, the grandson later teamed with one of the founder's sons (the grandson's uncle) and effectively ousted his father and brother – with whom relationships had soured – from control. The grandson's brother then tried to claim half of the grandson's option. The family descended into total chaos with control continually shifting between the two factions. Eventually, the entire family grew weary of the fight and decided to sell the business to outside parties.[6]

Family story 5: a family squabble split another Asian family business into four separate companies, making the entire enterprise vulnerable as a result of divided attention from the core business. The youngest of four brothers clandestinely set up companies of his own. He also invested in businesses he deemed strategically imperative, taking advantage of relationships he had developed with the government and participating in a governmental programme designed to foster economic growth in rural, undeveloped areas. The younger brother was supplanted as chairman by the elder brother and the entire conglomerate was reorganised. Although the brothers eventually worked out their disputes amicably, the question remained whether the conglomerate family business could grow as well with each brother's focus now in a different direction as it had when the family was still united.[7]

Family story 6: the son of a European entrepreneur took over when his father passed away. The son built the father's idea – which was a base-level forerunner to a major beverage chain – into a chain of 39,000 locations. He then diversified into other retailing areas, catapulting both enterprises to market leader positions. The son began to buy stakes in other companies, growing the family's holdings substantially. After four decades, the son suddenly found himself no longer involved in any of the family businesses. There was 'complete destruction of trust between the board of directors and himself'. When the father died, he left an ambiguous will which led to a power struggle between the son and his siblings for control of the company. The son won out. Later, his decision to take the original business public divided the family irreparably. Although the son had made the family wealthy beyond their imaginings, the son's 'prickly personality', the forcible way he overtook control, and the fact that the rest of the family had been shut out for four decades finally was avenged in ousting him from the helm. The son and his sister were bought out completely. The mother sided with her other three sons. The family's holdings became subject to intense foreign competition, lower prices in the marketplace, and new governmental restrictions on sales of certain items. The family rift has, so far, yet to be healed.[8]

These are summaries of stories highlighting families of wealth which were featured in *The New York Times*, *The Wall Street Journal*, *Forbes*, and other news sources. Articles used for sources and in which the names can be found are notated.

There seemed to be little looking deeply into the palm of the hand, yet the cycles move on.

---

[1] Vietnamese monk, activist and writer. Born1926: http://thinkexist.com/quotations/family.

[2] Based on information contained in Adamy, J., 'Father, son and gum: as other dynasties fade, a fourth-generation CEO shakes up Wrigley by tossing out his dad's rule book', *The Wall Street Journal,* March 11 2006.

[3] Based on information contained in Maremont, M., 'Court documents present insight into breakup of Pritzker empire', *The Wall Street Journal,* January 11 2006: http://online.wsj.com/article/SB113694882504643459.html.

[4] Based on information contained in the following media reports: Maremont, M., 'Pritzker family dispute leads to end of $15 billion empire', *The Wall Street Journal,* December 11 2002: http://online.wsj.com/article/SB1039564376921100393.html; Maremont, M., 'Pritzker's settle family lawsuit; cost: a fortune', *The Wall Street Journal,* January 7 2005: http://online.wsj.com/article/SB110504452074819125.html; Maremont, M., 'Court documents present insight into breakup of Pritzker empire', *The Wall Street Journal,* January 11 2006: http://online.wsj.com/article/SB113694882504643459.html.

[5] Based on information contained in: Nocera, J., 'At Dow Jones, it's all about family', *The New York Times,* August 20 2005.

[6] Tripathi, S., 'Singapore's feuding Jumabhoys', *Asia Inc.,* June 1996: www.saliltripathi.com/articlesAsiaInc/June96AsiaInc.html; The Phoenix Group: Bawiga, R., Debil, G., de la Cruz, H., Fabrigar, E., Moscoso, L.V., Leonida, C., and Lucero, A., 'Chapter 8: Polygamy and family squabbles', College of Management, University of the Philippines Visayas, January 26 2002: http://pabs.netfirms.com/chapter8.htm.

[7] Based on information contained in: Erickson, J., and Mooney P., 'Hope takes on the world: China's largest private company is branching out', *AsiaWeek,* October 1997: www.asiaweek.com/asiaweek/97/1010/biz2.html.

[8] Dukcevich, D.E., 'The torn Herz family', *Forbes Faces,* February 2001: www.forbes.com/2001/02/09/0209facesherz.html.

Chapter 1

The Generational Wealth Management Continuum^{SM}: a new approach to family wealth management

'The father buys, the son builds, the grandchild sells, and his son begs.'

Scottish Proverb[1]

'There's nobbut three generations atween a clog and clog.'

Lancashire proverb[2]

'*Avô rico filho nobre e neto pobre.*'

Portuguese proverb

'Shirtsleeves to shirtsleeves in three generations.'

American proverb

The search for ways to successfully defy the famed proverb quoted above is an age old and ongoing global concern. Therefore, if you found any part of the six stories summarised in the Preamble to be personally familiar, it is because the familial elements in these stories can be considered universal. Families of wealth the world over can easily identify aspects of these stories in their own relationships whether the wealth is $20 million, multiple billions, or somewhere in between. The adamant, seemingly immovable, 'sticking with what works' attitude illustrated in the first story can be found in patriarchs of family businesses with assets of all sizes. It is not a trait reserved for the super wealthy. Neither are mandated legacies nor demands for complete, unquestioned trust.

The six stories elicit two primary questions, each directly related to defying the fulfilment of the edicts of the Proverb cited above: 'What are the roots of family dysfunction around wealth?' and 'How important are family relationships to the successful management of material and financial wealth?' These questions apply to every culture – every family whom the world would consider extraordinarily successful in traditionally accepted terms.

In the family wealth industry today, families and their advisors are giving these concerns more attention but the idea of making them a vital focal point in wealth management is quite early in its development. Why should such concerns be a focal point at all? Portfolios grow and perform without considering these questions; family businesses function without finding answers to them. Thus, the importance of the two questions in and of itself becomes a point of discussion. The answer lies in understanding that families of wealth today face exponential complexities which are rarely robustly addressed.

This book explores these complexities from a different perspective. It seeks to guide readers on a journey beginning with the family and leading to its wealth rather than from the current trajectory which views the family from a business and wealth management perspective to find applications for

5

organising the family. This alternative concept may seem counterintuitive. In reality, it is the most natural and organic order. Approaching wealth management – and governance, for that matter – from the family perspective will facilitate the discovery of a more robust, common sense approach to wealth management as well as to family organisation.

We will begin by picking up on a universal theme outlined by the six stories in the Preamble – family dysfunction. Dysfunction is a symptom of a much deeper problem. In the early stages, its progression is easy to dismiss in favour of 'more pressing' issues. Although every family has some dysfunction, families who come to understand their particular version and its progression may prevent its development to a chaotic level which subverts an effective decision making process. Understanding the nature and origins of dysfunction opens new dimensions and creates greater transparency for wealth management.

As we begin our journey, we will drill down into this progression by exploring:

- the nature of family dysfunction and its connection to the way family members interact (family dynamics);
- the foundation from which family dynamics are formed;
- a new definition of family wealth;
- a set of family assets rarely included in the traditional portfolio management paradigm; and
- the introduction of a new approach to family wealth management.

An exploration into the foundation of family dynamics leads us to a new definition of family wealth. Whether homogenous or dysfunctional, the dynamics of family serve as the initial conduit through which wealth is either fostered or dissipated. Understanding their nature and how they are formed offers insights which empower families to postpone the fulfilment of the proverbial dissipation of wealth until well beyond the third generation.

The nature of family dysfunction

Every seeker of knowledge begins his or her journey for answers and solutions by asking questions. In an attempt to partially answer the question seeking the roots of family dysfunction around wealth, we note the study conducted by Roy Williams and Vic Preisser over a period of 20 years with 3,250 global families of wealth.[3] Participants in the study indicated that the source of family dysfunction lies in the realm of communication, trust, and the lack of understanding by family members of their roles and responsibilities. The second question which addresses the importance of family relationships in wealth management indicates there may be a deeper problem which lies at the heart of these issues.

Generational viewpoints set up the way family members interact with each other. There are two types of generational perspectives: social (archetypical) and familial (chronological). A social generation is defined by a specific span of years into which people are born who experience social and economic times as a group and in such a way that a 'group persona' develops. These generations are labelled to identify their 'location in history'.[4] In America, labels such as GI, Silent, Boomer, Gen-X, and Echo (or Millennial) are used.

Familial generations are labelled chronologically and only apply to families with significant wealth. The first generation label of 'G1' refers to the wealth creating generation. Subsequent

generations are labelled 'G2', 'G3', 'G4' and so on. Any members of the chronological generations will also be members of a social generational cohort or archetype. Both types of generational
perspectives directly affect views on parenting, communication and relationships, and the roles of
family members, all of which, in turn, affect one's concept of self worth and, ultimately, the family
wealth. Poor self worth – or a lack of acknowledgement or appreciation of one's abilities by others
– has been linked to addictive behaviours[5] at worst and an inability to make joint decisions[6] at best.

Generational biases regarding expected behaviour, work ethic, roles and responsibilities all
contribute to the family's particular set of dynamics. These biases set in motion a full range of
interactions which colour the family's internal relationships in a way that fosters either homogeny or
relationship crippling dysfunction. All decisions relative to the management, transfer, or protection
of the family's wealth are made as these biases function dynamically in the background.

Exhibit 1.1

Determinants of family dynamics

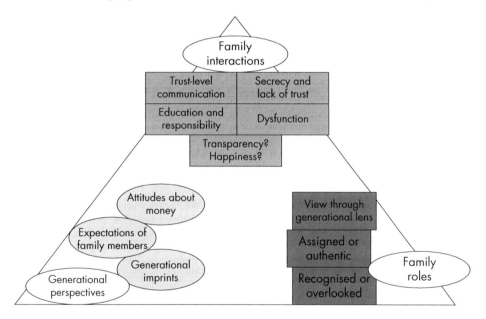

Source: graymatter Strategies LLC. All rights reserved.

Signs of dysfunction in families of wealth surround us. They are topics of great interest and
the media love to highlight them. They seem to relish each instance in which the familiar Proverb
appears destined to come true. Otherwise, we would not so easily have found the six stories which
were cited in the Preamble!

As much as the media enjoys reporting on the dysfunction of prominent families of wealth,
they also like to create 'trends' out of such families' activities. One recent example is the giving

of the bulk of family wealth to charity and not to heirs. The presumption on the part of families is either: (a) the heirs will be 'spoiled' by the wealth; or (b) the heirs are not responsible enough to manage it well and, thus, the wealth will be squandered. Although, according to philanthropy professionals, this trend is more perception than reality – this is even more true in light of the 2008 crisis – the principle involved points us to an important illumination, primarily that 'there is a continuing misprision that family wealth is financial as opposed to human and intellectual'.[7] The arbitrarily pre-determined disposition of wealth significantly in favour of a philanthropic entity – or any other type of entity – and away from heirs leans heavily toward the view of wealth as financial and, therefore, potentially ruinous to heirs. As well, the pre-determined and arbitrary segue of the family business to the eldest son may also be viewed as a decision based in the view that wealth is financial.

This is certainly not a statement against philanthropy, nor is it an implication that grooming a successor for the family business is a mistake. Philanthropy increasingly serves as a vital component of a successful family's multi-generational wealth management strategy. And eldest sons who genuinely share the passion and have the talent for running the family business may make fine stewards. Rather, it is an attempt to bring critical awareness to a second misprision – a misprision born from the growing fear that children of wealth will become spoiled by simply having the decision of what to do with the wealth left in the children's hands. The notion that heirs are destined to fulfil the Proverb – destined to become the famed 'third generation' – and that the *only* prevention or cure is for founders or current leadership to dictate the financial wealth's dispersion based on that notion does little to circumvent the Proverb's fulfilment. In fact, it may well accelerate its fulfilment by fostering deep-seated resentment, consciously or sub-consciously, expressed or not.

I would argue that wealth is *not* ruinous to heirs; poor communication, broken trust relationships, and keeping heirs in the dark about their roles and responsibilities until they are of a certain age, when they suddenly are expected to have learned such responsibility completely by osmosis, most certainly are. The statistics formulated by the survey cited above support such a conclusion. I would further propose that attitudes about wealth vary according to the perspectives of each generation – both archetypical and chronological – and that recognition and understanding of this truth is the key to unlocking the Proverb's hold on family wealth dissipation. These are the sources of family dysfunction. These are the silver-coated bullets which lie ready to be fired in any family of wealth at the most critical points of future determination.

Family dynamics, work ethic, and the pursuit of happiness

Whatever the situation or the wealth decision at hand, thinking of wealth as financial and pre-empting heirs' opportunity to make responsible decisions regarding it equates to parents imposing their own wishes on their children, inadvertently compelling them to 'steward another's dream' while sacrificing their own.[8] The sacrifice of one's dreams precludes the fulfilment of an innate right to the pursuit of happiness. The concept of James E. (Jay) Hughes, Jr. that founders or current family leadership should nurture the heirs' dreams, making them capable of truly stewarding the founder's dream at a later point in their lives *only* after they have realised their own dreams[9] is one that would give great pause in the majority of controlling generations' minds. Such a concept describes a different form of leadership which may seem paradoxical, indeed; but it is the only kind of leadership that truly can forestall the fulfilment of the proverb. *It is the only path through which the wealth can survive.*

Mortimer J. Adler described 'Great Ideas' as those ideas which are 'basic and indispensable to understanding ourselves, our society, and the world in which we live'.[10] In a discussion of one Great Idea, Aristotle's theory of happiness – the theory which inspired the authors of the American Declaration of Independence – Adler concludes, 'Hence, if everyone has a natural right to the pursuit of happiness, and if that means that happiness must be attainable by all, then we know at once, do we not, that power over other men cannot be a part of human happiness – for if it were, happiness would not be attainable by all. The pursuit of happiness must be co-operative, not competitive'.[11]

Independent family advisor Barbara R. Hauser has addressed the right to the pursuit of happiness where wealth is concerned. Reflecting the misunderstanding that wealth is financial, she notes that wealth is thought largely to be detrimental to heirs, spawning laziness and depriving heirs from the 'privilege' of hard work. She posits that the assumption that people work only to earn money implies that people would naturally choose not to work if that choice were made available to them. Further, that work would hold a much lower status in a civilised society if that were indeed the case, indicating that work would have no purpose other than to provide food, shelter, and the necessities of life. 'Parents and advisors who want children to work in traditional jobs are selecting other people's work. This is to give children a weary load. This is to put their souls in a ferment of revolt.'[12] Of course, this is perfectly aligned with all other decisions that equate to 'stewarding another's dream'.[13]

In actuality, the notion of work as a source of fulfilment, even of following one's heart, draws us nearer to the true value of work and the benefit the resulting wealth can have on individual family members as well as the family as a whole. For by comparing possible life fulfilment through work one loves to do – therefore, deriving pleasure from it as well as satisfaction from resolving challenges – with the mandate that work should be hard and that life should be a struggle, it becomes easy to see the contrast between a life well lived and simply, a life. The former offers growth and recognition of responsibility; the latter spawns oppression and misery.

A new definition of 'wealth'

In line with that illumination, family dysfunction can hardly be equated with joy. To the extent that dysfunction may be thought of as a result of wealth, the happiness and fulfilment of the family – or the lack, thereof – can logically be tied to the view of work since it is the primary instrument of wealth creation as either life fulfilment or as a catalyst for dysfunction in the family. If we expand the ideology of work to include any productive function within a family so that it not only refers to one's occupation but also to the roles family members perform relative to other family members, the family wealth, and the family business if one exists, a new vista emerges. A larger view of wealth, its influences, and its effects on the family can be entertained. The result of such a view is a more accurate definition of wealth – that of the family members themselves and the human and intellectual capacities they possess.[14] However, this definition is still incomplete.

The human and intellectual capacities of family members must be fostered by supportive and nurturing relationships – from within or outside the family or both – to create material wealth in the first place. In my view, this comprises a third set of capacities possessed by family members: social capacities. They are the pivotal ingredients without which the intellectual and human capacities cannot function on the path toward material and financial wealth creation.

Thus, the relationship ingredient – the set of interactive dynamics present within the family –

determines each family member's social capacities and is, therefore, critical to the ability of family members to regenerate the wealth. Family members may have exceptional capacities from the human and intellectual aspects; however, if those capacities have no social outlet through which to gain support, they may never be developed.[15]

Including the effects of family relationships makes the new definition of wealth even more robust, since it is these relationships which determine the extent to which family members' capabilities within the human, intellectual, and social realms are enabled to flourish. Therefore, we can define a family's authentic wealth as *the intellectual, human, and social capacities of families and the relationships that nurture them.* The term 'authentic' is a powerful one, especially in reference to wealth. It, of course, implies that what is traditionally thought of as wealth is not the family's true wealth at all. *This is because we assign material wealth its own perceived role that it was never meant to perform!* When material wealth functions properly within its own 'authentic' role, the true wealth of the family is regenerated[16] and *greater amounts of material and financial wealth are the by-products.*

By employing such a definition, it becomes clear that one generation's views on work and the roles family members perform can easily clash with those of another. If views on work and roles clash, the financial and material wealth effectively can be used by family leadership to manipulate the actions as well as to distort the views of other family members to support unquestioningly those of the founder (or current leadership), leading to 'power over other men' that 'cannot be a part of human happiness'. When multiple generations live simultaneously within a family, complexities inherently arise from the sheer number of people, notwithstanding the multiple perspectives of each. Each family member playing on the views of the others can entrench dysfunction quite solidly.

So where does this leave the financial and material wealth? It places it squarely into its proper role – its most effective role; that of a tool chest by which the family's authentic wealth can be fostered. *Financial wealth is a facilitator for enriching lives; it is the by-product of the materialisation of the family's real wealth, its authentic capacities.* Authentic wealth serves as a connector among generations. It softens the 'my way or the highway' approach of GIs and Silents; it balances the workaholic, establishment rejoining excess of the Boomers; it offers a logical 'bottom-line' approach for cynical Gen-Xers; and it fosters community for Echoes. It spans generations of both types – archetypical and chronological – enabling connectivity among generations who, otherwise, might have little or none.

When allowed to occupy its authentic role, money can be a tremendous gift – a gift that flows from one generation to the next, offering the best opportunities for a life well lived.

The relationship between the evolution of energy and the measurement of time

Successful founders engage in a process of 'materialising'[17] their intellectual, human, and social capacities into what we traditionally think of as 'wealth'. The energy that was once just an idea becomes material in form through the creation of an operating company. The materialisation process begins when the idea becomes expressed through a recordable format (the written word) and culminates in the creation of assets to which a monetary value can be assigned. After developing the initial idea, the founder employs his or her social capacities to garner funding in the form of seed capital. Once funding is secured, the founder's social and human capacities combine to gather enough people – physical bodies – to pragmatically implement the idea. Thus, families of wealth beat the odds of the business success and significant material and financial wealth is created.

The energy which fosters ideas is constant; it doesn't disappear, it simply changes form. One of the forms energy takes is matter. Matter evolves through a cyclical process of creation and deterioration exactly as described in the famed Proverb over the span of three generations.[18] This process is directly tied to the way we – human beings – evaluate progress through the measurement of time.

Exhibit 1.2

Authentic asset cyclical flow

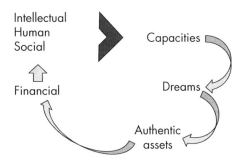

The critical point for families and their advisors in flourishing the wealth is the recognition that the materialisation of wealth, like the evolution of matter, is a cyclical process rather than a linear one. This realisation becomes the foundation for a family's journey toward regenerative wealth flourishing – a process this book is dedicated to exploring in depth.

In the wealth advisory world, this tangible form of energy comprises what are commonly called the family's assets. Yet, there are other types of assets just waiting to be materialised but for which the process becomes thwarted at worst, stymied at best. They are embedded in each family member's human, intellectual, and social capacities. These are the authentic assets of the family. The catalysts for their materialisation are the relationship structures found in the dynamics which shape the family's ability to communicate and build trust. These relationship structures are embodied within the perspectives held by each generation represented within the family. They hold the key for wealth flourishing.

Incorporating authentic assets into the family wealth portfolio

Regeneration of the wealth, whether of the original pool of wealth or by creating additional pools, can only happen if the family and its advisors truly understand the expanded definition of wealth that includes the sources of its creation. When we consider the components of the conceptual family enterprise, it quickly becomes clear that there is much more involved than the management of an operating company or a group of material and financial assets. The expansion of the family business concept to include relationships of multiple generations of family members as well as the management and staff of the corporation goes a long way toward addressing the various forms of wealth which may be present.

The term 'family enterprise' expands the notion of family business succession to include the relationships, roles, and multiple generations of family members.[19] However, the focus and related discussions and activities still emanate from the context of the business. I propose that this is a misalignment which does not optimally serve the family's interests. The focus on the business is a logical one; the business is the vehicle through which the intellectual, social, and human capacities of the founder(s) transformed the vibrant energy contained therein into a tangible form.

Most often, every activity after this materialisation point seems either to be connected to or emanate from whatever the business of the family might be, whether it is an operating company, several operating companies, or the management of investment capital. Relationships and communication among family members become defined in terms of the business. Disbursement of assets and/or dividends occurs first among family shareholders of the business. The business continues to create monetary wealth which is turned into financial investments, segued into trusts and other estate planning and tax structures, and dividends are distributed to maintain lifestyles – all emanating from the original operating company.

This misalignment then creates a view that we have a business with a family attached, rather than a family who owns a business or a business entity which has metamorphosed their authentic assets into a tangible form. Issues of communication, trust, and the education of dynamic stakeholder owners within the family become viewed from the perspective of the life of the business instead of the life of the family. The materialised assets and all related considerations come to dominate the family's interactions, how they view each other, and the decisions they make about the tangible wealth. Little provision is made for managing the authentic assets and fostering their growth. In fact, the authentic assets may go completely unrecognised.

By approaching wealth from the family perspective rather than from that of the business, it makes sense to incorporate the *sources* of traditional assets into the portfolio of the family. Doing so brings awareness of their existence to the attention of governing generations as well as to that of family advisors. If we think organically, we begin to realise that families and their advisors spend the bulk of their time focusing on only 25% of the family's entire portfolio of wealth! The other 75% – the intellectual, social, and human capacities of family members[20] – may be addressed in some fashion but it is rarely, if ever, connected to the financial and investment piece and treated as a set of actual family assets to be included in the portfolio.

Are these elements of family wealth truly assets? If we think of them as the source from which material wealth comes into being, several applications may be made. From the aspect of copyright ownership, for example, under US copyright law an idea is not protected until it is reduced to a tangible form. This fact causes the creator of the idea to make intense efforts to guard the idea – even after it is written down – until a tangible or financial asset from that idea may be formed. A book begins as an idea. Those thoughts and ideas are written down and a copyright attaches immediately to the tangible expression of those thoughts and ideas. In US law, while copyright ownership vests in the author immediately upon creation of the work, copyright law affords stronger protections once a work is registered with the US Copyright Office.[21] Thus, the idea becomes a tangible, legally protected entity.

The intellectual capacity from which the idea sprang forth becomes a resource which can then be turned into a material asset. In developing a working definition of an asset, the International Accounting Standards Board's (IASB) World Standard Setters Meeting in September of 2006 cites the IASB's and the Financial Accounting Standards Board's uses of the phrase, 'Future economic benefits'. In reference to the phrase, it proposes that a working definition of an asset should assess, '… whether something with the capability of generating future cash inflows, or reducing future cash outflows – an economic resource – exists at the present time'. It cites the example of a 'lottery ticket or an unexercised stock option is a present economic resource even though future economic benefits might not flow from that resource'.[22] It goes on to propose the working definition of an asset as, '… a present economic resource to which an entity has a present right or other privileged access'.[23]

If we consider an idea which has been formulated and placed in written form as a present economic resource, we then must determine if there is an entity which has rights and/or other privileged access to that idea. Since no family is exactly like any other family (because no other family has those exact same people as members), Hughes cites each family's 'differentness' through the family's affinity with each other as the establishment of the family as a separate entity, larger than any one of its individual members.[24] This entity of family certainly has rights and privileged access to an idea which might be considered a present economic resource. In this light, we can conclude that intellectual capacities are indeed assets.

Further, an economic resource requires the use of other assets to foster its change in form from energy into a tangible material asset which can be counted on a balance sheet. A gold, silver, or copper mine which has been discovered definitely exists but will never be transferred into financial capital if the ore is left sitting in the mine. It is indeed an asset – an economic resource as defined above – and the owners of the mine have rights and access to it. Yet, if the ore contained therein has no access to the marketplace, it has little or no recognised value. No one knows how much ore is contained in the mine. It requires extraction, refinement, and delivery to a marketplace which is willing to exchange currency for the ore, transforming it into goods that may be sold or financial capital which can then be used to buy equipment to mine more ore and also to improve the quality of life of the owners.

Similarly, an idea may exist as a present economic resource but it will never become transformed into financial capital or material wealth unless the owner of the idea can secure funding for development through a viable social network. Further, unless human beings can be hired to implement the idea to develop a product or service, the product or service cannot be taken to a marketplace and exchanged for currency.

In light of these definitions, we can assess that families, as entities, possess four different types of assets along with rights and privileged access.

1 Intellectual capacities – 25%.
2 Human capacities – 25%.
3 Social capacities – 25%.
4 Financial and material assets – 25%.

Total assets of the family – 100%.

Thus we have clearly identified intellectual, human, and social capacities as 75% of the family's wealth.

At this point, two important distinctions need to be made. The reader may have heard references from various consultants to the above components of family wealth as 'capital' – human capital, most commonly, intellectual capital, and social capital. Throughout this book, I substitute the word 'capacities' for the word 'capital' out of a conviction that the term 'capacities' more appropriately describes the unlimited nature of the authentic wealth of family members, especially in the stages before those capacities become tangible in any form. Secondly, there has been considerable debate whether social capital should be viewed as a by-product of human and intellectual capital or whether it should be treated as an independent form of family capital. Again, the only aspects of family wealth I view as 'capital' are the financial assets. Intellectual, human, and social forms of wealth are 'capacities' of limitless potential.

In addressing this ongoing debate, it is my firm belief that neither the intellectual nor the human capacities of family members may be fostered to a tangible form without the employment of the social capacities of family members. I would further note that there are families in which social capacities are not employed. Family members rarely see each other and have no desire to be in relationship, signifying high levels of family dysfunction. Therefore, the intellectual and human capacities have no support system within the family to nurture their development. This goes back to the very definition of wealth developed earlier in this chapter. It is the foundation for my opinion that social capacities are separate components of the family's authentic wealth and, like a family's intellectual and human capacities, should be viewed as assets of the family.

On that basis, we can easily see that there is a more complete portfolio of family assets consisting of four forms of family wealth. This becomes a critically vital point in fostering a family's success in transitioning the wealth from generation to generation to generation. The most common denial of this authentic wealth occurs when the founding generation attempts to impose its dream upon its heirs by expecting them to steward the founder's dream before they steward their own.[25] The assignment of roles based on the perceptions of the wealth creator's generational imprint serves as the transmitter of this denial – yet another clue to the impact of generational perspectives on family wealth.

From this viewpoint, it becomes clear that management of all forms of a family's assets in an integrated fashion is an absolutely essential ingredient in postponing the fulfilment of the edicts of the Proverb and in providing optimal wealth management service to families of wealth.[26] To incorporate the management of these assets into the management of the traditional portfolio, we must construct a richer, more robust approach to wealth management.

The Generational Wealth Management Continuum[SM][27]

Now we come to the framework that will guide families and their advisors toward postponing the fulfilment of the edicts of the Proverb. It must be a framework that is flexible enough to encompass all forms of the family's wealth. It must also be a framework which acknowledges the integral relationship between the various forms of wealth and the components that foster their growth. Lastly, it must be sequential in nature, yet function as a consummately integrated collective which follows a cyclical progression.

A continuum by definition is 'a coherent whole characterised as a collection, sequence, or progression of values or elements varying by minute degrees'.[28] By placing the components of what we now call Consummately Integrated Wealth Management within a continuum, we more appropriately see the effects that each progressive component of family wealth management has on the next. By understanding each component and its sequential effects on the ones that follow it, a process unfolds that offers families the option of allowing the fulfilment of the edicts of the Proverb to happen naturally or of postponing that fulfilment so that wealth may truly become what it should be – a gift by which family members' lives are enhanced in a meaningful, fulfilling way.

Based on these characteristics, we can logically name this framework or structure the Generational Wealth Management Continuum^{SM}, (the Continuum) as shown in Exhibit 1.3.

Exhibit 1.3

Five components of the Generational Wealth Management Continuum^{SM}

Family system	Family governance	Translation	Implement strategies	Ongoing monitoring
Generational perspectives	Identify needs	Behavioural finance overlay	Investment policy	Benchmark: family goals
Roles	Identify goals		Goal-based asset allocation	Benchmark: investment goals
Family dynamics	Design strategies		Asset location	Monitor data points: familial investment
Identify authentic assets			Manager selection	

As Exhibit 1.3 depicts, the Continuum houses five basic components, each with subcomponents that flesh out the breadth and depth of service today's families of wealth require. The Continuum also illustrates the appropriate sequence of what we now call 'consummately integrated wealth management'. Of course, the nature of integration is not necessarily sequential or singular. Rather, it tends to follow a basic sequence, then revisits necessary areas – possibly multiple times – to authentically further the process. The act of integration is to 'form, coordinate, or blend into a unified whole'.[29] It is a concept that fits perfectly with the needs of families as outlined in Alderfer's ERG Theory, so named to reflect its three levels of needs: existence, relational, and growth.[30] Instead of fitting into a sequential progression illustrated by Maslow's often cited pyramid of the Hierarchy of Needs, Alderfer's approach employs a simpler structure and has received greater empirical support than Maslow's approach. Alderfer suggests that the fulfilment of different levels of needs may be pursued simultaneously within a structurally prescribed order.

This is exactly the way families function. Often, family consultants will require the family to stop all decision making and focus on the dynamics of the family and setting up an appropriate governance system, following in straight sequential order in similar fashion to Maslow's hierarchy. This methodology works contrary to the nature and to the needs of families. As exemplified in Alderfer's approach, families have multiple needs which must be addressed at once. Unexpected events occur; new needs arise which require satisfaction; stages of life change causing changes in leadership or revisions to the family governance system. The process must be interwoven with the family's ongoing concerns; this is the only way to adequately address them.

A deeper examination of these two theories in Chapter 15 will show even more interesting corollaries to the needs of families and strategies for satisfying them. For now, they illustrate the flexibility of integration within the more ordered structure of a continuum.

The progression of the Continuum^{SM}

The components of the Continuum^{SM} progress from the foundation of generational perspectives which determine roles family members occupy as well as the way the family interacts. This circles back to our discussion of family dynamics at the beginning of this chapter. As noted above, these components do not always occur in order; however, the conceptual order offers guidance in creating an optimal service model for families of wealth today.

Here are brief descriptions of the five components of the Generational Wealth Management Continuum^{SM}.

The family system

The way family members interact with each other is dependent upon the roles which are either assigned by the generational perspectives within the family or recognised as authentic. The longer family members function within either a perceived or an authentic role, the more firmly entrenched that role becomes in the family member's life and the greater determinant that role becomes in the family member's future. The needs of the family are also determined based on these roles and interpreted through the dynamics of the family. These elements form the family system. It is from these roles and the family dynamics in play that the family's needs are identified. This is also the optimal point at which the family's authentic assets may be recognised.

Based on the needs that are identified from the roles family members occupy (either perceived or authentic), goals are set and strategies are designed for achievement. It is from this first component in the Continuum that all other components emanate. If this initial component is not fully understood and the authentic assets are not appropriately recognised, supportive systems for their flourishing will not be put into place and the family wealth – in all forms – will be diminished.

Family governance

The role of family governance works hand in hand with the family system to consciously support the flourishing of all forms of its wealth. One point of integration is reached when advisors are called upon to help the family develop and implement the strategies it has designed to achieve its goals. As we will see in Chapter 13, these advisors may be located in the family office (which has its own governance system separate and apart from the family), or within whatever entity or combination of external resources the family has developed that serves as a family office surrogate.

It is also the task of family governance to design protective strategies for the family's authentic assets. These strategies are outlined within the family constitution which also contains what may be called the 'investment policy' for managing these authentic assets.

Translation

Then comes the task of translating the goals of the family system into a language which can be used to develop financial and investment goals. Aspects of behavioural finance[31] may be used to prioritise goals and identify potential behavioural risks such as decision risk, framing of decisions, and mental accounting. Other hidden risks such as relationship risk[©32] associated with the family's authentic assets are identified. These risks along with traditional investment risks and behavioural risks are integrated to form a robust risk management strategy. The behavioural overlay to the generational maze of attitudes about wealth serves as a conduit through which a more direct satisfaction of the family's goals may be achieved.

Implementation of strategies

The financial and investment goals must then be prioritised and the time horizons for accomplishment and risk parameters for each noted in the investment policy. A subportfolio is created for each goal. After asset location issues are identified, managers and/or investment structures are selected and assets are allocated accordingly. Finally, optimisation occurs across the entire portfolio.[33]

Once the subportfolios are designed and all accompanying constraints are identified, due diligence is performed and managers are selected to implement the investment strategies. Asset location issues must also be considered in the implementation phase since whatever happens in one subportfolio affects what happens in the overall portfolio. Integration of risk, return, and tax considerations become part of the portfolio's ongoing monitoring and review.[34]

Monitoring and review

Monitoring of the entire portfolio of family assets becomes an ongoing process connected not only to financial and investment performance, but also benchmarking against the achievement of the family's goals for fostering its authentic wealth. Changes that affect a family's authentic assets include issues affecting communication and trust, the education of heirs in their roles and responsibilities, stage of life and leadership transitions, changes in circumstance, and the process of transitioning material and financial wealth to next and future generations. All of these areas have data points which may be monitored in the family's day to day management of all forms of its wealth. A system which monitors the family's authentic assets as well as the financial and investment assets offers a more robust management approach and empowers a family to be proactive in working with the cyclical nature of wealth flourishing.

Exhibit 1.4

Seven steps of the Generational Wealth Management Continuum^{SM}

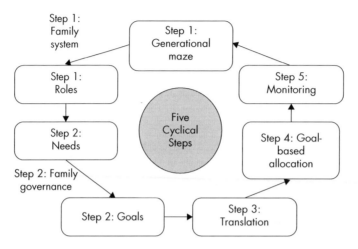

As we see in Exhibit 1.4, the five components of the Wealth Management Continuum^{SM} break down further into seven sequential steps, each of which may be revisited as necessary throughout the process. The entire process can be entered at any point where the family's needs lie; working back from there to address the necessary foundational components does not in any way make the process less effective. In fact, it makes the Continuum^{SM} timely and relevant, offering the flexibility of addressing multiple levels of need simultaneously.

For example, as new members enter the family entity either by marriage or partnership or by reaching the age where one's authentic assets are being recognised, new needs may arise which could alter the goals set by the family either through change or expansion of those goals. Or a change in leadership may require revisiting the family's generational maze and recognition of authentic wealth. Although a cyclical progression has been laid out, the monitoring step may uncover the need to revisit other steps, not necessarily in sequential order and not necessarily in singular fashion. A change in roles will also create a change in needs and, possibly, goals. Thus, a cyclical pattern of generational discovery becomes instituted that proactively supports the development of the family's authentic wealth.

The journey to discovery

The outline of the Continuum^{SM} which now has been created sets the stage for a deeper level of discovery. We began this chapter with a discussion of family dynamics and the dysfunction they can create. It is easy for founders and wealth creators to think of the resulting materialisation of their personal wealth as belonging only to them. On the surface, that would seem to be true. However, no wealth creator achieved his or her success without the help of others along the path to materialisation. And no wealth which has been materialised affects only the life of the creator(s). Spouses who live with these founders and the children who grow up in homes where material wealth is abundant are most obviously affected. If the wealth is significant enough, future generations will also be affected by the wealth. If siblings and/or cousins were partners in the materialisation, their spouses and progeny also benefit.

As future generations are born and new members join the family through marriage or life partnership, greater authentic wealth is brought to the family. The authentic assets of each family member hold the promise of material wealth regeneration and the hope of defying the Proverb. This is the reason a deeper, more complete approach to wealth management is needed. Hughes notes there are two kinds of families; one which is linked by blood who simply own assets together and another which is linked by affinity of relationship for whom the material wealth becomes a gift for generations to come.[35]

Teddie Ussery, founder of Family Office Matters LLC, notes, 'this is what holds a family together – not an asset base or the foundation or the business. It's the common thread of value, culture, and legacy that every family member has to embrace and the realisation that the assets belong to everyone in the family. If one family member chooses to think differently or to go in a different direction, the rest of the family has to support that one. It doesn't mean everyone has to do the same thing with their assets and their future. That lesson is one of the most powerful things a family can learn.'

By exploring the nature of generational perspectives and the powerful influence they carry in decisions made about the wealth, we may begin to discover the keys to managing a family's entire portfolio of wealth more successfully from generation to generation to generation. With this realisation, I invite you to join me on a journey of discovery following the path of the Continuum^SM through which we will weave a new story of family wealth management.

---

[1] Spencer, P., 'Shirtsleeves to shirtsleeves in three generations,' *Pennsylvania Fiduciary Litigation,* Spencer Law Firm, July 18 2008.

[2] Ibid.

[3] Williams, R. and Preisser, V., Preparing *Heirs,* (San Francisco, CA: Robert D. Reed, 2003), pp. 17, 36, 43. The study mentioned here is reported in this book published in 2003 as placing the success rate of the Proverb's fulfilment at 70%. Other sources, not necessarily scientific, place the fulfilment rate at 90%. Either number certainly begins to bring the weight of the problem home.

[4] Strauss, W. and Howe, N., *The Fourth Turning: an American prophecy* (New York, NY: Broadway Books, 1997), p. 16.

[5] Rubino, J., 'The importance of self esteem in the treatment of drug, alcohol, and other addictions', Treatment Centers, March 2010: www.treatment-centers.net/self-esteem.html.

[6] Any references throughout this book to the terms 'joint decisions' and 'joint decision making' refer to concepts presented in *Family: a compact among generations,* (see p. 122) and are used with permission from its author, James E. Hughes, Jr.

[7] Hughes, James E. Jr., Personal interview, August 2007.

[8] Ibid.

[9] Hughes, James E. Jr., Personal interview, October 2006.

[10] Adler, M.J., *How To Think About The Great Ideas: from the great books of Western Civilization,* (Peru, IL: Open Court, 2000), p. xxiii.

[11] Adler, M.J., 'Aristotle's *Ethics*: the theory of happiness II', the Mortimer J. Adler archive: http://radicalacademy.com/adleraristotleethics2.htm.

[12] Hauser, B.R., 'The Next Generation and the pursuit of happiness: Part One', *The Journal of Wealth Management,* Fall 2005, pp. 18–24.

[13] Hughes, James E. Jr., Personal interview, October 2006. All references to 'stewarding another's dream' or similar phrases point to the work of James E. Hughes, Jr.

[14] Hughes, J.E. Jr., *Family Wealth: keeping it in the family,* (New York, NY: Bloomberg Press, 2004), p. 4. It should be noted that Hughes and other professionals use the terms 'human and intellectual capital' in describing the authentic capital of the family. There is a distinct difference of thought between the author's concepts of authentic wealth and those in the industry who refer to family's talents and abilities as capital. The author views the use of the word 'capacities' as a meaningful expansion of the thought processes addressing the authentic wealth of the family rather than simply an opposition to the use of the term 'capital'.

[15] As indicated, an ongoing debate exists regarding the independence of the social capital of families from their intellectual and human capital. Hughes and Peter Karoff, renowned author on philanthropic and social issues, have differing views; Hughes feels a family's social capital is entirely dependent upon the family's intellectual and human capital. Karoff views social capital as separate and apart from intellectual and human capital. From the author's perspective, there are two important differences of note. The first is the use of the term 'capacities' as noted above in association with intellectual, human, and social wealth of the family. The second is the author's view that neither the intellectual nor the human capacities of family members may be fostered to a material form (the concept Hughes uses to note the transformation of energy into matter in application to the materialisation of family wealth, see p. 15 of *Family: a compact among generations*) without the employment of the social capacities of family members. The term 'authentic wealth' is used in place of Hughes' term 'authentic capital' for the purpose of illustrating that these capacities of family members can and should be treated as assets in the expanded family portfolio. This is the author's opinion and is not to be confused with the current debate on the independence of social capital (rather than capacities) or the concept of authentic capital, which is rightly associated with intellectual and human capital, rather than the concept of authentic wealth which lends itself more toward developing those capacities as family assets. More information about the debate between Hughes and Karoff on the independence of social capital may be found on p. 100, footnote 1 of *Family: a compact among generations*.

[16] Wealth Regeneration® is a registered service mark owned by Laird Norton Tyee and is used throughout this book Laird Norton Tyee's permission.

[17] 'Materialisation' is the term used by Hughes to describe the process transforming a family's energy into a material form. See *Family: a compact among generations*', p. 15.

[18] Hughes, J.E. Jr., (2007). *Family: a compact among generations,* (New York, NY: Bloomberg Press, 2007), p. 15.

[19] Jaffe, D.T., 'Stewardship in your family enterprise,' (Pioneer Imprints, January 2010), p.3: www.pioneerimprints.com.

[20] See note 14 above.

[21] See generally, United States Copyright Act, 17 U.S.C.A. §§ 102, 201, 411, 412 and 504.

[22] International Accounting Standards Board, 'Information for observers, World Standard Setters meeting. September 2006, London, Agenda Paper 1A, section 7b: www.iasb.org/NR/rdonlyres/8049CA20-8EA4-4E9B-BBDD-1988CEB6D78E/0/WSSAGENDAPAPER1A.pdf .

[23] Ibid, section 9.

[24] Hughes, James E., Jr., Personal interview, August 2007.

[25] Hughes, James E., Jr., Personal interview, October 2006.

[26] The concepts of integrated wealth management and optimality for the client are attributed to Jean L.P. Brunel. See Brunel, J.L.P., *Integrated Wealth Management*, 2nd edition, (London: Euromoney Books, 2006).

[27] The terms 'Wealth Management Continuum[SM]' and 'Generational Wealth Management Continuum[SM]' are the marked property of graymatter Strategies LLC.

[28] Merriam-Webster Online Dictionary: www.merriam-webster.com/dictionary/continuum.

[29] Merriam-Webster Online Dictionary: www.merriam-webster.com/dictionary/integrate.

[30] These comparisons are sourced from 'ERG Theory', a publicised comparison with implications for business management at www.netmba.com/mgmt/ob/motivation/erg.

[31] Brunel offers the insight that behavioural finance can be employed to translate the family's systematic goals into a financial language which make it possible to create appropriate investment goals on the family's path to optimality.

[32] The term 'relationship risk' is a service mark owned by graymatter Strategies LLC.

[33] Brunel, J.L.P., *Integrated Wealth Management*, 2nd edition, (London: Euromoney Books, 2006), p. 203. Any references to goal-based allocation throughout this book are based on Brunel's goal-based asset allocation model which identifies four

basic goal buckets with which investors identify in their daily lives: income, liquidity, capital preservation, and growth. Other buckets may also be identified as opportunistic investments or trades, operating businesses, and collectibles.

[34] In Brunel's goal-based asset allocation model, subportfolios are created and risk parameters and constraints identified for each; optimisation then occurs across the entire portfolio.

[35] Hughes, J.E. Jr., *Family: a compact among generations,* (New York, NY: Bloomberg Press, 2007), p. 3.

Part 1:

The foundation of the family system

'The greatest revolution of our generation is the discovery that human beings, by changing the inner attitudes of their minds, can change the outer aspects of their lives.'
William James

Chapter 2

The stealth influence of generational perspectives on wealth management decisions

'Each individual family is a part of the family of man and is thus affected by the history of every member of our larger human family. Yet each family is different as a result of its specific ancestors' experiences but none is unique since all are parts of one large family, the family of man.'

James E. (Jay) Hughes, Jr., Family Wealth: keeping it in the family

So we embark on our quest to understand the mystical stealth power of generational perspectives and how they influence every aspect of our lives – particularly wealth related issues – for as long as we live. A complete exploration, however, requires the determination that generational perspectives are, indeed, the most impactful in this regard. Therefore, this chapter attempts to settle the question of whether generational perspectives, cultural influences, or personality carry the greatest influence over the decisions families make in managing their wealth. Setting forth a premise stating such, it then makes the case that generational perspectives are indeed the bedrock forces influencing every aspect of wealth management. To understand the power of these forces, we must understand their nature and what makes them such an integral part of the wealth management equation.

Social generations become labelled by archetypical reinterpretations. The seven chapters within Part 1 will explore the archetypical generational responses of larger society. Interwoven with those responses will be the views of familial or chronological generations. Each type of generational perspectives has a set of foundational views and characteristics as well as a collective identity by its members.[1] Baby Boomers, Gen-Xers, and Echoes have their respective characteristics from a larger society view; founding generations, second generations, and third generations are characterised from their progression in the fulfilment of the Proverb, making these characteristics common within the social subset of families of wealth.

From this point forward, we will refer to the two types of generations as archetypical (for social generations) and chronological (for familial generations). Referring to the two types of perspectives in this manner allows a more direct understanding of their nature and their influence on family wealth decision making.

It should be emphasised that both types of generations are cyclical. They are in tune with nature. The natural law of entropy (also a cyclical progression) contributes to the fulfilment of the edicts of the Proverb. Correctly interpreted, that means families of wealth have two choices: they can either try to beat the natural law and deny the effects of the Proverb which, actually, makes the fulfilment of its edicts quicker and more certain or they can work with the laws of nature in a way that regenerates[2] their wealth – and the spirit of family.

The second note of import is that 85% of the reasons families succumb to the edicts of the Proverb has to do with factors other than management of the material wealth. In the Williams Group survey, participants were asked to identify the reasons that the Proverb's ratio of fulfilment is so high.[3] Survey respondents gave lack of communication and trust within family relationships a 60% attribution; lack of clarity regarding the roles heirs should play garnered a 25% attribution and, further, that heirs do not understand the responsibilities those roles carry.[4]

The journey chosen for this book is to find the keys for working *with* the natural laws of nature to postpone the fulfilment of the edicts of the famed Proverb rather than trying to deny them or escape from their power. On this road to discovery, we will find that generational perspectives and the roles family members occupy are inextricably linked to the decisions families make about their wealth. In the process, the very definition of family will rise to a new level, illuminating that family means more than what we personally want out of life.

There are five skills which are crucial to the success of wealthy families today.

1 Recognising dysfunction as a divider of family wealth that undermines family cohesion and well being.
2 Acknowledging the critical role of generational perspectives and family dynamics in making wealth management decisions.
3 Understanding the difference in cyclical and linear time measurement and the role each plays in a family's success.
4 Understanding the power of generational cycles in defining the family and fostering affinity in an effort to postpone the Proverb's fulfilment.
5 Learning how the historical Turnings of generational archetypical roles along with the expectations inherent in chronological generational roles affect family relationships and, consequentially, the family wealth.

This chapter will go deeper than the introduction of Skills One and Two offered in Chapter 1 and will firmly establish how an understanding of the impact of generational perspectives goes beyond personality and behavioural influences to enrich communication, trust, education, and other critical wealth management components which impact family success.

The critical role of generational perspectives and family dynamics

Modern society revels in attempting to apply sound-bite type solutions to symptoms, only to face the same problems – usually in even more severe situations – over and over again. This feeds the media interest in prominent families' dysfunction around their wealth. There are plenty of stories to tell – six are included in the Preamble – on Family Systems and each family reading this book can recite its own elements.

There is no doubt that dysfunction is a divider – of family members and of family wealth. Rather than the direct result of possessing material wealth, it is my firm belief that the cause of dysfunction lies more fundamentally within the dynamics of the family – the manner of relationship between family members and how they treat each other. These dynamics are embedded within each family's unique maze of perspectives present in the generations currently alive. Having significant material and financial wealth only exacerbates a pre-existing problem. This leads us to conclude that generational perspectives are the root causes of family dysfunction and, therefore, exert their influences directly on wealth management decisions.

But is this premise correct? According to Hughes, 'Philosophy teaches that all ideas remain worthy of consideration until and unless they are found to be truly fallacious' and that '... truly good ideas, as philosophy teaches, are timeless'.[5] In that light, I take delightful pleasure in launching the premise to sail upon its own waters through the oceans of time. One of the first tests of the premise might be to examine the thoughts of other professionals working with families of wealth in these areas of concern. What is the primary influence on wealth management decisions?

To explore that query in depth, a panel has been assembled that represents my colleagues, family wealth professionals ranging from private wealth management professionals at large financial services firms, to wealth and business psychologists, to consultants who work with families of wealth on issues from governance to family office recruiting to multi-generational wealth management – in essence, professionals from across the board.

Our panel members include: Teddie Ussery, founder, Family Office Matters LLC; John Benevides, president, Family Office Exchange; M.J. Rankin, president/CEO, The Rankin Group; Joline Godfrey, founder and CEO, Independent Means, Inc.; Natasha Pearl, CEO and founder of Aston • Pearl; Donald J. Herrema, Executive Vice Chairman, Kennedy Wilson International, Inc.; Richard L. Luscomb, Ph.D., Clinical Psychologist, Germantown Psychological Associates, P.C.; Thomas J. Handler, J.D., P.C., Handler Thayer LLC; and Barbara R. Hauser, independent family advisor at Barbara R. Hauser LLC.

Let us now join our guests in the conference room and see what they have to say about the influences on wealth management decisions in families of significant wealth.

Moderator: Our topic of discussion concerns the influences that come to bear on family wealth management decisions and, in turn, how family relationships are affected by these decisions. Which do you think carries the greatest influence on wealth management decisions in families of wealth – cultural influences, generational perspectives, or personality?

Ussery: I think it's a combination of generational perspectives and personality, especially from the perspectives of the second and third generations. The first generation had what Hughes calls a 'dream which it materialized'[6] that it wants to protect. The second and third generations certainly want to continue to protect it but they also want to put their own mark on it. Each generation has to reinvent the dream for the wealth to continue.

Moderator: What influence does personality have?

Ussery: The second generation is very important because they move from the first generation into decision making at the family level. Leadership is critical at that juncture. If the family cannot agree on leadership or if real leadership does not emerge – even in the form of an outside council – it may jeopardize the family's success. When women in the family marry, the influence of the spouses combined with each generation's desire to reinvent the dream can change the wealth dramatically. This is where personality comes in. And that's where conflict can arise.

Moderator: And the legal and tax structures employed to protect and pass on the wealth introduce the concept of wealth location ...

Benevides: As I think about wealth location in terms of asset allocation, goals, and governance, each of those may have a different hierarchy of influence. If you look at governance structures, I would say cultural influence is probably the leading factor. I'm not really clear in terms of personality – in terms of governance, personality would probably be third or would tie with generational perspectives. The cultural influence is strong here in the US since our roots are based in a democracy, so we understand that as a principle at our core. While other countries have *become* democracies, the cultural history is more rooted in a top-down, patriarchal or clan-leader system.

So I would say culture has the most influence in terms of setting up the governance structure and how that structure will evolve. In terms of generations, judging from our current benchmarking work across the families, you see differences depending on which generation is at the top and what age range they represent. In terms of asset allocation, there may be some cultural variance you could point to, but generational perspectives are definitely Number One. Personality would follow that and culture would be third.

Rankin: It's really hard to generalize when talking about families and family offices. Each family is so unique. It depends on the family, their values, and the culture that's been created – who they are, where they've come from, what they want in the future – these are the critical influences. Additionally, you have to understand the unique characteristics that motivate people from their generation(s) and how that impacts their own values and attitudes, their ancestry, and how much they understand the tradition of who they are, how the money was made, and their perspective on it.

Then you get into the psychological dynamic of the family to help them better understand the decisions they make. That's why I think one of the most influential factors impacting families and family offices is probably the culture and personal values. Clearly defining the culture, traditions, and personality of the family impacts the perspectives of the generations.

Moderator: Joline, as a family wealth educator, how would you answer this question?

Godfrey: 'Who you are' is a product of your culture and your history and what's going on in current events. Certainly, for the younger generation, whether it's teens or 20-somethings, there's a much more powerful cultural influence than in practically any other generation before them. They're so inundated and saturated by it. So in a way, culture is the biggest variable regarding everything related to money and one's values.

Pearl: I would put generational first and I would definitely put personality second. There's a lot of awareness today among most families, traditionally, that the wealth has been dissipated by the third generation – usually *in* the second generation *by* the second generation family members! That said, I think the second generation has become more acutely focused on proactively taking steps so that doesn't happen to them. They want their kids to grow up with the idea that they are family wealth stewards, not spenders. But our clients do tend to share certain psychographic characteristics and that's true no matter where they stand in the generational continuum.

Herrema: Those are all important! I think I could argue for almost any ranking I could give you. But I'm going to take a little liberty with personality and say that if personality means 'lifestyle', I would rank it Number One. I would put cultural influences Number Two and generational perspectives Number Three. Generational perspectives are different if you're talking about a first generation source of wealth rather than a second or third. So I think generational perspectives are important, but it depends on when the wealth was created.

Moderator: Don, in your opinion, how does lifestyle portray the influence of personality?

Herrema: I put personality first because certain individuals like to live a certain way regardless of ranges of wealth. That dictates a lot of things. For example, a person who spends $5 million a year may feel he can only stay in a $20,000-a-night hotel and that he has to have household help of every variety wherever he happens to be. Another person who has $15 million may feel like he's living on a shoestring. Yet another $15 million person who only spends $1 million per year may feel he has a very comfortable lifestyle.

Moderator: From a psychological standpoint, which influence seems greater over wealth management decisions?

Luscomb: Money issues can arise from all three – generational perspectives, cultural influence, or personality. But in terms of wealth management decisions, absolutely generational perspectives are the most influential. Let's take a broad look at what's happened over the last couple of generations. The fathers coming out of the WWII [World War II] generation produced very highly motivated, entrepreneurial, initiative-based kids. Those kids came out of the [19]50s and took the world by storm. They grew up with a strong work ethic and were very conservative.

They, in turn, produced a generation where the guidelines were not as clear. So we then had a generation of parents who went out of their way to make sure their children had everything they didn't have growing up. As a result, the third generation has never had the value of money or a work ethic instilled in them. There are a few kids who do work hard and I tell them, 'The world will be your oyster because your peers will be standing around wondering what you are doing'. That's a broad, cultural brush of people who grew up from 1905 to kids born in the 1980s.

Handler: I rank them generational, personality, then cultural. Cultural factors could be Number One in some cases but it's not the predominant factor. As a general proposition, the way people are raised and what they experienced are going to inordinately determine how they respond. Personality will come into play because some people are simply more driven, controlling, or capable than others.

Children and grandchildren are viewed as potential successors. How they live their lives, how much talent they have, their backgrounds – all of that is scrutinized. And inheritances will vary based on who's giving the gift and who's receiving it. The way the previous generation or two treat, interact with, and educate the current generation has a massive impact on how they're going to make decisions.

Hauser: I would put cultural traditions first, generational perspectives second, and personality third. Cultural traditions are the larger community in which you form your values. You may not even be aware of them – they're the ingrained assumptions you make and within those cultural traditions, people are aware that different generations have a slightly different stance on it. But they share the cultural ideas.

Moderator: So how do generational perspectives come into play?

Hauser: The senior generation believes in duty and hard work – life's not supposed to be fun. Their kids are the baby boomers who really haven't had the chance to control any wealth. They've been kept in the dark in terms of family wealth and don't have the training or expectation of using it in any serious way for their own life goals. The younger generation sees that after the bubble burst, it was difficult to find employment anywhere. They don't have this set of rules and there's a lot of angst about what to do with themselves.

Moderator: Thank you all very much for some wonderful insights.

By looking at the definition of a generation, we discover that, just as the comments of our panel reflect, generational perspectives are quite closely related to cultural influences. According to the American Heritage Dictionary, a generation is 'a group of generally contemporaneous individuals regarded as having common cultural or social characteristics and attitudes,' as well as 'all of the offspring that are at the same stage of descent from a common ancestor'.[7] Since the term 'culture' is used within the definition of a generation, one could almost assert that their influences are the same. However, a closer look at the nature of the two reveals quite a different story.

William Strauss and Neil Howe, renowned authors on generations and their perspectives, define a generation in an entirely different way. They define a generation as 'the aggregate of all people born over roughly the same span of a phase of life who share a common location in history and, hence, a common collective persona ... and each phase is associated with a specific social role that conditions how its occupants perceive the world and act on those perceptions'.[8] This squarely gives a generation a different power – a unique position of influence. It gives it a place in the world as well as a place in time.

Birth Spectrums© and generational imprints

From these definitions we can add our own definition of a generation as 'a group of people born within a specific period of years corresponding to a particular set of social and economic experiences'. The specific period of years corresponds to the particular phase of life, and can be named the Generational Birth Spectrum©.

Exhibit 2.1

Birth Spectrums and generational imprints

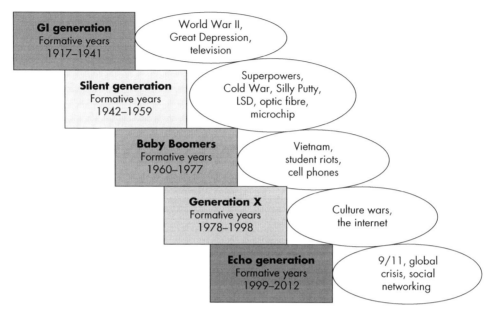

From our panel members' comments and in light of these definitions, it makes sense to view cultural influences as the impact of social conditions on communication and interaction[9] or as traditions that are handed down or as generally accepted social behaviour. Generational perspectives refer to the basic mode of reference – a generational template, if you will – that subconsciously guides our way of thinking and behaving.

Behaviour most certainly can be influenced by culture, but one's basic generational template is built during the formative years based on a historically dictated archetypical role and is tied more closely to the collective experiences and responses of people at the same stage of life. The question then arises, just how strong and long lasting are these generational perspectives? And are they truly the predominant influences on decision making?

Jung spoke of attitude types that are biologically hard wired into mankind. These archetypical behaviours are so entrenched in the 'collective unconscious' that nothing could weaken their hold.[10] Mannheim's work (circa 1970) confirms the formation of an initial set of impressions which give meaning to one's life experiences during the mid to late teens. These impressions create a predisposition 'for a certain characteristic mode of thought and experience, and a characteristic type of historically relevant action'.[11] This set of impressions creates a generational lens which colours our natural view of the world. Everything we experience after this natural view is formed derives its meaning through this lens, regardless if that experience serves to verify or negate our particular world view. 'Even if the rest of one's life consisted of one long process of negation and destruction of the natural world view acquired in youth, the determining influence of these early impressions would still be predominant.'[12]

Almost 30 years later, Strauss and Howe further described a generation as possessing 'a common collective persona' as noted above. This points to specific characteristics resulting from the collective responses shared by people born within a specified period of years.[13] Therefore, we can reasonably conclude that each of us, as a human being, has a predominant, permanently formed frame of reference directly resulting from an imprint of perspectives which we share with other members of our particular generation – perspectives which colour our attitudes towards wealth, how money should be used, how we should live our lives, and every other aspect of our existence. As we will see, this is a critical notion in the examination of the process through which wealth management decisions are formulated within families.

Generational perspectives or personality?

We may also conclude that generational perspectives go beyond personality in impacting the decisions families make about their wealth. For example, if we look at two entrepreneurs – one Silent generation and one Gen-Xer – we will see that they share common personality traits. They will both be driven, they will both be idea generators – they may even be good delegators. But their basic approaches to their respective entrepreneurial ventures will be entirely different. For example, the Silent generation wealth creator will likely have secured financing for his or her venture through traditional outlets such as bank loans or professional investors. The Gen-X wealth creator may have got a group of friends together and started his or her enterprise out in the garage or inside a university dorm room with little or no start-up capital. The Silent generation entrepreneur will take a different approach to growing the company than the Gen-Xer. The Silent would look to hire employees in-house and who live in close proximity to the business's operating headquarters.

The Gen-Xer will tend to more readily employ technology to operate leaner, more efficiently, and to produce a product or service faster. He or she may outsource services which are used occasionally and may have little regard for where an employee lives since everyone will be connected by computer interface. The entire business may have generated itself through the internet. It could have begun as a hobby or as the recognition of a societal need which transformed itself into a money-making venture. With easy and inexpensive access to the masses, growth can occur exponentially. Employees can be located across the globe with supply chain, delivery, and other options outsourced wherever economies of scale present themselves.

The Gen-X entrepreneur may use less traditional models of operation and hierarchy. In fact, there may be little or no hierarchy in a Gen-X entrepreneurial enterprise. Relationships with employees and opportunities for contribution or advancement will also differ with the two entrepreneurial ventures. Both may be equally successful; the Silent generation entrepreneur may also embrace technology and more efficient business processes. But the Gen-X entrepreneur will have a more fluid approach to growth, with greater ability to change course to adapt to changes in the marketplace. If the business develops in an unexpected manner, the Gen-Xer will likely have greater flexibility, enabling him or her to follow the marketplace's lead. The Silent generation entrepreneur may tend to stick closer to the original idea for the business, discounting messages – even blatant ones – from the marketplace which may unexpectedly show alternative revenue streams to be more successful.

The generational 'lens'

Based on the conclusion that our generational 'lens' colours almost every aspect of our lives, the next step is to examine how generational factors become translated into the decisions families make about their wealth. Strauss and Howe state that 'common beliefs and behavior of a generation show its members to be different from people born at another time. They are the means by which a generation moves history'.[14] Each family – regardless of wealth – is comprised of members of multiple generations. As in society at large, the perspectives of family members based on their generational imprints 'moves' the history of the family, in essence, preserving or destroying the family legacy – what we will refer to throughout this book as the Family Story.

As the oldest social institution in the world, there are correlations that can be made from larger society and brought down to the entity that has been characterised as the foundation of society, the family. 'In fact, a nation or a state is often described as a large family, and a family is often described as a society in miniature.'[15] Therefore, we can appropriately refer to the family as a 'mini-society'. Since the members of a family are also members of generational cohorts, the archetypical generational templates outlined in the work of Strauss and Howe are present in every family regardless of the amount of material wealth. Families of wealth additionally have the perspectives of chronological generations emanating from the generation who originally created or materialised the wealth. Most often, chronological generations match the fulfilment of the edicts of the Proverb and the wealth disappears by G3 or G4. The first generation creates the wealth and the second generation either spends it or lets it sit there with little effective management. By the third generation, the sheer numbers of people benefiting from the wealth have increased in a way that naturally diminishes the wealth and, through the lack of stewardship of the second generation, members of the third generation are forced to do work which may or may not bring them joy and fulfilment.

How do we recognise a generation? From the archetypical perspectives, generational personas are definitively separated by birth spectrums© with specific beginning and end points.[16] What is a generational persona? 'A distinctly human and variable creation which can embody attitudes about family life, gender roles, institutions, politics, culture, lifestyle, money, and the future.' According to Strauss and Howe, a generation possesses all the capabilities of a person – the ability to think, feel, and do. It can behave in a conservative manner or a reckless one; its nature can be 'individualist or collegial, spiritual or secular'. It shares the characteristic of 'being fuzzy at the edges' like other social categories such as race, class, religion, or nationality; yet, it differs from other social categories by possessing 'its own personal biography'. The core personality of each generation emerges as it continues through its lifecycle. Not every member of a generation will possess all the characteristics of the archetype but every member will be forced to reckon with it over the course of his or her lifetime. According to Martin Heidegger, 'the fateful act of living in and with one's generation completes the drama of human existence'.[17]

There are three attributes that identify the persona of a generation: a perception of membership by people born within the specific generation's birth spectrum©, beliefs and behaviours which are common across the generational cohort, and a commonality of being born within the specified range of years – the location in history. The perception of membership emerges during adolescence and continues to form itself during and immediately after college, military experience, marriage, and the initial work experience. Members of a generation who are born early in the birth spectrum© acquire these attributes at an older age than those born later since they are the ones who initially shed the identity of the previous generation.[18] This accounts for the 'fuzzy at the edges' nature of the various archetypical cohorts.

Further, since each generation occupies its own place in time through its particular birth spectrum©, the manner in which time is measured becomes paramount to the success of postponing the fulfilment of the edicts of the Proverb. To fully understand the position of each generation, its role in society at large, and the 'pass-through' impact of generations within our mini-society of family, it becomes essential to understand the effects of measuring time both from a linear and a cyclical perspective. This is the task of Chapter 3.

---

[1] Nadler, Reena. Associate, LifeCourse Associates, Great Falls, VA. Personal interview, May 2010.

[2] Wealth Regeneration® is a registered service mark owned by Laird Norton Tyee and is used throughout this book Laird Norton Tyee's permission.

[3] Williams, R. and Peisser, V., *Preparing Heirs,* (San Francisco, CA: Robert D. Reed, 2003), pp. 17, 36, 43. The study mentioned here is reported in this book published in 2003 as placing the success rate of the Proverb's fulfilment at 70%. Other sources, not necessarily scientific, place the fulfilment rate at 90%. Either number certainly begins to bring the weight of the problem home.

[4] Williams, R. and Peisser, V., *Preparing Heirs,* (San Francisco, CA: Robert D. Reed, 2003), pp. 17, 36, 43.

[5] Hughes, J.E., Jr., *Family: a compact among generations,* (New York, NY: Bloomberg Press, 2007), p. 63.

[6] Ibid, p. 15.

[7] American Heritage Dictionary of the English Language, 4th edition, Houghton Mifflin Company, 2000: http://dictionary.reference.com/browse/generation.

[8] Strauss, W. and Howe, N., *The Fourth Turning: an American prophecy,* (New York, NY: Broadway Books, 1997), p. 16.

[9] The North Central Regional Education Laboratory: www.ncrel.org/sdrs/areas/issues/students/earlycld/ea4lk22.htm.

[10] Strauss, W. and Howe, N., *The Fourth Turning: an American prophecy,* (New York, NY: Broadway Books, 1997); also Wikipedia, 'Jungian archetypes': http://en.wikipedia.org/wiki/Jungian_archetypes.

[11] Mannheim, K., 'The problem of generations,' *Psychoanalytic Review,* 57, 1970, p. 389. This is found in Mannheim's comments regarding the 'tendency 'inherent in' a social location'. Strauss and Howe in their writings also speak of defining generations in association with a social, experiential location.

[12] Strauss, W. and Howe, N., *The Fourth Turning: an American prophecy,* (New York, NY: Broadway Books, 1997), p. 16. The power of generational perspectives over the entire life of a person is further emphasized in that, 'For even in negation our orientation is fundamentally centered upon that which is being negated, and we are thus still unwittingly determined by it'. Strauss and Howe also point to the power of generational influences in political elections and world events in their book, *The Fourth Turning*.

[13] The terms 'birth spectrum' and 'generational birth spectrum' are the copyrighted and service marked property of graymatter Strategies LLC.

[14] Strauss, W. and Howe, N., *The Fourth Turning: an American prophecy,* (New York, NY: Broadway Books, 1997), p. 66.

[15] Fernea, E.W., 'The family in the Middle East', Center for Middle Eastern Studies, The University of Texas at Austin, 1984–2009.

[16] Strauss, W. and Howe, N., *Millennials Rising: the next Great Generation,* (New York, NY: Vintage, 2000), pp. 40, 41.

[17] Ibid.

[18] Ibid, p. 39.

Chapter 3

Cycles of regeneration ... the matter of time

'More recently, the West began using technology to flatten the very physical evidence of natural cycles. With artificial light, we believe we defeat the sleep-wake cycle; with climate control, the seasonal cycle; with refrigeration, the agricultural cycle; and with high-tech medicine, the rest-recovery cycle. Before, when cyclical time reigned, people valued patience, ritual, the relatedness of parts to the whole, and the healing power of time-within-nature. Today, we value haste, iconoclasm, the disintegration of the whole into parts, and the power of time-outside-nature.'

William Strauss and Neil Howe, The Fourth Turning

To further develop the premise that differences in generational perspectives are the source of family dynamics and the root of all family dysfunction, we turn now to the 'location' of generations in time. This part of our journey will introduce us to two tools which will facilitate a more complete understanding of the influence of generational perspectives on wealth management issues – the evolution of energy and the cyclical and linear measurement of time. The notion that generations have a specific location in time is dependent upon an understanding of cyclical time measurement. The essential foundation laid by an understanding of cyclicality connects us to the edicts of the 'shirtsleeves to shirtsleeves' Proverb. The Proverb itself looks, feels, and sounds negative. Through the exploration of time and its impact on generational perspectives, this chapter will explore the Proverb's nature more fully and determine if, in fact, a negative outcome is unavoidable.

As delineated in Chapter 2, we note that there are two different types of generational perspectives: those which cyclically reinterpret archetypical cohorts through the course of each century and those whose origination begins with the founders and creators of the family wealth. America has labelled the archetypical generations GI, Silent, Baby Boomer, Gen-X, and Echo (or Millennials). Chronological (or Proverbial) generations are referred to as G1, G2, G3, G4, and so on. They primarily refer to the generation's position in time relative to the distance from the wealth creating generation. Thus, this latter set of generationally-sourced perspectives only applies to families of wealth within the context of this book.

Either type of generation becomes identified through the measurement of time. Both types of perspectives are essential for our purposes, since families of wealth are also composed of people born within a larger society generational cohort. Therefore, we apply the first set of perspectives from the standpoint of understanding the socio-economic influences that shaped the imprint of each generation in the family and through which we can identify the dynamics that are at work within the family. The second set of generational perspectives offers the realisation that views of wealth change the farther each generation gets from the original wealth creators. Keeping these two types of generational perspectives in mind, we will focus more on the archetypical type in the first half of this book and overlay the influences of the chronological during the second half.

The five skills identified in Chapter 2 are critical to families' abilities to apply their understanding of these concepts in a way that will significantly enhance the flourishing of their wealth in all its forms. To flourish means to grow luxuriantly, thrive, fare well, or prosper.[1] What a magnificent thought, that of a family growing its wealth luxuriantly to benefit living as well as future generations as the gift it truly can be! Even in times of economic uncertainty such an endeavour is not unrealistic. In fact, such times often yield unforeseen opportunities.

Times of economic crisis show us the true nature of wealth – that material wealth can be adversely affected by factors beyond our control. The real wealth of the family, however – its family members and their limitless capacities – holds continual potential and is bursting to be developed. That wealth is the authentic legacy for wealth creators and family leadership. If a family develops a consummate understanding of its true wealth and its exponential potential, management decisions regarding the material wealth yield significantly better results. This is particularly important during times of crisis. These are the times when: (a) the authentic wealth may actually buffer the material wealth against unfavourable market and other external forces; and (b) the family may be offered the greatest opportunity for leveraging the future growth of all wealth forms. The way in which time is measured has a great deal to do with the manner in which families of wealth experience such crises.

This chapter begins by looking at the nature of time measurement within our global society. We will observe that crises such as the Great Depression, World War II, 9/11, and, most recently, the credit crisis of 2008, which are experienced in society at large, are spawned from the generally accepted societal view of linear time progression.[2] It proceeds to show how cyclicality is integrated into family wealth and concludes by exploring an unfortunately convenient modern-day example of linear time imposition.

With these thoughts in mind, we will address skills Three and Four which encompass:

• understanding the difference in cyclical and linear time progression measurement and the role each plays in a family's success; and
• understanding the power of generational cycles in defining the family and fostering affinity in an effort to postpone the Proverb's fulfilment.

Through such an examination, this chapter will explain the differences in time measurement from both a linear and cyclical perspective and the relevance of those differences to our purposes, subsequently illustrating the essential nature of skills Three and Four to family wealth management success.

The nature of time measurement

As noted earlier, Strauss and Howe, refer to each generation as possessing a 'common collective persona'.[3] The interpretation and experience of each phase of life is coloured by this persona which holds perspectives unique to each generation and is further interpreted by differences in personality. A 'long human life' equates to 100 years and is the basis for the creation of the marker of time called the 'century'. Use of a long human life span to measure time goes back to the Etruscans who viewed history as a seasonal cycle of growth, maturation, entropy, and death. Time as measured by cycles has no end; it experiences completion and regeneration continuously. Its weakness is found in its inability to help human beings feel some sense of progressive development. It does not accommodate modern ideas of creativity, originality, and self improvement[4] – ideas which undoubtedly contribute to the psychological health of human beings.

The linear view of time has an absolute beginning and an absolute end which Strauss and Howe say began with the Fall from Grace, proceeds through trials, failures, revelations, and divine interventions to end in redemption and re-entry into the Kingdom of God. Linear time's great achievement is an 'endowment to mankind' that allows the definition of moral and material goals, fostering a sense of heightened satisfaction when those goals are reached and an effort to improve by applying new strategies to accomplish the same end when they are not. But the journey is never repeated.[5]

The weakness of linear time measurement, the authors assert, is the estrangement of people from the eternal – the grounding force that fosters meaning in life. By considering our social destiny to be ultimately within our own control and the direction of our lives to be self-determined, we deny ourselves the rich experience of participation 'in a collective myth that is larger than ourselves'.[6] Thus, our efforts to 'flatten natural and social cycles often meet with only superficial success'. We may simply be substituting one cycle for another or worse, we may be altering a cycle from its normal regularity of occurrence, causing cycles to occur less frequently and with more devastating effects.[7]

This happens in families during the reign of each governing generation. In analysing the failure of governing generations to even recognise change much less try to accept or understand it, Strauss and Howe note that each generation views successive generations as simply an extension of its own. In other words, a Silent wealth creator expects his or her Boomer or Gen-X children to do things in the same manner as they were done while the children were growing up. In subsequent chapters, we will find this to be a characteristic not reserved for American families; it is a characteristic shared across the globe.

As those children become adults and begin to express different ideas, the fear that the youthful generation will indeed perform its proper role of reinterpretation and 'forging a fresh path'[8] is the incentive for trusts that are set up to 'protect' the wealth (or the children from being 'spoiled') or used as leverage to manipulate behaviours. However, if the next generation is denied its opportunity to individuate in this way, the resulting dysfunction leads to the development of a family's own brand of a Great Event as described below. If those Great Events occur within a family of wealth who is well-known, the media will happily give them public exposure as with the six stories of the Preamble.

How linear time imposes itself

The view of governing generations alluded to above is a perfect example of linear time imposition. The resistance to change comes from the encapsulated view of one generation that things will always – and should continue to – be done the way they did them. It is a 'linear extension of the recent past'.

The linear time view is pervasive throughout the global society. Yet, the foundation of the manner in which families function is grounded in cyclicality. Linear time imposes an artificial progression that defies equilibrium or the state of balance and harmony. When artificial impositions stray too far from the natural cyclical progression, nature forces a return to the natural flow with some type of extreme event. Strauss and Howe call these corrections Great Events and define such an event as an 'emergency so fraught with social consequence that it transforms all of society's members, yet transforms them differently according to their phase-of-life responses'.[9] A Great Event in a family of wealth transforms the dynamics of the family, usually in a way that masks the fact that the event is the entire family's problem, not just the family member's who seems to be at the heart of the event.

In larger society, the impact of each so-called 'Great Event' is shaped differently depending on the age of the person experiencing it. An event that is successfully resolved results in a lasting memory which identifies a 'unique location in history' and fosters the generational persona.[10] Such events as World War I, the Great Depression, Pearl Harbor, Watergate, 9/11, and the bear market of the early 2000s shaped the lives of those who experienced them. It is too early to know the full effects of the credit crisis of 2008, yet the view of a major restructuring of the way the world (society at large) functions – financially, economically, and as a global society – is clearly within the realm of possibility.

We are beginning to see that there may be a connection between the manner in which such crises develop in larger society and the manner in which crises develop which are experienced by families of wealth. In *The Fourth Turning: an American prophecy*, Strauss and Howe compare the cyclical succession of generations over 100-year periods with the seasons of time. Just as the four seasons of summer, fall, winter, and spring turn over the course of a year, generations have four 'Turnings' over the course of a century, the span of a long human life. They explore the fixed patterns of the 'seasons' of history, citing also the fixed patterns of generational turnings in which each of four archetypes – the collective persona – makes a personal connection with the society and culture in which it lives. In similar fashion to the seasons of nature over the course of a year, the turnings are 'in the same order' century after century 'as successive generations pass through life'. Each turning is dominated by four generational archetypes which occur in the same order century after century and are reinterpreted by each new generation.

Interestingly, the span of the chronological generations which fulfil the Proverb's prophecy also come close to occupying the span of a century. However, these generations are identified relative to their distance from the creation of the material wealth, not through birth spectrums©.

The way to make sense of the four Turnings of generational archetypes is to view them within the normal flow of life. The archetypes identified by Strauss and Howe are 'expressions of the enduring temperaments and life-cycle myths of mankind'.[11] History imposes these archetypes over each of the four Turnings, creating in each Turning a new grouping of generations Strauss and Howe call 'constellations'. Within these constellations, our memories are coloured by the 'emotional complexion' of our stage of life at the time of the dynamic event.

Markers of childhood are coloured by dreams and innocence; markers of later life bear the cares of maturity and signify the way a person has shaped events and influenced younger people. As we age, we remember the markers that mattered and enshrine them. The linking of biological aging and shared experiences which are reproduced across turnings and generations make history relevant on a personal basis,[12] tying family members together and fostering joint decision making on important family matters.

The effects of both methods of time measurement can been translated to the smaller society of family and their roles in determining family communication through the powerful lenses of generational perspectives. Ignoring or attempting to 'flatten' the natural generational cycles by imposing a linear view of time progression attempts to prevent the inevitable reversion of energy from a material form to its pure state. It is an effort doomed to failure.

Exhibit 3.1

The flattening of natural generational cycles

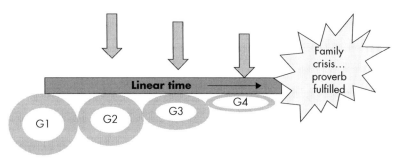

Yet, that is what the majority of families of wealth and advisors of all ilk unwittingly attempt to do! Traditional asset protection tools are a ready example. These tools are quite valuable when employed for their best purpose – that of mitigating risks which are beyond our control. But when they are employed without the benefit of cyclical time recognition and are not designed to consider the family's authentic wealth, their seeming effectiveness can ultimately become compromised or circumvented even under the best, most 'iron-clad' situations. They can actually contribute to the fulfilment of the edicts of the Proverb. Often, this manifests itself in 'problem' family members, 'unforeseen' personal situations, and a necessity to make less than desirable wealth management decisions – the effects of which touch the entire living family as well as future generations.

From this application, we can conclude that the crises families experience as a result of conflict around wealth issues – and which foster the fulfilment of the Proverb – also are born from the way families measure time. It is within this context that the influence of generational cycles becomes apparent, opening the door to the flourishing of all forms of family wealth. Cyclical time creates the pathway through which larger society evolves. This evolution usually occurs in an upward spiral.[13]

Exhibit 3.2

Cyclical rejuvenation: chronological generations

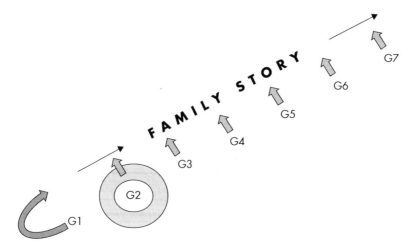

Through cyclical wealth regeneration,[14] families can create a path in which the wealth created by the first generation wealth owners can be rejuvenated by successive generations (G2, G3, G4, and so on) so that it continues to benefit G5, G6, G7, G8 and possibly G9, G10, and more.

This is why it is so important for families and their advisors to recognise the power of the energy cycle in the creation of material wealth. In doing so, we also come to recognise the importance of acknowledging the cycles of time, of life, and how any attempt to ignore such cycles goes completely contrary to the very nature of wealth creation. The cyclical materialisation of wealth and the measurement of time are innately intertwined as we are about to see as we explore the nature of time measurement and its effects on every facet of our lives.

The cyclical nature of family relationships

By showing the validity of the four Turnings and the associated archetypical roles throughout the annals of history to the current times in which we live, *we can discern pathways of communication and consensus for family wealth decision making through acknowledgement of the influence of generational cycles.* In applying the four archetypes to the smaller society of a family, we see that generational perceptions result in 'gut-level differences in values that involve a person's beliefs, emotions, and preferences' based on the social and economic experiences of the people born within the generational birth spectrum©.[15] Whenever generations try to work together – as in making decisions jointly[16] about family wealth – these differences become especially poignant. Each generation has its own set of core personal values based on the social and economic events experienced during childhood – the 'Great Events'.

Values guide thinking, conviction, and behaviour; differing values may lead to confrontation in any situation where a group of people of different ages is confronted with issues related to wealth; religious beliefs; music, fashion, and food preferences; and/or moral convictions.[17] Knowledge and understanding of generational differences can mean the difference in family consensus or total impasse; the fulfilment of edicts of the Proverb ... or their postponement.

Looking back at the second family example in the Preamble, we can see a perfect illustration of linear time progression being carried to an extreme. The mandated, imposed family legacy of keeping the wealth intact had failed to allow each generation to put its rejuvenating magic to work; there was no genuine 'buy-in' by subsequent generations which would have allowed them to own the legacy for themselves and reinvent it, as Ussery stated, to establish their 'mark' or contribution to a renewed version of that legacy. By the time the wealth reached chronological G4, the linear extreme snapped and the wealth was split into 11 pieces. Similar insights can be gained from the first and third stories. The linear progression of the first was not carried to quite the extreme of the second, but the third certainly was. The financial wealth of each family was eroding, and wealth as defined by family members, their intellectual and human capacities and the relationships that bind them, was suffering as well.

These principles also hold true for families of other cultures. All global cultures hold generational secrets of the real meaning of family that families of wealth would do well to know. By looking at families only through an American lens, we miss the essence of family and of family wealth. The true richness of family wealth can be seen only through a much wider lens – a lens that allows American families to view European, Asian, Middle Eastern, and Latin American families; a lens that works both ways to allow families of other cultures also to view the merits of American families; a lens that not only sees financial and other assets of monetary value, but the true wealth of the family – the intellectual and human capacities of its members and the relationships that make them the larger, separate familial entity.

Within which Turning are we now living and how is it affecting families of wealth? Six cycles (centuries) of turnings have been confirmed in history since the Renaissance. Each cycle had four turnings which, in turn, produced four generational archetypes. When Strauss and Howe wrote their book in 1997, they stated that we were in the seventh cycle of Modernity and in the Third Turning of our age. Although it is too early to define with confidence, it is my belief that with the Great Event of 9/11, we entered the Fourth Turning predicted by Strauss and Howe to begin around the year 2005. The basis of my conclusion is the following. Of the list of possible predictions Strauss and Howe list in their book in 1997 for the next Great Event, this one leaped to my attention:

'A global terrorist group blows up an aircraft and announces it possesses portable nuclear weapons. The US and its allies launch a pre-emptive strike. The terrorists threaten to retaliate against an American City. Congress declares war and authorizes unlimited house-to-house searches. Opponents charge that the president concocted the emergency for political purposes. A nationwide strike is declared. Foreign capital flees the US.'[18]

Though not exact in its prediction, the similarities to actual events since that fateful day in 2001 could be considered rather startling: the 9/11 airplane strikes, the later accusations that the American president concocted 9/11 for political purposes, the declaration of the War on Terror, the phone tapping by the American president, the investigation into the wire tapping, the announcements by

Iran regarding its nuclear capabilities, and the fact that foreign capital has been moving out of the US as a result of the stringent hurdles imposed by the Patriot Act.[19]

This was the first event which ushered in the period of Crisis and what I believe will prove to be the beginning of the Fourth Turning. True to historical form, 9/11 was only the ushering in of the crisis period. Its effects rang true with the Great Events that ushered in other Fourth Turnings in history. It served as a catalyst for a mood change for the country, even the world. According to Strauss and Howe, there is a time span of anywhere from 15 to 25 years between the catalyst and the resolution ushering in the next First Turning or heroic period. That heroic generation is already born.

A regrouping which energetically brings society together under a common cause typically occurs from one to five years after the catalyst[20] (9/11 occurred in 2001; the apex of the credit crisis occurred in 2008 – both events occurred in September of their respective years). Two months after the 2008 credit crisis hit, American society forcefully reunited to elect whom it – and indeed, the world – hopes will be the agent of America's return to greatness as its new president.

An example in modern times

The relevance of time measurement is direct. It has to do with the way we experience crises, both from the perspective of society at large and also within the mini-society we call 'family' as well as how we respond to these crises based on our generational template. The fullness of the effects of the 2008 crash remains to be seen; however, a closer look at how the crisis developed depicts a perfect storm of the imposition of linear time progression upon the natural cycles which govern every aspect of life.

At this point in time, the financial markets in the US had experienced a 50% loss, capitulating over the previous 17 months from a high of 14,164 to a low of 6,547.[21] Although the crisis resulted from the imposition of linear time measurement, its effects were entirely cyclical.

To gain a better understanding of the underlying cyclical forces that were being flattened, I asked Jean L.P. Brunel to chronicle the forces leading up to the credit crisis of 2008.[22]

Gray: Jean, to what event do you attribute the origins of the 2008 crisis?

Brunel: The crisis can be traced back to 1971 when the Nixon administration decoupled the US dollar from the Gold Standard, therefore ending the Bretton Woods agreement, the first example of a fully negotiated monetary order intended to govern monetary relations among independent nation-states. This resulted in the translation of a gross domestic product (GDP) surplus into the first deficit.

Gray: Would you chronicle the events following which led to the issues faced by the markets during this most recent crisis.

Brunel: The Tax Reform Act of 1986 exacerbated the problem by phasing out over the next five years the ability of individuals to deduct interest from non-mortgage debt service. This shifted individuals toward using equity lines of credit since it was the only tax deductible source left available to them.

By 1989, the use of such credit increased consumer spending relative to disposable income to unprecedented levels. The political intention was to offer more Americans the ability to realize the 'American Dream' of home ownership. This expanded use of credit spawned an increased and more broadly based use of leverage, encouraged by the lack of legal and regulatory constraint in using credit secured by real estate for non-real estate expenditures. The financial world subsequently enhanced the ability of banks to extend credit through the pooling of mortgage loans for securitization. Banks incented the extension of such credit to create additional mortgage loans which could be sold and pooled for securitization. The focus thus shifted from providing high quality loans to creating as many loans as possible with high credit ratings to enhance sales.

Gray: Thank you, Jean, for this historical explanation.

The absence of the gold standard and the setting aside of appropriate regulatory constraints flattened the cyclical disciplinary practices of reining in activities which had strayed too far outside the formerly prudent criteria. This eventually led to the financial meltdown which began in the US and spread to Europe and other parts of the world, spawning what may result in one of the most severe global recessions in history.

Indeed, as of this writing, families across the globe are being forced to come to grips with aftermath of this financial, economic, and societal upheaval. The Echo generation, now in its formative years, will carry the effects of this upheaval throughout its lifetime. It will forever colour this generation's view of the world in ways we cannot anticipate. Since the situation is at hand, we have the opportunity to explore the linear progression to the point of crisis, illustrating in current times the havoc which can be wrought by the imposition of linear progression upon cyclical nature.

Application to family wealth

Skill Three: understanding the roles of cyclical and linear time in family success

Since we have established that the family can validly be viewed as a mini-society, the same natural cycles borne out in the generational archetypes of society at large, can also be said to be present in families. As in society at large, any attempted flattening of those cycles within the family mini-society will eventually yield similar results. In essence, a family can be defined by its cycles of generations, thus lifting the concept of family to that of a separate entity – an entity larger than our individual selves.[23] Viewing the concept of family in this way allows us also to broaden the definition of family wealth to include not only the human and intellectual capabilities of each family member, but also the relationships that nurture those capabilities to fruition. With the notion of family as a separate entity, we can begin to see that a family is really a mini-society. Based on this broader foundation, we can apply the larger societal influences of the cycles of history to the smaller society of what we call 'family'.

We can also see how cycles of generations influence our approach to wealth management issues. The comparison of the two entrepreneurs from different generations in the previous chapter easily offers a glimpse of the reinterpretation of wealth generating factors which are present in the similar personalities of entrepreneurs. If such differences in approach are ignored (flattened) in an effort to continue the older generation's 'legacy' or way of doing things, the younger generation entrepreneur will either have a much more difficult road toward the materialisation of his or her dreams or it will simply become impossible for those dreams to be realised.

The Wrigley story in the Preamble is a perfect example of this. The younger generation was an idea generator just like his father. The wealth was already in the process of deterioration and the lifeline to the business which was being thrown out in the form of the younger generation's ideas was pushed away by the older generation's attempt to continue in a linear fashion. Only when the first generational cycle was complete was the second generation able to employ its regenerative effects and to literally regenerate the material wealth through the realisation of its ideas into profits and a higher stock price.

Skill Four: understanding the power of generational cycles in defining the family

If we employ the modern focus on linear time and essentially deny the relevance of generations, we eliminate the significant life altering events that enable us to link past to future or to define our lives within the context of a larger entity. It is as if they never happened. In this paradigm, we have nothing to which to compare our lives; there is no path with which family members can connect with the larger concept of family. Family is the testing ground for defining who we are and who we are not. Family members who see themselves linked by 'affinity and who act from a common philosophical base have the greatest possibility of successfully enhancing the individual development and growth of their members and, thus, dynamically preserving themselves for at least five generations'. Families who see themselves as linked only by blood will rarely survive – much less overcome – the cycle of diminishing wealth. Family is 'the place we leave to individuate and where we most want to return to tell the stories of our lives to those most willing to listen'.[24] *In essence, family is the cycle of generations that defines our 'differentness' through our affinity with each other.*[25]

Each family 'culture' has what Oswald Spengler describes as a 'founding idea' which establishes the family's differentness. The birth and expansion of this new civilisation subsequently yield concentric circles (or cycles) of believers and adherents radiating from that founding idea to continue bringing the idea to life within each generation, with the result that the larger entity of family adopts it as its unique and special gift.[26]

Further, Hughes notes that families must continually bring life-generating energy and dynamism into their wealth management processes if they are to postpone the fulfilment of the edicts of the Proverb. He introduces the word 'dynamic' as a critical component of wealth preservation.[27] In linear thinking, each generation would simply be a continuation of reproduction that increases the number of family members into what we refer to as a 'family tree'. *It is linear thinking that wealth can be preserved only by the investment process and tax and legal structures that lull us into misidentifying wealth as financial. Cyclical thinking brings the continuum of family back in line with nature by realising that each generation is not merely a succession of biological beings but the opportunity for each generation to make a contribution which rejuvenates the family wealth – in its truest definition – so that real progress can be made within the larger familial concept.*

Now, let us explore a bit more deeply the respective impact of linear and cyclical models on the entity of family. The cyclical nature of life, the corresponding 'seasonality of history', dynamic wealth preservation, and the rejuvenation of family wealth are in direct conflict with modern linear thinking. As modern people, we tend to view life as a progression, not as a continuous series of cycles or seasons. This linear view gives us a *feeling* of accomplishment, of progressing. The cyclical view, the 'dynamic of aging and dying enables a society to replenish its memory and evolve over time'.[28] Thus, in order for society to *truly* evolve, it must balance the natural realities of cyclical time with the creativity, originality, and self improvement offered by linear time. Strauss and Howe say that Plato, Polybius, Arnold Toynbee, and Arthur M. Schlesinger, Jr. all point to generations as the source of cyclical change.[29]

Yet linear societal thinking has led some to believe that generations should no longer be considered – they are no longer important and have no bearing or application to life today, much less to family wealth decision making. This thinking was brought to life for me during a chat with a fellow attendee at a 2006 family office conference. In response to his query, I was explaining my thoughts regarding the influence generational perspectives have on family wealth management decisions. The gentleman flatly stated that generations were no longer relevant in a global society or in wealth management, for that matter – clearly a view of continuum along a linear pathway toward human 'improvement'.

As noted earlier, the stories of the dysfunctional families in the Preamble illustrate some of the effects of employing a linear view of time while denying the relevance of generations which, as we know, are cyclical. In each of these families, the combination of weakened generational links and tunnelled linear thinking caused the family wealth – by any definition – to suffer significantly. Hughes asserts that if a family successfully reaches its fifth generation, it will have created a system that supersedes luck as the chief ingredient for success.[30] Note that all the media stories on the pages before this chapter depict families in their third or fourth generations, not yet having reached the fifth generation intact.

The lines of successful families such as the Weyerhaeusers, the Laird Nortons, the Rothschilds, and the Pictets are now in their sixth, seventh, and eighth generations. Has their success been rooted in linear progression or in a renewal by each generational cycle of dynamic wealth preservation – or both? Must we give up the achievement and creativity enabled by a linear time view in order to benefit from the natural, underlying progression of cycles? I believe not. The evidence of economic progress is clear in the opening of markets in countries such as China, Indonesia, and India where, although quite early in the process, economic prosperity is beginning to be accessed by larger segments of the general populations. Their ability to weather the current environment and foster this prosperity will be a key element in the way the current crisis plays out. *The importance of cyclicality cannot be stressed enough at this critical point of evaluating the factors which determine family success and, from a larger perspective, the impact on society at large.*

Since both measurements of time offer value, Strauss and Howe offer a happy compromise between the two in the realisation that time is simply a measure of cyclicality. It is the measure of tides flowing in and out, the orbit of the earth around the sun, celebration of seasons heightened by the extremes of winter and summer with transitional periods of fall and spring, the seasons of a human life marked by the succession of generations through Crises and Awakenings transitioning through Unravellings and Highs. Cycles of time are evident in our everyday lives. Companies who prosper are aware of the business cycle and plan accordingly; they continue to grow. Investors may watch financial cycles or electoral cycles; their investments may atrophy or may continue to prosper. We speak of crime waves and waves of opinion; yet life goes on.[31] Rather than abandon one view of time for another, we can work toward some type of equilibrium that will allow significant postponement, if not full elimination, of the 'shirtsleeves' Proverb.

What we must realise – indeed what we are being forced to realise – is that the linear progression of technology – from the age of the cave people all the way to the internet and beyond – does not belie the importance of the cyclical nature of humanity. The signs of technological progress are everywhere. We see them in the news and we incorporate them into our lives every day through the latest iPods, cell phones, and new Windows operating systems. Recognising that the generations of family cycle within the progression of technological development opens the door for the wealth of the family in all its forms to flourish generation after generation.

Cyclical history and family wealth

The wealth situations faced by families today are the direct inheritance of the attitudes, actions, and considerations given the family wealth by individual family members belonging to generations past. If later generations can gain some understanding of the basis for certain decisions, opportunity may arise for understanding the underlying love and care inherent in those decisions. Every wealth creator wishes his or her progeny to benefit from the family's good fortune. Often, simply learning how other family members feel about decisions that have been made, or that are about to be made, can improve family dynamics – or at least open better communication within the family. Such communication can foster better education of family members, creating future family leaders who will help the family weather challenges more effectively, reducing damage or erosion of the entire portfolio of financial, intellectual, human, and social capacities.[32]

With the explanation of generational archetypes available to us from Strauss and Howe, it seems that the generational connection to family wealth management would already be part of the wealth management process. Interestingly, as the authors chronicle the history of generational archetypes from Euro-American experiences, they note that although generational issues rise to the surface more persistently as societies progress, 'the more modern a society thinks itself, the more resistant its people become to legitimizing generational change as an *idea*'.[33]

So accustomed are we to thinking in linear patterns, it is difficult to think of wealth in terms other than financial and other assets which can be assigned a monetary value. As the chapters unfold, this book will view families through several different lenses or perspectives. But there is one set of perspectives that underlies all views, whether or not families are blessed with the gift of material wealth – the perspectives of our primary frame of reference, the generational template into which we were born. As we will see in the following chapters, this holds true for families all over the world. We will also see how these generational perspectives colour each family member's view of the world, of each other, and of their particular role regarding the family wealth.

1 www.thefreedictionary.com/flourish.
2 Strauss, W. and Howe, N., *The Fourth Turning: an American prophecy,* (New York, NY: Broadway Books, 1997), pp. 43–46.
3 Ibid, p. 16.
4 Ibid, p. 11.
5 Ibid, pp. 8–15.
6 Ibid, p. 11.
7 Ibid, p. 13.
8 Strauss, W. and Howe, N., *Millennials Rising: the next Great Generation,* (New York, NY: Vintage Books, 2000), p. 60.
9 Strauss, W. and Howe, N., *The Fourth Turning: an American prophecy,* (New York, NY: Broadway Books, 1997), p. 58.

[10] Ibid.

[11] Ibid, p. 19.

[12] Ibid, p. 15.

[13] Strauss, W. and Howe, N., *The Fourth Turning: an American prophecy,* (New York, NY: Broadway Books, 1997), p. 105.

[14] Wealth Regeneration® is a registered service mark owned by Laird Norton Tyee and is used throughout this book Laird Norton Tyee's permission.

[15] The terms 'birth spectrum' and 'generational birth spectrum' are the copyrighted and service marked property of gray-matter Strategies LLC.

[16] Hughes, James E., Jr., Personal email, March 2007.

[17] Hicks, K., *Boomers, Xers, and Other Strangers: understanding the generational differences that divide us,* (Wheaton, IL: Tyndale House, 1999), p. 4.

[18] Ibid, p. 273.

[19] Ip, G., 'U.S. may be losing its appeal to foreign investors, according to report,' *The Wall Street Journal,* February 12 2007, 3:37 EST.

[20] Strauss, W. and Howe, N., *The Fourth Turning: an American prophecy,* (New York, NY: Broadway Books, 1997), p. 256.

[21] The high of 14,167 was reached on October 9 2007 and the low of 6,547 was reached on March 9 2009: www.the-privateer.com/chart/dow-long.html; http://dowjonesclose.com/.

[22] Brunel, Jean L.P., Personal interview, September, 2008.

[23] Hughes, James E., Jr., Personal interview, October 2006.

[24] Hughes, J.E., Jr., *Family: a compact among generations,* (New York, NY: Bloomberg Press, 2007), p. 4.

[25] Ibid. Hughes is the originator of the concepts of 'family affinity' and 'differentness' used within this definition.

[26] Ibid.

[27] Ibid.

[28] Strauss, W. and Howe, N., *The Fourth Turning: an American prophecy,* (New York, NY: Broadway Books, 1997), p. 16.

[29] Ibid, p. 15.

[30] Hughes, James E., Jr., Personal interview, August 2007.

[31] Strauss, W. and Howe, N., *The Fourth Turning: an American prophecy,* (New York, NY: Broadway Books, 1997), p. 13.

[32] Gray, L., 'Generational perspectives and their effects on goal-based allocation,' *The Journal of Wealth Management,* Spring 2006, pp. 1–11.

[33] Strauss, W. and Howe, N., *The Fourth Turning: an American prophecy,* (New York, NY: Broadway Books, 1997), p. 63.

Chapter 4

The Generational Maze^{SM}:[1] the key to family wealth success

'The wisest families understand that differences of opinion are matters of legitimate perspective, not differences of irretrievable personality. They know that if they attribute differences to personality rather than to perspective, they will slip into saying things like, "There's just no hope – you've been like that since you were three. You're acting just like you did when you were a kid". Instead, they accept that it is natural and valid to disagree, and this acceptance enables them to have empathy for one another and permits real communication to occur.'[2]

John L. Ward, Perpetuating the Family Business

Chapter 3 identified 'family' as the cycle of generations that defines our differentness through our affinity with each other. It noted Strauss and Howe's assertion that the 'dynamic of aging and dying enables a society to replenish its memory and evolve over time'.[3] In the same way, the smaller society of family is replenished as each older generation dies and each new generation assumes leadership. In families of wealth, the generations radiate chronologically from the establishing generation of family to bring new life to the founding idea. Although the basic idea itself remains, it is reinterpreted and redefined by each generation through its particular archetypical template, allowing the idea to be proliferated as the Family Story – or the family legacy as it is often called. Thus, the family wealth is rejuvenated – given new life – from one generation to the next.

How does this rejuvenation come about? Is there a secret to its emergence? This chapter will lay the groundwork for the process, enabling chapters following to illustrate how the generational archetypes identified by Strauss and Howe 'show up' in the people whom we love, with whom we live every day, and with whom we share that special bond called 'family'.

It will use the analogy of a maze to show the complexity generational perspectives add to family relationships – the dynamics at work in the way a family functions. A maze can be difficult to navigate; it takes unexpected twists and turns; and it has many paths going in different directions, theoretically toward the same end. Mazes show how easily families can lose their way within a particular combination of generational perspectives and are, therefore, an ideal tool for visioning a family's journey together.

For, as important as each of the generational templates is, their combined effects translate into a powerful conglomerate force.[4] The impact on the successful rejuvenation of family wealth across the globe lies squarely within each family's singular maze of relationships. Hughes states the fusion of these relationships is essential to the materialisation of dreams – it is one of the four virtues necessary to the family's existence; hence, the maze of generational perspectives becomes a critical factor. In fact, it is *the* determinant factor in the transformation of family members' human, intellectual, and social capacities into matter.

These five chapters tie together the essential ingredients for families to weave their multiple generational perspectives into a unique design from which supportive dynamics for the materialisation of dreams are born and may be sustained.

To begin, this first chapter in the collective five will:

• define a generational maze^SM and describe how it functions; and
• describe the generational archetypes identified by Strauss and Howe.

Since Strauss and Howe state that 'America offers the world's clearest example of the generational cycle at work',[5] a look at American generational perspectives will serve as a comparative foundation for the examination in Chapters 6 and 7 of the generational perspectives of other cultures of the world. Chapter 6 will focus on generational perspectives of European and Latin American families; Chapter 7 on the generational perspectives of Asian and Middle Eastern families. Generational perspectives are also affected by gender. These will be the topic of Chapter 8. The five chapters together set up a framework from which we can extract the important influence generational perspectives have on the roles of family members and the dynamics of the family, key components in the quest for family success.

More importantly, within the context of these chapters we can offer an anchoring element to which families of all cultures can return time and again to renew their confidence in the flourishing of their wealth in all its forms across generations. To discover that anchor, we first turn our attention to the mazes within which the generational templates function.

The Generational Maze^SM of perspectives

The descriptions of the individual archetypical templates only scratch the surface of the power that awareness of the templates and the four Turnings holds for us. In order for this knowledge and the Turnings to positively impact the fusion of relationships within families of wealth, we must become aware of each generational archetype's historical development as well as its behavioural response to the turnings of its lifetime. The combinations of archetypical behaviour during any one cycle or Turning create the aforementioned generational maze – the generational perspectives emanating from the templates alive within the family structure as the family experiences the seasons of a long human life.

If we hypothetically put a family in a maze, each member will follow his or her own direction – some may take the same path, others may take different paths; however, each will ultimately find a way out. A maze has individual paths which turn abruptly in different directions yet lead to a point of clarity at the edge. Not all paths are continuous; some are dead ends. And more than one path may lead to a clarifying conclusion. Navigated independently, the journey may be more difficult and may take longer due to the misguided choice of turns which may result in dead ends. If family members navigate together, they can more successfully find the way to clarity for all – and there will be a group of people who love each other and enjoy each other's company along the way and with whom to celebrate when they do! This journeying together better prepares younger family members to navigate the mazes they will encounter in their own time. As older generations pass on, their energy is preserved. As new generations are born, new mazes are created, resulting in a garden full of a related cycle of mazes to delight the eye and offer robust experiences to all.

As time goes on, the garden's character and shape will change. Old mazes will disappear; the new ones carry reminders from generations past to guide the way.[6] Each generation will have its own maze to navigate – its own particular generational combination offering the opportunity for rejuvenation. Therefore, the mazes become a smaller, much more limited version of the Turnings at work within each family system.[7]

The four Turnings of generational archetypes

To assign relevance and/or significance of the four Turnings introduced in Chapter 2 and their associated archetypes to family wealth decision making, we must first develop an understanding of the turnings themselves. According to Strauss and Howe, the four generational turnings of a century identify four archetypes by the seasons of their births. The roles played by these archetypes are dictated by collective societal unconsciousness:

- into a first Turning, or the High, the Prophet generational role is born (Boomers);
- into a second Turning, or the Awakening, a Nomad generational role is born (Gen-Xers);
- into a third Turning, or the Unravelling, a Hero generational role is born (Formerly GIs, soon to be Echoes); and
- into a fourth Turning, or the Crisis, an Artist generational role is born (Silent generation – GI children).

The most recent First Turning, the American High, occurred from 1946–1964; the Second Turning, the Consciousness Revolution, from 1964–1984; the Third Turning, the Culture Wars, from 1984–2001;[8] and the 2010s will begin to feel the effects of the Fourth Turning, ushered in by the Great Event of 9/11.

The Fourth Turning is a period of crisis whose outcome can be either disastrous or can result in complete renewal. Strauss and Howe wrote their book as a wake-up call to America for its survival; we can use the same information for our purposes as a regenerative wake-up call to families of all cultures to defuse the effects of the powerful shirtsleeves Proverb.

Exhibit 4.1

The cycle of generations

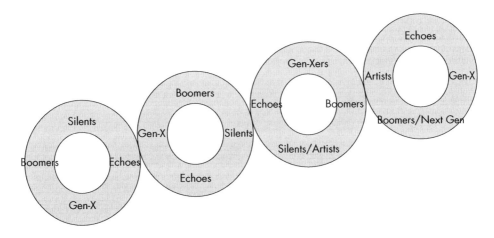

Generational mazes

	Prophet (Boomers)	Nomad (Gen-Xers)	Hero (GIs/Echoes)	Artist (Silents)
First Turning High	Born	Elder	Midlife	Young adult
Second Turning Awakening	Young adult	Born	Elder	Midlife
Third Turning Unravelling	Midlife	Young adult	Born	Elder
Fourth Turning Crisis	Elder	Midlife	Young adult	Born

If G1 is a Silent:

They are elders (Artists now 66–86) while a new generation of Artists is being born (now 0–9)

G2 are midlifers Boomers (Prophets now 46–65)

G3 are Gen-Xers, young adults (Nomads now 29–45)

G4 are Echoes, children (the new Heroes now 10–28)

In Exhibit 4.1, we can see the positioning of generational perspectives over the course of a lifespan with respect to the four archetypes of Prophet, Nomad, Hero, and Artist. The four Turnings and their corresponding archetypes indicate the naturally assigned roles that each generation is destined to occupy. We can see that by developing awareness and understanding of these larger generational roles, we begin to comprehend the generational templates that subconsciously determine modes of reference, attitudes toward wealth, and communication styles of family members. With that, we can refine our focus on generational perspectives and the meaning we can extract for families of wealth.

The generational template as a lens

The sphere of influence of a generation may at times seem difficult to identify until a couple of cycles later. Early and late birth spectrum© members of any generation may parent the next two generations – for example, late birth spectrum© GIs parented Boomer children along with early birth spectrum© Silents; late birth spectrum© Silents parented Gen-Xers along with early birth spectrum© Boomers. In any case, the early birth spectrum parents will carry the dominant influence in shaping the world of the children two generations out. Looking back, it is easy to see the GIs were in control of social institutions (schools, the medical profession, the media) during the coming of age of early birth spectrum© Boomer children so GI leadership determined much of the institutional structure within which Boomer children grew up.[9]

During the transition from one generation to the next, this factor can cause complexities in relationships due to the overlapping of influences. Within these complexities lies the possibility of viewing family relationships through a different lens rather than using the generational templates to simply typecast people into groups defined by birth spectrum© lines of demarcation. In families, when grounded in altruistic love, the perspectives held by each generation can be used as a foundational starting point for the fusion of relationships. Therefore, a family's generational maze is the mechanism through which the flourishing of the wealth in all its forms is either fostered or impeded. When used as a lens, the generational mazes become a fluid conduit through which to promote deeper understanding of the roles of family members and barriers to communication by recognising not only the more apparent characteristics but also the nuances of archetypical transition.

The usefulness of the Turnings in providing lights along the paths of the maze is quite clear. Their ebb and flow easily represent the turnings in family relationships from one generation to the next. Some generations turn sharply from the preceding ones; others are more conforming – all quite reflective of the cycles of family. Each turning is equally important and provides balance and continuity within the cycles of nature.[10]

Just as cultural influences in society along with the economic conditions of the times contribute to the formation of a collective persona for each generational archetype, each generational maze[SM] of the mini-society we have identified as 'family' reinterprets the family culture – the personification of Hughes' founding idea of differentness – in its own way. Each family member responds to this ever evolving dynamic throughout the various stages of life using his or her generational template© as a consistent subconscious reference point. Therefore, we can conclude that a family's culture – the dynamics of the family – is determined by the particular maze of generational archetypes alive in a family at one time. It forms the backdrop for the family's 'Great Events'.

By viewing a family tree as cycles of generations rather than simply as a line of descendants, we can get a clearer view of the members of each generation in the family, both from an archetypical and a chronological generational standpoint. Exhibit 4.2 shows each generational system of branches within the overall family tree which can be used to understand the characteristics which may shape each generation's outlook toward life, work, and money.

Exhibit 4.2

The Generational Family Tree^{SM} I[11]

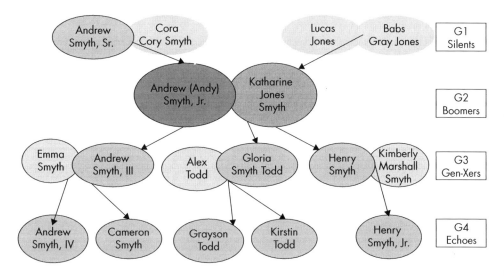

A Generational Family Tree^{SM} makes it easier to see the overlap of chronological generations with archetypical ones. Exhibit 4.2 shows a family with four generations which are pretty clearly delineated. Exhibit 4.3 has been depicted quite a few years later and shows the family with a new and slightly more complex generational mix. Here, the generational maze^{SM} of the same family has changed with the addition of Echo daughter Babs – sister to Andrew, IV; Gloria; and Henry – who was born 11 years after the youngest Gen-X child Henry. In this view, since Henry is a late birth spectrum© Gen-Xer, his wife Kimberly is a member of the Echo generation. Although Babs is a member of the Echo archetypical generation, she is also a member of the G3 chronological generation. This can make a significant difference in establishing the elements of communication and trust, roles and responsibilities within the dynamics of the family. Such a diagram might have been helpful to the Preamble family illustrated in Family story 2; it might have created a different set of dynamics which would have enabled the patriarch's legacy to have remained intact, at least in some aspect.

Exhibit 4.3

The Generational Family Tree^{SM} II

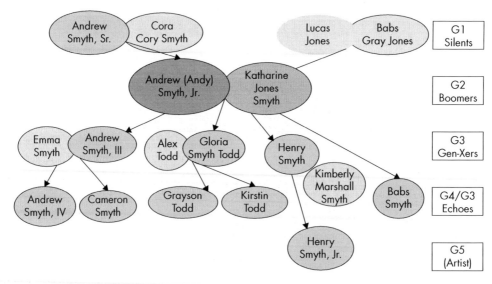

After looking at the Generational Family Tree^{SM} and identifying which generations are represented by whom within the family's particular generational maze^{SM}, we can begin to note some of
the characteristics which personify each larger generational cohort. This would give us some idea
of basic views which might be present in a particular generation of the family, keeping in mind
that personality differences may interpret those characteristics differently.[12]

Understanding the larger society archetypical characteristics

Translating the templates to our smaller society of family requires recognising the power of the
Turnings in and of themselves which facilitate the reinterpretation of the archetypes. On a larger
society level, Strauss and Howe state that the Turnings wield sufficient influence to determine when
and if leaders who 'can galvanise and inspire' come to power. Forsyth also notes the power of
such group dynamics:

> 'The tendency to join with others in groups is perhaps the most important single characteristic
> of humans, and these groups leave an indelible imprint on their members and on society. To
> understand people, we must understand their groups.'

He goes on to list a variety of areas in which group dynamics affect both individuals and society at
large.[13] This supports Strauss and Howe's contention that the crisis backdrop of a Fourth Turning

is powerful enough to cause the voting public to place people of greatness in the highest offices of the land at the very time society needs them. As cases in point, the authors cite the rise of both Abraham Lincoln and Franklin Delano Roosevelt. Both were Prophets who possessed the leadership qualities required at the point of Crisis or a Great Event and each was well prepared for the events which faced them. Lincoln faced the greatest civil strife in history at that time and Roosevelt faced the Great Depression and World War II.[14]

Why did these exceptional people not rise to leadership earlier? The nature of Third Turnings or Unravellings prevents the public from seeking out leaders who possess intelligence, vision, and integrity. Translating this to our own time, we saw low voter turnout a decade ago and a lack of a challenger strong enough to unseat a public official who even may be held in low esteem by the larger society. Interestingly, leaders of integrity and vision have little interest in holding a high public office during a Third Turning. Electing a leader of Lincoln's or Roosevelt's ilk during the Unravelling would have disrupted the natural cyclical flow, causing early onset of the Crisis and only intensifying the destructive nature of the roles being performed at the time and fostering a disastrous resolution. Only after the first spark of Crisis occurs and the Fourth Turning begins do great leaders emerge and seek power. Only then will the populous see that it needs a saviour and award power to those capable of rescuing society once again.[15]

The 2008 election of Barack Obama as president of the United States yielded the highest voter turnout since 1968.[16] This was seven years into the Crisis (Fourth Turning) based on the 9/11 induction which I identified and three years after the predicted onset by Strauss and Howe. Obama's election was the reflection of a societal mandate for strong new leadership, falling right in line with a society that feels the need to be rescued.

The four Turnings of family

In applying the four turnings to the generational cycles of families, we must again refer to the difference in linear and cyclical time. The nature of financial capital in and of itself is inherently linear. It may grow or diminish but each of those conditions occurs in a sequential fashion. Financial capital has no defined or certain end. The true definition of wealth goes beyond the linear; the secret to fostering family wealth over the period of a long human life or beyond lies in the regenerative[17] potential of the generational cycles – the 'turnings' of family. This realisation illuminates a dichotomy among the different forms of family wealth. *How can we understand this dichotomy in a way that equips us to choose a form of entropy which puts us in sync with the cycles of nature and allows us to be participants in rejuvenation instead of becoming entropic victims?*

The quest to find an answer to this question compels us, in our journey to delve into the source of family functioning, to explore the generational templates at a deeper level. Exhibit 4.4 shows the generational archetypes as they cycle through different stages of life. From here, we will attempt to understand how these archetypical influences make an appearance in the dynamics of family interaction which, in turn, affect decisions regarding the family wealth.

Exhibit 4.4

Strauss and Howe's generational cycles

	Prophet	**Nomad**	**Hero**	**Artist**
Childhood	Post-Crisis children increasingly indulged	Nomadic children grow up under-protected during an Awakening (2nd Turning)	Newly born Heroes are increasingly protected as they become post-Awakening (2nd Turning) children	Artists become overprotected children since they grow up during a Crisis (4th Turning)
Young adulthood	Narcissistic crusaders of an Awakening (2nd Turning)	Alienated young adults in the aftermath of the Awakening	They become the heroic young team players during a Crisis (4th Turning)	They become sensitive young adults in a post-Crisis world
Midlife	In midlife, they cultivate principled morality	In midlife, they become pragmatic leaders during a Crisis (4th Turning)	Heroes become hubristic mid-lifers, full of energy for their task	In midlife, they become indecisive, breaking free during an Awakening
Elderhood	Elder Prophets become the leaders who guide navigation of the next Crisis (4th Turning)	Late in life, Nomads become tough post-Crisis elders	As powerful Elders, Heroes are attacked by the next Awakening	Artists become empathetic as post-Awakening elders

Source: The Fourth Turning. Used with permission. Strauss, W and Howe, N., *The Fourth Turning: An American Prophecy,* (New York: Broadway Books, 1997), p. 84.

To understand how financial wealth operated in the lives of the generational templates of recent history leading up to our time, we must first understand the history of 'Old Money' myths. These myths were legendary, instilling an honour-bound responsibility to nobly lead society, lifting the masses to a higher level through cultural and educational pursuits. As we will see through the archetypical generations of recent history, the concept of class based in honour and dignity has eroded, fostering a society – and an inherent class system – bound instead by the extremes of privilege and poverty.[18]

According to Aldrich, the transition from wealth's personification of class in America based on property ownership to the more common use of the word 'class' as an adjective in front of some-one's actions or attire ('she's a class act' or 'that's a classy outfit') was a direct result of World War II.[19] The Hero archetype, who were young adults at the time, were the cataclysmic force in the last Fourth Turning, of which World War II was the culmination. Hence, it serves us well to begin our examination with the generational maze into which those Heroes were born.

Although the numbers of this generation are practically non-existent,[20] its ideals continue to mesmerise the generations of today. Tributes such as Tom Brokaw's 1998 book *The Greatest Generation*, renewed production of World War II movies such as *Saving Private Ryan, Schindler's List, Letters from Iwo Jima, Flags of Our Fathers*, author Ken Burns' 2007 public television series, 'The War',[21] and, most recently, the celebration in New York City on the 65th anniversary of V-J Day of a statue to commemorate the famous Times Square kiss between a sailor and a nurse, keep the memory of these glorious Heroes alive. Note that the fascination with this generation has resurged in the latter years of the most recent Third Turning Unravelling and the early years of the Fourth Turning Crisis period which we are now experiencing. This signifies our current longing for a hero to save us; since the new hero generation has not yet come into its own, the previous hero generation is the only generation to which we can look. Since the generational imprint occurs during our formative years,[22] a look at the cultural and economic influences at work during the GI generation's childhood has implications for the archetypical development over the last century.

The GI generation Heroes wielded the strongest influence on society in history until their Boomer grandchildren made an even greater impact. Historically, the Prophet archetype provides the leadership which facilitates the 'saving' of society by the Hero young adults during a Fourth Turning. Rewinding the Turnings back to the time when the former Hero archetype was born, we find ourselves in the Third Turning (Unravelling) of 1908–1929, the period of World War I and Prohibition. Descriptions of Hero generations before the Greatest Generation have been called Arthurian, Elizabethan, Glorious, and Republican.[23]

Generational imprints are the result of the social and economic conditions at the time of their maturation. Generations do not follow in perfect linear order. The GI generation were parents to both Silent and Boomer generation children; Silents were the children of both Lost and GI genera-tion parents; Silents were parents to both Boomer and Gen-X children. A generation is defined by its birth spectrum[©]. What happens to each generation separately is only part of the picture; of more importance to history is what happens to generations together. 'They age in place and overlap like tiles on a roof, overlapping in time, corrective in purpose, complementary in effect, altering every aspect of society from government and the economy to culture and family life.'[24]

The next 'Great Generation' is growing up before our eyes. They are the children of Boomers and Gen-Xers and they 'echo' the Boomer generation in superficial ways, yet they reinterpret many of the characteristics of the generation Tom Brokaw dubbed 'The Greatest Generation'. This is why they are referred to as Echoes and also as Millennials. Having been born during a resurgence of adoration of the child as well as completely within the modern technological age, this generation is commanding a media following like no other in history.

The American public is mesmerised with this generation. As it began to come into its formative years in 1997 – the years when the generational persona is imprinted – the national mood began to be lifted along with an economic revival during the presidency of Bill Clinton. The transition from the dismal Gen-X period was reflected in the abandonment of all things Gen-X. CD sales began to plunge; movies such as *Beevis and Butthead* no longer held appeal. Taking their places were movies like *Scream* and *Titanic*; expressions like 'collaborative learning', 'back to basics', 'zero tolerance', and 'standards of learning' began to emerge.[25]

The unprecedented media attention has created a generational consciousness earlier in the Echo life cycle than in any other upcoming generation in American history. Early in this generation's birth spectrum©, there was confusion about the dividing line between Gen-Xers and Echoes. A group called Generation Y, born between 1974 and 1980 were first latched onto as the new generation after the Gen-Xers. The characteristics of Generation Y overlapped with those of the Echoes. Later, Generation Y became the first segment of the Echo birth spectrum©.[26] The turning of the Boomers from child despisers to child adorers gave birth to an early fascination with the Echoes.

Echoes have received much more attention from adults than their Gen-X predecessors ever did. Each generation is identified by the years in which it is born. The early birth spectrum© members are the ones who define the break from the previous generation and the start of a new one. The early birth spectrum© Echoes (as with every other generation) are the ones who have set the identification points for their generation. As with every other generation, they have carried a few characteristics from the previous generation with them; thus, the celebration of the Echoes by adults is mixed with criticism of residual Gen-X characteristics. But the characteristic standards are set and later birth spectrum© members will attempt to 'exceed those standards with further improvements in attitudes and behaviours'.

Recalling the cyclical reinterpretation of the generational archetypes, the Echo generation will be everything the Boomer generation was not. Trends associated with the Echo generation will be opposite the trends which are associated with the Boomers. They are emerging against a backdrop of global markets where, despite recent economic hiccups, the wealthy still become wealthier, technology continues to reign, and the chasm between rich and poor continues to widen.[27]

They cannot imagine writing a term paper with pen and paper. They cannot imagine a world without video games, or what it feels like to be discriminated against because of their race or gender. At the point in life when early birth spectrum© Echoes were forming their generational imprint (15–17 years old), they had never experienced a recession. They had only seen the capital markets go up; they had never felt the effects of a foreign crisis; they had only seen the wealthy become wealthier. Even today – after one of the most significant economic crises in history, they may still feel only peripheral effects. In any case, they do not know what it is like to stand in a bread line (nor do Boomers in the US) or to have fuel rationed (US Boomers experienced this is 1979). Rather, they are the ecologically minded who have always recycled and who cannot understand why alternative forms of energy are just now being developed.

How will the tiles of this generation overlap with the others in the family's generational maze[SM]? Will they indeed overlap or is this generation so separated from the other archetypes that its tiles will only lie side-by-side with the previous archetype? How will the new generational garden affect the nurturing of the authentic wealth and the management and distribution of the material wealth in families? The answers to these questions will be very interesting indeed and will be explored more deeply in Part 4.

As we consider the various characteristics of both archetypical and chronological generations, we must understand the psychological issues which surround family wealth from each generation's viewpoint. Should distributions to heirs be equal no matter what? Should a full share of the wealth be bequeathed to less competent heirs or should more be provided to an heir with greater needs? What should be the ratio of wealth left to family foundations compared to the amount left to heirs? Should spouses of heirs be included in family meetings? What about heirs who seem to display no interest – should they be included in the meetings? As we explore these issues more fully throughout the course of our journey, we will see the value family advisors may offer when they are also educated to understand the Generational Wealth Management Continuum[SM]. An advisor's role is not to become a full-fledged psychologist to the family. However, an advisor with sufficient knowledge and skill can help families open a dialogue among their members that can lead to a more unified family wealth focus – a highly valuable service, indeed.

To understand the perspectives of generations of both types, we must look at them individually and within the various cultures of the world. Today's families are more culturally diverse than ever before. As the Echo generation begin to have their own families, this phenomenon will only increase. The next four chapters open the door to the perspectives of American, European, Latin American, Asian, and Middle Eastern generations as well as to the different perspectives of women and men within a generation. It is my hope that examining generational perspectives from a multi-cultural approach will equip families to fully enjoy the richness of their particular generational mazes.

---

[1] 'Generational Maze' and 'Generational Family Tree' are service marks owned by graymatter Strategies LLC.

[2] Ward, J.L., *Perpetuating the Family Business: 50 lessons learned from long lasting, successful families in business,* (New York, NY: Palgrave Macmillan, 2004), pp. 13, 14.

[3] Strauss, W. and Howe, N., *The Fourth Turning: an American prophecy,* (New York, NY: Broadway Books, 1997), p. 16.

[4] Ibid, p. 99.

[5] Ibid, p. 95.

[6] Ibid.

[7] It should be noted here that by indicating there are versions of the Turnings within the generational mazes of the smaller society of family in no way suggests that family generations develop a common persona and, therefore, define a new type of generation which is indigenous to the family. Rather, the archetypical generations represented by family members also represent the times in which these archetypical generations live and, therefore, represent the influence of the Turnings within the family. The two are connected to each other. Each individual family member's interpretation of his or her generational archetype weaves together to form the family's generational maze which, indeed, is indigenous to that particular family and to no other.

[8] Ibid, p. 123–38.

[9] Ibid, p. 80.

[10] Strauss, W. and Howe, N., *The Fourth Turning: an American prophecy,* (New York, NY: Broadway Books, 1997), p. 100.

[11] The names of family members in the Generational Family Tree I and Generational Family Tree II are completely ficti-tious and have been made up arbitrarily by the author. Any seeming association with or connection to any real person is purely coincidental and unwitting.

[12] It must be remembered the notation Strauss and Howe make that, although each individual may not share all of the archetypical characteristics of their generation, each individual will have to deal with those characteristics throughout

their lifetime, making their generational template every bit as much a part of their generational archetype as those who do embody the archetypical characteristics.

[13] Forsyth, D.R., *Group Dynamics,* 4th international edition, (Stamford, CT: Thomson Wadsworth , 2006); Professor, endowed chair in ethical leadership, Jepson School of Leadership Studies, University of Richmond: www.richmond.edu/%7Edforsyth/gd/; www.amazon.com/Group-Dynamics-4th-International-2006/dp/B001T42J32/ref=sr_1_2?s=books&ie=UTF8&qid=1281910440&sr=1-2.

[14] Strauss, W. and Howe, N., *The Fourth Turning: an American prophecy,* (New York, NY: Broadway Books, 1997), p. 309.

[15] Ibid.

[16] National Voter Turnout in Federal Elections: 1960–2008: www.infoplease.com/ipa/A0781453.html.

[17] Wealth Regeneration® is a registered service mark owned by Laird Norton Tyee and is used throughout this book Laird Norton Tyee's permission.

[18] Lasch, C., *Revolt of the Elites and the Betrayal of Democracy,* (New York, NY: W.W. Norton, 1996), p. 7.

[19] Aldrich, N.W. Jr., *Old Money: the mythology of wealth in America,* (New York, NY: Allworth Press, 1996), p. xvii.

[20] Burns, Ken. According to the 2007 PBS seven-part series 'The War', 1000 members of the GI generation die each day.

[21] Fiorani, F., *New Illustrated History of World War II: rare and unseen photographs 1939–1945,* (Newton Abbott: David & Charles, 2005): www.amazon.com/New-Illustrated-History-World-War/dp/0715321021/ref=pd_bbs_sr_2/104-7149888-1235964?ie=UTF8&s=books&qid=1188872000&sr=1-2.

[22] Strauss, W. and Howe, N., *The Fourth Turning: an American prophecy,* (New York, NY: Broadway Books, 1997), p. 55.

[23] Ibid, p. 123–38.

[24] Ibid, p. 99.

[25] Strauss, W. and Howe, N., *Millennials Rising: the next Great Generation*, (New York, NY: Vintage Books, 2000), p. 38.

[26] Ibid, p. 40.

[27] Ibid, p. 45.

Chapter 5

Generational perspectives in America

'In their reconstruction of it, history was a concrete and personal thing, a continuous story in which they and their forebears and their descendants were directly involved. In their eyes, it bound the past to the present, the distant to the near-at-hand; it made unknown people important, ordinary places extraordinary, common things significant …. From childhood, they had listened and remembered; now, they were travellers from another age, the last survivors of a time and place that was almost lost and forgotten.'

John Egerton[1]

The perspectives of generations within the family weave together a particular tapestry of family dynamics which set the foundation for the development (or lack thereof) of 85% of the ingredients for success. At any stage in a family's cyclical generational progression[SM],[2] an education about its unique maze of generational perspectives can change the dynamics at work within the family. This can happen fairly quickly and as the result of a single insight or it can happen over a period of years as multiple insights gradually unfold. The greater understanding a family has of the generational perspectives behind the dynamics at work in the family's relationships with each other, especially in wealth related issues, the greater hope the family has for postponing the fulfilment of the Proverb's edicts.

The only way a family can make these discoveries is by beginning a dialogue specifically designed for that purpose. It can be an enriching and fascinating experience for families to do this! Many families today are already involved in researching their genealogies and filling in their traditional family trees. Families create archives which tell the stories of generations past, educating current and future generations on the stories that make their family different than any other and which offer a singular identity for each member who joins either through birth, marriage, or life partnership.

A brief review of archetypical generational history sets the backdrop for fostering such a dialogue. The individual responses to archetypical imprints of American generations filter in to the family's personality in hidden and unanticipated ways. There may be unspoken rules which govern family interaction which no family member might dare to challenge. Yet, younger generations continually 'surprise' older ones in both pleasing and disappointing ways – a testament to the generational perspectives at work in family leadership.

So we begin with an overview of American generations, just to have a place to start and to follow the global tendency to use American generations as a benchmark.[3] In doing so, this chapter will:

- describe the way American generational mazes have influenced American family relationships during the recent Turnings of history; and
- show the effects recently regenerated archetypical templates are having on today's family relationships.

To set the backdrop for this chapter's exploration, we can chronicle a series of generational approaches to wealth transfer. The GI generation carried on the legacy of the industrialists who created the initial wave of wealth for so-called anchor families such as the Rockefellers, Phipps, and Morgans. Their Silent children picked up the torch and are now in the process of handing it to their Boomer children. In the early days – the days of the industrialists and even the early birth spectrum[©4] GIs – wealth management decisions were uncomplicated. There were only the immediate family, the parents, and siblings to consider. A single generation possessed total control and answered to only one 'boss' – the founding industrialist who had created the family fortune. For such a founder, many of the following questions would have held little relevance.

Upon the industrialist founder's death or relinquishment of control, these questions would be asked.

- Should the family wealth be dispersed among the family?
- If so, which family members get how much of the money?
- Should the money be invested collectively?
- What about family members who want to take a large segment of their portions in cash now?
- How will that affect the founder's legacy?
- If invested collectively, how much 'say' does each family member have in investment decisions?
- Should the founder continue to carry the weight in decision making until he or she is ready to pass the torch to the next generation?

A founding industrialist would have never questioned if the wealth should be dispersed among the family – it was to be handed down to the elder son. There might have been some interest in pooling the wealth, but more from the standpoint of making business investments with other entrepreneurs. As the numbers of generations grew, along with each generation's interest in the family wealth, more of these questions had to be answered, and answered directly. But founders sought to maintain control as long as possible, often for years after their death, to ensure the money which they had worked so hard to accumulate would continue to support succeeding generations. As the early generations passed on, heirs began to assume control and multiple generational influences began to have impact. Today, as the Boomers contemplate their plans for their own legacies, there are many more family members to consider and many more issues to address.[5]

Generational attitudes toward wealth

Attitudes toward wealth also have their roots in generational perspectives. Personality may be an overlay and is often the focus. Knowing one's money or financial 'personality' can be helpful, but understanding the underlying forces behind those attitudes can open a deeper and much more meaningful door to understanding attitudinal differences. Silents may have adopted the attitudes of their GI parents or may have become more lenient in an effort to have closer relationships with their Boomer children. As a result, Boomers may have considered wealth their right to do with as they please, creating the Boomer 'B' classification denoting less responsible siblings to their Boomer 'A' counterparts.[6] Generation X is, by definition, another transition generation, like its Silent grandparents, mirroring characteristics of both the previous and immediately succeeding generations and creating a generation gap of its own with its Boomer parents.[7] Understanding the importance of generational perspectives involves a discovery process. Attitudes toward wealth differ with each successive generation and each generation's attitudes are shaped by its formative experiences as well as its historic archetypical role and its chronological generational role. These attitudes affect the relationships between family members, their advisors, and the manner in which the wealth may be managed or transferred.

Since attitudes and perspectives about wealth affect relationships with family members, family advisors, and the community at large, we will examine the characteristics of each archetypical generation along with its typical attitudes toward wealth. These insights will provide an initial screening, if you will, for opportunities to open communication and get to the heart of understanding the relational dynamics within the family's generational maze.

GIs

GIs were born between 1900 and 1924. By far the largest and most powerful generation up until their Boomer grandchildren, GIs were the 'confident and rational problem-solvers of twentieth-century America, the ones who knew how to get things done'.[8] They were between 17 and 34 years old when Pearl Harbor was attacked and, staunchly patriotic, they readily defended the freedoms of their country. Their parents were the 'Lost' generation, the adults most affected by the Great Depression and who served in or came of age during the Great War of 1915 (World War I). The wealthiest members of the Lost generation felt the Depression cut their fortunes in half, but the half that remained was sufficient to re-invest in the then-fledgling economy, planting the seeds for the great wealth to be handed down to the Silents and Boomers during the 1950s and 1960s. The GIs reaped the initial fruits of these wealth seeds and became the most significant contributors to the American way of life. Their 'never say die' attitude toward problem solving gave new spirit to the country. An unprecedented collective energy for life was infused back into a country weary from two world wars and a dire economic crisis – all of which had previously been unthinkable. The GIs dominated everything – even the White House. They contributed a generation of US presidents from JFK to George Bush, Sr. But the GI persona also spawned cultural complacency and a super machismo. They were the quintessential patriarchs, knowing what was best for everyone and thinking totally 'in the box'.

The GI generation transformed every stage of life it experienced – a legacy its Boomer grandchildren would emulate and which the Echoes are now reinterpreting. Staunch in their beliefs, confident in the American government, and focused intently on self-sufficiency, GIs often were rigidly stalwart in their efforts to secure their legacy according to their own standards. GIs, perhaps ironically, were also generous philanthropists, feeling a strong personal obligation to provide for the future and to give back to society.

GI perspectives on wealth: The GIs brought specific values to bear in the management of the family wealth. They were heroes who saved the world; they were the self-appointed caretakers of the family wealth. With the limited investment options available for individual assets in the 1940s, 1950s, 1960s, and 1970s, things were relatively straightforward and simple when it came to wealth management. The GI generation was accustomed to being in control without question. Early GIs were adults during the Great Depression; later GIs spent their formative years during the Depression and came of age during World War II. All GIs were determined to make things better for their children. Thus, their word was indeed family law.

Their 'unquestioned' control created family dynamics where children (and even spouses) were likely kept in the dark about family wealth management, planting the seeds for the rebellious attitudes of the Boomer generation. Family governance was in the hands of the patriarchs. The patriarchs left everything in the hands of the trustees, who were held to very little accountability. In the days of the GI, this mode of control made sense. When translated to today's times, it fails to adequately serve the family.

Box 5.1
Family quandary: GI generational family dynamic

'There was only one trustee and he was so busy, everyone was afraid to ask questions. They were getting all kinds of money and didn't feel they could complain, yet they had issues that needed to be addressed. They just didn't have a forum, which left a lot of the burden on the trustee and left the family members just out there in the dark.'

Anonymous

The Silent generation

The year 1938 has been identified as the most successful time to be born, naming the Silents the most successful generation in the process. This generation, born between 1925 and 1942, grew up during the last stages of the Great Depression as Franklin Roosevelt instituted his New Deal. They came of age during the McCarthy era and the beginning of the Cold War. The children of the mighty GIs were christened the Silent generation by a November 5 1951 *Time Magazine* cover story describing a generation of outward conformity, constantly afraid to overtly express their own views due to McCarthyism and the nuclear threats of the Cold War. In their early years, the Silents blindly followed in the footsteps of their GI parents; later, the influence of their Boomer children would hold sway, establishing the foundation for the social disruption of the 1960s and 1970s.

The Silents were 'sandwiched' between the two largest, most powerful, and influential generations to date – the GIs and the Boomers. Despite no readily identifiable distinction of their own, Silents planted the seeds of change through Martin Luther King, Elvis Presley, William F. Buckley, Woody Allen, Carl Sagan, Jimi Hendrix, and Martha Stewart. These seeds of change would be radicalised by their Boomer children in the 1960s.

Early birth spectrum© Silents benefited from the unprecedented employment opportunities after World War II. They contributed some of the great musicians and thinkers of the time (Jimi Hendrix, Bob Dylan, John Lennon; William F. Buckley, Allen Ginsberg, Gore Vidal). But the Silents never produced a US president.

Silent perspectives on wealth: the attempt to identify wealth attitudes among Silents can be tricky. The Silents (think Grace Kelly, Elvis Presley, Natalie Wood) were overpowered by both their GI parents and their Boomer children since they were too young to participate in World War II and too old to be subject to the Vietnam draft. Now in their seventies and eighties, however, the Silents are stewards of the second significant phase of wealth transfer to flow to the Boomers.

Having become 'keepers of the wealth' between the two such powerful generations, Silents want a voice of their own – and someone who will listen. But they also may find it difficult to talk about wealth with their children. Silents may have adopted the philosophy of their GI parents that financial matters are not to be discussed. They may fear their children are greedy or will try to take control before they are ready to relinquish it. Many in this generation constantly fear they do not have enough, although their savings and investments tell a different story. Silents are likely to have been successful in business, yet not lived to match the level of their success.

And just as they planted the seeds of change during the 1950s, Silents are laying the foundation for a new type of retirement – an active retirement with more control and autonomy in their golden years. Silents have spurred the growth of retirement communities as an alternative to nursing homes. Groups of Silents are beginning to invest together to build private retirement communities, pooling their resources to provide living quarters for a dedicated nursing professional 'on staff'.[9] In short, Silents are doing what they have always done best – paving the way for their Boomer children to make the most of what they (the Silents) started.

The Boomers

Born between 1943 and 1960, the Boomers (think Hamilton Jordan and Jody Powell, Gilda Radner and Oprah Winfrey, Oliver North and William Bennett) grew up never experiencing economic hardship even approaching the degree of their parents or grandparents and, in what would become characteristic defiance, decidedly opposed the idea that any particular set of values was more valid than another.[10] They grew up with optimism and a determination to live life according to their own terms.

Because of the size of their population segment, Boomers received more attention than their GI predecessors for changing attitudes, social mores, and outlooks on life and wealth.[11] Following the legacy of their GI grandparents, Boomers have uniquely and firmly implanted their mark on every stage of life they have experienced. But Boomers lives are much more fluid than their GI, linear, age-defined grandparents. Better educated and experimental than their Silent parents, they like trying new things. They are more directly involved and more tolerant of others' ideas. Medical advances and the extension of life expectancies will allow the Boomer generation to continue their legacy of redefining the life stages through which they pass.

Boomers are entrepreneurs who, after having led successful careers at large companies, are starting second businesses after being laid off or retiring early. Boomers born during the early part of the designated spectrum are already becoming the new seniors. They travel, ignoring any constraints related to age which might have previously hindered their parents, go back to school, and use their previous success to fund what they want to do later in life. Especially in light of the foundation being laid by their Silent parents, Boomers are expected to completely redefine the word 'retirement'. They are already putting their stamp on the legacy, changing the meaning of retirement and seeking to remain vital and active for the remainder of their lives.[12]

The GIs and the Boomers have changed attitudes, social mores, and outlooks on life and wealth in ways that no one could have foreseen or comprehended. These changes are translating profoundly into the manner in which wealth is managed, used, and transferred – especially for the significantly wealthy.

Boomer perspectives toward wealth: wealth carries mixed meaning for members of the Boomer generation. Many have witnessed the adverse effects that mammoth inheritances have had on some of their peers. These Boomers grew up to become members of the very 'establishment' they so ardently rebelled against in their early years. Thus, the descriptions of Boomer A and Boomer B[13] to differentiate between Boomers who either learned from their mistakes or who never made them and those who made mistakes but never learned from them. However, the stigma which may have been well-earned by so-called Boomer B siblings may unfairly mask the work ethic and sense of responsibility felt by a Boomer A who simply may not have inherited the business acumen of his or her ancestors. Boomers also have been handed wealth they did not know about, or at a minimum, had no idea how to manage.

Box 5.2
Family quandary: Boomer generation family dynamic

'The widespread image of "trust babies" who shun the responsibility and hard work required to continue growing their wealth is unfair to many inheritors who do inherit the work ethic and a sense of responsibility but cannot be expected to have the skills their parent or grandparent acquired over decades. And the job they inherit is, in some ways, more difficult than the one the founder was doing.'

Kenneth Kaye and Sara Hamilton

Despite their self absorption, generally rebellious attitudes, and the desire to do everything on their own terms, many Boomers who have become the stewards of the family wealth are acting – rightly or wrongly – to prevent the disincentive visited upon their peers by focusing more attention on the effects their wealth might have on their children and grandchildren. This new focus is driving the growing interest in philanthropy, which promises further changes in governance issues and advisory involvement in the education of new generations. The family foundation is becoming a type of training ground for family members as young as eight years old and parents are seriously pondering the wisdom of leaving their vast wealth in totem to their children and grandchildren.

Many Boomers are deciding to leave their children only enough wealth for 'the basic necessities' and gifting the bulk of their wealth to charity – without discussing this choice with their future inheritors. This trend has been in place for about a decade and has tremendous implications. It could change the acceptance of wealth and the people who have it from a societal standpoint. Society at large could benefit greatly if huge portions of wealth are given away to worthy charities. Bill and Melinda Gates, Warren Buffett, Ted Turner, George Soros, and others are in the news regularly for the philanthropic choices they make.[14]

But is limiting the wealth passed on to succeeding generations the proper way to accomplish these worthy ambitions? Ironically, such a decision is a redirection of the same rigidity exercised by their GI grandparents and Silent parents. Rather than preserving the wealth for their progeny, however, these Boomers seek to preserve the work ethic of their children, providing enough for the children to be comfortable, but not enough for them to be 'spoiled'.

Succeeding generations are becoming better educated through the rising interest in philanthropy as an educational venue. Such training will render future generations more capable of making wise decisions as adults. Without precluding the emphasis on philanthropy, questions arise. Is it not the inherent right of heirs in some sense to inherit the family wealth? Is it not also their right to make their own decisions regarding the wealth – to do with that wealth what they wish?[15] Equipping succeeding generations with the tools required to make wise choices regarding philanthropy and wise management of the wealth may indeed be a more equitable option than simply predetermining their lack of ability or interest by limiting the amount of inheritance. The unintentional effects of the attempt to prevent the spoiling of children will be explored in a family example in Chapter 20.

Obviously, this is a question that must be explored by each individual family, but it is also a thought process which can be guided by trusted wealth advisors, especially those having earned the relationship level of personne de confiance.[16] If Boomers do plan to leave the bulk of their wealth to their children, concern about their children's feelings come into play.

Box 5.3
Family quandary: Boomer generation family dynamic

I've got four children but only one is a business person. Should I name that person as the executor or should I name all four kids? Another of my children is very rich on his own and doesn't really need my money. I'm afraid of how he will feel if I don't leave him any money. What do I do?

Along with the Boomers came the civil rights and feminist movements. The civil rights movement laid the foundation for the multi-cultural society we have today, an influence on family wealth which will become greater as future generations become more involved.

Generation X

The very term Generation X denotes a transition generation. Like their Silent predecessors, Gen-Xers are a 'bridge' generation and have been labelled cynical slackers, rightly or wrongly, because they were the so-called latch-key kids of the 1980s and 1990s, seemingly forgotten by their Boomer parents who had become absorbed with the accumulation of wealth, power, and prestige. Born between 1961 and 1980 with more wealth and time on their hands than any generation before, many Gen-Xers looked to television and other less than desirable sources for role models. But Gen-Xers grew up having to fend for themselves, which gave them great self-reliance and the ability to quickly adapt to change.

Gen-Xers are also a transition generation in the sense that they grew up in the midst of the technology revolution. The advent of the PC in the late 1980s and the Internet in the mid-90s occurred while they were still teenagers. They came of age in the 'wired' world. They feel a disconnect with their Boomer parents, rejecting Boomer workaholic values and choosing more balanced lives and closer relationships to family. Gen-Xers are also more tolerant of cultural and other differences in society due to their connection with a more global community.

Gen-Xer perspectives on wealth: Gen-Xers want clear communication regarding wealth issues. They want to know how decisions are made and want to be part of the decision making process. They want their opinions to be heard and valued. They value quality of life over money – approximately 40% grew up with parents who were either divorced or separated – but they are driven and industrious. The portion of the US female population in the workforce grew from 18.8% in 1900 to 59.8% in 2002. Having grown up with working mothers, Gen-Xers are very entrepreneurial. In 1993, when Xers were between the ages of 25 and 34, they created 70% of new businesses. Because of their adaptability, they are better suited for today's career realities than older people in the workforce,[17] which may make adapting to Boomer decisions to leave the majority of their wealth to charity that much easier. They may simply decide to create their own wealth; indeed, they may have already done so. They likely will have several careers; they create their own job security by their adaptability and being able to transfer the skills they learn to each successive job or business they create.

The Echo generation

The Echoes, born between 1982 and 1995, are so called because they are expected to have the greatest influence as a generation since the Baby Boomers; as well, they 'echo' the characteristics of the last Hero generation, a generation Tom Brokaw dubbed the 'Greatest Generation'. Their numbers slightly surpass those of the Boomers, but they represent a smaller part of the population as a whole. Regardless, their numbers are sufficiently significant to draw the attention of sociologists, demographers, and marketing consultants.[18]

The Echoes are the first generation to be totally 'plugged in' to technology and a globalized mode of living since birth. They are also the first generation since World War II to be confronted with higher academic standards than the generation preceding them and to show early signs of meeting those standards. They strive to meet higher academic, social, and behavioural standards than Gen-Xers. Echoes feel they have few adult role models, and since community service was added to the list of high school graduation requirements which affected them, Echoes are more civic minded. It is predicted that the Echo generation will wipe out the downbeat image of their Gen-X predecessors and replace it with a youth image of upbeat and engaged. Howe and Strauss predict this will have 'seismic consequences for America' over the next decade.[19]

Echoes today spend over $170 billion a year of their own and their parents' money. The first to grow up with computers at home, they tend to be over achieving, over managed, and overpressured. Their entire lives have been spent in some type of organised activity.[20] Part of this may be the combined result of competitive parents racing to see whose child is achieving the most and the problems caused by the latch-key Gen-Xers. This generation is the world's most multi-cultural – about one third – as well as its most tolerant with a desire for everyone to participate in community. They are educated, motivated, and have a greater desire to get along with their parents than Gen-Xers. They are considered the 'on-demand' generation with information constantly available to them from multiple sources.[21]

Echo perspectives on wealth: the Echo generation clamours for education about and inclusion in the family wealth engine. They are an active and involved version of the GIs, wishing to make their marks on wealth decisions and stewardship. Families concentrating on providing such involvement for their Echo members want advisors and wealth managers who consider these desires.[22]

The Echo generation is hard working and optimistic. Like the Boomers, they expect to live their lives on their own terms with access to whatever it takes in terms of technology and information for them to accomplish their goals. If one venue does not give them what they need, they quickly try something else. Like Gen-Xers, Echoes view jobs as educational opportunities to learn needed skills which can be leveraged to gain a new position or start a new business of their own. Echoes are more conservative and want the approval of their parents, since they grew up with the expectation of high achievement. They are opinionated and want to feel what they have to say is heard and considered important. They are accustomed to having money to buy what they want. They want to be knowledgeable of and involved in family wealth decisions.

The multi-generational landscape

It goes without saying that the variety of generational perspectives can create myriad possibilities regarding the dynamics of a family. Opening the conversation between family members may be difficult. Founding entrepreneurs may be elderly GIs who no longer have direct control over the management of the wealth, but whose 'take charge' approach may still be in force through their Silent generation children. Keep in mind, this 'take charge' attitude is how the wealth was created in the first place, so this attitude may simply reflect GIs' tendency to stay with 'what works'. It may be difficult for the Silent children and the GI founder to share information about the family wealth with Boomer children and Gen-X or Echo grandchildren who may be in their early twenties and want to know about and be instrumental in making decisions regarding the wealth.

The wealth situations faced by families today are the direct inheritance of the attitudes, actions, and considerations given the family wealth by individual family members belonging to generations past. Often, simply learning how other family members feel about decisions that have been made or that are about to be made can improve family dynamics – or at least open communication within the family. Such communication can foster better education of family members and upcoming family leaders will be better able to help the family weather challenges more effectively, reducing damage to or erosion of the entire portfolio of family assets including financial, intellectual, social, and human capacities.

Against this backdrop of American generational mazes, we expand our exploration to other cultures of the world, recognising the tremendous potential of looking at the rejuvenation of family wealth through the generational cycles at work across the globe.

---

[1] Egerton, J., *Generations: an American family*, 20th anniversary edition (Lexington, KY: The University Press of Kentucky, 2003), p. 12.

[2] The term 'generational progression' has been marked by graymatter Strategies LLC and refers to the upward cyclical progression of generations, both archetypical and chronological, in families of wealth who successfully defy the Proverb.

[3] Margolis, D.R., 'Women's movements around the world: cross-cultural comparisons', *Gender and Society*, 1993, p. 381: www.jstor.org/stable/189799.

[4] The term 'birth spectrum' has been marked by graymatter Strategies LLC and refers to the point at which a person or

group of people is born within the designated birth years for a named and publicly recognised generation.

[5] Gray, L., *The New Family Office: innovative strategies for consulting to the affluent,* (London: Euromoney Institutional Investor, 2004), pp. 107, 108: www.euromoneybooks.com/default.asp?page=4&productID=3178.

[6] Brunel, J.L.P. and Gray, L.P., 'Integrating family dynamics and governance in strategic asset allocation,' *Journal of Wealth Management,* Winter 2005, p. 42.

[7] Howe, N. and Strauss, W., 'The new generation gap,' Part I, *The Atlantic Online,* December 1992: www.theatlantic.com/issues/92dec/9212genx.htm.

[8] Howe, N. and Strauss, W., *Generations: the history of America's future, 1584 to 2069*, (New York, NY: Morrow/Quill, 1991), pp. 28–30. www.lifecourse.com/books.html.

[9] Brown, P.L., 'Growing old together, in a new kind of commune', *The New York Times,* February 27 2006.

[10] Gray, L., *The New Family Office: innovative strategies for consulting to the affluent,* (London: Euromoney Institutional Investor, 2004), pp. 107, 108. www.euromoneybooks.com/default.asp?page=4&productID=3178.

[11] Howe, N. and Strauss, W., *Generations: the history of America's future, 1584 to 2069*, (New York, NY: Morrow/Quill, 1991), p. 28: www.lifecourse.com/books.html.

[12] Gray, L., *The New Family Office: innovative strategies for consulting to the affluent,* (London: Euromoney Institutional Investor, 2004), pp. 107, 108. www.euromoneybooks.com/default.asp?page=4&productID=3178.

[13] Brunel, J.L.P. and Gray, L.P., 'Integrating family dynamics and governance in strategic asset allocation,' *Journal of Wealth Management,* Winter 2005, p. 40.

[14] Gray, L., *The New Family Office: innovative strategies for consulting to the affluent,* (London: Euromoney Institutional Investor, 2004), pp. 107, 108: www.euromoneybooks.com/default.asp?page=4&productID=3178.

[15] Hauser, B.R., 'A child's "station in life": inheritance rights and expectations,' *Journal of Wealth Management,* Winter 2001, p. 10.

[16] Hughes, J.E., Jr., *Family: a compact among generations,* (New York, NY: Bloomberg Press, 2007), p. 240.

[17] Lankard, B.A., 'Career development in Generation X', ACVE Publications, 1995: www.cete.org/acve/docgen.asp?tbl=mr&ID=57.

[18] 'The Echo Boomers,' CBS News 60 Minutes, September 4 2004: www.cbsnews.com/stories/2004/10/01/60minutes/main646890.

[19] Howe, N. and Strauss, W., *Generations: the history of America's future, 1584 to 2069*, (New York, NY: Morrow/Quill, 1991), pp. 28–30: www.lifecourse.com/books.html.

[20] Ibid.

[21] Ehlers, M., 'What's up with Gen Y?: Here comes a group that rivals the boomers'. *The News & Observer,* February 5 2006: www.newsobserver.com/690/story/396515.html.

[22] Gray, L., *The New Family Office: innovative strategies for consulting to the affluent,* (London: Euromoney Institutional Investor, 2004), pp. 107, 108.

Chapter 6

Generational perspectives in Europe and Latin America

'In Europe, family trees go back to the Middle Ages. I think that's probably the biggest difference between Europe – and probably Asia, as well – and North America. Europe is an old continent and an old continent may have certain rules which may or may not be written but which are strongly held within those families.'

Pierre-Alain Wavre[1]

Although generational cognisance seems most prevalent in America, generational factors are an underlying force in all cultures. According to Strauss and Howe, the origin of American generations began with the European Renaissance which became 'the true Western threshold into modern history'.[2] Therefore, if we limit our view of generational perspectives as distinctly American, we again leave out important elements in the wealth regeneration[3] formula. Only by looking at the perspectives of generations in different cultures can we fully understand the implications for our own families in effectively managing our wealth.

Generational perspectives are somewhat different in every culture, yet the effects of two historically dynamic and powerful generational forces (the GIs and the Boomers) continue to affect global societies in similar fashion. This is not to say the effects from those two generational forces are the same in every culture; however, various cultures do share some generational commonalities and, in some ways, are interwoven with their American counterparts.

The Boomer influence is still predominant at this point and is contributing to the aging of the global society as well as to world-wide issues of healthcare, the redefinition of retirement, and the way older people live and define themselves. Now, the Echo generation is also beginning to make its impact, causing families of wealth to grapple with issues and challenges completely foreign to the psyches of their founders.

There are two primary benefits of examining generational perspectives of the world. First, generational influences have woven themselves in and out of the various cultures of the world more poignantly over the last century. Therefore, we simply cannot understand nor fully appreciate the various cultural traditions – nor can we fully understand our own – without knowing a bit about the anchor of history to which their identity is tied and, thus, to which individual families are tied. Families in other cultures view the link to their generational past differently than Americans view theirs. In a globalised world where families increasingly are becoming more culturally diverse, it is impossible to enrich the spirit of family within *any culture* or to authentically rejuvenate the family wealth without understanding the various generational backgrounds.

This chapter will spring off the foundation of American generational perspectives to examine generational influences in Europe and Latin America. It will take a brief look at the history of both cultures, the traditions passed down through the generations, and how they shed light on the changes that are occurring now. We will look at these changes and draw lessons that can be learned from families of wealth in Europe, Latin America, Asia, the Middle East, and America.

In preparation for our global generational voyage

By definition, a generation is formed by social change, either against a certain economic backdrop or as the instigator of economic change. *It is the economic change that captivates the attention of families of wealth and their advisors most; the social change, although impactfully present and influential, is addressed but is most often left in the background with little or no connection to or inclusion in the economic wealth management portfolio.* In reality, the two are inextricably linked and cannot be separated. So, the fact that we humans continually try to separate them evokes an imposition of linear time that undermines cyclicality and wealth rejuvenation.

Thus, we identify the various archetypical cohorts of history based on other socio-economic events such as cycles of war and peace or based on various societal and economic responses to upheaval within various countries of a specific culture.

The history of early generational distinction begins in the early days of modern Europe when the elite were the only segment of society who had the power to break free from tradition and 'redefine the social roles of whatever phase of life they occupied'. The 'New World', offered this opportunity to people of any class; all they had to do was find transport. Certainly the promise of economic change was as attractive as the opportunity for social change. People who could never dream of owning land before now had a much greater possibility of making that dream a reality. It was an opportunity to 'start fresh'. According to Strauss and Howe, the promise of social [and economic] change has been the primary pull in attracting immigrants from across the globe to America from the 17th century to the present. Today, with the issue of passage practically moot, the opportunity to 'share in the redefinition of social roles and hence to join in what makes the generational cycle turn' is open to anyone.[4] Economic change along with social change, once again. As marketers began to label the various generations of America, the social consciousness of generational delineation was perpetuated.

The Echo sea change is occurring on the back of the vast economic changes instigated by the internet which came into being as the Gen-X generation was coming of age. They are 'echoing' the effect of the Boomers after World War II, who basically upended the social order on the back of a wave of economic prosperity introduced as the Silent generation was coming of age. They are also 'echoing' the previous Hero archetype, the GIs. This reinterpretation of the same archetypical role from the previous century is innate in every new generation. Like their GI and Boomer predecessors, the Echoes are already showing themselves to be strongly influential, particularly from a global and group perspective.[5]

The Echoes are the first generation in which each of its members was being born into a completely wired and globalised world. Technology has infiltrated practically every aspect of life; the influence from a generation born into such expansive social and economic change is destined to have enormous power. Awareness of this generation's impact is becoming more vital to families of wealth today. A family's generational maze creates its identity. 'Family' denotes 'a symbolic continuity which transcends individuals and generations, interweaving the past with the present and the future. It links successive generations, joining kinship lines by means of complex webs of social alliances, and transmitting identity to its members'.[6] That is why the concept of family is so important and why both types of generations within a family are such fundamental influences.

The influences of chronological generations in sync with the famed Proverb and is no respecter of culture. This is why families all over the world fear the Proverb and assess its rate of fulfilment at such a high level. The more subtle influence of archetypical generations varies from culture to culture although the generational persona of stronger generations is a worldwide experience. Each archetypical generational response will be shaded by cultural components.

As centuries of archetypical Turnings have unfolded, so have the various cultural responses to what is called 'modernisation'. Change in the modern world seems to spread from America to Europe, to Latin America, to Asia and the Middle East. So we will take a look at cultural generational characteristics beginning with Europe and Latin America, moving on to Asia and the Middle East in Chapter 7.

A history of family tradition

Change in the European family landscape is occurring against the backdrop of a continent steeped in history and tradition. Yet, the rate of change is not the same across all European countries. Changes in the traditions of Latin American families are also uneven across various Latin American countries, influenced by exposure to societal changes as well as varying stability of each country's political regime which, of course, carries significant economic implications.

As we venture into the realm of multi-cultural generational perspectives, we also have to realise that we are doing so with the broadest brush, touching the tip of the multi-cultural generational iceberg. There are many sub-cultures within the broad categories we are examining – so many that it would be impossible to address them all. And, as with the American generational categorisations, we must take care not to use these categories as stereotypical labels, but as an initial gleaning from which we can gain enough insight to see the individual components that add meaning. A basic understanding of the history of family systems in other cultures provides a foundation from which to gain more complete understanding of why generational factors are once again becoming a necessary focal point in our time and how such an understanding can serve families of all cultures in their quest to postpone the fulfilment of the Proverb's edicts.

European and Latin American generations of history

The differences in family systems among the cultures of the world seem to be tied to the degree of practical proximity to the patriarchal systems dating back centuries. This, in turn, has been primarily tied to religious mores, particularly in the realm of conjugal relationships and the hierarchy of patrimony.[7] In European families before the Renaissance, decisions about education, marriage, and work were traditionally dictated by the church. With the Renaissance was born a cycle of modernisation. These are the cycles which determine the generational perspectives present in European families, cycling from control by the state to religion and back to the state. Family relationships during this period of vast change responded in cyclical fashion to imperatives of church, of state (and its judicial system) and, to some extent, of landlords as well as the marketplace.[8]

Whether Christian, Muslim, or Confucian, the degree to which these systems are held within the family varies across the globe. These are real, not just theoretical, differences. However, they vary from family to family and from culture to culture. Family systems in Europe are not homogenous throughout the continent despite the dominance of the Christian religion for over a millennium and a half. Neither are those within Latin American countries, although they remained more closely aligned to the patriarchal system until World War II. The democratisation of families has intensified over the last 50 years and has ushered in three basic changes for both European and Latin American families.

1 The view of the family as a productive unit has declined. Where the family unit used to be tied to the working of the land or, more recently, to succession issues in a family enterprise, this is no longer 'a given'.
2 The power of the patriarchy has waned as individualism has increased, offering greater autonomy among family members. Although patriarchal values are still spoken of in reference to family arrangements and relationships, these values are no longer the central feature of contemporary European or Latin American families.
3 The religious tenets that emphasised the connection between human sexuality and reproduction have fallen by the wayside, evidenced by the increasing numbers of births outside marriage. Reproduction is no longer the primary focal point of sexual practices and such activity is no longer confined to the marriage.[9]

Latin American families have also been more subject to the political systems of the countries in which they live. The economic instability caused by political situations continues today to define the perspectives of Latin American generations.

Box 6.1 shows Latin American generational characteristics from the turn of the 20th century. We can see the cycles of political involvement and nationalist interests, cycles in community involvement, and the greater involvement of women in business. These are the perspectives of Latin American generations as viewed from the head of a Latin American family office.

Box 6.1
Latin American generations

1901–1924: this generation was very conservative and traditional, what one might call 'machistas' who were very authoritarian, politically active, not involved in community, mostly involved in the business. They felt that women had no role in business.

1928–1947: a little more progressive, this generation is still very traditional and family oriented with little involvement in politics.

1958–1967: there is greater community involvement with this generation as well as greater numbers of women getting educated and involved in business; still very family oriented.

1966–1982: this generation is not traditional, is very business oriented, yet it questions the way businesses have traditionally been run. Women are more educated and have developed their own businesses outside the family business; this generation grew up in the midst of very nationalist, volatile political situations.

In early modern Europe, migrations of multiple ethnic groups brought along with them various religious practices; for example, Jewish immigrants held to practices based on Old Testament laws that had been modified by the Christians; Muslims maintained Near Eastern practices in a determined way; and the lifestyle of the nomadic gypsies of Rome added their own influence. Although class differences have always been present,[10] there were two primary axes of difference in early modern Europe, according to Goody. One had to do with differences in the main Christian denominations in post-Reformation times, characterised as between the north and south or northwest and the rest, or in some cases as West and East. Second between recent demographic divide of industrial capitalism in Europe (not mercantile capitalism) essentially between civil law (*le droit écrit*) and common law jurisdictions (what is customary).[11] Of course, today, this distinction between civil and common law is the dividing line most commonly recognised in European countries although traditional patriarchal systems have remained underlying components to varying degrees.[12]

In many cases, the written code in early modern Europe may have been more patriarchal than the family itself. This was, perhaps, the reason legal backing for the code was required – it was an indication of the variance of actual practice. There was also a wide variety of relationships that the traditional European patriarchal flavour still represents. The basic principles of honour and shame seem to have been carried forward in the south, much more than in the north of Europe where there was more individual choice of marriage partners and greater equality in the marriage. There was also greater affection displayed between parents and children. These elements seemed more evident in the nuclei of smaller families which many historians and sociologists cite as the 'embryo of the modern family living in smaller households'.[13]

The main differences for larger families were evident primarily in less adult attention and less expenditure per child – quite logical in families with greater numbers of people – both of which had a significant impact on education. Love between spouses had more to do with how long the couple had been married as well as the economic backdrop of the country in which they lived. These differences in families of northern and southern Europe affected how people chose their spouses – more arranged marriages in the patriarchal systems of the south and more individual choice in the north.[14]

Laurence Stone notes a massive change in world view and societal norms in Britain between the 16th and 19th centuries where societal changes seeped into family relationships, primarily through customs, legal structures, power, and sexual relationships. He labels this radical change 'Affected Individualism', noting its singular importance in Western history over the last 1000 years. It is against the societal changes of this time period, early modern Europe that Western civilisation emerged.

Interestingly, this period of enormous change begins at roughly the same point Strauss and Howe cite that time began to be measured in saecula. So we have a sort of weaving in and out of generational influences between Europe and America, intermingled with the establishment of American generational labelling. The traditional patriarchal systems saw greater change in the northern countries of the European continent, including Britain; changes which were transported to the New World where the opportunity for social change became open to anyone, not just to the elite.

Puritanical forces through Calvinist roots created a new type of patriarchal control against which the American women's movement rose up beginning in the 19th century as well as the movement for greater ethnic equality, most notably during the American Civil War (also in the 19th century).

Through these significant social (and economic) changes came further demarcation of the generational archetypes in America. The European continent did not experience similar social revolution and, with the export of generational power from the elite to the New World offering access to anyone who could procure passage, it is easy to see why generational distinctions did not hold the same fascination for Europeans.[15]

Rather, Europe's generational cycles were characterised more by war and peace. Britain's Toynbee identified an alternating rhythmic cycle, punctuated by quarter-century wars which occurred approximately each century since the Renaissance. There were five repetitions of this cycle as outlined below.

1 The Italian Wars, 1494–1525 (the Overture).
2 The Imperial Wars of Phillip II, 1568–1609 (First Cycle).
3 War of the Spanish Succession, 1672–1713 (Second Cycle).
4 The French Revolution and Napoleonic Wars, 1792–1815 (Third Cycle).
5 World War I and World War II, 1914–1945 (Fourth Cycle).

Therefore, a European family's generational maze might resemble Exhibit 6.1.

Exhibit 6.1

European generational maze

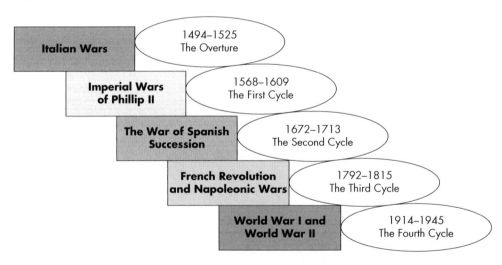

Source: graymatter Strategies LLC. All rights reserved.

A comparison of the generational cycles of Europe and America since the 19th century is shown in Exhibit 6.2.

Exhibit 6.2

Comparison of European and American generational cycles

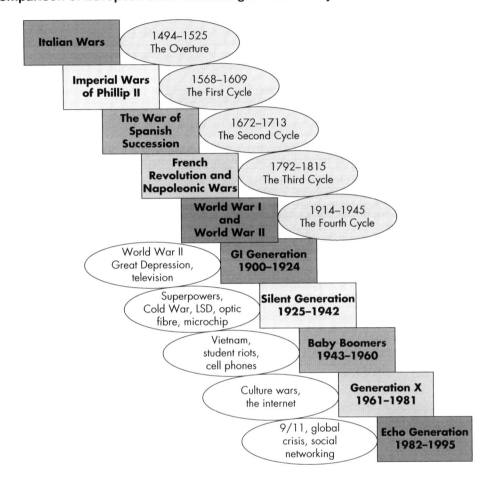

Source: graymatter Strategies LLC. All rights reserved.

In the generational sequence in European history, we can see primarily that earlier modern Europe displayed greater affection and individualism in families while later generations held more authority over children, especially in the south. Over time, power over these decisions migrated to the government and, later, to the individual. In more recent years, this authority has waned. Older generations no longer hold power over spousal choices or decisions of vocation or habitat.[16] The timing of this evolution in family relationships varies from country to country, having occurred earlier in the northern countries with the increased independence supported by both society and government and resulting in less tension among family relationships across the continent in modern times.

The changing generational dynamic in Europe

One of the greatest changes that have occurred in European and Latin American families over the past few centuries has been the shift from family fusion as a mandate to fusion becoming a choice. When agriculture was supplanted by photo-industrialisation and then by industrialisation, the family was no longer tied to access to land in the same way and in the end, the element that had held the family together had been permanently altered. Those transformations had radical effects on domestic life and were pushed further by the Second Industrial Revolution later in the 19th century and by the socio-economic changes (or Third Industrial Revolution) that followed World War II.[17]

As Affective Individualism began to infiltrate successive generations, the basic thread of change seemed to involve earlier generations of families displaying both affection and individualism.[18] Later generations saw a shift to greater parental authority over children. This tradition has been modified over the years – older generations no longer determine future marriage partners, the type of work their progeny will do, nor where they will live.

The economic reasons for multiple generations living under one roof have virtually disappeared, yet the social reasons for maintaining close family relationships remain. For example, in Switzerland, elder generations desire to live in close proximity to their married children to gain social and moral support during their later years and to be closer to the grandchildren.[19] For the most part, the range of relationships Europeans include in their concept of 'family' has rarely extended past the descendants of the grandparents. This would include immediate aunts and uncles, siblings of the parents, and their children who would be first cousins.[20] Although what seemed to be closeness in previous generations has shifted, the concept of what constitutes 'family' still holds. Interestingly, a generationally-based change in the range of relationships is occurring. As Boomers have aged and life spans have lengthened, Boomers in Sweden and France now usually belong to a family structure with four living generations; in Spain and Italy, the greatest likelihood of living in a multi-generational household lies with the Boomer generation.[21]

In a continent that has traditionally not been as fascinated with generational labels as America, global generational changes are lacing themselves within the vestiges of tradition. For the European family – as with families of other cultures steeped in centuries old tradition – this presents the challenge of incorporating significant change coupled with the preservation of a historical cord that has grounded them for centuries. For example, later age of marriage for both sexes and the tradition of having unmarried live-in servants are general features of European families dating back to the Middle Ages. Today, the percentage of families with unmarried parents is significant and growing, and live-in servants are largely a thing of the past. This presents new and challenging governmental issues, inheritance issues, and business succession issues. The two most common statistics shared across Europe are the rapid increase in births outside of marriage and the fact that these births actually reflect the number of unmarried couples having children rather than births to single mothers.

The questioning of traditional values, many founded in religious beliefs, has occurred for decades and Latin American families are no exception to this experience. As in other cultures, the abandonment of traditional mores to make way for the acceptance of new ones creates additional conflict through the redefinition of family roles, relationships, and responsibilities previously considered inherent to those relationships. 'The redefinition of familial relations, roles, and obligations as the basis of stable expectations between family members is a gradual and complex process.' Such changes happen slowly, are 'constantly fluctuating, and are never unidimensional'.[22] Current generations have grown up in different countries and different social and economic backdrops relative to their experiences with various historical periods. Many families in Nicaragua, Guatemala, and El Salvador have experienced civil war for years but the resulting post-war societal changes are quite individual.[23]

In Nicaragua, families became more global and invested less in their own country, signifying their roots are no longer Nicaraguan. Guatemalans felt more confident in their country after the wars so their view is exactly the opposite. Many families in El Salvador sought asylum in the United States and other countries and took their businesses along with them. After the political situation stabilised, many El Salvadorian families returned.[24] Most Latin American families, however, have come from a very patriarchal history where the eldest son inherits the wealth and the control of the family.

'In Latin American families, the second generation often doesn't become actively involved in the family's wealth management decisions until the patriarch dies. It's also more likely that the oldest son would be in a more prominent position than the oldest child in a US family,' notes Herrema.[25]

The eldest son in a Latin American family also tends to be expected to take over the family business as well as leadership of the family. 'In Latin American countries, Dad speaks and it happens. Mom heavily influences Dad but it is as it always has been. This is a very entrenched, dominant, and persuasive part of the Latin American culture,' notes Benevides.

According to Herrema, 'If a third son in a Latin American family wants to strike out on his own, it might mean no longer being a part of the family picture and wealth and that's hard. And it's much less likely than in the US that a daughter would ascend to the most-important-child role. In Brazil, this might be different. Brazil has the one of the most modernized approaches of the Latin American countries. It's one of the BRIC countries and its size and potential are being realized. It's becoming more like a westernized country in terms of wealth creation, industry, and banking.'[26]

Such change, however, is spreading throughout the Latin American region at different rates and to different degrees.

Class, tradition, and generational change

In France and Germany, it is still a common expectation for the next generation to inherit and run the family business. German, Austrian, and Swiss families work very hard. The oldest grandson is king and they try to groom him to run the show. He inherits everything and he is responsible for taking care of everyone else. So he is educated and trained to ensure that the family will survive. It is very autocratic but he is the decision maker. He does not know he can go out and hire experts to figure it all out. But that is changing. As families become more international, it is becoming more difficult to cling to those original notions.[27]

Property ownership and class have been inextricably linked in European families. For years, the large wealth in England has been property based. Since there was no revolution there, the land is still a primary asset that is inherited. The land usually carries a title with it such as Baron or Count. This is something not found in the US.[28]

The British appear to have abandoned their traditional system to a large degree but in reality, the nobility largely still owns and controls Britain and there is still a great schism between the nobility and the rank and file. It is still a very class based society. Ninety percent of the British Isles is controlled by about 300 families.[29]

Property is also a large part of inheritance in France, although the revolution caused a significant amount of property to change hands. There once were three basic class distinctions in France. In keeping with our 'ties to religion' focus, classes would be divided into the Aristocracy (or Nobility), the Church, and everyone else. If we focus completely on the secular world, we see a titled aristocracy which may have status and property but may not have much in the way of financial assets. Most work of the Nobility was farm related. Traditionally, the family assets – like the family castle – have been maintained almost at all costs. People might be cash poor but quite wealthy in assets, which may present a radical change in lifestyle when the patriarch becomes deceased. The financial strain of the upkeep might be more than current generations can afford. They have a few options. They can re-guild the Coat of Arms by marrying someone outside the aristocracy who has money – typically a member of the Bourgeoisie who may have created new wealth and who crave aristocratic status – making it possible to maintain the castle for a few more years. Or the family may resort to opening all but the family living quarters to the public and charging admission for tours in an effort to keep from having to lose an asset that has meant so much to the family's legacy.

In some cases, a scion may take over the family business – a move which may succeed long enough to secure a favourable buyout, may add new life to the business and succeed of its own power, or which may fall flat on its face. For example, in the 1990s, Club Med which had been owned by Gilbert Trigano was taken over by son Serge who was then replaced by former Disney CEO Phillippe Bourguignon. Bourguignon attempted a relaunch of the company which proved to be unsuccessful. In the case of the Bouygues Group which was founded by father Francis the year son Martin was born, Martin grew up in the industrial works and construction company (which built the Roissy terminal at Charles De Gaulle Airport), took over from his father in 1989 and successfully led the firm into an entirely different business segment by purchasing a television network and growing it into a highly diversified media group.

In cases where the succession was a failure, there was no choice other than to sell. This has led to degeneracy in the patrimony.

In Switzerland, there is still the Noblesse or those privileged by birth which goes back 200 or 300 years in some families. 'It's the idea that the family history is deeply rooted to a certain region, a certain land and the blood comes from one place,' says Wavre.

Family dynamics and generational attitudes toward wealth

Comparing American and European perspectives on work reveals distinct differences in attitudes. In Europe, work is not necessarily viewed as something people admire. For example, an American might spend a relatively short period of time working on a project that becomes a huge success, then embellish the efforts by saying, 'I worked my tail off', with an added emphasis of, 'I made this myself', regardless of the number of hours it actually took to achieve that success. Credit for similar success in Europe would more often be given to the parents even if the person did create it autonomously.[30] One example of this might be a family whose wealth was originally created by previous generations, then the assets seized during a time of political uncertainty or by military invasion. Succeeding generations may recreate the wealth but they will give credit to the previous generations to maintain the family's identity and retell the legends of hardship and perseverance.

European families are more careful about showing their wealth and older families saw the family office as a way to protect the privacy of the family as well as to provide security. 'People forget about the time in Italy or Germany when people were kidnapped – it wasn't so long ago and people tend to forget very quickly. So, there have always been family offices in Europe to protect and manage the wealth,' Wavre explains.

Another reason for attempting to 'hide' the wealth is the way most European countries have imposed their tax systems. In England and Scotland during the 18th century, there was a tax instituted on the number of windows in a house. France instituted a tax on windows and doors from 1798 to 1926. Families resorted to hiding assets – in this case, by bricking or boarding up windows and doors – in an effort to avoid these taxes.[31] In the 1960s and 1970s, France instituted a tax on bathtubs and sinks! A wealth tax still exists in many European countries in lieu of or in addition to some type of income tax although, in recent times, Finland, Iceland, and Luxembourg have abolished it. The tax is, in essence, based on one's net worth[32] – something that would definitely include the family castle along with windows, doors, bathtubs, and sinks.

Contrasting European, Latin American, and American Generational perspectives

In contrasting European, Latin American, and American generational perspectives, there is much to be learned. As more and more families become culturally diverse, their family dynamics are changing radically. This sets up an even greater likelihood that the misunderstanding of generational perspectives will lead to family conflict – both within the family and within the business of the family. Industry professionals in Europe have long understood that awareness of cultural differences is key to adequately serving families of wealth. The generational changes occurring globally are now bringing the importance of generational differences to the forefront of family wealth management.

'Fifty years ago – and still for the older families who have carried the tradition for centuries – just owning the company and having the capital was enough. Now, families with new wealth realize you also have to manage it well,' Wavre continues. He says families realise that if they do not have the talent for managing the company, they will not be able to keep the wealth. If the next generation has the talent, they can be trained to take over after the founding generation. But if they do not have the talent, highly talented management can be brought in and the next generations trained to be top level board members so they will know how to protect their interests.

Some European countries still hold on to strong traditions but people in advisory positions are realising how many of their clients are interested in issues of governance and other family wealth related issues. 'The generation who lived through the war [World War II] is very different because, even though things were better after the war, people became much more conservative. They went through a very difficult period, especially in Europe, so this has become a trait – it's really in their stomachs. The next generation went through 1973–1974 and the deep recession – the oil crisis – so they also have known some hard times. But the new generation – the younger ones since 1979 – you can't say they have gone through a very difficult period yet. That's a big difference. When you inherit wealth and that is the case, you tend to be more concerned about philanthropy and other things. It's taken for granted that the wealth will be there. The older generations remember the hard times and that changes the way they handle the relationships and the way they manage the assets. So in that way, perhaps generational perspectives are gaining more importance since we live in a more open world,' explains Wavre.

Families in Europe are beginning to focus more on how to create structures through which these generational changes can be managed more effectively. They are familiar with the family office concept but are learning much more about family governance and the benefits or creating a more organised way of interacting. Europe, traditionally, however, has separated family business issues from more family related issues but that is changing, although at different rates throughout the continent. Grégoire Imfeld, client relationship manager at Pictet et Cie makes the point that 'it's difficult to generalize about Europe because it's so multicultural. It's difficult to talk about trends because it differs depending on the region. People are still focused on the financial side but they're very curious about the family governance issue and they want to know more about it'.

Pictet's Vera Boissier, senior vice president, senior relationship manager, and head of a family office team says that one of the biggest concerns of European families is education. 'It's absolutely key. Because a lot of the children have studied in the US and also because, in Europe, you have some countries which are old Europe and much more conservative. But other countries want to catch up and want to know what's going on. The concept of family governance is emerging and you now find people are more open to these ideas.'

'As a result of the 2008 crisis, more family problems are coming to light – they have always been there but now, families and their advisors are seeing that these issues need to be addressed. Families are realising they are not as equipped as they thought to navigate these waters on their own,' Boissier continues.

Boissier notes that many families were running a successful business, then tried to create an investment business for their families. 'The business was going well and there was excitement, then they let things go. Now, it makes sense to go back to the industry they understand. They're more secure in what they know,' she explains. 'So now they're coming to organizations like ours who are more professional and objective and have organized process that specialize in family office functions.'

She also notes that European families today are looking for sustainability. 'The objective is to pass things on to the next generation so their priority is not necessarily aggressive growth. They are looking at multiple generations and passing on the values that one generation should not waste the resources of the other one. There should be something left for the next generation to develop.'

Wavre contrasts private family services in Europe and the US in earlier times. 'The private bankers played a role in the US as a type of a family office for years. At that time in Europe, the offerings of banks and family offices were different and family offices were more often developed as a stand-alone resource.'

It is no longer enough to focus on the investment or wealth management side alone. The crisis peeled back beyond those focal points to reveal the underlying issues that affect a family's success, of which generational perspectives are also the foundational element. The connection between issues of family dynamics and how they affect the management of the wealth are becoming more and more realised. This points to the critical need for institutions with family office segments to work hand in hand with the wealth management and other segments to provide a more robust experience for their family clients.

American professionals who think they do not have to concern themselves with multicultural perspectives are operating in the dark. America is more culturally diversified than ever and more families of wealth are finding their children marrying people of other cultures with different generational histories and different attitudes toward wealth.

'In America, the individual is king – that's in our culture,' notes Patricia Angus, CEO at Angus Advisory Group. 'Cultures in other countries often have a greater sense of connectedness within the family. Today, in America, some families are learning more about what that view of family could do for the future generations of their own families.'[33]

Wavre notes there are two root differences between the way Europeans and Americans approach family wealth – the fact that European families go back many, many centuries so the bloodline is very important and also the differences in the legal system and the way wealth is passed over to the next generation.

According to Herrema, Latin American families sometimes are more linked to family than US families. US families often will go their separate ways but Latin American families tend to be more involved in the family business. Part of that could be that the opportunities in the US are more plentiful than in Latin American countries. There is more of a multi-generational closeness and there may be tighter control of the wealth in Latin American families.

'Europeans don't worry about the same issues as families in the US. They [families in the US] don't have the Calvinist work ethic and belief that life shouldn't be fun. There are countries like Italy where they're, obviously, having fun all the time and yet, their economic productivity is higher than in the US. So Americans have a peculiar view of the value of hard, boring work!' explains Hauser.

'Europe also has different inheritance rights,' Hauser says. 'They are fixed and do not have trusts, so from birth, the children know they are going to have half or a third, depending on the country and the number of siblings. So they grow up living with this knowledge about their inheritance. The big family wealth in Europe still has the family name attached to it very visibly out in the marketplace. So they have to be careful about how they behave since the family brand is so visible.'

Wavre says, 'My sense is that the younger generations in the US and in Europe are converging. I would guess that there were more differences 10 or 20 years ago than there are now because of globalization and because the new generation has not experienced difficult times. Everything is becoming more international. Today, communication is easier [because of technology] and so it's even more important to send the next generation abroad if you want to form them to take over the business or to train them well.'

And yet, sending the younger generations abroad may no longer be enough. According to Boissier, European families have become more knowledgeable about the family office industry, particularly in gaining knowledge about family governance issues and becoming more organised in their communications and decision making. One catalyst for this has been the education of the next generation with many children studying abroad and coming back to share the knowledge from their management studies with their elders. 'The family office concept is known in every country in Europe now. Many families tried to do it themselves at first. Then the 2008 crisis came along and they realized that perhaps they were not very well organized and they didn't have the right people involved.' When it comes to performing family office roles, trusted long-time family advisors or perhaps family friends may or may not be the best choice as the family office setting may require more sophistication or broader professional experience. Although the well-educated children brought a bank of knowledge to the family, they lacked the experience in the family business that the elder generation had gained over time.

Families virtually handed the leadership reigns over to the younger generations whose lack of experience may have not served the family well during the crisis.

Imfeld notes, 'Over the last three years, the financial crisis has had a significant impact on the family dynamics. Latent problems that were ignored while the markets were good began to surface in the aftermath of the crisis.' Before the crisis, families paid little attention to how much was spent compared to how much was earned. 'Can I cover my costs? These types of questions really emerged during the crisis,' he says. 'All of these factors may lead the way back to a more authoritarian approach where the elder takes a much stronger lead and break what was thought to be a transition period. As a result, the next generation may become more spectators than active participants.'

And yet, there must be a better way to manage generational change than the 'all or nothing' approach outlined above. The point of sending younger generations abroad to be educated is for them to come back and contribute to the success of the family. Perhaps a blending of the knowledge younger generations acquire with the experience of older generations might serve families better. Changes should happen progressively; the ancestral way of doing things does not have to be upended in order to open a path for new ways of doing things. This is a lesson that families in all cultures might wish to learn; it is a lesson that leads families down the path to their authentic wealth and the importance of consummately integrated management of all assets within the family portfolio. In all cultures, issues of family dynamics emanating from differences in the perspectives of a family's generations are becoming as important as issues of investment and asset allocation. Becoming aware of these factors and recognising their importance are essential for families wishing to foster all forms of their wealth.

1 Wavre, Pierre-Alain, Managing Director and Head of the Pictet Family Office, Pictet et Cie, Personal interview, February, 2007.

2 Strauss, W. and Howe, N., *The Fourth Turning: an American prophecy* (New York, NY: Broadway Books, 1997), p. 92.

3 Wealth Regeneration® is a registered service mark owned by Laird Norton Tyee and is used throughout this book Laird Norton Tyee's permission.

4 Strauss, W. and Howe, N., *The Fourth Turning: an American prophecy,* (New York, NY: Broadway Books, 1997), p. 95.

5 Strauss, W. and Howe, N., *Millennials Rising: the next Great Generation,* (New York, NY: Vintage Books, 2000), p. 29.

6 Salles, V. and Tuirán, R., *The Family in Latin America: a gender approach,* (New York, NY: Sage Social Science Collections, 1997), p. 151: http://csi.sagepub.com/cgi/content/abstract/45/1/141.

7 Ibid, p. 142.

8 Goody, J., *The European Family,* (Malden, MA: Blackwell, 2000), p. 13.

9 Salles, V. and Tuirán, R., *The Family in Latin America: a gender approach,* (New York, NY: Sage Social Science Collections, 1997), p. 142: http://csi.sagepub.com/cgi/content/abstract/45/1/141.

10 Goody, J., *The European Family,* (Malden, MA: Blackwell, 2000), p. 100.

11 Ibid, p. 102.

12 Ehlern, S., *Global Private Wealth Management: an international study on private wealth management and family office services for high net worth individuals,* Doctoral Study (London, Zurich: Ferguson Partners Family Office, 2006–2007), p. 438. For a more comprehensive elaboration of civil and common law.

13 Goody, J., *The European Family,* (Malden, MA: Blackwell, 2000), p. 102.

14 Ibid.

15 Strauss, W. and Howe, N., *The Fourth Turning: an American prophecy,* (New York, NY: Broadway Books, 1997), p. 95.

16 Goody, J., *The European Family,* (Malden, MA: Blackwell, 2000), p. 153.

17 Ibid, p. 14.

18 Ibid, p. 153.

19 www.everyculture.com/Sa-Th/Switzerland.html.

20 Goody, J., *The European Family,* (Malden, MA: Blackwell, 2000), p. 3.

21 Ogg, J., 'The Baby Boomer generation and family support: a European perspective', 2006: .icsw.org/doc/0041_5e_Ogg_Eng_Abstract.doc.

22 Salles, V. and Tuirán, R., *The Family in Latin America: a gender approach,* (New York, NY: Sage Social Science Collections, 1997), p. 143: http://csi.sagepub.com/cgi/content/abstract/45/1/141.

[23] Anonymous source, Personal interview, July 2007.

[24] Anonymous source, Personal interview, July 2007.

[25] Herrema, Donald J., Personal interview, January 2007.

[26] Herrema, Donald J., Personal interview, January 2007.

[27] Handler, Thomas J., Personal interview, February 2007.

[28] Wavre, Pierre-Alain, Personal interview, February 2007.

[29] Handler, Thomas J., Personal interview, February 2007.

[30] Anonymous source, Personal interview, October 2007.

[31] Wikipedia, 'Window Tax': http://en.wikipedia.org/wiki/Window_tax.

[32] Wikipedia, 'Wealth Tax': http://en.wikipedia.org/wiki/Wealth_tax.

[33] Angus, Patricia M., Founder and CEO, Angus Advisory Group LLC, Personal interview, April 2007.

Chapter 7

Generational perspectives in Asia and the Middle East

'Compared to Americans, there's much less of a sense of an individual self among Asians. They experience themselves as far more embedded in a net of extremely close emotional relationships. They have what might be called a familial self, one that includes their close relationships in their own sense of who they are. This kind of self simply does not exist in the West to nearly the same degree.'

Alan Roland[1]

In contrasting generational perspectives of various cultures, we find clearer distinctions between American generational perspectives and those of Asian and Middle Eastern families. The concept of modernisation helps in comparing American, Asian, and Middle Eastern perspectives and also in completing the global generational perspectives picture. Modernisation is defined as 'the transformation of a society from a rural and agrarian condition to a secular, urban, and industrial one'.[2] The spread of modernisation from 17th century Europe to other parts of the world occurred at different rates. Keep in mind, all cultures of the world are still involved in this process, a concept which makes the Echo generation's wave of influence that much more impactful.

Within modernisation, the importance of the individual gradually overtakes the importance of family or the community as the basic unit of society. 'Modernisation is a continuous and open-ended process ... which must be measured in centuries.'[3] And so, we have another element to the generational cycle which is based on societal and economic change. Strauss and Howe cite the 1500s (the 16th century) as the first 100-year period to be named a 'century'. This, in conjunction with the advent of modernisation in 17th century Europe, sets us on the way to our current time, the vast global change that is and has been occurring, how it has affected families of wealth since World War II, and how the Echoes are creating their own global footprint. As this new generation comes of age, they do so within the developmental timeline of modernisation their culture is experiencing.

What does all this mean for the consummate family wealth portfolio[SM]?[4] By looking at the generational perspectives of various cultures and the history of how they were formed, we ground ourselves in a pivotal fashion that allows us to balance the developments of our current time against the history and legacy of times past. This allows us to stop treating the symptoms of family wealth dysfunction and discover the source of the issues. We can balance the best components of the old with the innovative advantages of the new. Subsequently, it opens the door for postponing the effects of the Proverb's edicts so that the gift of wealth can be continuous for five, six, seven generations or more. An incredible legacy for any family.

This chapter will highlight the history of modernisation in a way that clarifies the magnitude of change being effected by the Echo generation, how they are affecting all societies and the families of wealth living in them. It will round out our examination of American, European, and Latin

American generations so that our global generational picture will be more robust and will begin to come much more clearly into focus.

The multi-cultural generational pathway

A generational sea change led by the Echo generation is threading itself through the globalised world. Like the Boomer generation, they are affecting every stage of life they enter, only in a much broader wave. They are echoing the effect of the Boomers after World War II. According to *Fourth Turning* co-author Strauss, 'We looked at several European and Asian societies – there are variations but basically they follow the same rhythm because WWII was such a large generations creating event', He notes that across the generational and cultural spectrum, 'we broadly have the same generations but there are variations – the birth year and the timing of generations in different cultures could be three to four years apart. And, of course, everything has its own cultural overlay. So being a Millennial [Echo] in Pakistan is not the same as being a Millennial [Echo] in England'.

And being a Boomer in America is different from being a Boomer in other parts of the world. For example, the Boomer generation in Japan is called the 'Dankai' generation, which is in the early stages of the country's mandatory retirement system. This Japanese version of the Boom was 30% greater in size than those born in Japan in the periods either preceding or following. Although the Dankai were born over a period of only three years, hardly a full generational birth spectrum©, they shared characteristics with the Boomer cohort of America. They, too, rebelled against the 'establishment'. They were called the 'Beatles generation', increased consumption, and raised life-style expectations in Japanese society.[5] In some ways, the generations of each culture are similar; in others, they are quite different.

How did each culture's generational perspectives lead them to the developmental space they occupy today? And what important elements can be gleaned in helping families regenerate their wealth for generations to come? The answer lies in a brief look at history. Once we know the path we have travelled, we can understand more fully the path we are currently taking and where it might possibly lead us. The path that generational cycles have travelled from a global perspective is the path of modernisation. This path encompasses the vast social and economic changes that have occurred in each culture, defining their respective generational lenses along the way.

Modernisation: a dually phased process

In similar fashion to linear time, modernisation seems to make progress in the initial phase and 'to carry the institutions and values of society along with it'. This sense of progress also is felt to be upward or forward moving. Then there comes a point where the success of the initial phase turns and begins to breed discontent while the push to continue on the same path becomes more compulsive. *One of the most important things to note about linear impositions is that the cyclical tide begins to turn even as the linear path increases momentum, leaving the travellers of the linear path increasingly exposed to higher levels of risk.* Expectations become so high based on the progress of the initial phase that demands for satisfaction become more and more difficult to fulfil. From the larger society perspective (and, ironically, also of the capital markets), these demands strain society and its resources to the point of threatening the very growth and expansion that the first phase accomplished, creating issues which may 'seem beyond the competence of the traditional nation-state. At the same time, the world remains dominated by a system of just such sovereign nation-states of unequal strengths and conflicting interests'.[6]

Exhibit 7.1

Cyclical underpinnings of modernisation and linear time

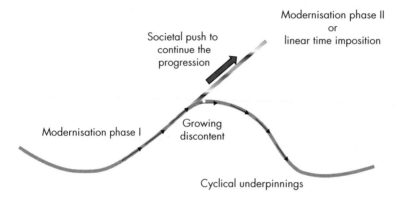

Modernisation phase II
or
linear time imposition

Societal push to
continue the
progression

Growing
discontent

Modernisation phase I

Cyclical underpinnings

Notably, modernisation is the second of only two 'quantum leaps' that have been identified through the social evolution of human beings; the first – the Neolithic or agricultural revolution out of the Stone Age – occurred in the third and second millennia BC and led to the development of urban civilisation.[7]

So there was this huge block of time from the first quantum leap out of the Stone Age (Paleolithic period) into the agricultural revolution which had an irreversible, sustainable impact on society and the economy. From the agricultural revolution came the creation of the plough which, in turn, created a social revolution of its own. From this single invention, more people could be fed. This led to massive growth in the world population and the establishment of families who worked together in what might be called the 'family business' of that time. The surplus of food made possible by this new and better technology allowed individuals so inclined to 'opt out' of the family business to become artisans, priests, merchants, and bureaucrats. From urban civilisation rose the ancient – and empirical – cultures of China and India, Greece and Rome.[8]

Until the 16th century, Europe was considered backward in its comparative development to Asian and Middle Eastern civilisations. As Europe experienced the Renaissance, a religious metamorphosis began. At the time, the world was dominated by contemplative religious practices found in Catholicism and the Eastern religions of Hinduism and Buddism. As Protestantism took hold in Europe, religion was brought to every person rather than reserved for priests. An overlay to Protestantism, Puritanism, emphasised the value of hard work and frugality. It was against this backdrop that the New World was developed, bringing the promise of social change out of the exclusivity of the elites and offering access to the common people. As these societal expectations bred seriousness and hard work, they also bred industrial capitalism and modern science.[9] And so the cycle continued.

As Europe colonised America, vast new resources created unprecedented wealth and physical power. This set the West on a different developmental path than the rest of the world. Philosophers speculated that the world might again achieve the greatness of the ancient Greeks and Romans. The advent of modernisation brought broader and faster developing changes. As the generational archetypes were reinterpreted alongside modernisation, powerful generations such as the Boomers brought vast and sweeping change. As the decades pass, the development of technology brings change at even swifter rates. These are the 'roots' of our modern day generational perspectives. Now we have a clearer path toward the foundation from which developed the various cultural generational perspectives of our time.

Asian generational perspectives

Asian cultures along with Latin American and Middle Eastern cultures have traditionally been heavily patriarchal. This section will look at two primary Asian cultures – Japanese and Chinese – to find similarities and differences within an overall eastern philosophy. In researching the generations of these two cultures, the amount of material discovered could inspire an entirely separate book! Therefore, I will highlight what I consider to be important generational factors for our purposes so that we may, hopefully, get a glimpse into the perspectives of these very old societies and extrapolate useful application to wealth management issues. We will also touch on the perspectives of Korea and India for generations since World War II, rounding out the Asian generational picture.

An important element in family owned businesses in some (not all) Asian and Middle Eastern cultures is the impact that polygamy has on the family business structure. In these cultures, men marry multiple wives to have more sons to ensure family business succession and to develop rivalry within the different branches of the family to see who will be the best candidates. This is a prime example of how what happens on the family side influences what happens in the business and investment side. Asian families do not separate 'family' from 'business' any more than they separate the 'self' as Western cultures do. Self is much more closely integrated with a web of relationships than as an entity independent from political, educational, and economic concerns.

The one exception to this may be Japan. In Japanese society, self is subordinated to societal conformity.

Japanese generations

Generational conflict has drawn comment throughout the lives of most Japanese currently alive. Since World War II, each new generation of young people has been targeted in some way, from the *taiyōzoku* of the 1950s who were seen as abandoning the discipline of their elders for their own hedonism, to protesters against the US Japan Security Treaty, and 1960s radicals reflecting the tumult of youth in that decade; to *shinjinrui* , who were seen as the 'new breed' of the 1980s, claiming to be so different from their Japanese elders as to no longer be 'Japanese', to *otaku,* who were seen as technophiles swallowed up by the world of computers and media and in the late 1990s, *kogyaru,* young women with artificially dark tans and hair dyed bright blond.[10] Now, there is the *Ojo man* or 'girlie man' who represents the quiet social revolution against the image of the macho

Japanese *taiyōzoku* salarymen, 'upon whose shoulders modern Japan was built'. It is a revolution that has seemingly been sought by Japanese for years as a result of the long economic downturn.[11]

It can be said that each generation of children is brought up to recreate the world of its parents. That is the only world they know. On the other hand, each generation has three options as they come into adulthood. They can reproduce the environment in which they grew up; they can create a completely different environment for their own children; or they can reshape the world they inherited from the older generations.[12]

In the 1960s as the post-war Boomer children came of age, Japanese demographics underwent enormous change. Agriculture, fishery, and forestry had been the primary industries and people began to leave these more rural industries and move into cities. In the late 1960s, early 1970s, student rebellions took place in Japan, France, Germany, and the US. During these years, the Dankai would have been in their late teens–early twenties. These rebellions coincided with the anti-Vietnam war movement. Unlike the revolts of previous generations, this was a younger generation's revolt against an older generation who had grown up in an entirely different environment.[13]

'Japan is a culture that wants to hang on to its traditions and its history,' says Thomas J. Handler of Handler Thayer LLP in Chicago. Therefore, the possibility of rejection of the standing social order creates great tension. The concern that the world of the elders will not be legitimised by the younger generation after their rebellion creates a period of crisis as younger generations enter adulthood.[14] The 1960s brought new ways of expression from Japanese youth in keeping with what American sociologist Daniel Bell termed, 'the sensibilities of the sixties'. Young people began to do what they wanted instead of what was expected of them. Another notable difference was a change in attitude toward the West. Before 1964, the Japanese government only allowed overseas travel for business or with a study abroad programme. In 1964, travel abroad was approved for the purpose of tourism. Where the previous generations had idolised American and European societies, this new generation was more critical. The new generation felt that they had more authority over their own lives; they no longer felt compelled to conform to older, established ways. Interestingly, the advent of television broadcasting in 1953 gave broader access to information. By 1962, 80% of Japanese households had a TV. Since the ways of the West were thought, at that time, to be worth striving to adopt, the western way of doing things spread quickly.[15]

The recent generations of Japan have turned 180 degrees from the early postwar generations, the first of whom were called the 'my home' generation. As a result of separation of fathers from families during the war, this generation focused less on being at work and more on time at home with family. A 'new family' generation followed who desired much closer relationships between men and women, parents and children. Then came the rebellious 1960s but Japan's version of student riots were short-lived having never caught on significantly within Japanese society. This generation was much less spirited than its global counterparts – much to the relief of the Japanese authorities of that period.[16]

The following generation was called 'crystal' and was materialistic and somewhat amoral. Next came generations who adopted their own fads and fashions including the *takenokozoku* who tanned their bodies and dyed their hair blond (the *kogyaru* mentioned above were predecessors of this group) and used their bodies to morph into whatever type of look they wish to achieve. This was a great departure for Japanese women who, in the decades before the 1970s and 1980s, would never have exposed their arms or their legs much less their backs.[17]

In his book, *Japan As – Anything But – Number One*, Jon Woronoff writes that relationships among Japanese generations are experiencing a significant gap between those who lived through post World War II confusion and poverty and the newer generations who experienced Japan's high growth in the 1960s and 1970s and its economic superiority in the 1980s and who are now government leaders. The entire institution of family is 'decaying and crumbling at alarming speed' and little of the family's digression can be attributed to modernisation.[18]

Fathers are groomed to be 'company men' from the time they graduate high school or college. College graduates are destined for higher level positions within the companies they work for all their lives. Even when at home, Japanese fathers seem to be absorbed in their work, being mentally absent while physically present and feeling relief when it is once again time to return to work. Mothers take over what they can but they cannot be appropriate role models for boys growing up nor can she teach her sons the 'man's language' of Japanese society.[19]

The Girlie Men or 'Herbivores' comprise 30% to 40% of the Japanese male population between the ages of 21 and 34. Their revolution is aimed at more gender-based workplace equality, making the workplace less 'spiritually crushing', and forging closer family ties. Indeed, one of the primary goals of younger Japanese is to enjoy greater pleasure in both their personal and work lives. More workers are expressing interest in changing jobs even at the high cost of sacrificing the opportunity of becoming an executive along the company-led path.[20]

They are in sharp contrast to the stoicism of the generation who emerged from World War II focused on rebuilding Japan into the second most powerful world economy. This generation's children, the Dankai, were followed by the 'Bubble Generation' of the 1980s as Japan seemed well positioned to dominate the world. Then came the dark decade that shifted global attention to the growing societies of China and India.

Japan has traditionally exerted great control over the development of its young. It supervises every stage of development from birth to preschool to primary school, secondary school, college, from college to work and then to corporate socialisation.

Today, the corporate socialisation aspect seems to have become the primary focal point. The pressures resulting from Japanese employers' demands on workers increasingly separate families from fathers, who are still the traditional workers. Long commutes, long hours, and the propensity of fathers to either work overtime or spend after hours time with colleagues rather than their families is causing a split in the long-admired Japanese institution.[21]

As a result, children only are able to define their roles through the companies they work for after they become part of the working world. Although society dictates that the father is to be looked up to, respected, and deferred to as an elder, he is never around and the offering of such respect to someone who is a stranger, in essence, becomes a duty rather than an honour. The mother ends up being an overbearing educator and family leader whose domination crushes the children's efforts to individuate. So relationships between generations have little chance to develop along the lines of the 'the traditional Japanese framework'.[22]

As well, the current leadership generation, sometimes called the Dankai Junior generation, is breaking the tradition of legitimising the long-established social order. The generation of the Democratic Party of Japan (DPJ) who, in the most recent election, upturned the 50-year reign of the Liberal Democratic Party (LDP), is leading Japanese society to greater choice and more openness, yet the undercurrent led by the Herbivores is seeking the more introspective life of the pre-war generation. The Herbivores are responding to the changed Japanese economy and reinterpreting the pre-war generational archetype, that of a less competitive, silent majority.[23]

All of this would seemingly point to change in the family, as well, but the impact of the younger generations to date seems to offer little weight toward narrowing the gaps between generations or toward rejuvenating the family as an institution.[24]

Economic influences

Because of Japanese society's seeming separation from the rest of the world and the singular experience of its economy since the late 1980s,[25] the economic impact on Japanese society is an even greater force in shaping its current generations. During the 1980s, the values of Japanese stocks and land increased enormously – tenfold in many cases – far outpacing values that grew through entrepreneurial enterprises. The seeds of phenomenal growth originated from the company man mandate, spurring innovation and productivity that became the envy of the world.[26] The stage for extreme growth may have been set by Nomura securities in the early 1950s with its 'Million Ryo Savings Chest' programme designed to help people save enough money to buy shares in the newly revived investment trust programmes. The programmes were designed to encourage people to save and were the first reinstitution of the investment trusts since the end of World War II. The programme was so successful that by 1962, over one million Ryo chests or 'piggy banks' had been distributed.[27] This was a significant precursor to government involvement in the banking system.

Eventually, the underpinnings of unprecedented growth began to cycle back, leading to frothy growth of land and stock values which continued until 1989 when prices began tumbling and the banking system entered a crisis which has yet to be fully resolved. Continued government intervention since that time has propped up the banking system and kept the Japanese economy from recovering. From 2003 to 2007, the government instituted savings programmes through a separate company the government created called the Japanese Post which enabled people to buy life insurance and access banking services through a government entity and, simultaneously, re-subsidise the banking system. Numerous bank bailout programmes followed such as the Financial Function Stabilisation Plan, the Financial Revitalisation Plan, the Financial Reconstruction Account, Financial Crisis Management Account, and the Early Strengthening Account. These were all instituted during the late 1990s.[28]

Over the period, the Post accumulated over $2.1 trillion in savings account assets and over $1.2 trillion in its insurance programme. The Post also was home to a government bond program equal to one fifth of Japanese national debt. The Post had been created to replace the Postal Services Agency and was instituted as a plan to privatise the post office which was the country's largest employer.[29] The hope was to revive the Japanese economy from the seemingly endless cycle of recession and deflation that had occurred since 1989 when the Nikkei average reached its peak of 38,957 before tumbling over 63%. The Japanese Post was indeed privatised in 2007; as of 2010, its success is still uncertain.

None of this has abated the spending habits which grew from the hugely inflated land and stock values. Much of the personal wealth, quite contrary to traditional Japanese propriety, is now being openly flaunted, contributing to the view that Japan is a market which guarantees foreign business success.[30] As the wealth is being handed down to the next generations and with the state of the family in limbo, new generations have little regard for traditional family culture – especially in caring for aging parents or of giving back to the community.[31]

Exhibit 7.2

Japanese generational identities

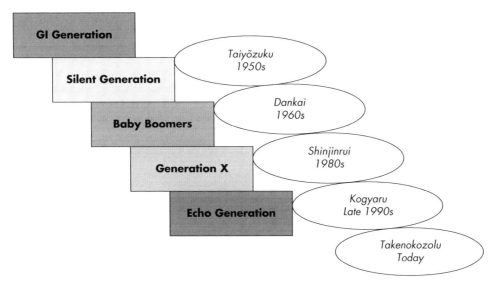

So we have the makings of significant social change most markedly in a country known for its conformity. The seemingly opposed generational forces indicate a great upheaval, typical of the Fourth Turning crisis period. In fact, Japan has had four different prime ministers over the last four years, the latest of which, on the day of this writing (June 2 2010), has agreed to step down.[32] Perhaps the Herbivores are the Japanese version of the next Hero archetype (the Echoes), paving the way for the children now being born – the next Artist cohort – to enjoy their pursuits for greater fulfilment. As events in the US and parts of Europe have mirrored much of what has happened in Japan – the propping up and subsequent crash of real estate values and the 'too big to fail' mentality guiding government intervention – it seems that the world's major economic powers may indeed be headed toward structural change from both economic and social perspectives. It will be interesting to see how this backdrop imprints the generations growing up within it.

Japanese Diaspora

Japan's native archetypical generations differ from those of the Japanese Diaspora, those who emigrated from Japan to the countries of North America and Latin America. The Diaspora generations follow a numerical order from the original emigrating generation rather than the original wealth creating generation or an archetypical generational sequence.

Box 7.1
Generations of the Japanese Diaspora

Issei – emigrant generation (G1)
Nisei – children of the emigrants (G2)
Sansei – grandchildren of original emigrants (G3)
Yonsei – great-grandchildren of original emigrants (G4)

The bulk of Japanese living in the western hemisphere emanate from Issei who emigrated between 1880 and 1924. A multinational group of sociologists gave the name Nikkei to encompass the entire group of generations emanating from Japan across the globe.[33] Interestingly, Nikkei is also the name of the Japanese stock exchange.

Box 7.2
Corresponding generations: Japan and America

Dankai generation (most like American Baby Boomers)
Hanako generation (most like American Gen-Xers)
Dankai junior generation (most like American Echo)

Notes Hauser, 'The senior generation in Japan is a lot like ours – duty, hard work, and life's not supposed to be fun. It was probably cross fertilized with our influence after World War II.' Obviously, the Diaspora generations have been heavily influenced by the culture of the countries to which they emigrated. For example, the evolution of Japanese Americans and Japanese Brazilians has been quite different. Japanese Americans hold lower ethnic status in the US and feel less tied to their homeland than Japanese Brazilians do in Brazil. However, when Japanese Americans return to the homeland, they have a better experience because of their higher socio economic status where Japanese Brazilians are viewed as minorities.[34] The Diaspora generations open up an entirely new vista for study, a study which will be reserved for more in depth treatment in a possible future publication.

Chinese generations

Chinese generational perspectives also are divided between native mainlanders and the Diaspora which emigrated to Singapore, Indonesia, the Philippines, Malaysia, Thailand, and Vietnam.

It is an understatement to say that mainland China has become a global focal point of growing economic power. As much as Japan seems to try to maintain its established social order, notes Handler, conversely, China is embracing the West very quickly on its own volition. We will begin by looking at the forces in recent history which laid the groundwork for China's open-armed embrace of the West, then move to the generations of the Diaspora.

The most impactful social change in recent Chinese history was the Cultural Revolution spanning 1966–1976, the years when Mao Zedong was in power. To understand why China is 'going western' so quickly, one must have at least a surface understanding of the significance of the Cultural Revolution. It was a vast upheaval, socially, politically, and, of course, economically. Cultural practice during this period, which greatly affected the everyday lives of every person in China, was rooted in the Chinese experience with western culture and power over the entire 19th century.[35] It was an effort to forward a Communist political agenda through elitist cultural pursuits. The ideology was this: by forcing a high level of culture as the standard for the appropriate way of life, China would be restored to its former days of power, making her once again wealthy and strong. The arts were a venue through which the stories of 'martial heroism and recent history' could be told. It was believed that the most effective way to lead the masses to a higher standard of life was through the arts.

Exhibit 7.3

Chinese generations

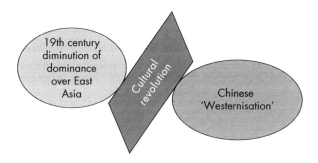

Political themes were expressed through eight basic models of opera which were repeated through film, dance, and fine art. The political elites of the time were constantly fretting over their control of cultural production and consumption. There were expectations that audiences in attendance would respond in 'appropriate' ways. Peking opera inadvertently became the standard bearer for correct production. It became the ideal through which the political elite envisioned bringing modernisation to China.

There was 'constant and repeated re-working of model works ... which we might now identify as cross-genre product tie-ins. A hero of a model opera would appear in posters, songs, comic books, even on pencil cases and enamel mugs'.[36] Although analysis of these 10 years primarily comes from the political point of view, there was a profound effect on the common people. During these years, young people began to leave the cities and populate the countryside where there was greater freedom of expression. The concerted institution of a standard, national culture almost obliterated the local culture, yet the local culture thrived underneath. Underground, it grew ever stronger. Because of the openness of creativity in the underground, this nationally oppressive period also became a highly creative time when works, 'both official and unofficial built on earlier developments and made possible a reorientation in Chinese cultural discourse since the 1980s'.[37]

The Cultural Revolution symbolically represents the two-phased effects of modernisation. The point of the Cultural Revolution was to produce a modern Chinese culture as a restorative from the diminution of Chinese dominance over East Asia in the 19th century. In applying oppressive control to 'ensure' the desired outcome, the project failed miserably, defeated by its own process. Yet, it sowed the seeds for the China of today, a growing participant in the global marketplace, producing unprecedented levels of wealth for a growing number of its citizens. 'The rise of the modern, Chinese consumerist world by the early twenty-first century perhaps marked a bigger break than the seemingly more startling changes immediately after 1976 [the year Mao Zedong died].'[38]

For the Diaspora, we will use the Singaporean Chinese as a representative example. The first emigrants were born during the time of the American GI generation. There are differences in the generations of the homeland and of the Diaspora, although they share a history that younger generations want to know and understand. However, the early generations of the Diaspora views their historical roots differently. They are not so willing to tell their stories to the younger generations because it reminds them of such a painful time in their lives.

Ussery describes the dilemma for Chinese American generations. 'The first generation may be born in China and later, may move to America. They may work hard to provide for their families – a responsibility they feel from their cultural background – and eventually, produce significant wealth. Their children are born in America and as they grow older, they develop a greater interest in their Chinese heritage. But as their children grew up, none of the stories of the first generation were shared – the experiences were too painful, in their eyes, to discuss. They left their homeland so that their children would have the opportunities offered by the American culture. They wanted to leave that life behind. So it becomes an issue of passing on those painful memories just as the second generation yearns to know and understand what the first generation went through – what gave them the drive to come to America and to create a new life and build a future for their family.'

Box 7.3

Chinese Diaspora: in Singapore

Born 1901–1924: these are first generation immigrants with low levels of education who are largely self-made through great hardship.

1924–1944: these are first or second generation immigrants. If from China, they are better educated, self-made, and also in professional careers.

1945–1964: these are well educated, often with tertiary degrees, at their prime, and have created or accumulated wealth but are still building. Many are scions of established wealth.

1965–1979: these are beginning to be established in careers, are sophisticated and well educated; lots of MBAs especially among heirs of wealth, involved in family business.

1979–1995: the educational opportunities for these seem limitless. They tend to favour US schools versus British or European. They are accustomed to the good life, are quite sophisticated in tastes, and not necessarily interested in family business; they may travel before settling down to a job. They tend to start their careers later than their parents did.

Greater percentages of older generations of Chinese who came to the US or Europe for education would return to their homeland. Increasingly, since the late 1970s, Chinese immigrants have chosen to settle down in countries where they attend school or university, leaving parents and grandparents in their country of origin. There is less of the transference of values in general among the Diaspora compared to mainland Chinese but families who have a well-respected or well-known patriarch (matriarchs of a certain generation are not given too much of the limelight) have an easier time in passing on family values. There are lots of opportunities for 'story telling' of history as families move into their third and subsequent generations.[39]

Getting the first generation to tell their story then becomes a key component in the family's long-term success because, although the second generation has everything the American culture offers, their roots are in China, and they want to understand and be a part of that culture.[40] Children born to Chinese immigrants in America – or any other country to which they emigrated – may not even speak the same language as their relatives on the mainland. This causes an automatic divide between generations, enough to disrupt the family story of generations gone before.

According to Angus, 'In many of the multi-national families with whom I've worked, the second or third generation comes to the United States to be educated and often, they stay here afterwards. They adapt to American culture while their families remain in their home country, which can create a cross-cultural gap within the family.'

In fact, communication among family members is one of the top challenges Chinese families of wealth face. Generations educated in the west may have difficulty with grandparents who only speak the 'mother tongue'. It becomes more difficult to transfer values if younger generations increasingly see parents and grandparents as old-fashioned and outdated. The perception of younger generations that their elders have a problem of 'letting go' – this is probably one of the most divisive issues in even the most successful Chinese families.

'There's an expectation that, if a Chinese first generation is here in America and they created the wealth, the second generation will carry the baton. That's the culture in the Asian world. And the second generation, who was born here in America, may want to create their own gifts and talents but because the culture of honoring one's parents is so strong, the first generation is "strongly encouraging" them to take the family business. So we end up with second and third generations that aren't very happy. This is a real issue – that of allegiance and honor,' explains Ussery.

Despite the gaps in generational communication, the Diaspora as well as mainland Chinese share cultural traits that contribute to the promotion of the family story. According to Handler, 'In contrast to the US, where we are generally effective at creating wealth and passing it on yet not as effective at passing on values, the Asian culture is very good at cementing and passing on values; truly something to be admired. In Asian families there may be several areas for improvement in passing on wealth, but on values of the family, the family history – who did what when, what war they fought in, what the family stands for – they are very good at ensuring these things are passed on. In short, in the US, it's the reverse. The wealth passes, on balance, but the values and structure may not.'

Generations of Korea and India

Although significantly more could be written about the generations of Korea and India, we will only do a brief overview for the purpose of providing a glimpse of cultures which may be poised to become more influential in the future.

During World War II, Korea was under colonial rule from Japan. Koreans who fought in the war were born Japanese citizens. The veterans who fought on the Japanese side came home, just freed from Japanese colonial rule, to fight a war on their own land as restored Korean citizens against the communist regime. The generation who fought these wars felt that they had lost everything since they had been under the rule of another country, then fought a devastating war immediately after their liberation. 'The two wars left the generation nothing but horrible ruins and desperate poverty.' But the Korean victory laid the foundation for the Republic of Korea that exists today.[41]

Korea still considers itself a very closed and patrilineal society with each generation feeling reciprocal obligation and responsibility within a single family. Eldest sons typically inherit the largest portions of their fathers' estates and one of the greatest concerns of South Korean families is to have a son to carry on the father's lineage and to perform ancestral rituals in the leadership of the family as well as at the family gravesite. Worship of ancestors was practically a religion, emphasizing that family members do not enter oblivion after they die; they remain a spiritual presence with the family. Until the 1930s, marriages were arranged and the duty of the wife was to produce a male heir.[42]

Older generation Korean families had tiers of kinship. The first tier would be the immediate household; the second would be the mourning group, consisting of all family members over four generations which is responsible for carrying out ritual ceremonies at the family gravesite. A lineage was the third level and might be comprised of a small number of households or a large group of households. This third tier was responsible for carrying out ancestral rituals for the fifth generation and above. The fourth tier was called a clan and its members shared surnames as well as remote generational origins.[43]

Korean society changed drastically under Japanese rule. Colonisation came about when King Kojong was forced to abdicate his throne so that his son could assume power. The son was not a strong ruler and was 'married off to a Japanese woman and given a Japanese peerage'. Japan then assumed rule, installing military officers and a governor general who reported to Japanese prime ministers. Japan used Korea as an agricultural source for the rice it so desperately needed. Korea was ruled as a conquered people and in 1919, students rose to protest in what has become known as the March First Movement. Social movements in the 1920s, although clamped down upon, laid the groundwork for influence well into the post-liberation period.[44]

When World War II came along, Koreans were treated as full Japanese citizens regarding their eligibility for combat. By this time, almost all industries as well as farmland was owned by Japan. Ideologies from the west infiltrated a land formerly Buddhist, Confucian, and shamanistic. By the 1930s, Koreans were being forced to speak the Japanese language and, in essence, transform themselves into Japanese people, even to the adoption of Japanese surnames. During the war, all Korean newspapers and magazines were shut down.[45]

The seeds of social reform and protest had been sewn and, by the 1960s, a democratic party rose to oppose the corrupt authoritarian rule of the Liberal Party under Syngman Rhee. Rhee had been elected in 1948 and was admired as a national hero who led the country through post-war negotiations with the US. As Rhee's reign grew increasingly dictatorial, a much more politically conscious society became a bigger and bigger threat to Rhee, finally causing Rhee to resign in April 1960.[46]

By the 1990s, Korean society began to digress from the traditional family and kinship tiers. The foundation of relationships was no longer as firmly rooted in lineage and the neighbourhood social scene. Relationships became more functional. The nuclear family of husband, wife, and children is supplanting the Confucian lineage-based ideal. Blood relations are still important, but ties within lineage have weakened, especially between urban and rural relations.[47]

Today, South Koreans view themselves as a 'tightly knit national community with a common destiny' within a rapidly changing world.

Generational perspectives in India have been given labels to coincide with the generations in America. Indian Traditionalists correspond to the American Silent generation. By the 1940s and 1950s, Traditionalists were well into their formative years, the years of generational imprint. Unlike American teens during this period, teens of India watched their homeland become an independent nation. Poverty reigned amid a period of nationalist pride coupled with familial and community loyalty. Adherence to traditional practices was commanded, yet the Traditionalists sought ways to participate in their country's new independence.[48]

India's Boomer generation saw the country come under a socialist economy and align itself with the Soviet Union after only 20 years of independence. Border wars abounded during this period and poverty was still prevalent. Like teens in the US during this period, teens in India lost faith in their political leaders and sought education in the UK or the US to equip them to work in those countries.[49]

The Indian version of Gen-Xers saw vast reform come to their country as the son of Indira Ghandi deregulated business, loosened restrictions on foreign imports, and trimmed the bureaucracy. India had traditionally had a strict social class distinction. The Caste system was losing its grip as education became attainable to more of India's best and brightest. Most still look to leave the country after their education but opportunities for success within India are growing and Diaspora are beginning to invest in the country's future.[50]

India's Echoes are witnessing vast economic growth similar to the Silent generation's experience in the US. Having access to such strong educational and economic opportunities, they accept opinions that differ from their own, are entrepreneurial and savvy, and are still influenced by the Western laws and customs under the former British rule. This makes them perfectly poised as savvy participants in the global community, adding yet another integral component to the global generational sea change.

Middle Eastern generations

The generational archetypes seem a bit harder to apply to the Middle Eastern culture, based on the degree to which each country has embraced modernisation. Islamic cultures are traditionally known to be much closer and interdependent than Western families. This of course varies from country to country and family to family, but without doubt family interdependence is much stronger among all Muslim families. Modernisation of societies in Muslim countries has been a much more recent phenomenon than in the West. In the West, there was an inexorable step-by-step process of modernisation that started in the 17th century – well over 400 years ago. But, the Muslim world's modernisation has happened mostly in our own time.[51] It has happened virtually over the course of a single generation.[52]

Beginning in the 1970s, modernisation of the societies started and progressed very fast. This set up a dichotomy of sorts, with modernisation weakening family ties. Family relationships have indeed changed, but they have not weakened significantly. Islam preaches family values, and there seems to be a resurgence of these values in Islam today.[53]

Middle Eastern families are facing unprecedented change and, therefore, are grappling with what future family life may look like. The family unit traditionally has provided everything that the state provides in Western cultures. The range of kin relations spreads wide to include not only so-called immediate family but also aunts, uncles, cousins, to several degrees on both sides of the marriage. In the past and to a great extent today '… the group served as an employment bureau, insurance agency, child and family counselling service, old people's home, bank, teacher, home for the handicapped and insane, and hostel in time of economic need' in return for their members' allegiance.[54]

Much of the Middle East was under Western rule until the early 20th century. In most areas including Turkey, Pakistan, Saudi Arabia, Egypt, Lebanon, and Morocco, the family is still the primary source of economic and social support.

John Sandwick, a specialist in Islamic wealth and asset management in Geneva, notes that, in a typical family in Riyadh, the father has absolute power within the family structure, and his rule is total and unquestioned. Children and wives do their father's bidding. The father is the centre of all decisions and guidance. The paternal-centric structure of Muslim families throughout the Islamic world is really what most distinguishes them from their western counterparts. Importantly, this is relatively unchanged. For example, imagine a 42-year-old son of a wealthy Saudi businessman in his late seventies. The father grew up in a vastly different world than the son. The father was raised in mostly poverty, sometimes hunger, and always in a hostile environment (Saudi Arabia is one of the most brutally hot places on earth). There was no air conditioning. There were no modern conveniences. There was a high rate of infant mortality, low rates of education, and poor overall nutrition. The oil boom of the 1970s and 1980s, however, showered the father with prosperity. His children, unlike himself, were able to study in the West. They have top-quality healthcare and modern diets. They travel to places the father could have never imagined when he was young. But, despite the enormous change in modernisation for the current generation, the relationship between father and son has not changed from the previous generation. He is venerated. His word is the law. No one dares question his decisions despite the fact that he does not have anywhere near the education and training of his son. Not until the father passes away will the son actually take control of the family business or indeed even the family's affairs. And, of course, the oldest son takes these responsibilities. Younger sons tend to treat older brothers with the same degree of respect and consideration that was reserved for the father during his life.[55]

Typically the survival of the Arab family business in this region depends on the father's thinking and acting in advance of his death. If he refuses to create an environment where generational change is possible, then the business begins to fail almost immediately upon his death. Unfortunately, the region is heavily populated with these kinds of companies.[56]

'Importantly, a lot of the region's most important businesses were established in the 1960s or 1970s. The young men who created these current powerhouses are all now in their seventies or eighties. Now is the most critical time to adapt and change the family business structure. A lot of the patriarchal founders don't see any need. They think the oldest son will handily take over and that will be that,' notes Sandwick.

'The primary business structure in the Middle Eastern world is a sole proprietorship and the wealth is not that old. For most people, it dates from World War II and that's if they're really, really old families. For a lot of other families, the wealth may date from only five years ago, so the issues are different,' says Joe Field, senior international partner at Withers Worldwide. The impact of polygamy in the Middle East is that after three generations, a family may well have 300 members, or more. So the number of family members to be served by the wealth presents additional complexities on top of the fact that the wealth is so new.

The concept of family is much broader in the Middle East than it is in the West. It tends to be inclusive of all issues, even political and economic matters because the family is the basic unit of social organisation and the provider of all human need. Westerners tend to separate family issues from business, economic, political, and other issues. As a culture that has begun facing the sweeping changes of modernisation most recently, the family concept is the focus of social change occurring throughout the region. The radical sweep of wealth into the oil rich countries like Kuwait and Saudi Arabia has changed the family dynamic and the roles of family members. Women traditionally are considered the hub of family life, around which all economic, personal, and political issues revolve. In Saudi, women are still not allowed to work outside the home. In Kuwait, they work for the purpose of enjoying a fulfilling career; in Egypt, the concept of women joining the workforce would have been unthinkable a single generation ago.[57]

The winds of change are also blowing toward the laws of most Middle Eastern countries concerning education and family planning. Advocates of change say that only by allowing women 'equal access to divorce, child custody, and inheritance can the traditional family structure survive and become viable in modern society'.[58]

Dubai might seem the perfect example – the perfect venue through which to witness the effects of modernisation within the Middle Eastern world. Sandwick notes that Dubai is a microcosm of the Arabian Gulf, but not always a reflection of the Arab culture and civilisation. 'What's happening in Dubai often has a very profound demonstration effect for changes in neighboring countries, but not in all things and all the time. In Saudi Arabia and indeed outside Dubai things haven't changed much.'

'In these countries, there are a limited number of tools available to deal with some very complex problems. As families modernize, they realize they have parallel issues to Western families. They're not identical, but they're similar enough,' says Field.

From an American generational perspective, it might seem that Middle Eastern families are experiencing a jump from the American GI generation to the Gen-Xers with the Echoes coming up right behind them! Quite a leap, reflecting the reality that the Middle East is experiencing modernisation over the course of a single generation as opposed to the multiple hundred-year transition of their Western counterparts. With the extremes of change ranging from Kuwait to Saudi with Egypt and Dubai in between, the family still is the interpretive force of values from the traditional into the modern world.

Sandwick gives an example of how younger Middle Eastern generations are maintaining traditional values within the dramatic shift. 'A young Arab from a prominent business family today has fully modern behavior and even modern values. He still retains strong cultural values that are often in great contradiction to the values we see in the West. He uses a mobile phone, drives a modern car, got his education in the United States, and vacations in the south of France. And, he is charming and talkative and fully integrated into the modern world. But, he still reveres his father, he has extremely close relationships with his siblings and near relationships, and nearly universally has a deep foundation in spirituality. He lives a Muslim life. Yes, he enjoys the family's wealth, but unlike many Western counterparts he does not have access to the riches that have been accrued. He doesn't fly private jets, he often stays at fine hotels but doesn't take the presidential suite, and while he dresses well he is not a fashion junkie. Muslims are by and large more modest when it comes to displaying and using their wealth. They don't as a rule, and with only a few exceptions, amass great art collections, they don't own magnificent palaces in exotic locations (but do have some very nice homes in their country of residence), and they don't ostentatiously show their wealth. This is not so much derived from Islamic law as the traditions of Muslim countries.'

Still, the generational sea change has not made an exception for Middle Eastern families from its influence. 'With globalization, the world's becoming a smaller place and the influences come inside the family,' notes Salim Omar, president of The Omar Group, CPA in Cliffwood, NJ. Education is the generational tool, serving as 'a kind of mediator' in the debate of the Middle Eastern family future. Education has tremendous impact on the family in light of the traditional role of women. As more women in more Middle Eastern countries begin working outside the home, as the education of women and girls increasingly is talked about in the media as the societal shift continues from an agricultural base to an urban one, and as connectivity through technology fuels even greater social mobility, Middle Eastern countries are experiencing their own version of a Fourth Turning crisis. Families are reorganising themselves in order to survive in the face of rapid and monumental change; social and economic change creating a new imprint on a generation thrust into a globalised world.

Field echoes, 'Connectivity is one of the tools of globalization. Another tool is the fact that kids are now going to the same business schools where, a generation ago, the father may have been a nomad living in the desert. The advancement of modern family management techniques has developed as a by-product of globalization – they would have evolved on their own even without the discovery of the computer.'

This is because there is a transition generation paving the way of change from the elders to the new Echoes, much like the Gen-X generational archetype. And yet, this does not mean Middle Eastern values are getting lost in the translation. 'I have one Saudi friend who is the oldest son, in his mid 40s, and by all rights and measures should take over when papa dies, which will be in the next ten years if statistics are correct,' relates Sandwick. 'The son is highly educated, talented and experienced, and without doubt he would do a magnificent job taking over the large family enterprise. But, he is preparing now to leave the family business, asking the father to pass on the crown to a younger brother and give him cash today for his portion of the future inheritance. Why? Because this son has five daughters and no sons. This alone precludes his oldest child, a girl, from ever becoming a family business leader. Knowing this in advance, my friend said he can never remain in the family business knowing in advance that his own oldest child would not be permitted to take the reins after his own death.'

As change challenges the traditional concept of family within the Middle Eastern world, families of wealth need tools to help them navigate. According to Hughes, Islamic families who have elected to use the forms and functions of systems other than their own answer the questions of how to handle a mandated legacy and have done better, which is not to say their system is not very thoughtful and can work, but in a modern society and economy, the capitalism of creative destruction and the evolution of business forms is somewhat advanced.[59]

'Families in this region do seem to have a much more powerful respect and veneration of the "old man" right up to the moment of his death. Very few families can make any changes whatsoever without his cooperation and, in fact, leadership. Getting the leader to make changes in advance of his death is an absolute requirement,' offers Sandwick.

'If a patriarchal society with deeply religious convictions works for many Muslims, and if Muslim family members are highly interdependent, then who is to complain? Indeed, westerners could look at the modern Muslim family with a bit of admiration. Sibling rivalries seem to be fewer, a father lives his life with respect and honor, and there seem to be less anxious heirs, not worrying about how much they will get when the old man passes away. That doesn't mean everything would be acceptable to our Western values,' says Sandwick.

'In America, the individual is king – that's in our culture,' notes Angus. Cultures in other countries often have a greater sense of connectedness within the family. Today, in America, some families are learning more about what that view of family could do for the future generations of their own families.

This is indeed the mode of thought with which we compare the generational perspectives of various cultures around the world. By understanding each culture's generational lenses and seeing the progression of generational archetypes through history, we can all adapt the best lessons from each to our own, creating a global connectivity of a different sort and on a deeper level.

1 Roland, A., *In Search of Self in India and Japan*, In: 'A sociological social psychology: self-types and their differences across generations and the life cycle', (Trinity University, Fall 2001): www.trinity.edu/mkearl/socpsy-6.html.

2 Encyclopedia Britannica, *History and Society: Modernisation*, Encyclopedia Britannica, 2006–2009: www.britannica.com/EBchecked/topic/387301/modernization.

3 Ibid.

4 The term 'consummate family portfolio' and 'consummate family wealth portfolio' are the service marked property of graymatter Strategies LLC.

5 Tsutagawa, K., 'Baby Boomers' retirement poses problems', *The Daily Yomiuri,* July 6 2004. www.globalaging.org/pension/world/2004/boomers.htm.

6 Encyclopedia Britannica, *History and Society: Modernisation,* Encyclopedia Britannica, 2006–2009.

7 Ibid.

8 Ibid.

9 Ibid.

10 Mathews, G. and White, B., (2004). *Japan's Changing Generations: are young people creating a new society?* (New York, NY: Routledge, 2004), p. 5.

11 Broughton, P.D., 'The rise of Japan's 'Girlie Man' generation', *Timesonline, The Times,* November 5 2009. www.timesonline.co.uk/tol/life_and_style/men/article6903043.ece.

12 Mathews, G. and White, B., (2004). *Japan's Changing Generations: are young people creating a new society?* (New York, NY: Routledge, 2004), p. 4.

13 Ibid, p. 19.

14 Ibid, p. 16.

15 Ibid, p. 18.

16 Woronoff, J., (1991). *Japan As – Anything But – Number One*, (Armonk, NY: M.E. Sharpe, 1991), p. 186.

17 Jolivet, M., 'The sirens of Tokyo', *The Courier UNESCO,* July/August 2001: www.unesco.org/courier/2001_07/uk/doss21.htm.

18 Woronoff, J., (1991). *Japan As – Anything But – Number One*, (Armonk, NY: M.E. Sharpe, 1991), p. 179.

19 Ibid, p. 180.

20 Ibid, p. 184.

21 Ibid, p. 179.

22 Ibid, p. 182.

23 Broughton, P.D., 'The rise of Japan's 'Girlie Man' generation', *Timesonline, The Times,* November 5 2009: www.timesonline.co.uk/tol/life_and_style/men/article6903043.ece.

24 Woronoff, J., (1991). *Japan As – Anything But – Number One*, (Armonk, NY: M.E. Sharpe, 1991), p. 186.

25 'Japan 1990 – United States of America 2006: the past as a window on the future, Part 1 of 5': www.gold-eagle.com/editorials_05/joubert031106.html.

[26] 'Japan 1990 – United States of America 2006: The past as a window on the future, Part 1 of 5': www.gold-eagle.com/editorials_05/joubert031106.html.

[27] Funding Universe company history: Nomura Securities Company, Ltd: www.fundinguniverse.com/company-histories/Nomura-Securities-Company-Limited-Company-History.html.

[28] Montgomery, H. and Shimizutani, S., 'The effectiveness of bank recapitalization in Japan,' Asian Bank Development Institute, 2005: www.apeaweb.org/confer/hito05/papers/montgomery_shimizutani.pdf.

[29] Wikipedia, 'Japan Post': http://en.wikipedia.org/wiki/Japan_Post.

[30] Hardach, S., 'Japan's big spenders flaunt their new wealth,' *The New York Times,* January 6 2008: www.nytimes.com/2008/01/06/business/worldbusiness/06iht-rtrfeature.9035419.html?_r=1&pagewanted=2.

[31] Woronoff, J., (1991). *Japan As – Anything But – Number One,* (Armonk, NY: M.E. Sharpe, 1991), p. 191.

[32] McCurry, J., 'Japan's Prime Minister Yukio Hatoyama resigns,' guardian.co.uk, June 2 2010. www.guardian.co.uk/world/2010/jun/02/japan-prime-minister-yukio-hatoyama-resigns.

[33] Wikipedia: http://en.wikipedia.org/wiki/Yonsei_%28fourth-generation_Nikkei%29.

[34] Arizona State University, 'The Japanese Diaspora: peoples of Japanese descent in the Americas': http://shesc.asu.edu/node/285.

[35] Clark, P., *The Chinese Cultural Revolution: a history,* (New York, NY: Cambridge University Press, 2008), p.5.

[36] Ibid, p. 4.

[37] Ibid.

[38] Ibid, p. 261.

[39] Anonymous source, Personal interview, November 2006.

[40] Ussery, Teddie, Personal interview, November 2006.

[41] Yang, S-h., 'A letter from a man of my father's generation', *The Chosun Ilbo,* January 2010.

[42] US Library of Congress, 'Traditional family life': http://countrystudies.us/south-korea/38.htm.

[43] Ibid.

[44] US Library of Congress, 'Korea under Japanese rule': http://countrystudies.us/south-korea/7.htm.

[45] Ibid.

[46] US Library of Congress, 'The Syngman Rhee era, 1946–1960': http://countrystudies.us/south-korea/11.htm.

[47] US Library of Congress, 'The Syngman Rhee Era, 1946–1960, "Family and Social Life in the Cities"': http://countrystudies.us/south-korea/11.htm.

[48] Erikson, T., 'Generational differences between India and the US', *Harvard Business Review* Blog, February 2009.

[49] Ibid.

[50] Ibid.

[51] Sandwick, John, Personal interview, November 2006.

[52] Fernea, E.W., *'The Family in the Middle East'*, Center for Middle Eastern Studies, The University of Texas at Austin, 1984–2009.

[53] Sandwick, John, Personal interview, November 2006.

[54] Fernea, E.W., *'The Family in the Middle East'*, Center for Middle Eastern Studies, The University of Texas at Austin, 1984–2009.

[55] Sandwick, John, Personal interview, November 2006.

[56] Sandwick, John, Personal interview, November 2006.

[57] Fernea, E.W., *'The Family in the Middle East'*, Center for Middle Eastern Studies, The University of Texas at Austin, 1984–2009.

[58] Ibid.

[59] Hughes, James E. Jr., Personal interview, August 2007.

Chapter 8

Generations of women

'We are the story – the ones who make the buying decisions that count, for certain, but also the ones the world comes to for wisdom beyond the struggle for power and with the perspective of compassion. We should be seen and heard.'

Laura Baudo Sillerman[1]

In every society, women have always been perceived as the centre of the family unit and the family unit as the foundational institution of society. Societal views of the roles of women within the institution of family have varied based on the Turning in which people were living and the associated archetypical responses. The entrance of greater numbers of women into the workforce in America in the 1960s and 1970s radically changed the dynamic of family life and also of society at large within the American culture. Feminist movements reverberated all over the world during the 1800s and 1900s and their effects are still being felt today.

This is why dedicating a chapter to women's generational perspectives – in all cultures – is a necessary component of the generational landscape which will serve us well. The roles of women and men within society and also within the family are critical component of families' abilities to preserve and regenerate[2] wealth for generations of the future. Regardless of culture, what happens to women affects what happens to the wealth.

Gender also plays a role in how generational views are shaped and it certainly plays a role in how wealth is managed. More importantly, it affects the degree to which the family's authentic wealth – regardless of gender – may be fostered as a contribution to the Family Story. Since women statistically live longer than men – in almost any culture – their roles significantly affect the way wealth is distributed. Today more than ever, women are involved in decision making around the family money. In a 2008 survey,[3] 88% of women said they are either highly or moderately involved in overseeing the family's financial and material assets. Over 50% of the women surveyed had family net worth or $50 million or more. Three fourths of them cited an operating company as the origin of their family's wealth and 25% of them had created the wealth themselves. Just fewer than 48% had inherited their wealth. Three fourths of the women represented either the second chronological generation or later.[4]

There are two other impactful components to gender-based generational perspectives: the way children and their upbringing are viewed and the ways in which children are educated, particularly as stewards of the wealth. Both of these perspectives affect trust-level communication and the roles and responsibilities of heirs – the two major components in determining family wealth success. In generations past, these two responsibilities fell largely to the mothers. Although fathers certainly weighed in on these two matters, it was the women who were with the children day in and day out, transmitting the messages the children received.

So we have four things to do in this chapter that have relevance to our purpose. The first is to gain an understanding of feminist influences within the four Turnings and the generational archetypes of each. The second is to look at the views toward children and toward the education of children within each of those settings. Thirdly, we must look at gender-based generational perspectives as a key to unlocking the authentic wealth of the women in the family – in general and specifically in various cultures of the world. And fourthly, we will posit some thoughts regarding current views of women and their roles (which also affect men and their roles) and determine the benefits received and lessons learned in our time.

Feminist influences within the four Turnings

The emancipation of women has been a topic of relevance since the 1800s, particularly as modernisation enabled the family to move away from an agriculturally based society to a more industrialised society. It must be noted that an exploration of women's generational perspectives cannot be separated from the ongoing effects of feminist movements across the globe. Although women are, obviously, participants in the archetypical responses of their generation, the gender factor adds another dimension to those perspectives. This, of course, has to do with the level of participation society expects women to have in all aspects of life, from defining roles of women in the home to the acceptance of women working outside the home, to the freedom women have to pursue fulfilling careers and to make a difference in society and political life, and in some societies, even to the number of children she can have.

These movements shape women's identities and redefine the roles of both women and men. It is essential to present the movements of various countries in as objective a format as possible. It is the intent of my focus to do so; however, since I am a woman – as well as an American woman – I ask the reader's forgiveness for any slight bias which may have unwittingly filtered in. Regardless of my own gender and nationality, the Women's Movement in the US has been used by countries around the world for comparison purposes, either lauding its successes or illuminating its failures.[5] Therefore, it is also used for comparison purposes in this chapter, just as the generational discussion in this first part of the book uses American generations to get the generational discussion rolling across cultures.

Strauss and Howe note that interest in feminist movements varies according to the archetypical cycles they identified which are reinterpreted during each saeculum. Betty Friedan said, 'The history of women's rights is like a series of gathering tidal waves, each sweeping over American institutional life at discrete intervals before sweeping out amid rips and eddies.' Similarly, gender roles participate in these cycles with feminism gaining popularity during an Awakening and causing the smallest gap in roles during an Unravelling. A Crisis will bring back the predominance of male power and feminine morality causing the gap between roles to be at its widest during a High. Prophet archetypes have as members impassioned women such as Susan B. Anthony and Hillary Clinton who are considered equal with their male counterparts. Their generations reaffirm the division of sexual roles both in public and private. Young Nomads minimise sexual differences while young Artists emphasise them. Both of these latter archetypes reverse course during mid-life. Friedan noted in *The Feminine Mystique* how younger women were thrown back onto the domestic 'pedestal' after World War II,[6] symbolised by TV shows of the 1950s such as 'Leave it to Beaver' (with June Cleaver cleaning house dressed in pearls and a perfectly ironed shirtwaist dress) and 'Ozzie and Harriett'.

In characterising the impetus behind the US women's movement, Phyllis Tickle, author and a founding editor of *Publishers Weekly,* says the origin of the suffragette movement in the 1920s was thought to have been political, but this notion was founded in a philosophical point of view that would never have gone very far. The movement in the 1960s built upon the successes of the suffrage movement but it certainly would not have had gender equality in the workplace as a goal without the sexual revolution, the release of the birth control pill in 1962, and the advance of technology to relieve women from domestic chores. She notes that at this point, for the first time in human history, the home shifted in function. 'The home went from a place where the providing mate – male or female – went forth to conquer the world to a place where everybody went forth to conquer the world. Then every part of the family unit came home in order to try to restore itself to try to go forth and conquer the world tomorrow,' she explains.

Some cite the release of the birth control pill (the Pill) as the impetus behind the women's movement in America. An article noting media commentary on the 50th anniversary of the Pill's release in America (May 9 2010) questions whether the Pill was actually the instigator of the modern feminist movement.[7] In light of the archetypical cycles identified by Strauss and Howe, we see that interest in feminism is also cyclically influenced and the underpinnings of the movement of the 1960s in America fall right in line with cyclical timing.

Looking back, however, we can see that the Pill did play a very significant part in altering family life. It was an element that offered families, not just women, greater choices in the roles their members might occupy. Fifty years after the Pill was released, couples proactively and jointly decide when to have their children – as well as how many to have; timing and number are no longer simply the natural – and undeterminable – result of the relationship between a man and woman. Discussions are now held among heterosexual couples regarding who should be responsible for which caretaking duties, or how the couple might switch off each other in caring for children and balancing the work load both inside and outside the home. It is no longer a question of which roles are more socially acceptable for men or for women. This has significantly changed the way families function and it has offered new role experiences for families of all levels of wealth.

Generational cycles influence attitudes toward women's roles in the following manner:

Exhibit 8.1

Cyclical archetypical interest in feminist movements

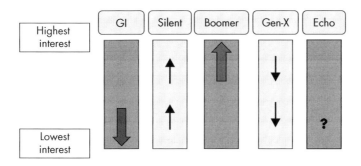

As the concepts of home and family as societal institutions shift, so do the gender roles linked to them. This has a great bearing on women's freedom to contribute to the regeneration of the family wealth. The cyclical sequence happens as follows. During Awakenings when gender roles are beginning to narrow, both women and men suffer confusion as they struggle to redefine their roles within the coming 'new paradigm'. During Unravellings, traditional roles may become more egalitarian with older males still holding on to vestiges of the roles women played in the past. Crises foster togetherness and protective modes as gender roles again begin to separate. Highs bring a new type of role separation against which the next Awakening will rebel.

The cycles of gender role views follow the pattern of the four archetypes in that each narrowing and each separation of roles between the sexes gets redefined against the social and economic backdrop of the time. If the cyclical progression spirals up, the redefinition of roles will evolve accordingly.

As the cyclical views of women's roles progress, both women and men will ideally have more choice about the way they lead their lives and will have greater options for fulfilment whether working in the home, outside of the home, or some combination of the two. Combined with greater involvement of fathers in caring for and educating the children, this holds promise for a more egalitarian upbringing for the children. In any culture, when fathers are more directly involved in caring for and raising children, the children experience a more complete maturation and educational process. In a world that is more broadly connected, children benefit from being more broadly prepared. This includes greater sharing of the caretaker and educational roles regardless of the working arrangements of parents. Even in a patriarchal society, the father's direct involvement with the children rather than the view of a distant figure who makes all decisions from afar has direct impact on the success of the family. The active involvement of both parents in their children's lives offers greater assurance that the Family Story will continue.

Views of children and education

Attitudes toward raising children shift quite rapidly at the onset of each new generation. The Gen-X generation was born at a point where the fertility rate was low and when society held a broad aversion to children. Boomers did not have time for children; they were too busy living 'adult' lifestyles in which children were not a comfortable fit. The experts of the day encouraged parents to let children grow up freely and uninhibited so they would become 'tough and self-reliant'. These were the days of the open classrooms which allowed children to educate themselves by choosing the activities to which they were naturally led.

There was also a sharp rise in the divorce rate and other activities that were harmful to children during this period. Alcohol consumption, drug abuse, abortion, and violent crime rose at unprecedented rates. Gen-Xers grew up as latch-key kids and welfare children. As they moved into the naturally self-defining formative years, they were viewed as the 'entitled' generation and nothing good could be said about them. Society's assignment of this generation's perceived role as 'outcast' (black sheep) prompted the perceived need to 'fix our children'. So there was renewed interest in education, in childproofing homes – childproofing anything and everything, for that matter. This was the time when flame retardant sleepwear and childproof tops for prescription drugs were developed. Gen-X 'marked a watershed for the way adults view and treat children and in what they expect from them'.[8] And in sync with the protecting and nurturing of Hero children within a Crisis, the new generation of children, the Echoes, are looked upon far differently than were the Gen-Xers, although the two generations overlap. Gen-Xers were considered to be 'beyond hope' and the Echoes still hold hope for the future.[9]

Having babies became a popular trend, particularly for older Boomers who now longed for progeny. Rather than being an imposition on an independent lifestyle, children began to be wanted, protected, and considered worthy. It was the first time since the early 1900s that a new generation was so desperately desired and the focus on the needs of children so dramatic. In true Boomer style, babies 'became the primary medium of self-discovery for their parents'. The new attitude brought about changed behaviour. 'Family values' became the mantra. Staying home to take care of the children once again became an acceptable priority – for men as well as women, even if it meant taking a job with less pay.[10] Except, this time, staying home became a choice – for either sex – rather than a pre-expected role for a single gender to fulfil.

Exhibit 8.2

Cyclical archetypical attitudes towards child rearing

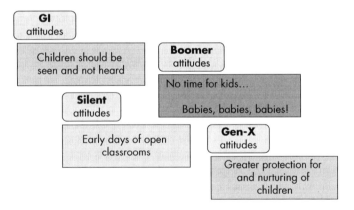

Source: graymatter Strategies LLC. All rights reserved.

From the late 1940s to early 1960s, American adults deliberately relaxed their style of parenting. They emphasised individualism and inner creativity rather than teamwork and external convention. Today's Boomers are the recognisable product of this style. As children, they showed from early to late birth spectrum[©] a progressive worsening in scholastic achievement, and in most measures of behaviour – crime, violent crime, suicide, self-inflicted accidents, sex, alcohol and illicit drug use. Trends in the Echo generation are running the other way. Boomers were brought up with more relaxed childrearing standards in an era of conforming adults. Echoes are being brought up within a completely opposite backdrop; they are being raised by non-conforming adults as childrearing standards grow tighter.[11]

Parallel to these are changing ideals in society at large as Exhibit 8.3 shows.

Exhibit 8.3

Changing ideals in society at large

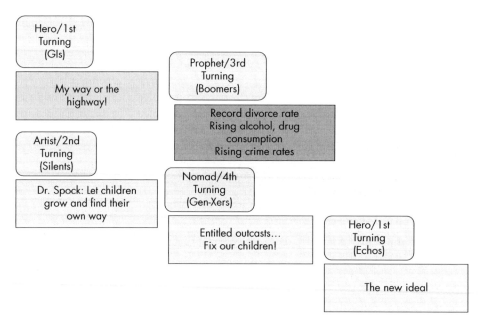

Strauss and Howe note that 'cyclical time endowed classical societies with a prescribed moral dimension, a measure by which each generation could compare its behavior with that of its ancestors'.[12] We have seen this most readily in the Asian and Middle Eastern cultures who still hold the family at the centre of their societies. The provision of life's necessities is either found through the family as a small society as it is in the Middle East or with the concept of family inextricably integrated with the family business as in Asia. As women of each generation compare their behaviour with those of their ancestors, we have the hope of greater family communication and trust when it comes to making decisions about the material wealth. This is because communication is an innate function of women's brains.[13]

Unlocking women's authentic wealth

From our brief visit in earlier chapters with the cultures of the world and their generations, we see that family is what ties generations together and the people who are at the centre of 'family' are women, in whatever roles they occupy. Women shape myriad decisions in the family and, even in the most patriarchal societies, the behind-the-scenes influence of women is strong. Women are the glue that holds the family together. They are also the nurturers of communication and education.

The makeup of women's brains is scientific evidence of this. The brain centres responsible for language and hearing in women's brains have 11% more neurons than men's. The centre for emotion and memory formation and observing emotions in others is also larger than men's. We can legitimately say, then, that women are 'hard wired' for 'expressing emotions and remembering the details of emotional events'. By contrast, men's brains are two and a half times larger than women's in the areas of sexual drive, action, and aggression.[14] This certainly does not mean that men cannot be excellent communicators and empathetic listeners or that women cannot be aggressive and decidedly proactive. However, a woman's brain is described as 'a machine ... built for connection', driving a female to be heavily 'invested in preserving harmonious relationships'. Women's brains were structured like this because the ability to read faces and voices is essential to understanding the needs of a baby, to sense when protection is needed by predicting aggressive behaviour from a male (who quite likely is larger than the female), or to band together with other females to 'ward off aggressive cavemen. This is a matter of life and death to the brain, even if it's not so important in the twenty-first century'.[15]

It is also critical to the configuration of a family and its ability to recognise and subsequently support the flourishing of each member's authentic wealth. Women's innate communication and relationship focus enables the kind of environment where each family member's authentic wealth can flourish. In nurturing the family's authentic wealth, Hughes notes that there are four basic virtues which are at the heart of successful family relationships: Fusion, Altruism, Beauty as Harmony, and Joy as an Expression of Love. Each subsequent virtue is a by-product of the virtue previous. Each builds upon the other.

Fusion

Fusion describes the relationship between two bodies of energy where each body contributes to the other in a way that the total combined energy is greater than either of the two bodies could emit on its own. Family members are definitely bodies of energy! Positive relationships between family members cause each person's energy to enhance that of the other and of the family as a whole.[16] Fusion is not to be confused with melding completely into another person so that one energetic body disappears into the other. Rather, they remain individual entities, contributing to each other in such a complementary way that a bond forms through which the energy of all joining bodies can be enhanced. Fusion is an innate virtue which may or may not have the opportunity to be realised. It is human nature to bond with others. The family is the primary institution through which intimate bonding can occur in a safe environment without losing the sense of self. At the same time, each member willingly modifies some of his or her individual preferences in order to participate in the group and enjoy the safety and comfort it can afford.[17]

Altruism

Hughes describes altruism in families as the seeking of individuals to know themselves through their interactions with others of the same purpose, all with the goal of mutual enlightenment. Altruism is much more than just a survival mechanism for the family. It is the mutual desire of each family member to enhance the journeys of the others while asking nothing in return. Altruism has no strings. There is no manipulation. It has no expectations or requirements to be 'paid back'. It is simply an innate desire to enhance the journeys of other family members in the process of fulfilling one's own. Altruism is also not complete self sacrifice. It does not deny the altruistic family member his or her own journey. It does not invite what might be called martyrdom of the spirit. Rather, it is an abundance of family spirit that has no room for fear of deprivation or a feeling of superiority but fosters the highest level of happiness and fulfilment for each family member.

Beauty as harmony

When fusion and altruism are present, the harmony produced is beautiful. There is camaraderie of spirit. If each generation understands that the mutual enhancement of each others' lives is a thing of beauty, harmony then reigns. Any dispute that erupts between family members is then shaded by the desire to maintain harmony. Harmony does not always bring blissful, total agreement among family members; rather, it fosters the ability to appreciate others' viewpoints without the need of either to force change in viewpoint. The harmonious solution of 'agreeing to disagree' notes respect of and honouring of others' views while continuing to be comfortable with one's own. Creating awareness and understanding of the perspectives of other generational perspectives within the family's generational maze lays the groundwork for this mutual honour.

Joy as an expression of love

The presence of fusion, altruism, and a beautiful harmony yields joy expressed as love of family. This joy can carry a family through any adversity, any separation, any challenge, including change of leadership, changes in life stages, unforeseen family events, and even financial catastrophe.

The virtues of family combine to enable the family to see another day, to rebuild its wealth, and certainly to regenerate it from generation to generation to generation. Women, then, are rightly positioned as the torch bearers of the family virtues. They are the agents of fusion and examples of altruism. Their brains are built for harmony. And the resulting joy fosters love and security for all. These are elements of authentic wealth for all women, underlying all abilities in whatever career women may choose, whatever philanthropic cause they may champion, and whatever leadership they may otherwise have to offer.

Women in cultures of the world

Although the generational labels of America have been used to describe the archetypical responses within each Turning, their use has merely been descriptive. As we have seen, cultures around the world also name their generations and the two strongest generations in recent history – the Boom generation – and the current Echo or Millennial generation are wielding global influence. The connection between family and society at large is different depending on the culture and the perspectives of generations; therefore, the view of the role of women both in the family and in society at large also varies according to culture and generation. In America and Europe, family tends to be viewed as separate from the business and from governmental provision of life's critical elements for survival; in Asia, the family is inextricably connected to the business; and in many Middle Eastern countries, the family continues to be considered the source of all necessary provisions of life.

This is not a book solely focused on the generational perspectives of women. If it were, we would be able to explore the perspectives of women in much greater depth across the globe. As it is, we only have the luxury of looking at a few representative countries in each culture.

European women

Women of Europe were granted the right to vote in: Norway, 1913; Denmark, 1915; Soviet Union, 1917; Austria, 1918; Germany, 1919; United Kingdom, 1928; Spain, 1931; France, 1944; Switzerland, 1971.[18]

The plight of women in France during the 18th and 19th centuries paved the way for the feminist movement there, coincidentally with suffrage in America and other countries of the western world. Life expectancies increased throughout Europe during this period but did so earliest and most markedly in France. After the Napoleonic wars, France experienced a vast aging of its population. The percentage of women who lived longer continued to rise but life expectancy for men stagnated until after World War I. As a result, the elder population in France doubled over a period of 150 years with the number of women significantly outpacing the number of men. This caused a major shift in the balance of power between men and women in France in the 19th and early 20th centuries. The shift affected French society in economic terms and also affected women's access to wealth as well as how families behaved.[19]

Women's wealth during this era consisted basically of dowries and their roles were as spouses and mothers. Since all the wealth passed by law to the children, the number of multi-generational households grew. Under Napoleonic law, women had no right to work, to spend money on their own, or to sign a contract. Whatever jobs women had were entirely dependent on their husbands' businesses. So the loss of a husband also meant a woman's loss of the ability to support herself sufficiently or to gain access to any meaningful means of support independent of family. Women were given the right to use a portion of the husband's property (called usufructus) but had no powers of ownership.

Even estate tax rates were lower for inheriting children than for surviving spouses. Not until the late 19th century were there changes in inheritance laws in France to benefit women. By the early 1900s, women had been given access to education, to industry and service jobs, and increased usufruct rights. By the end of the first decade of the 20th century, married women had the right to spend money as they wished and also to go on maternity leave.

The consequences of these changes reverberated throughout French society. Women benefited from a huge redistribution giving widows rights to not only inherit money but also property, as well as the right to sell that property. Wealth inequality in France was high during the first half of the 19th century but was significantly more equal by the first half of the 20th century after World War I. 'Gender matters in explaining wealth distribution and its evolution'.[20] Because of female longevity and the change in wealth distribution laws, the gender gap narrowed. This progression is consistent with Strauss and Howe's assessment of the cycles of gender gaps, using American Turnings as a guide.

Today, European women have careers and share fiscal responsibilities; they may own property or manage the investments. As in America, equitable pay with men for the same job performance is still not a reality.

Latin American women

Women were granted the right to vote in: Venezuela, 1946; Argentina, 1947; Peru, 1955.

For women in Argentina in the 1800s, the advent of electric illumination became symbolic of the arrival of spiritual light. It fostered the hope of progress, great hope that the future would make all things right – that women would have the power to reform their own roles. The evolution toward human perfectibility could not turn and retreat into barbarism, equated to the oppression of women. This view was reinforced by North American women's advances which were widely publicised in the Argentine press. Argentine women believed they would be lifted from the then current backwardness toward a new state of civilisation which, in their eyes, was already observable in France, England, and most notably in the US. However, to admire the US was to reject Argentina's Spanish cultural roots. Women focused on the roles of Anglo-Saxon women who enjoyed rights and freedoms unheard of in Spain. This fascination equated to a radical critique of Argentine culture. The implicit accusation of backwardness was an insult in an age of progress.

Models of history always begin with a state of past savagery, evolve to a middle state of enlightenment, then point to a future golden age of civilisation. A family where the mother had no authority and, thus, could not practice the enlightened love of which she was uniquely capable became symbolic of savagery. The symbolism of Eve's fall had provided patriarchal society with a justification for restricting women's freedom. Nineteenth century ideas of progress relegated Eve to the distant past. The Virgin Mary's divine motherhood exonerated womankind and marked the end of the primitive era of Eve. Homes became oases of happiness and delight against the barbaric society created by man. Emancipationists and anti-emancipationists shared the view that if women could not create homes modelled on the image of Mary, the Lady Mother who redeemed the image of women from Eve's downfall, all society would suffer. Yet, the emancipation of women in the second half of the 1800s was thought to be so dangerous to the social order as to possibly unleash anarchy.[21] So was the struggle for women's rights in Latin America.

Today, depending upon the country, women's rights in Latin America are still being won. Costa Rica inaugurated its first female president, Laura Chinchilla, in May 2010. She is the fifth female president of a Latin American country. In the 18 years between 1990 and 2008, 15 Latin American countries rewrote their constitutions to include provisions of equality between women and men, even to the point of specifying situations which undermine women's equal treatment. However, material support and agency direction for implementing the new laws is deficient. Many governments place little substantive emphasis on the importance of the laws;[22] many also are using women's rights as a political tool. That said, Latin American women enjoy greater equality than women in other countries outside of the Organization for Economic Cooperation and Development (OECD) which is comprised of advanced capitalist democracies.[23]

Asian women

Japanese women were granted the right to vote in 1946.

In Japan during the time of the women's liberation movement, women were viewed as subservient, yet women were the ones who were responsible for managing the household finances. It was a responsibility passed from mother to daughter and spread throughout Japanese society.[24] In Japan, family represented 'nurturing, enduring, and non-contingent relations governed by morality'. Family has also historically been and continues to be an institution that is oppressive for women. In

114

Japanese villages, there was the structure of a farm economy or small business economy. Women worked under the authority of their husbands, were not allowed to earn income or have any control over economic resources. They could not meet people and form relationships outside the family. In typical Japanese villages, family life consisted of a unified household where men walked down the street separately from the women. Families attended family events such as weddings and funerals together but sat on opposite sides of the room.[25]

So the push for women's rights began with the focus of reforming the oppressive patriarchal society rather than for women's suffrage. Women's education became a focus as a result of political leaders' beliefs that an educated female population would raise diligent, patriotic sons. Women's rights advocates saw it as an opportunity to advance women's rights in Japanese Society. It was a period of significant cultural upheaval in Japan and women's suffrage became a focal point amidst cultural change.[26]

In the middle of the 19th century, millions of women in Europe, Latin America and Asia left their homelands and came to the US to find work. They were considered 'cheap labour' and came over with their families. Men and women earned a family wage and often had destitute relatives back home to support. Women's labour was, therefore, essential for survival. [27]

The first Japanese generation to emigrate – called Issei – to America did so between 1909 and 1924, beginning with the Gentlemen's Agreement and ending with the Immigration Act of 1924, for the time, ending immigration from Asian countries. This first wave settled in the Bay Area before World War II where they formed communities and had children. The second generation – the Nisei – were born between 1918 and 1940. The next wave came after World War II and were called 'war brides' since they married American soldiers who were either stationed in Japan or who worked with the post-war occupation. Most of these women entered the States between 1950 and the mid 1960s. They shared the circumstance of growing up or reaching adulthood during the war, suffering the dislocations and hardships caused by the war and its aftermath, and having to adjust to life in the US as wives of ex-servicemen. There was already an established way of Japanese life to which they had to adjust and become a part.

The Issei established stable communities to shield their families from the hostile society in which they now lived, one that devalued people of colour. The Nisei shared the experience of growing up in a stable ethnic community that provided anchor and refuge in such a hostile society. Issei women maintained the traditions from their homeland. Although 'women started out in a peripheral role in organization of the community, they have emerged over time as its prime movers'.[28] Women who were educated passed on the language, literature, and art to the next generations. Every day traditions in Japanese culture, including food, folk medicine, peasant lore, and customs from their communities in Japan were transmitted by all Issei women.

An intact family system characterised by strong kinship bonds and clear ethnic identity enabled the Issei and Nisei to withstand economic and psychological hardships and to develop a positive sense of self.[29] Their largest challenge was in keeping the family together while they acted to overhaul the family structures that subordinated them. The lack of a coherent system left the war brides more vulnerable to these external forces, and they suffered greater personal disorganisation as a result.

China

Ironically, women's rights in China came in with the Communist regime during the Cultural Revolution. Mao Zedong believed that a power which was equitable to its women would be viewed as equitable by the world. Women became soldiers, marching right along with their male counterparts and reading the same books. They became educated and took jobs outside the home. Women were also allowed to hold the power of command, making them actually more dominant than men during this period. After the revolution, women lost some of the equality they had experienced under Mao. The influence of Western culture offered women a new sense of freedom. Many Western concepts such as choosing one's own husband, divorce, and fashion consciousness were adopted.[30]

Today, despite guarantees that a 'minimal but significant number of women' serve 'in all legislative assemblies', the complaint is made that government assurances contradict what is a daily experience of gender discrimination. Less access to higher levels of education and a continued preference for sons along with incidents of violence against women continue.[31]

For the Chinese Diaspora of today, there is less bias in including female members of the family in the business enterprise. Female members have been included in the management of private wealth or philanthropic activities but control and management of family business is still very much preserved for male heirs.[32] In Indonesia, some businessmen still disinherit their daughters in favour of their sons. The daughters receive nothing outside a significant dowry.

Middle Eastern women

Women were given the right to vote in: Lebanon 1953, Egypt, 1956; Yemen, 1970; Jordan, 1974; Iraq, 1980; Kuwait, 2005.

There is a great deal of interest from the West in emancipating Middle Eastern women today. And, of course, levels of Western style emancipation vary from country to country. Except in the medical field, Saudi Arabia still has restrictions on women working in a mixed gender environment. Things have changed in the last decade; more women are venturing to work outside the home and over 45% of businesses are owned by women. But Saudi women's involvement in politics is very shy,[33] whereas women in Kuwait have more freedom and work simply to have fulfilling careers.[34]

In Egypt, women have been forced into the workplace just so the family can survive. Egyptian women's ability to hold a job in the workplace would have been unthinkable as recently as a generation ago. Most women tend to work in lower paying jobs, although a few have entered traditionally male professions of law, engineering, medicine, teaching, business, and diplomatic service. In this way, the economic conditions run contrary to the ideal practice of family.[35] Though Egyptian women were pioneers in all movements concerning gender issues, it was not till the last decade that the changes started to show an impact. Today, almost as many women are educated as men. Women are an important working force and, like men, are working abroad in the Gulf countries. They share in the political arena in the parliament, cabinet, and legislative bodies.[36]

In 1960, there were fewer women in Muslim countries working outside the family than any other sector of the world. Those numbers increased so rapidly that by 1981, women comprised 18% of the Egyptian industrial workforce. This has eroded the ideal of the family as the primary institution since the number of women going into the workforce has mandated that life sustaining services become the responsibility of the state rather than the family. Some in the Middle East feel that men must reassert their role as protector and supporter of the family while others contend that the participation of both sexes in the working world enables a better future for everyone. Women need to work so the family can stay together, whether 'family' refers to the nuclear family, the extended family including multiple wives (in some countries and not as familiar as in the past), or the family of all Muslims.[37] In Lebanon, women make up about 30% of the workforce.

Education of women is still a contention in many Middle Eastern countries. With the impact of modernisation and industrialisation brought on in recent years by the oil wealth, more women are working, education and the media are increasing, and people are leaving rural areas and moving to cities. Middle Eastern social scientists view this transition as a significant improvement over old traditions and the large, extended family structure. What is actually happening, however, is the reinstitution of the family within the modernisation process. The changes are being viewed as ways to strengthen the family unit rather than diminish its importance and relevance. Thus, families are 'reorganizing and regrouping in answer to modern needs', despite the debate around the roles of women within it.[38] In another trend that is noticeable, women are not only following their husbands to work abroad, but are being offered jobs on their own, mostly in the gulf counties. Some are even going to Europe and the US to study and work.[39]

Feminist movements across the globe: what went wrong ... or right?

The stark realisation we must face is that we currently are in the Turning in which interest in women's equality begins to wane and that the largest gender gap occurs during Highs, with interest growing again during an Awakening. *We must realise that the next Awakening is two Turnings away.* Already, we can see the effects of the beginning downturn in interest. Evidence of this may be found in the United Nations Women's Treaty which shows increasing numbers of countries stating their reservations about agreeing to ensure women's equality.[40] Today, many consider women's rights to be a non-issue, that equal treatment is established and is now 'a given', or simply taken for granted. Yet, many women work more than men while getting paid less than men do for the same work.

Others think women's rights are only an issue in Middle Eastern countries. In fact: (a) some Middle Eastern countries are much more progressive than others; and (b) the rest of the world certainly has not come full circle with rights on employment, compensation, child care, and many other cultural, political, and economic issues. 'Gender equality furthers the cause of child survival and development for all of society ....'[41] As importantly, gender equality enables family wealth to be enriched with the authentic wealth of its women. *Without access to the authentic wealth of all family members, regeneration of the wealth will be compromised, at best.* And the Proverb has one more ally to its fulfilment.

Two Awakenings ago, 1886–1908, saw the formation of women's suffrage groups around the globe. If you notice the years in which women were given the right to vote in various countries, they overwhelmingly line up in European countries and in the US between 1908 and 1929, the subsequent Unravelling (the Turning where gaps in gender roles are at a minimum). The following Awakening (1964–1984) saw major legislation for women's rights in various countries of the world.

The US movement has been viewed as more successful than the British movement with greater public acceptance of the movement's goals and achieving changes in policy as a result. It has also been criticised as being politically motivated, 'deficient in theory, overly spontaneous, and politically naïve'.[42] So the advancing of women's issues is certainly not a 'one-size-fits-all' concern. At the International Women's conference in Nairobi, it was emphasised that 'feminism must deal with survival issues if it is to be relevant to women's lives throughout the world'.[43]

The feminist movements in Western Europe were largely fragmented into radical, decentralised groups which criticised the US movement as trying to sweep too broad a brush with a liberal focus that was too heavy. It is also felt in other parts of the world that measuring women's roles in the Middle East and in developing countries by Western cultural standards equates to imposing the standards of Western-style liberal democracies[44] which do not recognise women's economic contributions through child raising, traditional housework, agricultural subsistence, unpaid jobs in family businesses, and voluntary work in non-government organisations (NGOs) and others. So-called traditional roles of women in India are considered an integral component of national identity, rendering feminism an 'irrelevant, Western notion reflecting a bourgeois, modernist perspective' in their view.[45]

In the Middle East, the experience with feminism varies and is more complex than simply applying a Western concept to what is assumed to be similar across the board for Islamic women. Other countries note that when feminist concerns conflict with traditional customs, the question must be asked, 'which values should be privileged?' Still others feel that treating feminism as a 'foreign import' is often founded in a male strategy to hinder its progress and maintain control over women. Additional support for this view states the view that feminism is a foreign import is 'a superficial misreading of history', and that 'the concept stands for a transformational process ... against women's subordination. Thus feminism was not imposed ... nor was it a foreign ideology'.[46] In the 1940s, a movement to remove the veil started in Egypt and moved on to Syria and Lebanon. This movement led to modernisation and Western-style living especially after World War I and until modern times. In the 1990s, a reverse movement occurred, requiring the veil to be the norm. So Egypt, Syria, Lebanon, and Tunisia, which were considered quiet Western in their way of life, were greatly affected by the call to return to traditional dress code. Although many women have followed the call, it has not stopped them from going to work or even living abroad.[47]

Whatever the view, women's movements in each country must fit that country's particular situation to be successful. There should be no 'ethnocentric assumption' that each country's feminist pursuits inevitably follow an evolutionary path toward the Western model.

On the other hand, paradoxes in the progress of feminism consistently exist in countries where there are constitutional guarantees of gender equality; yet these governments in practice fail to endow their societies with the rights proclaimed.[48]

In the US, personal observations regarding the American Women's Movement in the 1960s render its success debatable. Rankin says, 'I appreciate why there needed to be some kind of a movement that gave women recognition and more choices, but there are times when I wonder if it was really the answer. In some ways, it created greater inequities in the marketplace, not from a money management perspective, but from a work ethic and job opportunity perspective. It became easier for some women to expect advancement in their jobs without having to work for it and earn their way. They were part of a minority group and felt that they could claim certain things that gave them an easy ticket. A lot of people rode that horse for a long time, which meant that the movement didn't teach the lessons it should have, which were that everyone should have access to opportunities and a fair workplace if they demonstrated that they had the skills, attitude and performance.'

What the US Movement did do was open the pathway. If it were not for the movement of suffrage in the 1920s and the Women's Movement of the 1960s, women's options today would be far fewer. The US Movement of the 1960s laid the foundation for Gen-X women to make the most of their opportunities and of their options.

Today, women are making more money; in many cases, more than their husbands. The number of households in which women bring home the larger paycheque grew from 17.8% in 1987 to 25.3%

Exhibit 8.4

Rates of voting right gains for women across the globe

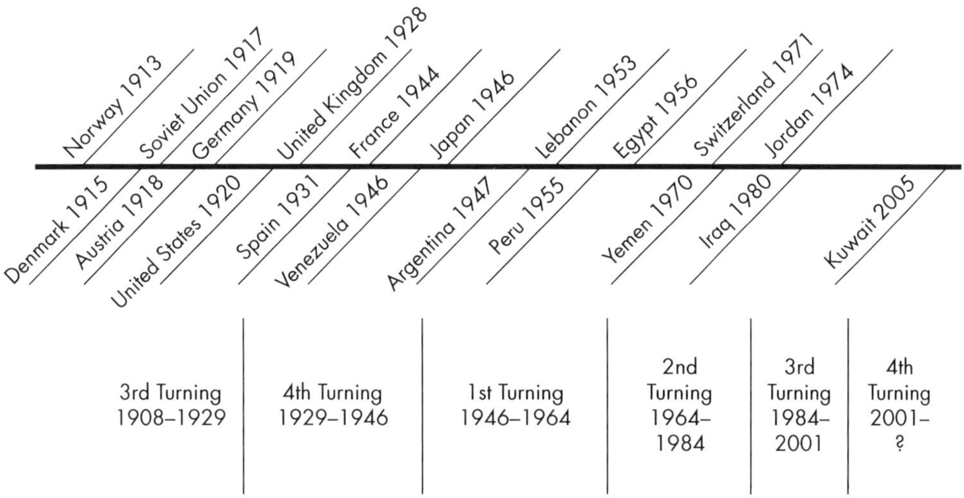

3rd Turning 1908–1929	4th Turning 1929–1946	1st Turning 1946–1964	2nd Turning 1964–1984	3rd Turning 1984–2001	4th Turning 2001–?

Source: graymatter Strategies LLC. All rights reserved.

in 2007. The increase in salaries of college educated women rose 34.4% from 1979. Men's salaries increased 21.7% during the same time period.[49]

This is nothing new. Boomer women have long out-earned their husbands due to their own ambition and the types of professional choices they made early in life. Still other Boomer women went back to their careers after the children were raised or as their husbands were either laid off, retired, or simply downshifted. That said, the overall rate of pay is still disparate, although that disparity is shrinking. In 2007, women in the 35 to 40 age group were paid 75% of what their male counterparts made. Between ages 25–34, they made 81% as much as men.[50]

The number of such families who have emancipated both sexes and either made role reversals or who now share traditional roles more equitably has also increased, especially among younger couples who increasingly expect more fluid roles and greater flexibility. The number of husbands pitching in with more traditionally female chores at home such as doing the dishes and taking care of children had risen to 34% by 2007 compared to 24% ten years earlier. And many are realising that such role sharing is not a threat to their masculinity.

And women of all ages are participating. Professional women now have a workplace that allows them to work part time and spend time raising their children. Many women, having had successful careers, have made the choice to stay home and have families. Many men, as noted earlier, relish the choice they have made to take a larger part in caring for the children.

Women who make more money say they feel gratification that they are no longer 'beholden' to their husbands. Instead of channelling their energies into finding a marriage partner, young women are now free to pursue personal ambitions. They also feel more fulfilled since they can contribute more to the household bottom line.[51] Today, women owned businesses in the US employ 23 million people according to a study conducted by the Center for Women's Business Research. That figure is almost double the number employed in the top 50 companies combined.[52]

What does it all mean for the future?

Whatever the ill effects of the Women's Movement of the 1960s, it broke ground for future generations of women to grow up in a world where they feel they have every option to live the kinds of lives they wish. In some cases, this is a mixed blessing. Tickle explains, 'I get email from young women saying it's impossible to do it all, so which part do they do? I think we're in real trouble unless we can bring up a generation of women who say: "OK, we're equal, we no longer have to prove that. Now, where best can we serve?" That's a real attitude shift.'

Many wonder what the future of feminism holds for women and for all of society, of which families are still a fundamental institution. When women are young, they are conflicted about which path to take – a career path or a relationship path. Hughes notes the conflicts of women at different stages of their lives and the positive and negative effects of the feminist movement. In sync with the information we now know about women's brains, he notes Jung's observation that the journey of young women is one of relationship. In the US, they now face the calling to launch a career at exactly the same point in their lives when they are also seeking to build those relationships. 'Unfortunately, the voices raised most strenuously about women achieving status through work appear not to have studied Jung and his disciples; if they did, they chose to ignore them. So now we have the suffering of the resulting trap, with young women burned out physically by its demands and finding all too often … that they "have no time, no time for anything" and absolutely no time for themselves.' He also notes that women's longevity likely gives them more options for pursuing their careers in the second stage of life than in the first.[53]

As women age, those who have delayed becoming mothers because they chose to have a career find themselves juggling quite a few balls all at the same time. Women who become mothers in their late thirties to mid forties can end up facing perimenopausal challenges while chasing toddlers around the house. With greater longevity overall, they may also find themselves having to care for aging parents, all at the same time.

The challenge in modern society is to 'help society better support our natural female abilities and needs'. The whole point in studying perspectives of different generations is to create awareness and to understand what will help families of wealth navigate their particular generational mazes successfully and in a way that will nurture all forms of their wealth. This positions generational perspectives as a vital tool families can use in wealth management – from practically any aspect. Within this, awareness of the differences in the brain chemistry of the sexes enables the authentic wealth of each to be more readily recognised, its productive and contributory deployment more easily facilitated, and confidence by both sexes in the roles that are appropriate for them to perform, regardless of the traditional labels those roles may carry.

How does this hope address the confusion that today's young women feel, as exemplified by the emails Tickle receives? 'Whether you like it or not, women have been the partner that filled in the cultural mores, that educated the children – that was the transferor of cultural mores. The social unit now has no form of intimate transmittal of values. So we're trying to do it with God knows how many eleemosynary organizations and those can only be accessed by changing your physical location. Going to a lecture is not the same as hearing it 16 hours a day from a parent or grandparent. We're in a society composed of citizens that have only been partially formed and it affects how we spend our money as well because we're constantly looking for diversion and/or the information on a way of being. What we're lacking now is a way of being,' she says.

A 'way of being' provides options that women – and by default, men – have not had before. Men can be equally adept both at transmitting values and at changing diapers – and some are very good cooks! In a perfect world, feminism will have accomplished the emancipation of both sexes to be fluid in their roles within the family so that the needs of the family are fulfilled appropriately and by the person most suited for the task, whether male or female. Tickle says that the US movement has to mature before society can get to such a point and she says, 'It's time! We've proved the point; now let's *do* something with it! No one says that for women to be women, men have to be weak and spineless.' If we are indeed living within a positive spiral of the generational archetypes, we can use the successes and failures of previous Awakenings to enlighten the Prophets who implement feminist achievements toward fostering both women's and men's authentic wealth. If we fail to achieve such a balance, the Movement of the 60s will have failed completely.[54]

Not only must a balance be achieved, but also a flexible one that allows roles to be fluid according to ability, desire, and need on the part of both women and men. At this level, chronological generational perspectives can become just that – generational perspectives without assigned roles that pre-determine what contributions family members should make based on gender or preconceived capabilities. This is where an understanding of the perspectives of generational cohorts is critical; the experiences early generations face 'establish patterns and shape the circumstances and choices of subsequent ones'. This allows both women and men to use generational perspectives of both types as well as knowledge of the Turnings as tools to navigate wealth management waters both now and in the future. It also empowers both men and women to be great leaders of the family.

[1] Sillerman, L.B., 'Generations of women moving history forward,' Women's Voices for Change, March 2007: http://womensvoicesforchange.org/generations-of-women-moving-history-forward.htm.

[2] Wealth Regeneration® is a registered service mark owned by Laird Norton Tyee and is used throughout this book with Laird Norton Tyee's permission.

[3] Willmington Trust and Campden Research in association with Relative Solutions, 'The New Wealth Paradigm: how affluent women are taking control of their futures', 40 participants between the ages of 40 and 65, minimum net worth of $25 million with at least one child. Fall 2008.

[4] Press Release, 'Research reveals affluent women taking control of their wealth,' Trusts and Estates, May 2009: http://trustsandestates.com/press_release/affluent-women-taking-wealth.

[5] Margolis, D.R., 'Women's movements around the world: cross-cultural comparisons', Gender and Society, 1993, p. 381: http://www.jstor.org/stable/189799.

[6] Strauss, W. and Howe, N., The Fourth Turning: an American prophecy, (New York, NY: Broadway Books, 1997), p. 111.

[7] Kantrowitz, B. and Wingert, P. 'Five myths about the Pill', Newsweek, May 6 2010. www.newsweek.com/2010/05/06/the-pill-turns-50.html.

[8] Strauss, W. and Howe, N., Millennials Rising: the next Great Generation, (New York, NY: Vintage Books, 2000), pp. 32, 33.

[9] Ibid.

[10] Ibid.

[11] Ibid, pp. 45, 46.

[12] Strauss, W. and Howe, N., The Fourth Turning: an American prophecy, (New York, NY: Broadway Books, 1997), p. 8.

[13] Brizendine, L., The Female Brain, (New York, NY: Morgan Road Books, 2006), p. 5: www.morganroadbooks.com.

[14] Ibid, p. 5.

[15] Ibid. p. 21.

[16] Hughes, J.E., Jr., *Family: a compact among generations,* (New York, NY: Bloomberg Press, 2007), pp. 88, 89.

[17] Ibid, p. 7.

[18] 'The long way to women's right to vote', http://history-switzerland.geschichte-schweiz.ch/chronology-womens-right-vote-switzerland.html; also 'Women's suffrage: a world chronology of the recognition of women's rights to vote and to stand for election': www.ipu.org/wmn-e/suffrage.htm.

[19] Boudieu, J., Postel-Vinay, G., Suwa-Eisenmann, A., 'Aging women and family wealth', *Social Science History 32(2),* 2008, pp. 143–74; DOI: 10.1215/01455532-2007-017, 2008.

[20] Ibid.

[21] Frederick, B., 'Women's views of their own history: Argentina 1860–1910', presented at the Latin American Studies Association meeting in Guadalajara, Mexico, 1997: http://lasa.international.pitt.edu/LASA97/frederick.pdf.

[22] Márquez, H., 'Women's rights laws – where's the enforcement?', *IPS News,* May 2010: http://ipsnews.net/news.asp?idnews=50560.

[23] Goodman, D., 'The struggle for women's equality in Latin America,' *Dissident Voice,* March 2009: http://dissidentvoice.org/2009/03/the-struggle-for-womens-equality-in-latin-america/.

[24] 'Japan 1990 – United States of America 2006: the past as a window on the future, Part 1 of 5': http://www.gold-eagle.com/editorials_05/joubert031106.html.

[25] Glenn, E.N., *Issei, Nisei, War Bride*: *three generations of Japanese American women*, (Philadelphia, PA: Temple University Press, 1986), p. 213.

[26] Wikipedia, 'Women's suffrage in Japan': http://en.wikipedia.org/wiki/Women%27s_suffrage_in_Japan.

[27] Glenn, E.N., *Issei, Nisei, War Bride*: *three generations of Japanese American women*, (Philadelphia, PA: Temple University Press, 1986), p. 3.

[28] Ibid, p. 213.

[29] Ibid, p 193.

[30] Baker, C., 'Position of women in Chinese history', BellaOnline, the Voice of Women, 2010: www.bellaonline.com/articles/art29973.asp.

[31] Margolis, D.R., 'Women's movements around the world: cross-cultural comparisons', *Gender and Society*, 1993, p. 388. www.jstor.org/stable/189799.

[32] Anonymous source, Personal interview, June 2007.

[33] Makhzoumi, M., President, Makhzoumi Foundation, Beirut, Lebanon, Personal email, May 2010. Throughout the sections on Middle Eastern women, Mrs. Makhzoumi has made comments clarifying the modern day activities of women in the Middle East, for which the author is extremely grateful.

[34] Fernea, E.W., *'The Family in the Middle East'*, Center for Middle Eastern Studies, The University of Texas at Austin, 1984–2009.

[35] Ibid.

[36] Makhzoumi, M., Personal email, May 2010.

[37] Fernea, E.W., *'The Family in the Middle East'*, Center for Middle Eastern Studies, The University of Texas at Austin, 1984–2009.

[38] Ibid.

[39] Makhzoumi, M., Personal email, May 2010.

[40] Deen, T., 'Women: reservations grow over UN Women's Treaty', *World News*, Inter Press Service, March 2010: http://web.archive.org/web/20040423160533/http://www.oneworld.org/ips2/mar98/unwomen.html.

[41] 'Women's rights; global issues: social, political, economic, and environmental issues that affect us all', (2010). March 2010: www.globalissues.org/article/166/womens-rights.

[42] Margolis, D.R., 'Women's movements around the world: cross-cultural comparisons', *Gender and Society*, 1993, p. 382. www.jstor.org/stable/189799.

[43] Ibid, p. 380.

[44] Ibid, p. 382.

[45] Ibid, p. 383.

[46] Ibid, p. 382.

[47] Makhzoumi, M., Personal email, May 2010.

[48] Margolis, D.R., 'Women's movements around the world: cross-cultural comparisons', *Gender and Society*, 1993, p. 388. www.jstor.org/stable/189799.

[49] Selvin, M., 'She earns more and that's OK,' *The Los Angeles Times,* February 2007: www.latimes.com/news/printedition/la-fi-wives4feb04,1,6064199,full.story.

[50] Ibid.

[51] Ibid.

[52] Mui, Y.Q., 'Women a big force in business, study finds,' *The Washington Post,* October 2009: http://www.washingtonpost.com/wp-dyn/content/article/2009/10/02/AR2009100205317.html.

[53] Hughes, J.E., Jr., *Family: a compact among generations,* (New York, NY: Bloomberg Press, 2007), pp. 88, 89.

[54] Tickle, Phyllis, Personal interview, November 2006.

Part 1 summary: the generational impact

Through our exploration of generational perspectives around the world and also of gender related perspectives, we have come to see the impact of larger society views on decisions families make about their wealth. From the GI 'my way or the highway' generation in America to the post-war *taiyōzoku* in Japan; from the Swiss Noblesse to the Chinese Cultural Revolution; from Betty Friedan to Carla Bruni-Sarkozy, the waves of generational change affect our relationships with family and our relationship to wealth in all its forms.

Unwittingly, we wander down the path toward traditional wealth management, focusing on the result and not the source of our wealth and the issues and complexities that come along with it, often missing the great gift it has the opportunity to afford us. Awareness and knowledge feed empowerment. And so the visualisation of familial generational mazes creating their family systems and serving as the foundation of their journey with wealth will determine if that journey is a short or a long one; whether it is a journey fraught with dysfunction and disappointment or guided by a harmony that ultimately brings them joy.

As angst-ridden as family dysfunction and the capital markets can make our lives, we have seen the power of cyclicality and the difference the way we measure time can make in the way we function in the world. As the forces of the family system and the impact of cyclical time converge, we understand the importance of developing the following skills for family success.

1 Recognising dysfunction as a divider of family wealth that undermines family cohesion and well being.
2 Acknowledging the critical role of generational perspectives and family dynamics in making wealth management decisions.
3 Understanding the difference in cyclical and linear time measurement and the role each plays in a family's success.
4 Understanding the power of generational cycles in defining the family and fostering affinity in an effort to postpone the Proverb's fulfilment.
5 Learning how the historical Turnings of generational archetypical roles along with the expectations inherent in chronological generational roles affect family relationships and, consequentially, the family wealth.

Placing the family system within the Generational Wealth Management Continuum^{SM} illuminates the critical importance of recognising the authentic assets of the family and nurturing their development. It also illustrates that our traditional approach to wealth management is sorely insufficient since we are not including the bulk of the family's assets – its authentic assets – within the portfolio to be managed.

Understanding how we live within our particular generation and how our generational imprint colours our view of the world enables us to move forward. It grounds us to a history larger than ourselves and defines us within a group offering safety and acceptance called 'family'.

All of this brings us to a place where we need structure to guide us in fostering the metamorphosis of authentic family wealth into a tangible form – a process through which we can become consciously proactive in working with the edicts of the famed Proverb and postponing its effects rather than unwittingly feeding its fulfilment.

The next step in the Generational Wealth Management process – the tool families design to serve them in this capacity – is called governance. Rather than an onerous and oppressive set of rules and regulations, governance serves families best in its authentic role as the portal through which authentic wealth comes to fruition. Part 2 explores how the roles family members occupy determine the type of governance structure they develop and the options families have for making their governance systems work better in accomplishing the goals they have set, whether those goals are personal, business, or investment management related. As we turn the page toward Step 2 of the Generational Wealth Management[SM] process and Part 2 of this book, we begin to make the vital connection between our dreams for our families and proactively making them a reality.

Part 2:

Family governance

'… boundaries are often thought to separate things rather than link them. However, while clear and proper boundaries may separate, in doing so, they allow individuals to grow and thrive, decisions to be made fairly and appropriately, and people to understand who they are and where they stand when they are together.'

Dennis Jaffe*

---

* Jaffe, D.T., 'Stewardship in your family enterprise', (Pioneer imprints, 2010), p. 105: www.pioneerimprints.com.

Chapter 9

Roles and the formation of family dynamics

'Behavior may be better predicted by understanding the roles people think they occupy. Personality factors may do no more than simply give style to one's basic role performances. In the extreme, the self can be conceptualized to be no more than the roles it plays. Take away one's roles and nothing is left.'

Professor Michael C. Kearl[1]

Family dynamics are where all the generational perspectives we have just explored converge. They come together either within the bonds of affinity, nurturing the development of each family member's authentic assets or they come together like a loaded time bomb just waiting for the right fuse to blow them up.

We established in Chapter 2 that the perspectives of generations – both archetypical and chronological – within the family hold the greatest influence on decisions made about the wealth. Generational perspectives are the fountainhead from which flow the roles family members occupy, setting up the dynamics of the family. From the dynamics of the family flow all other components – needs the family have and ultimately, the goals they set to fulfil those needs. By the time the dynamics of the family seep into the traditional wealth management process, the statistical likelihood that the edicts of the Proverb will be fulfilled is already set. Knowing this, it would seem that families and their advisors would spend a great deal of their time trying to understand the dynamics that are going on in the family. Both encounter their effects in just about all their dealings.

Many an advisor can attest to the fact that an otherwise seemingly very loving family can erupt – sometimes quite abruptly – into chaos when the topic of money enters the conversation. Relationships disintegrate, often with permanent damage in the aftermath. And many a family experiences what might be considered small disagreements but which, over time, cause communication to completely break down and result in breach of trust.

This chapter will conduct a deeper exploration into the impact of generational perspectives on the way family members interact and the roles they occupy. It will serve as one side of a book-end type of role discussion which comes full circle in Chapter 15 where roles are more pointedly discussed within the goal-setting process. The order of development is this: generational perspectives determine the roles family members perform, from which the dynamics of the family are defined; those roles, expressed through the dynamics of the family, present needs for which leadership sets goals for satisfying. These goals are then taken to advisors and the family issues piece translates into the traditional wealth management piece.

That is the way the process happens but that is not typically the way families or their advisors view it. Within the wealth management industry, the topic of family dynamics is beginning to receive greater attention, although only on a surface level from my observations. So, in keeping with the efficiency of starting where people's attention already is, we will begin at the family dynamics piece and drill down in a sort of backward fashion, beginning with an investigation of the nature of family dynamics and why families and advisors need to dig deeper. We then will discover how generational perspectives either 'assign' perceived roles or enable authentic roles to emerge, setting the stage for the set of dynamics which lie at the heart of the family's success or failure. Lastly, we will delve into the importance of the roles family members occupy within the family structure and the critical difference between perceived roles and authentic ones. Through this process, we will be able to see how the infiltration of archetypical generational perspectives intertwines with the expectations set through chronological generational perspectives to play into the hand of the fateful Proverb.

Families and their dynamics

The best way to foster understanding of a concept is to first define the object of investigation. The American Heritage Dictionary defines the word 'dynamics' as follows.[2]

adj.

1 a. Of or relating to energy or objects in motion.
   b. Of or relating to the study of dynamics.
2 Characterised by continuous change, activity or progress ...
3 Marked by intensity and vigour; forceful.
4 Of or relating to variation of intensity, as in musical sound.

n.

1 An interactive system or process, especially one involving competing or conflicting forces ...
2 A force, especially political, social, or psychological: *the main dynamic behind the revolution.*

Observable dynamics in families surely include energy, intensity, continuous change, and vigour and may at times include objects in motion. Hopefully, they also include progress. But examination of the interactive process forging the political, social, and psychological views of individual family members into a unified decision-making model is often set aside or completely overlooked in favour of making the decisions deemed urgently at hand – those pertaining to the management of financial assets.

Although passing over such examination for lack of time, perceived lack of relevance or simply due to a deep-seated desire to avoid the 'sensitive' side of wealth management issues has heretofore been accepted as the norm, the consequences of doing so have plagued families for time immemorial. When a practice becomes so widely accepted and is rarely, if ever, questioned, the resulting dysfunction also becomes universally accepted and unquestioned. Assets perform, perhaps in optimal fashion from portfolio management tenets, but not in optimal fashion for the family as a whole, much less its individual members. Heirs lack understanding when a will is read and assets get dispersed. Resentment is carried for years (perhaps decades) between siblings. Wealth creators' intentions may be worthy but actual results ultimately end up missing the mark.

This is called 'end-gaining',[3] rushing to gain the desired end result without taking the time to follow the necessary process. It is a compelling delusion that makes us feel the quickest way to get where we want to go is by skipping the proper due diligence and ground work for ensuring success in lieu of 'getting it done'. This often presents itself in families through a lack of discussion with family members on issues that affect their lives or arbitrarily making decisions on behalf of family members from the governing generation's interpretation of what is in the rest of the family's best interests. Sometimes, it is the result of the desire of a few family members to push through a decision they think will benefit the family with the behavioural-based fear that, if certain aspects of the project are known, other family members will scuttle it. It can also masquerade as inviting input from the family and the family giving the input they think leadership wants to hear so that 'family input' becomes another version of 'form' over 'function', the fallout for which can be seen in the case study at the end of Chapter 12.

In reality, this is the most *inefficient* way to meet an objective. And a project about which decision makers fear some family members will be resistant either requires discussions to explain the benefits in a way that the resistant family members will understand or the project should indeed be scuttled. It may be quite possible that these family members can see a less beneficial side of the project's effects that we may not envision in our haste to 'get it adopted'. In such a case, we are framing a decision the way we wish to see it, without taking into consideration all the potential risks involved. In hindsight, it is always easy to see how things could have been done better. Then we have to do what we can to make reparations.

Participation in end-gaining ensures that, at some point, we will have to retrace our steps (if possible) to mitigate the damage (if possible) after we have temporarily and only seemingly achieved our goal. Likely, the event or family crisis that forces the mitigation attempt is some time down the road, making the problem immensely more complex and damaging than it might have been.

By taking time on the front end to ensure an authentic process, families actually save time instead of wasting it as they might think. Conversely, the very thing family leadership fears will happen is actually predisposed to happen through the end-gaining attempt. The efficiency of the authentic process can be proven by the principles of calculus. Calculus is the mathematical measurement of change. There are two parts to calculus, the derivative and the integral. The derivative tells you the rate of change; the integral tells you by how much. If you toss a ball into the air, its positive derivative (how fast it goes up) will be slower than its declining derivative (how fast it comes down). Just before it changes direction, the ball will momentarily be at a standstill. This is referred to as having zero derivative. This zero principle at peaks and troughs has practical application. We employ it whenever we are looking for the most efficient way to do something – the fastest way to get where we want to go.[4]

Steven Strogatz, professor of applied mathematics at Cornell University, uses the example of finding the quickest way to cross a meadow, one which is half covered in snow which the wind has piled high, clearing off the other half in the process. Typically, we think the shortest distance between two points is a straight line. We extrapolate 'shortest' to also mean 'quickest'. But in this case, walking the straight line, because of the rate of change in a person's walking speed to get through the deep snow, would actually be slower than walking a longer path which avoided the snow. If two people started on opposite ends of the meadow and raced to get to the other side, the one who analysed the situation and took the time to go around the snow covered half would beat the one who went straight through. We know this through the employment of the calculus derivative.[5]

By skipping the investigation into family dynamics and the effects of the generational maze within a family, our minds delude us into thinking we can reach the decision component much more rapidly. The price we pay, however, is much dearer in the long run, takes an immensely greater amount of time to exact, and can literally affect the bottom line of the investment portfolio.

For example, let us imagine a family attempting to navigate the 2008 crisis. Perhaps the family had received some good consulting advice and spent time and money setting up a governance system that created a family council, advisory committees, education committees, and an investment committee. Although they had set up these committees and populated them, they had neglected to empower the committees to review the decisions that had been made by investment committee members who were in charge of managing the family's investment portfolio. Family members were not informed on a regular basis about investment activities and results for fear that the application of the investment policy would be disrupted by family members who are not experts and, therefore, may not understand the risk implications involved.

As important as it is not to have too many decision makers, especially in areas where they lack expertise, it is extremely important for family members to have transparency around the decisions experts make on their behalf and to have the power to make necessary changes if they are in agreement that such changes need to be made. In other words, the family council may agree as a body that changes needed to be made in the investment committee because the performance of a particular member (not necessarily a particular investment or investment philosophy) has not kept up with the needs of the family, yet they have no power to effect that decision.

By not empowering the family committee to take such action, the aftermath of a crisis like the one we had in 2008 might create a significant need to talk to family members after the fact about what happened to the family funds and why they might not be able to depend on receiving the same amount of dividends to which they had become accustomed. This, of course, could take a great deal of time. It could also involve emotional angst and the need to reassure and calm family members who would be affected.

If the committee were indeed empowered to take actions it agreed were necessary – or even prudent – ineffective investment committee members, or committee members focused on taking more risk than the family might need in particular market environments, could be removed and more conservative members might be installed. By doing so, the resulting damage from an event like 2008 might be less severe, or avoided altogether if the family decided not to invest in certain areas as a result of the market climate. An option to invest in these areas could be offered outside of the family portfolio for those individuals who felt compelled to have exposure.

Lastly, let us take a minute to think back and add up the financial cost as well as the time and energy cost over a period of 10 or 15 years multiplied by the number of family members involved to develop and populate a governance system with a family council, advisory committees, education committees, and an investment committee. Now add the time and cost of the phone calls and conversations which may have had to be held after the crisis to explain why the dividends would be reduced. Then add in the actual amount of loss experienced by the investment portfolio. The result is how much this end-gaining decision actually may have cost this family, a significant bottom-line figure that reaches far beyond the capital losses of the portfolio.

Following a more authentic process, of course, does nothing to guarantee a more favourable outcome. And the above example in no way indicates that the governing generations' intentions of this family might not have been worthy. But the more authentic process does guarantee both the productive use of time (forming *and empowering* the governance system), the saving of time (not wasting the time spent setting up the governance system; not having to make the phone calls after the crisis), vastly reduced amounts of emotional angst (interpreted as health risk of added stress for all family members involved), and circumventing possible damage to family relationships by empowering family members in their authentic roles. *Looking back to the equation we employed in the paragraph above, the authentic process enhances the family's bottom line even if the financial losses in the portfolio had been the same.*

Employing such a process requires transparency and the opportunity for family members to act as well-educated, dynamic stakeholder owners for the benefit of the family as a whole.

The generational bias

In larger society, we live our lives within a social context which we individually do not create. Where roads are built, which teachers are hired, the quality of public service areas such as parks and libraries, how fast the snow is cleared off of streets – even the racial and economic balance of the schools our children attend is not decided by the people making up the society. Society creates institutions such as marriage, political parties, corporations, the military, and the family within which the roles people play define us. C. Wright Mills (author of *The Sociological Imagination*) notes, 'to understand the biology of an individual, we must understand the significance of the meaning of the roles he has played and does play; to understand these roles we must understand the institutions of which they are a part'.[6] Within the institution of family we find singular generational mazes, a family's own particular dynamics, and generationally-based expectations for the behaviour of its members.

When we look at individual families, we see perspectives emanating from the four generational archetypical templates as well as the chronological generational order from wealth creation exerting a powerful influence over the making of decisions. Another word that can be used for this influence – in reference to both types of generational perspectives – is bias. Although the archetypes identified by Strauss and Howe directly apply to larger society generational cohorts, their influence – or bias – seeps into the family through the generational archetypical lenses. The larger society archetypical influences do not vanish simply because we are looking at a much smaller society called 'family'. Although they do not collectively create their own 'persona' within the family structure, common archetypical characteristics do make their way into the family simply because family members are also members of a larger society generational cohort. Even if, as individuals, they do not conform completely to the characteristics of their generation, they deal with those characteristics and are, therefore, affected by them.[7]

Every generation is shaped 'by their beliefs and behaviors and their location in history. These in turn are shaped by older generations who themselves belong to older generations who came before them. Generations are created young by history, then go on to create history themselves,' according to Strauss and Howe.[8] The governing generation's values, management styles, and outlooks on life define acceptable family behaviour and the way the family business is conducted. In the process, the governing generation subconsciously assigns roles to family members that fit within the value system it holds dear, the management style it believes is best, and the boundaries of what it deems is acceptable behaviour. This is why knowledge of widely held generational attitudes can be a powerful tool for families wishing to defy the Proverb.

How generational perspectives assign roles

Family dynamics may be dually identified as clues to the deeper level of homogenous family function or as symptoms of family dysfunction, particularly around the family wealth. The basis for the functional or dysfunctional state is embedded in the underlying generational perspectives, both archetypical and chronological, the roles those perspectives may assign to family members, and the resulting expectations for behaviour. At no other time in history have generational perspectives held such active and direct implications for wealth management and wealth transfer considerations. Greater longevity means three, sometimes four – in rare cases, five – generations may be living at one time. Multiply those numbers by the numbers of family members within each generation and complexities arise in wealth management which were never envisioned by founding wealth creators – or their advisors – as recently as a generation or two ago.

Whatever the generational frame of reference of family leadership, it will colour leadership's perception of the roles family members should perform. In turn, each family member's generational template will shape his or her own role perception. As leadership imposes its own template by consciously or subconsciously assigning roles to family members, the manner in which family members interact with each other also is determined. Hidden rules become part of the family's framework or 'personality'. The degree of openness and communication among family members is determined. These dynamics are the framework through which the assignation of roles – either authentic or imposed – occurs. These roles may or may not enable the family member's authentic wealth to flourish.

Assigned roles have a great effect on the life choices family members may have. Once such roles are assigned, needs associated with those roles are identified and motivation enters in to satisfy them. For example, a family member who is viewed as the 'black sheep' may cause leadership to identify a need to 'protect' the material wealth from the 'irresponsible' actions of that family member. Whether the family member is indeed an irresponsible black sheep or if this is merely a perceived role assigned by leadership seems irrelevant to leadership's – and to family members other than the black sheep – identification of the need to protect the material wealth. Leadership is subsequently motivated to set certain goals, either alone or with the help of other family members or external advisors, designed to fulfil the need to protect.

Or an eldest son may be viewed as more competent than his siblings to take over the family business simply based on leadership's perception with no effort to understand either child's true passions or abilities. Needs are identified, goals are set, and mechanisms put in place to segue control of the family business to the adult child who is perceived to be the most appropriate person to fill that role. This is a chronological generational bias which completely ignores the fact that a younger son – or perhaps a daughter – might actually have the passion and talent to carry the business to new heights of success. In some traditionally patriarchal families, as sons have proven to have greater spending ability than passion for the family business, patriarchs have turned their focus to daughters as possible grooming candidates for succession. This is the result of the patriarch's understanding that an assigned role (elder son taking over the business) may not be an authentic role.

Another example is the archetypical role assignment based on the view of appropriate gender roles. The GI generation (during a High when gaps in gender roles are widest) certainly felt appropriate roles for women and men were quite different. The Boomer generation (during an Unravelling when gaps in gender roles are at their narrowest) saw a giant leap of women entering the workforce and men becoming significantly more involved with the care of their children whether or not they actually gave up their jobs to become primary caretaker. This is certainly an example of how larger society archetypical roles affect family life!

Roles, whether archetypical or chronologically based, either open or close choices family members have to develop and possibly materialise their authentic wealth. In the case above of the father's expectation that the son will take over the business, this chronological generational bias may completely mismatch the expectation of the father to the authentic wealth of that particular son. It asks the son to steward the father's dream instead of his own. Unless the son chooses the father's dream for himself by reinterpreting it through his own generational lens, and unless the father is willing to allow the son the freedom with which to do that, this type of generational bias has the power to affect the health of the business.[9] This, of course, affects the wealth of the overall family, every investor in the business if it is private, and if it is public, every shareholder who invested in the business through the public markets.

In the case of acceptable gender roles, can you imagine the obstacles which would have been faced by a GI father wishing to stay home to care for his children while his wife worked? Of course, this was less than a realistic possibility for most at that time because larger society made caring for the children strictly the role of women and women were a rarity in the workplace. If a daughter had indeed had more talent than the son, she may never have had the opportunity to develop that talent, even to the point where she could prove her abilities in the workplace setting. Considering the stark difference in societal attitudes and expectations in the GI and Boomer generations regarding appropriate gender roles, it is easy to see how these influences affect family wealth.

Such expectations emanating from generational perceptions also affect how family members interact with each other, what we refer to as family dynamics. A GI or Silent patriarch may wonder why his daughters are not more interested in the family's affairs and also may experience consternation at what he perceives are spendthrift and frivolous activities in which his daughters are engaged. Over time, those role assignments (spendthrift, socialite) continue to widen the chasm between the father and his daughters which most certainly affects the way he treats them as well as the way he manages the wealth while he is still living and the plans he makes to distribute the wealth after his death.

If, however, the dynamics of this family are examined more closely, we observe that while the patriarch is talking during family meetings, his eyes naturally divert to the daughters' husbands, functioning completely away from the brain-embedded penchant for connection which operates to make these women feel their father has no interest in what they think. Moreover, the social activities the daughters are involved in, labelled as 'frivolous' by the patriarch, are instead active fundraising work in an area to which the patriarch has made contributions and about which he has told stories to all three of his children. Thus, we have family dynamics which inhibit communication and trust, we have generationally assigned roles which completely camouflage the authentic wealth of the daughters – at least in their father's eyes – and we have a perceived role the patriarch is occupying which introduces more risk to the family wealth in multiple ways – a topic for discussion in greater depth for Chapter 18.

Understanding roles of family members

Now that we see that there are indeed generational biases which determine the dynamics of the family and that these generational biases assign roles that may either be appropriate or inappropriate based on the authentic wealth of family members, we can take a look at the different types of roles family members occupy and how those roles factor into the way the family wealth is managed.

Archetypical roles

Since every family member is also a member of a generational archetype, we'll start with the roles each archetype plays within the larger society. Like the four seasons of the year, the four archetypes govern the formation of the four generational 'seasons' of each century. As no winter, spring, summer, or fall are exactly the same as the last winter, spring, summer, or fall, neither does any generation reinterpret its archetype in exactly the same way.[10] But, like the seasons, there are basic characteristics which can be expected, against which we can observe individual variations.

Strauss and Howe note that each generation has the freedom to choose which role it will play based on a limited number of choices pre-scripted by the societal collective unconsciousness.[11] These role choices fall within the realm of the social role of each archetype as follows.

- The Hero's archetypical role is to establish social order (from the previous Crisis).
- The Artist's archetypical role is to maintain the status quo.
- The Prophet's archetypical role is to unravel the previous social order.
- The Nomad's archetypical role is to lead society through the next crisis.

Each member of the cohort experiences four basic stages of life and each stage has a particular social role to fill. In childhood we are nurtured and receive values. With young adult vitality, we serve institutions and test the values we received as children. Midlife power enables us to manage institutions and apply the values we learned and tested. The leadership of elderhood enables us to transfer those values to the next generation.[12]

The last three stages are aligned with the three stage-of-life roles that Hughes identifies: apprentices in youth, leaders in midlife, and mentors and educators as elders.

Based on the larger society archetypical roles, Strauss and Howe make broad generalisations about the nature of archetypical childhood, youth, middle age, and elderhood.[13]

- Hero children grow up increasingly protected; as young adults they become heroic team members; in midlife, they demonstrate energetic hubris; they are powerful as elders and are the subject of attack during the next Awakening.
- Artists grow up overprotected during a Crisis; are sensitive young adults; indecisive leaders in mid-life; and empathetic elders.
- Prophets are increasingly indulged as children; they are narcissistic crusaders in young adulthood; moralistic, principled mid-lifers; and wise elders during a Crisis.
- Nomads grow up as underprotected children; feel alienated as young adults; are pragmatic leaders in mid-life; and tough elders during a post-Crisis era.

Do individuals vary within these generalised characteristics? Of course. However, knowing the larger society characteristics may help GI or Silent parents understand why their Boomer children were narcissistic young adults; or Boomer grandparents understand why their Echo grandchildren are overprotected; or why their Gen-X children surprise them so with their leadership in mid-life.

Family roles versus individual roles

As we bring roles down from the larger society level to the family, the first thing we realise is that there are individual roles and also family roles. In a family of wealth, there are also family business roles – roles family members play relative to whatever the family business happens to be (operating company, group of investments, a particular type of assets the family owns together, and so on). According to Hughes, every family member has two roles: that of Dynamic Stakeholder Owner[14] and that of altruistic supporter of other family members' dreams.

We can conclude from this that a successful family is made of dynamic stakeholder owners and as such, requires a dynamic wealth management process – one that clearly matches the dynamics of the family. The only way to match the dynamics of the family is to understand the origin of those dynamics. If a family wishes to change its dynamics to foster the flourishing of authentic wealth, it must examine the roles each family member is performing to ensure the authenticity of those roles. The role of dynamic stakeholder owner is an authentic role for every family member since it allows the family member's authentic wealth to contribute to the overall wealth of the family, whether by materialising his or her authentic wealth or developing that wealth in a way that contributes to the wealth of the family.

Exhibit 9.1

Dynamic Stakeholder Owner[15] chart

Dynamic (social capacities)	Stakeholder (intellectual capacities)	Ownership (human capacities)
Networking	Ideas	Structure and organisation
Ways of communicating	Strategies	People power
Generational perspectives	Delegation	Responsibilities
Marketing	Individual stake	Realised ROI
Family dynamics	Incentives	Roles
Influence	Wishes and dreams	Family identity

Source: graymatter Strategies LLC with permissioned use of 'Dynamic Stakeholder Owner'.

As we see in Exhibit 9.1, the nature of each word used to describe this type of role flows into the flourishing of the authentic capacities of family members and match each area of authentic wealth. The capacities listed under 'Dynamic' are active and require the social involvement of human beings. Having a stake in something inspires intellectual capacities such as new business ideas and strategies, the ability and wisdom to delegate, to personally envision the value of future individual return, and the fulfilment of wishes and desires. As an owner, human capacities of structure and organisation, people power, the realisation of investment return, roles people occupy, and the family identity.

Dynamic stakeholder ownership springs from the virtues of family discussed in Chapter 8. It is a purposeful educational process that should begin as early in life as possible. It is much easier to grow up with the values inherent in dynamic stakeholder ownership than to try to instil them after the fact, although that most certainly can be done.

Outside dynamic stakeholder ownership, authentic wealth of family members may be discounted, camouflaged, or go completely unnoticed. Pursuits which lie outside of a governing generation's interpretation of what is 'acceptable' and worth investing time, money, and energy to develop may be the one thing that carries a family to greater heights of material wealth or social influence. It may also be the one aspect of wealth creation which, completely unrelated to capital markets, could carry the family through a severe or extended crisis.

For example, becoming an artist or a musician or a writer could seem to be a non-contributory pursuit, especially if that role is viewed generationally as an inappropriate role and thus, not supported by the dynamics of the family. What if the artist had the potential to be another David Hockney? Or the musician, another Jean-Yves Thibaudet? Or the writer, another J.K. Rowling or Beatrix Potter? Certainly, the writing of children's fantasies does not hold the same attraction for support from families of wealth than starting and running a technology company might. Is that talent, however, necessarily any less authentic or its potential any less meaningful for the family's future from a wealth materialisation standpoint?

It is impossible to dynamically manage the authentic wealth of the family without knowing and understanding the authentic roles of the family members. By employing generational perspectives as a vital tool, families discover their authentic wealth – wealth they may never otherwise fully be aware of or fully understand how to appreciate. So, how do we recognise authentic roles?

An authentic role:

1 illuminates the authentic assets of each family member;
2 offers fulfilment and happiness to its occupant;
3 expands the feeling of safety and belonging while at the same time, validating the individuation of family members;
4 demands a more efficient form of governance and interaction; and
5 expands the possibility spectrum; that is, the wealth of the family or its ability to materialise wealth.

Awareness and knowledge of the various perspectives of each generation enables family members to discuss their abilities and passions without fear of judgment or criticism, which often is the result of one generation simply doing things differently than another or one generation having a different outlook on life than the other. Hauser notes that the older generations took a very serious approach to life and viewed having fun as being immature. 'Their kids were the Baby Boomers who really haven't had the chance to control any wealth. They've been kept in the dark in terms of family wealth and don't have the training or expectation of using it in any serious way for their own life goals. The generation after the Baby Boomers sees that after the bubble burst, it was difficult to find employment anywhere. They don't have this set of rules and there's a lot of angst about what to do with themselves.' This example weaves both archetypical and chronological perspectives together, noting the older (G1) generation's belief in hard work, then switching to the Boomer (G2) generation's chronological role of maintaining the wealth, and the Echo generation's characteristic of 'not having a set of rules'.

Handler gives a perfect example of chronological generational differences. 'One of the struggles the entrepreneurial generation has had in recent years is in figuring out why the younger generations don't understand what the older ones are doing or why. The younger ones have grown up with servants and butlers and cars all over the driveway and when they're asked to do certain things, they accuse the older generation of "controlling their lives". It's not reasonable to expect them to have the same perspective,' he notes.

With all this in mind, we see the need to drill down to family members' authentic roles. When we realise the context within which family members are responding to our behaviour, we can take a step back and create better understanding.

Authentic roles

When two people come together with the purpose of forming a family, their generational imprint has already been formed. They have predisposed ideas of the roles each of them occupy and they begin a discussion through which those ideas form the dynamics of relationship between them.[16] As they form their dynamics together, roles they occupy can be classified in two categories: family roles and family business roles. Family roles are simply that – any relationship within the family – spouse, sibling, parent, child, grandchild, and so on. These seem obvious and perhaps irrelevant but they factor in to a greater degree than one might think. Family business roles are any role a family member occupies that has to do with whatever the business of the family happens to be at the time. They include founder, CEO, trustee, beneficiary, benefactor, family office executive, and so on.

As the founding generation (G1) of two people come together, their initial familial roles may include:

- spouse;
- sibling (if they each have them);
- child (of each of their parents); and
- grandchild (if their grandparents are still living).

Their family business roles may include:

- founder;
- co-founder;
- CEO;
- private equity partner; and
- owner.

As their family grows and children are born, grow up, and start their own family units, the familial roles add:

- parent;
- grandparent;
- protector;
- family relationship facilitator;
- peace keeper; and
- educator/mentor.

The familial roles of their children may also include:

- spouse;
- parent;
- child;
- sibling;
- grandchild;
- black sheep;
- successor apparent;
- family relationship facilitator;
- protector;
- peace keeper;
- family spendthrift; and
- family disruptor (addiction, mental health issues).

The family business roles of all family members may be added to the business roles above:

- trustee;
- beneficiary;
- benefactor;
- family office executive;
- entrepreneur;
- family leader;
- family committee member; and
- board member.

There are any number of roles which could be added to this list, some of which will be indigenous to a particular family's 'differentness'.[17] Which of these roles are likely to be innately authentic? Certainly these since they are states of being, either through birth or by relationship choice:

- spouse;
- parent;
- child;
- grandchild;

- sibling; and
- cousin.

And possibly these:

- peacekeeper;
- protector; and
- family relationship facilitator.

But not necessarily these:

- protector;
- family relationship facilitator;
- black sheep;
- family addict;
- family spendthrift;
- family leader;
- successor apparent; and
- family office executive.

Someone who is considered the family's Black Sheep could simply be a subsequent generation member who views life and his or her purpose in it differently than the founding generation (G1). He or she could also be a Gen-X child to Silent parents, a Boomer child to GI parents, or any other generational combination. His or her talents may lie in art or music instead of in the family 'tradition' of doctor or lawyer – or entrepreneur.

We can apply the litmus test for authenticity by looking at the example of Black Sheep. We can look at this person and ask ourselves, does this person's role expand the feeling of safety and belonging while, at the same time, validating his or her own individuation? Do the talents of this person make room for or illuminate the authentic assets of other family members? From the founding generation's viewpoint (still viewing the person as the Black Sheep), the answer to both questions would definitely be 'no'. However, if the founding generation, in this case, were to ask the designated Black Sheep what he or she really wanted to do in life, that answer might change (on both counts) to 'yes'.

Someone occupying the role of Family Peace Keeper may actually hate conflict and may be playing that role out of self preservation rather than from authenticity. His or her authentic role may actually be Entrepreneur but the role of Peace Keeper occupies so much of his or her time, energy, and attention that the authentic role becomes thwarted.

Noting the importance of roles within the family, Ussery notes, 'Roles in the family are critical. The more inclusive the family can be of the gifts and talents of each family member, the more the family can develop an identity. The strengths and weaknesses of each family member should be identified in order to define the specific roles that should be fulfilled. You decide what needs to be done, then you match people's vocations with their avocations.'

The following case study illustrates how generational perspectives translate into roles family members occupy and also how the dynamics of family affect communication and trust regarding the material and financial wealth. It further implicates the impact of generational role perceptions on goal formation and on goal-based allocation. Although certain aspects of the family scenario are fictitious, the family's situation is based on a conglomerate of real-life family examples.

Family case study[18]

Take, for example, a family with a total of $225 million, one third of which was originally invested in four private companies the GI founder found attractive late in his life and which the Silent children have inherited. The Silents have since added investments in four more private companies. In the original four, the family had a controlling interest, however, two of the companies have since merged with larger companies; in the newer investments, there was only a minority interest. One of the minority interest companies is teetering on the brink of failure and the family will most likely experience a loss.

There is a management team which includes a Boomer child (one of two brothers) of the Silents (the heirs) who has shown interest in learning about new companies as well as one of his three Gen-X sibling children. The other Boomer son and the other Gen-X siblings know there is family wealth, but they have no idea how much or about any of the investments. They resent the fact that one sibling of each generation does have this information, although they are not sure how much is really known. This entire situation has set up distrust among the two sets of siblings and between the younger Boomer son and the Silent parents. The Gen-X management team member is particularly upset about the impending failure of one of the companies, although the family only holds a minority interest, and feels that too great a portion of the family wealth is exposed to private equity concerns. The family wealth is extensive and he feels the focus should change from continuing to grow the wealth to preserving it for future generations. He is able to talk to his Boomer father but the father feels helpless to change things since his Silent parents feel they are honouring their GI father (the founder) by successfully continuing his pattern of investing. The Boomer parent feels stuck since the Silent heirs have made it clear they expect the older Boomer son to carry on the investment tradition.

With all the secrecy regarding the wealth, there is little consideration of the current needs of the other two Gen-X siblings. One wishes to start a business of her own since she has a keen interest and genuine talent for clothing design. Her parents have sent her to the right schools to develop her talent, but support for her abilities has stopped there. She has earned an opportunity to study in Paris with a major fashion designer but, since her funds are in trust until she is 35, she has no way to fund the opportunity herself. Her Boomer parents feel she should learn the value of 'real work', and have offered to provide a nice apartment in a major city while she builds a career in another field. She can later fund her dream herself from any savings she may accumulate.

Regardless, all three Gen-X siblings wish to know about the extent of the wealth and how decisions are made regarding its management and future distribution.

The assets of this family are currently divided as follows: income from the private equity investments (30%) flows into liquidity (5%) and capital preservation buckets (40%); the assets in trust (25%) are in conservative growth buckets; and the Silent parents receive income from a Charitable Remainder Trust (CRT) that was set up by the GI parent founder. An astute, generational-perspectives-conscious wealth advisor could approach the Silent parents, who are both in good health and only in their early seventies, and ask them what they fear might happen if information about the family wealth and how it is currently invested were given to the entire family. How do they weigh the value of maintaining secrecy about the wealth since it has grown to its current size compared to the needs and concerns other family members may have? She could also ask them about their feelings regarding continuing to grow the wealth since the older Boomer son has successfully generated other wealth to leave his own legacy to his family and the younger Boomer son is also more than self sufficient, although not as successful as his brother.

The advisor could propose the idea that the Silents serve as educators to the Gen-Xers and fulfil their need to learn about managing the family wealth in a prudent manner now that the wealth is of fairly significant size. This could open the door to communication with both generations succeeding the Silents. When the Boomer parents see the interest of their Gen-X children in learning about preserving the family wealth through good management, they may feel better about funding the Gen-X daughter's Paris opportunity, especially if she agrees to reconsider her career track if certain measures of success are not attained.

The family wealth allocation may then be shifted to a possible allocation of 10% private equity, 15% liquidity to fund the Paris opportunity and provide a better 'emergency' fund for the elderly Silents, 50% capital preservation, and the 25% growth in the trusts to provide additional capital for the Gen-X daughter's business if she passes her success measures. The Boomer parents agree to make a family loan for the daughter to start her business if she successfully meets the previously agreed upon measures. The income stream for the Silents remains from the CRT.

Implications

By addressing these concerns and needs of each generation and highlighting the danger to the family legacy of keeping succeeding generations in the dark, it may be possible to open a conversation between all four generations to discover feelings about the wealth, how it should be managed, and why. The wealth can then be reapportioned as time goes by to serve the needs of the family and to promote the family's intellectual, human, and social capacities which will preserve the family legacy for generations to come. In the case cited above, one result could be the comfort the Boomer parents might feel from providing the promise of well-earned support for their daughter's dream. On one hand, they would be improving the relationship with their daughter by supporting her talent; on another, if she surpasses the measures used to gauge her success and the parents end up giving her start-up money for her new business, they could consider themselves to be carrying on the family tradition of investing in new businesses – something that should also make the Silent grandparents happy.

Even if Silent heirs are not willing to open such communication, the Boomer children may be. Dialogue among the latter generations can initiate a foundation for a more cohesive future focus for the family wealth after the Silent 'keepers of the wealth' have passed on. In the case where Boomer parents have either created their own wealth or inherited wealth from their Silent parents and are concerned about spoiling their children, opening a dialogue early enough in the process – before Gen-X children enter the work force or Echo children come of age – may allow parents to see the motivation and sense of responsibility characteristic of the younger generations.

As noted earlier, successful management of a family's authentic wealth requires dynamism and life-generating energy to defeat the proverb – the key word here is dynamism, what Hughes calls a critical ingredient to wealth preservation. This means taking the time (instead of end-gaining) to know family members well and to help them know themselves so that the authentic wealth of each has the opportunity to emerge, develop, and regenerate the family's wealth – possibly in surprising and unforeseen ways. The only way to discover authentic wealth is through communication, trust, and leadership. These are the topics of focus for Chapter 16.

---

[1] Kearl, M.C., 'Self types and their differences across generations and the life-cycle,' Trinity University, San Antonio, TX, Fall 2010: www.trinity.edu/mKearl/socpsy-6.html.

[2] Six entries found for *dynamics*: http://dictionary.reference.com/search?q=dynamics.

[3] A term used in connection with the Alexander Technique: http://www.hilaryking.net/glossary/end-gaining.html.

[4] Strogatz, S., 'Change we can live with', *The New York Times*, April 2010.

[5] Ibid.

[6] Lareau, A., *Unequal Childhoods: class, race, and family life*, (Los Angeles, CA: University of California Press, 2003), p. 15.

[7] Strauss, W. and Howe, N., *The Fourth Turning: an American prophecy,* (New York, NY: Broadway Books, 1997), pp. 68, 69.

[8] Strauss, W. and Howe, N., *Millennials Rising: the next Great Generation*, (New York, NY: Vintage Books, 2000), p. 33.

[9] Hughes, James E., Jr., Personal interview, August 2007.

[10] Strauss, W. and Howe, N., *The Fourth Turning: an American prophecy,* (New York, NY: Broadway Books, 1997), pp. 106, 107.

[11] Ibid, p. 74.

[12] Ibid, p. 54.

[13] Ibid, p. 84.

[14] Hughes, James E., Jr., Personal interview, August 2007.

[15] Term used with permission from James E. Hughes, Jr., personal interview, August 2007.

[16] Minuchin, S. and Fishman, H.C., 'Family therapy techniques,' President and fellows of Harvard College, 1981 and 1996, p. 16.

[17] Hughes, J.E., Jr., *Family Wealth: keeping it in the family*, (New York, NY: Bloomberg Press, 2004), p. 31. Hughes refers to a family's unique identity that sets it apart from any other family as its 'differentness'.

[18] Gray, L., 'Generational perspectives and their effects on goal-based asset allocation', *The Journal of Wealth Management,* Spring 2006, p. 9. This case study was taken from the previously published article listed here.

Chapter 10

The three forms of governance: an introduction

'The best form of governance depends upon the nature of the specific enterprise.'

Lee Hausner and Douglas Freeman[1]

Quite a few books have been written on the topic of governance relative to family wealth and some of the best ones are listed in the bibliography of this book. In my work with families of wealth, however, I have found the word 'governance' to be quite a misunderstood concept. It seems to function as one of the all-encompassing, catch-all words the family office and wealth management industries overuse to the point of losing its original meaning. For that reason, I find it much easier to break the concept of governance into three segments which are aligned with the respective needs of the family entities they serve so that families and their advisors can better understand what governance truly is, the full scope of the benefits it has to offer, and how it should indeed serve them as a family of wealth.

The concept of governance is such that its role of serving the family is often misinterpreted as a set of rules to be followed. I believe that does the concept of governance a grave disservice which also means its most valuable benefits are eluding many families.

In this chapter and the four following, we concern ourselves with the issue of governance as it applies to three primary entities of the family: the family itself, the business of the family, and the family office – another service entity whose role often becomes perceived rather than authentic. Governance is the place where the progression of generational perspectives, family roles, and family dynamics meet. The three come together as the family make decisions about all forms of its wealth, consciously and dynamically or subconsciously and with inertia. Thus, we have come to a crux point of our journey of exploration and the process of testing the over-riding premise of this entire body of work. For it is from the entrance of governance on the family wealth field that generational views, family roles, and family dynamics are solidified; it is the point at which family leadership begins to make decisions that will affect family members' lives for generations to come.

Another intriguing aspect of governance is the view that only large families need it. Any family in its second generation needs a governance system even of the simplest form. Usually, smaller families – and many larger ones – wait until issues surrounding the wealth are so entrenched, it is almost impossible to think of effectively making decisions together.

These chapters offer plausible solutions to these problems. If you can stretch your mind a bit, we can expand the processes of family systems to open new possibilities. Perhaps we can try thinking of governance through a different lens. In real terms, governance is the opposite of an onerous set of guidelines or a family rule book. It is the doorway through which all the discussions we have had so far are translated from philosophy into pragmatic utility by the family. I like to call family governance the 'keeper of the joy'. When governance is formed effectively, that is its most authentic role.

Therefore, I urge readers to ponder these four chapters within the context of the entire book. If such is beyond the reader's internal control, reading these chapters apart from the whole will serve some purpose – hopefully, it will incite the urge to read what comes before and after! *Extracting the governance chapters independently through an urgent, although sincere, desire to 'get a system in place' will result in misapplication of the very principles of governance which are so critical to a family's success.* Governance has a specific role within the scope of the Generational Wealth Management Continuum[SM]. Please remember as you read these chapters that any form of family governance is designed to provide a means for the higher functioning of the joint decision making[2] process – no more and no less. Governance is not the end all; it is a tool which can be invaluable in fostering the growth of the family wealth.

At this juncture, everything we have discussed enters the process of translation into practical application for the family and its advisors. Each of the previous chapters points its subject matter to the formation of the governance structures within the overall Generational Wealth Management Continuum[SM] described in Chapter 1. Further, the discussion of governance does not end here. Like a mortgage-backed security, governance is a flow-through entity, only with a different type of principal and interest, the 'principal' in this case is the family and the 'interest' is the materialisation of its authentic assets. What flows through governance seeps into every aspect of managing the family wealth.

Governance also serves as a conduit for a family's strength of unity – its 'affinity' according to Hughes. The relationship between the three forms of governance can make the family practically impermeable and is depicted in Exhibit 10.1 in a triangle shape, the strongest of the geometric shapes. Exhibit 10.1 employs the triangle to show the strength of support the governance systems can offer the family's three types of entities. This only works when the proper hierarchy is in place with family governance dominant and on top with family office governance and family business governance supporting the other two sides.

Exhibit 10.1

The three forms of governance: the Family Governance Triangle[SM] [3]

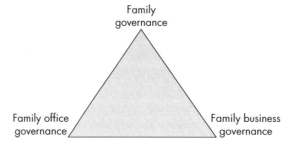

Source: graymatter Strategies LLC.

With family governance taking the lead, we see that the family office and the family business get their directives from the family and, in turn, support the development of the family's authentic wealth.

Essential points of application follow in the next four chapters for the purpose of creating a robust integration of the complete cycle of the Generational Wealth Management Continuum^{SM} from beginning to end – from consideration of a family's particular generational maze to a dynamic, highly customised, and successful strategic allocation of all of its forms of assets and their flourishing so that they may be used to fulfil lives and to flow back to nurture the authentic wealth of future generations.

Here is offered a different approach to governance, both in concept and in function. It is assumed that the reader has already developed significant knowledge about running a business and thus, the day-to-day particulars of business governance. Therefore, our treatise will offer an examination of: (a) family governance; (b) family office governance; (c) those aspects of corporate governance which pertain to fulfilment of the family's goals and needs for the successful growth of its authentic wealth as well as its financial capital; (d) how each form of governance differs; and (e) how each is essential to the others' overall service to the family.

Clarification will be brought first by defining governance relative to our discussion. To lay the proper foundation for considering the implications and proper positioning of governance, the three family entities to be governed will be explored on the basis of the needs and goals of each. With this foundation laid, these four chapters will examine the appropriate governance issues for each entity based on the purpose the governance system for that entity is to serve. Finally, the three forms of governance will be brought together conceptually under a single umbrella to support the goals of the family – including goals of dynamic wealth preservation of all its forms of capital and avoidance of the Proverb's edict. The fourth of the governance chapters (Chapter 14) highlights a successful seven-generation family with fifth-generation leadership to illustrate how the three forms of governance work together in practice.

Governance is a service process

The word 'governance' brings to mind a variety of denotations. Through a Google search one can find definitions related to corporate, clinical, water, technology, or electricity governance, among others.[4] From these, we can deduce that the definition of governance hinges upon the particular entity being governed. Therefore, we may also logically conclude that, since the family, the family office, and the family business are different entities with different needs, a different form of governance must be adopted to serve each. This is not to say that three separate governing bodies must be formed, although it may prove beneficial for some families to form more than one; rather, the conceptual separation of these three forms of governance within the overall management of the family and its enterprises holds the key to successful translation into family goal achievement.

Note also that the notion of governance is connected to the concept of service. Its most perfect design emanates from the needs of the family identified from the roles they occupy within the family's particular generational maze. Thus, for the purposes of our discussion, governance will be primarily defined as the portal through which the family's goals may be translated into a pragmatic format or system for achievement. The key result of the examination of these three forms of governance, how they function within each family entity, and how they support each others' effectiveness must be to effect the implementation of systems which will actively integrate the principles of joint decision making on a day-to-day basis for the ultimate purpose of achieving the family's goals over the span of a long human life – and even beyond.

Governance can be a mighty force in preserving the wealth of the family but only if it is employed in a manner that supports the definitions of *family, family wealth, and wealth transfer* formulated in previous chapters. Families of all types – regardless of net worth – have some sort of governance system either by design or by default. Every family, regardless of size or chronological generation, makes decisions. Successful families make purposeful decisions based on input from all family members within the expanded definition of family wealth.

Governance is the means to an ever-changing end within a particular goal. The goal is to foster the family wealth in its truest definition from generation to generation. Therefore, there can be no specific, immovable end designated for the governance process – only periodic benchmarks along the way to accomplishing the ultimate goal of fostering the wealth. Such a goal is designed to span a minimum of 100 years – the span of a long human life. Certainly, no generation can effectively foster family wealth through rigid dictates over such a period of time even through the most iron-clad structures. In fact, the attempt to set up such a governance structure for even 25 years – the approximate span of one generation – with no provision for change tempts the limits of the linear time view outlined in Chapter 3.

Drawing on the importance of the cyclical view of time, we note that life is itself in continual motion, accomplishing small achievements of ebb and flow all the while moving toward its ultimate goal of sustaining its own form on the planet century over century. In like fashion, families – made up of living beings – naturally thrive when they govern themselves in a flexible manner within the context of the generational cycles they experience, keeping their eyes on their ultimate goal. Thus, any effort by a single generation to staunchly 'protect' future generations in iron-clad fashion from being ruined by the wealth will inevitably fail. It is an illusory type of 'control'; after the controlling generation is deceased, subsequent generations usually find a way to do things the way they want. The stories in the Preamble give testimony to this in more than one instance.

What may appear to be an achievable benchmark within a single generation of leadership almost certainly will not be as meaningful to future generations – or even current ones. Thus, the proper focus of governance is any reasonable benchmark which can be attained within the broader goal or legacy of fostering the wealth from generation to generation. This melds with Brunel's observation that family legacies are universal in the sense that they do not focus solely on the question of financial wealth or philanthropy. They are larger than any such singular focus. Rather, a legacy 'is inherited or learned by each generation and then re-interpreted by that generation into the legacy that it will pass on to the next one'.[5] That re-interpretation by each generation gives cycles of generations spanning 100 years or longer the opportunity to fine tune adjustments to the governance structure at regular intervals, minimising the risk of a major linear time adjustment which can destroy families and maximising the opportunities a family has for materialising its authentic wealth.

Another way families and their advisors may think of governance is through the development of a family mission statement and/or family constitution. There is almost an over emphasis by families and advisors today on getting such documents in place with the result that, often, the essential work of building a shared vision through long discussion required to make these documents truly valuable instruments for the family gets overlooked. In today's increasingly fast-paced world, many families ask advisors and consultants to 'just tell us what we need to do'. The documents are created over the span of a few days – possibly during a family meeting – and leadership is happy because something is in place and the documents may seem to work ... for a while. Without the hard work required to educate the family members and to enable them to offer valuable, thoughtful input, any seeming benefit gained by the creation of the documents may be short-lived.

When these documents are the result of a family's efforts over multiple generations to thought-fully structure a process which values the input of all family members for the benefit of all family members for generations to come, their benefit becomes much longer lasting. What a gift *that* would be to future generations! The ability to see how decisions were made over past generations along with the changes that were implemented along the way! Knowing also that these decisions and changes were made jointly with a larger goal in mind would allow future generations to see the how the virtues of the family were nurtured along the way.

Advisors wishing to serve families through a different role and who understand the importance of leading a family thoughtfully through such a process help make such a gift even richer. But when 'governance' has been developed over a weekend meeting for the sake of being able to say, 'we have a family mission statement and we have a family constitution', the resulting documents have embedded within them the greater likelihood of fostering the natural fulfilment of the law of entropy rather than an energising force for the family wealth.[6]

Effective governance is a set of processes and systems which have been carefully designed and considered by leadership based on input from the family and voluntarily adopted by all family members specifically to serve the family and to protect as well as to foster the family's authentic wealth. It cannot be over emphasised that the primary ingredients in successful governance are: (a) input from all family members and careful consideration of that input by family leadership within the larger concept of family; and (b) voluntary buy-in from family members with the understanding that their input has been acknowledged, recorded, and valued even if it has not been directly imple-mented in the decisions at hand. These ingredients must be consistently included in the process of making any decision involving the family or the family's concerns.

As human beings, we may occasionally forget the reasons these ingredients are essential. Lessons sometimes have to be re-learned even by the most successful families. M. Laird Koldyke, chairman of the Laird Norton Company and managing partner of Winona Capital Management relates an experience where the board led an initiative for creating a vision for the future of the Laird Norton Company, the family, and the family's multiple businesses. 'When the recommendations, which involved some significant changes, were sent out to the family members, we got an unexpected response. The family felt that a small group had coalesced around an idea and made leaping decisions on behalf of 300 people which hadn't been fully discussed. We did not appropriately communicate to the family to get the acceptance and buy-in for these initiatives.' Koldyke notes that the value learned from this experience was *the realisation that the process by which family decisions are made is every bit as important as the merits of the decisions themselves.*

As noted earlier in this introduction, there are three distinct forms of governance which should be considered, at least from a conceptual standpoint, based on three distinct entities within which wealthy families function. Each of the governance systems for the three entities supports the same goals – to serve the family and foster the materialisation of the family's authentic wealth. That is the basis for their relationship to each other and, hence, their role in supporting the continued development of the family wealth in all its forms.

Now that we have defined governance, offered a general overview of the governance process, and identified the three entities involved in governing family wealth, let us take a deeper look at each. First, we turn our attention to the entity of the family.

---

[1] Hausner, L. and Freeman, D.K., *The Legacy Family*, (New York, NY: St. Martin's Press, 2009), p. 55.

[2] Hughes, James E., Jr., Personal interview, August 2007.

[3] The Family Governance Triangle[SM] is a service mark owned by graymatter Strategies LLC.

[4] Definitions of 'governance' on the Web: www.google.com/search?hl=en&client=firefox-a&rls=org.mozilla:en-US:official &hs=cHS&defl=en&q=define:Governance&sa=X&oi=glossary_definition&ct=title.

[5] Brunel, J.L.P., 'Letter from the editor', *The Journal of Wealth Management*, Spring 2007, p. 1.

[6] Hughes, J.E., Jr., *Family: a compact among generations,* (New York, NY: Bloomberg Press, 2007), pp. 15, 32.

Chapter 11

Family governance

'... the process by which family decisions are made is every bit as important as the merits of the decisions themselves.'

M. Laird Koldyke,[1] the Laird Norton Family

The definition of family as the cycle of generations that defines our 'differentness'[2] through our affinity with each other distinguishes the family as an entity[3] larger than its individual members. We have now come to a point which will determine whether we may indeed proceed with the discussion of governance with any validity. Although I believe the above definition to be comprehensive, there are elements which further qualify the existence of a family. Thus, at this critical point, we must determine if there is indeed a family – or not.

So the task presented here is to:

1 decide if there indeed is an entity called 'family' which may be well served by a valid and effective form of governance;
2 in light of the above, create an understanding of the essential nature of the family's needs from a governance perspective;
3 investigate the nature of effective family governance; and
4 compare various governance structures and their ability to foster the family's authentic wealth and, subsequently, its tangible wealth.

Do we indeed have a family?

Hughes describes the characteristics of a family as follows: 'In a world of risk to ourselves and our dreams, we have to find a group to join that seems to offer us the security within its system to be safe and to fulfill those dreams.'[4] Being a part of such a group – a family – involves giving up some of our individual freedom in order to join this 'government' that is interested in our individual safety and in assisting us in the achievement of our dreams and the aspirations they inspire. Such a group – a family, our mini-society – provides the opportunity for the achievement of the individual goals of its members while achieving the needs of the entire group it serves,[5] an objective that would seem to be impossible. Part of the task of this chapter is to show how this objective can indeed be achieved.

There is a vast difference in a family as defined by a biological connection or blood relation and a family which, while comprehending the different individuals within and determining the values each generation wishes to cherish, is its own governing self – its own energetic entity as Hughes describes. Such an energetic and flourishing entity possesses and celebrates the four virtues which were outlined in Chapter 8. *According to Hughes, if a family does not possess these virtues, it ceases to be a family in the larger sense of a separate entity to which individual members can feel they belong.*[6]

Families can be enriched by the values they attempt to pass from one generation to the next. Indeed, the issue of governance is often brought into play within this context. But values alone are not enough, as they may change over time; a family's virtues, on the other hand, are part of its innate composition. They are consistent from generation to generation and make up the legacy – the family story – which the family passes on and which each generation adopts anew. This is why Brunel's conclusion that legacy is universal is so poignant. Without the recognition of family's innate virtues, we have no true entity of family; there is no legacy to pass on, which makes our discussion of family governance a futile exercise.

Joshua Pianko, private wealth advisor at an investment bank, refers to the family virtues as 'the family truths'. Inspired by the Preamble to the United States Declaration of Independence, a family's conceptual or symbolic statement that 'we hold these truths to be self-evident' within the interaction of its members (the family dynamics) reflects the identity the family wishes to pass on to future generations and the affinity through which each family member will be connected.

The virtues of family identified by Hughes – fusion, altruism, beauty as harmony, and joy as an expression of love – indeed reflect the family's truest identity, it's most authentic nature. They are the vehicle through which the family values are transferred. Each generation reinterprets the family virtues to rejuvenate the family's authentic wealth. Through this reinterpretation, each generation makes its unique contribution to the family story.

This is not just an American phenomenon; it is a global one. Nor is it prescriptive for a Western approach to family governance. In every culture, the family's innate truths are reflected through its heritage. The connection from current generations to generations past enables the family's most authentic – and most effective – structure of governance to be formed. Cultural influences refine this structure to keep the family's cultural heritage alive while fostering the authentic wealth of each family member. The family truths weave themselves throughout every decision making process the family encounters, holding testament to the truths which preserve each family's cultural identity as well as its authentic wealth. We saw how the generational perspectives of each culture discussed in Chapters 5, 6, and 7 impact the way family members relate to each other, the roles they occupy, and how decisions are made about matters of wealth. Every family in any culture has its singular generational maze colouring every aspect of decision making about its wealth.

The virtues of family, also known now as the family truths, are integrated into various discussions in this book. For now, we will adopt the position that the family as a separate entity, celebrating its virtues, does indeed exist. Thus, we have the basis for continuing our exploration of family governance.

What is … and is not … family governance

Family governance is the most critical structure governing the three entities identified in the introduction to these chapters on governance since the goals to be achieved are to be served by both the family office and the family business. The family governance structure creates the guidelines for governing not only the family, but also for governing every other family entity or sub-entity. The family council, family assembly, or other designated body is the manifestation of family governance and has the responsibility of:

1 housing and ensuring the fairness of the system through which decisions are made by the family;
2 reviewing its own systems as well as those of other governing bodies to ensure the dynamic nature and viability of all governing bodies; and
3 managing the relationship between the three entities being governed.

The family governance system must be the most flexible of the three forms. If the family governance piece is properly formulated to sustain an energised system of decision making within the larger goal, the probabilities of creating an overall process through integrated systems which support and enhance the wealth of the family are greatly increased.

M.J. Rankin agrees that family governance is the critical beginning point. She notes that consensus must be built within the family about mission, vision, and mutual and individual goals and objectives – the governance structure cannot just be what the patriarch thinks it needs to be. When there are new generations in the family, it is important to set up a governance structure that identifies who is going to take responsibility as a board both from an internal and external perspective – how decisions for the family will be made, what individual roles will be, what responsibilities need to be taken. Once the family governance structure is formed, it has to be determined if family members will be active in the family office. 'What is the family board and how do they run this operation of employees who work for the family to do certain things? Does a member of the office sit on the board or not?' These are essential questions – the answers to which are determined through the family governance system.[7]

Some families leave it to the family office to institute a family governance system. Thus, many family governance issues inadvertently are lumped in with the governance and functions of the family office. In that case, the family does not view itself as a separate and distinct entity, missing entirely the fact that the functioning of the family determines how well both the family office and the family business function. This is a mistake families also make when they are trying to set up a representative form of governance. Rather than have family representatives on the family council where they are most appropriate, they have family representatives on the board. This, once again, confuses the roles of the three governance structures so that one type of governance is trying to function within another's role.

When family governance functions are simply assumed by the family office – or are set up through the family business organisation – a great opportunity for family unity and identification is overlooked. This essentially robs the family of the opportunity to bring its authentic wealth to the forefront and to fully recognise the forces which influence their decision making.

From an asset management perspective, missing such an opportunity can become very costly. If we consider the assets of the family to be human, intellectual, and social as well as financial, it becomes easier to see that confusing family office governance with family governance is much like expecting returns from an investment which it is not designed to give. For example, the expectation that a dividend paying stock will perform like a growth stock simply because both investments happen to be in high performing companies; or expecting so-called hedge fund strategies which have a significant correlation to the equity markets to perform markedly differently than those same equity markets. The same type of opportunity costs exist for the asset called 'family' which we are systematically attempting to manage if the family office is designated as the governing entity for the family.

An appropriate role of the family office could be to offer support and advice in assisting the family in establishing a governance system; this can sometimes prevent biases and long-standing disagreements from colouring or impeding decision making.[8] However, the most effective way to neutralise such impediments to decision making is for the family to understand its generational biases, the resulting roles family members are occupying, and to recognise its authentic wealth. This removes perceived fears and threats which may inhibit joint decision making.[9] The family office is then free to serve its proper role of assisting the family in achieving the goals it has set, formulated from the needs identified from the roles family members occupy. Ultimately, the family itself is the only entity which knows itself well enough to design a long-lasting, flexible system of governance which will serve it well for multiple generations.

Family governance is the portal through which the family gains the necessary input for joint decision making. As evident in the case studies throughout this book, a lack of consensus can totally derail attempts by advisors to appropriately serve the family, causing the family to sabotage its own success. In this respect, it is important to note that governance merely provides the venue through which joint agreement may be achieved; the root causes of consensus building problems lie within the influence of generational perspectives and the resulting dynamics of the family.

In an effort to separate family governance functions from those of the family office, we can look at a brief list of services developed by the family based on an assessment of the needs of individual family members and the family as a whole. Particular needs will vary from family to family as they will arise from the dreams of family members and the desire of the family to support those dreams. We should note here that the dreams of family members represent the intellectual assets of the family and the future contributions to the family wealth by the next generations. Thus, as noted in Chapter 1, the dreams of the family may be considered an asset of the family which should be protected and encouraged to grow.

Some general needs applicable to most families and which might be considered within the realm of family governance involve the following areas.

1 Education, regarding:
   - family history and the family virtues[10] – how they enrich the legacy of the family;
   - the critical roles individual families within the family system play within the larger concept of family;
   - individual roles and responsibilities; and
   - family business matters as well as the duties of being a beneficiary and how to be a responsible stakeholder owner.
2 Structure and processes for application to the family bank:
   - for educational purposes;
   - for entrepreneurial purposes; and
   - for temporary support.
3 Structure for expressing ideas and opinions and receipt of validation by leadership.
4 Events which foster family unity:
   - activities for the 15 and under crowd;
   - media for recording the dreams of 14 and 15-year-old family members;
   - keeping the family history alive; and
   - getting to know other family members, fostering the family's spiritual assets.
5 Planning family meetings and agendas.

6 Intra-family marketing to support the flow of information and sense of connection.
7 Interviewing family advisors.
8 Stewarding the next generation's dreams.
9 Demystifying 'unspoken' rules of the family.

This list is by no means complete and many of these functions may seem to fall within the realm of the family office. Indeed, some of the functions may seem to be duplicated by a first glance at both lists (the family office list can be found in Chapter 13). However, the difference in the governance functions of the two entities becomes evident as we look at their respective roles, which are starkly different. The role of the family is to make decisions that will sustain and foster the family wealth. The role of the family office is to serve the family in implementing those decisions and to make internal decisions for operation, protection, and wealth management within the guidelines the family has set forth.

For example, the function of education within family governance will first consist of a joint decision by the family that certain forms of education are needed. A family member then expresses the need for such education to the family office and, if the family member takes an active role in the family office, may oversee the planning and funding of those educational projects. If the family member is not active in the family office, the function of education from the family perspective may consist of expressing the need and outlining the components to be implemented by family office staff. The family member still plays the role of 'project manager' for implementation of the educational projects. However, the family member in that role may be responsible for overseeing the larger educational project for the family with the family office executive assigning staff to accomplish the tasks.

Exhibit 11.1

Family governance relationships

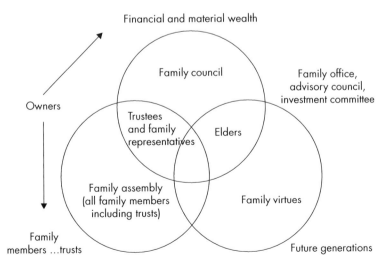

Source: graymatter Strategies LLC.

In essence, the roles set for family members within the family governance process are complementary to the implementation of those functions within the family office, showing that, although the roles of each entity are different, they complement each other. The family office's role in implementing the family governance functions is to serve and support the family in the goals it has set for that particular function to accomplish. The role of family governance is to design the actual decision making process and to develop guidelines to be used by the family office and the family business and the other supporting entities of the family in serving the family and supporting the family's goals.

The family accomplishes these tasks through the board or family council it elects, which may or may not include outside advisors as well as family office executives. Nonetheless, the governing body is the reflection of the goals and desires of all family members and its members are charged with fulfilling those goals to the maximum level possible while working toward the ultimate goal of fostering the family wealth. In actuality, this governing body is charged with receiving and processing input from all family members and working with family leadership to pragmatically implement a process that will work for the family, subject to buy-in and approval from all family members. Parameters regarding the use of the family bank are an example of the guidelines a family may have set up. Outlining who is allowed to benefit from the family bank, the process for applying for funds, and what criteria will be used for granting a family member's request are all decisions to be made through the process of family governance and implemented through the governance process of the family office. This is one point where the questions of 'Who is a family member?' 'Who should have voting privileges?' and 'Who qualifies for family office services?' come into play.

The nature of effective governance

Recall that a family begins with two people who subsequently have children. The first decisions this couple makes as a family are the values they agree are important and, subsequently, the guidelines for raising children. This is the foundation for family governance and, later, for deciding who is a family member and who is not.[11] Family rules – either spoken or unspoken – become established. Those rules may be carried over from previous generations and adopted anew by the new family or they may be new rules the family decides to implement as a result of dissatisfaction or unhappiness experienced under the previous generation's reign. At the early stages of development, family governance consists of family meetings between parents or between parents and their minor children.

As the number of family members grows, family governance must adapt. By the time the second generation has children, the larger concept of family kicks in and thoughts emerge toward creating guidelines for the newly formed separate family entity. As the family grows, each branch develops its own rules. But in an effective family governance system, the branches maintain their individuality *within the larger concept of family as a separate entity*. Hughes notes the importance of each individual family system within the larger concept of family, placing the success of decision making systems by the third and fourth generations as heavily dependent upon the success of independent joint decision making by the constituent families. The strength of the individual branches' governance systems is equally vital to the success of the larger family governance system based on the ability to jointly make positive decisions that foster active participation in the larger entity to which they naturally belong. Joint decision making at all levels fosters 'affinity governance' and is essential to the long-term success of the family. Hughes notes that simply arriving at the realisation that each family unit or branch within a system of family governance is implementing a joint decision-making process can help a family understand the implications and meaning of family governance.[12]

The Laird Norton family is a perfect example of how such a seemingly paradoxical approach can actually work in a successful family 150 years old with hundreds of family members. Koldyke explains, 'The legacy of the Laird Norton family is the ability to be adaptive and proactive not only in creating wealth but also in creating opportunities for future generations. The most important things are the ability to survive, to create wealth, and to keep the family together. By the time you have 300 family members, it's difficult to say they will all share nuclear family values at any single point in time. We're not a unified culture because (a) we don't want to be – our diversity is our strength – and (b) we're just not.' Note the mention of diversity as the family's strength. Such diversity adds to the richness of the experience of family and keeps the governance process vital and dynamic from one generation to the next.

Hughes lists five characteristics of families who govern themselves well.[13]

1 They are highly inclusive, encouraging participation and expediting new family members to full participation.
2 They have highly articulated practices for the development of representatives.
3 They have active training and development programmes to provide necessary coaching and mentoring to future family representatives.
4 They have highly developed educational programmes to ensure all family members are equipped as full participants in family governance.
5 They have procedures in place ensuring that the minority on any issue is protected and they have given elders the authority to enforce that protection.

Governance by consensus is basically a simple process but it is one which has an enormous compounding effect. Think of the concentric circles that result from dropping a pebble into the water. Each circle begets another. By considering the long-term compounded results of a proposed decision, families may master the art of making more positive joint decisions than negative ones, allowing the positive results to compound through multiple generations over a human life span of 100 years.[14] In other words, by making more positive decisions jointly than negative ones, each generational cycle builds upon the successes of the previous one, strengthening the family by continually fostering the family wealth.

This notion has even broader implications. Considering the Proverb, an ever-present threat in the minds of families of wealth, we can recall the proposition of eliminating the third generation as a strategy for fostering family wealth. The power of the second generation in its roles and responsibilities sets the stage for long-term success for the family. The family governance process can play a significant supporting role in this regard: *if family governance is successful as measured by the tenets set forth in this chapter, it will indeed present each generation the opportunity to become the 'second generation' all over again, resulting in the permanent demise of the proverbial return of the 'third generation' to shirtsleeves or rags.*

The influence of generational cycles on family governance

As noted earlier, 'By showing the validity of the four turnings and the associated archetypical roles throughout the annals of history to the current times in which we live, we can discern pathways of communication and joint decision making through acknowledgement of the influence of generational cycles'. For example, *Silent generation* leadership may wish to set stricter guidelines for family bank grants than *Boomer* leadership. The generational templates we use as our primary frame of reference explain what may seem to other living generations to be unreasonable responses, expectations, or requirements.

In that context, we can position governance as the venue through which the definitions of family, family wealth, and the roles of generational archetypes converge. Therefore, our next task is to become cognisant of the current generational maze present in the particular family for which governance structures are being designed. Recall from Chapter 2 that each family possesses a singular mix of generational perspectives at work overlaid with cultural influences and the nuances of personality. We recap below the generational archetypes[15] likely to be alive in families today according to the point in the cyclical turnings in which we live.

- A few members of the GI generation, born 1901–1924 (Heroes, today's elder elders).
- The Silent generation, born 1925–1942 (Artists, today's elders).
- The Boomer generation, born 1943–1960 (Prophets, today's mid-lifers, soon to move into elderhood).
- The Gen-Xers, born 1961–1981 (Nomads, today's young adults and approaching mid-lifers).
- Echoes, born 1982–2001 (the next Hero generation, the oldest of whom are entering their early and mid-twenties, the youngest of whom are children of late birth spectrum Gen-Xers).
- Yet to be named, born 2002–?? (the next Artist generation, still being born).

The family governance structure is based on the dynamics of the family which, in turn, are determined by the generational perspectives of family members. Governance will take on different characteristics depending upon which generation is in the position of leadership. Notice the number of generations which may be alive at once in today's families. Longer life spans have inadvertently created unprecedented opportunities for families from a governance perspective. The thought of having four or five generations alive at one time would have been laughable to families only a few decades ago. Families today can draw on the experience of the elder generations – and even elder, elder generations, in some cases – and have them bolster the roles of mentor and educator, offering access to a depth of wisdom unavailable to families in earlier times. Family stories told by great grandparents add a valuable dimension to the family history. Recorded family history on a page becomes transformed to real life through the very ones who made it! And grandparents have the opportunity – through learning about the generational templates and how they apply to their particular family's generational maze – to let go of their need to control, allowing them to accept their children and grandchildren for who they are, not for who the grandparents want them to be.

Coupled with the amazing opportunities afforded by significant wealth, the opportunities for fostering the wealth of the family become endless. Input can be gathered from the different generations from old to young from a vertical perspective and also horizontally across the members of each generational archetype. Such broad-based input can drive an exceptionally successful family governance process. The opportunity to properly position the longest-lived family members,[16] the family trusts, also comes to the forefront. Although trusts are most often considered vehicles for financial wealth protection and transfer, they are more accurately viewed as instruments of relationship. Older generations can educate the future beneficiaries of the trusts about their roles and responsibilities, setting the stage for a partnership level relationship with trustees in which beneficiaries, through a representative form of family governance, team with trustees to become educated and dynamic stakeholder owners.

In such a relationship, the older generations – and possibly the trustees themselves – can emphasise to future trust beneficiaries the love which went into the creation of each trust – especially if the trusts have been created to function at their highest level – easing the potential for discomfort and dissatisfaction beneficiaries may experience through responsibilities they will inherit rather than choose.[17] Thus, we see that governance is much more than just putting together a family mission statement, family constitution, or a family council or board – it is a process for nurturing the virtues of the family and enabling each family member to incorporate them into his or her life. It is the portal through which each family member has the opportunity to transform his or her authentic wealth into a tangible form.

Exhibit 11.2

Current generational Turnings

Source: graymatter Strategies LLC.

In Exhibit 11.2, we note once again the current generational constellation, to use the language of Strauss and Howe, from a visual perspective. Viewing the various archetypes, their archetypal roles at work, and the stage of life each archetype is experiencing offers multiple dimensions to the effort to build consensus among family members. The generational perspectives which may be present include the GI/Silent 'my way or the highway' directives, the sense of duty and the ethic of hard work with little entertainment of the role of wealth in pursuing fulfilment or happiness, concerns about spoiling the grandchildren or great grandchildren; the Silent/Boomer more active retirements, higher cultural pursuits, greater interest in social causes, and their own sense of power based on their sheer numbers and redefinition of each stage of life they have entered; the Gen-X template of entitlement, access to information and researching things themselves rather than depending solely on advisors, their desire to know more about the family wealth, their desire for more active involvement in decision making, and their interest in having more balance in their lives between work and leisure; and the Echoes, who are just coming to maturity and are the first completely global, wired generation. As such, they expect information to be at their fingertips 24/7, their values are more traditional and conventional, yet they are plugged in to the world community, and thus, their new definition of 'privacy' (see Chapter 2). They are achievers and parent pleasers. Their parents may be late Boomers or early Gen-Xers.

It is essential to consider the elements of the generational archetypes in formulating a successful family governance structure. As important as the governance structure is, it is merely the culmination of the discussions of the preceding chapters covering the impact of generational perspectives on effective communication and the roles of family members, the critical importance of the second generation, the generational impact in the formation of family dynamics and the formation of family goals, and the examination of the family's true wealth versus its perceived wealth. Each chapter leading up to and including this one plays a part in outlining the work a family must do in the effort toward reaching the fifth generation, 100-year milestone. Even reaching such a milestone only prepares the family for reaching other milestones in a successful history. The work of one generation in no way guarantees the success of the next. But each generation can add to the previous generation's work by compounding the virtues of the family through its own interpretation and application of those virtues.

Such a body of work can indeed seem daunting to families at the outset. John P.C. Duncan adds that it can even make a family wonder if it's worth going through. 'For almost every family, the ultimate purpose of wealth is to help each family member reach his or her potential and to help society, but there's no guarantee of that result. Conversely, if families do not do this work, the wealth is guaranteed to have the opposite effect.'[18] In other words, not doing the work can ensure successful fulfilment of the Proverb. By viewing governance as Hughes suggests – 'as a compact between free persons for their better joint success' – families can indeed see the process as a positive body of work which will enrich the quality of their family life. Citing John Locke's *'Two Treatises on Government'*, Hughes notes that individuals are much more likely to be voluntarily involved in a system which wields authority over them if they have had an active part in developing that system.[19]

Models of governance structures

The models depicted in Exhibits 11.3 to 11.7 compare various types of governance structures and list the benefits and disadvantages below each. These models illustrate basic structures which can and should be customised for the family's particular needs. It is much easier, of course, to build an effective model from scratch starting most often with the second generation. However, basic educational elements should be put into place while G1 is still in leadership and as G2 rise as apprentices. The age at which apprenticeship should begin can range from age eight (or even a bit younger) to age 24 (or older). The idea behind apprenticeship is the luxury of being able to practise making decisions within the safety net of parental or leadership's ultimate governance.

This enables the extension of trust on the front end and the ability to learn from mistakes that are made. It is, in my opinion, a much better way to protect assets over the long term since young apprentices have the opportunity to develop confidence in their decision making abilities, will see the need to be educated so that they are capable of making informed decisions, and will naturally rise to their responsibilities as dynamic stakeholder owners. Mistakes will indeed be made. And people of all ages respond much more productively to being given a second chance out of trust and the ability to learn from their mistakes than from being shamed by them. Thus, governance becomes most effective when reviewed on a regular basis and adjusted to fit the needs of the family through each generational cycle. In this way, it serves the family in its most authentic role as a living, breathing service element that guides the family in achieving its goals.

A patriarchal governance system which is grounded in cultural mores may work for a family if the patriarch understands the true nature of ownership and encourages input from family members at some level. As well, assurances are given family members that their input will be acknowledged,

Exhibit 11.3

Patriarchal governance

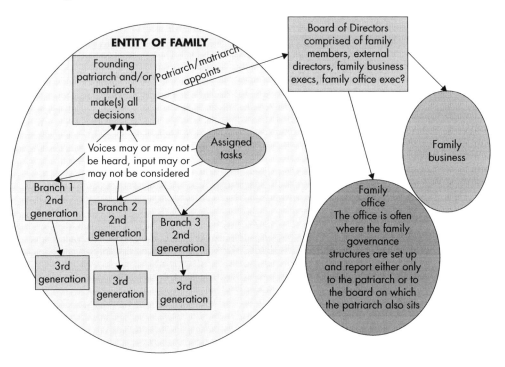

Source: graymatter Strategies LLC.

recorded, and considered. The patriarch still makes all the final decisions, but he does so based on the input he receives. If the patriarch sets up a committee of advisors which include family members, the family may feel that they have at least some representation in the decision making process. If family members do not feel that they have ownership or if they feel that nothing they say or do matters regarding the decisions that are made, the system will have limited success.

Patriarchs often feel they know best for the rest of the family and they wish to 'control' how the wealth is used and distributed in order to take care of the family. This becomes an authoritarian form of governance. Although this springs from love for the family members and a desire to protect the wealth for their ultimate benefit, it most often creates the opposite results. The illusion of control can make this system work for, possibly, a generation but it is unlikely to be truly effective for multiple generations. Most often, things change radically upon the death of the patriarch.

Even if the second generation subscribes to similar values as the patriarch or promises to uphold the values of the patriarch, the new leadership will want to make its own mark. Strictly patriarchal systems do little to foster dynamic stakeholder ownership by family members. Quite often, the second generation becomes a steward of the first generation's dream without having the opportunity to realise its own dreams. This fosters disunity and, rather than consistently building

Exhibit 11.4

Authoritarian governance

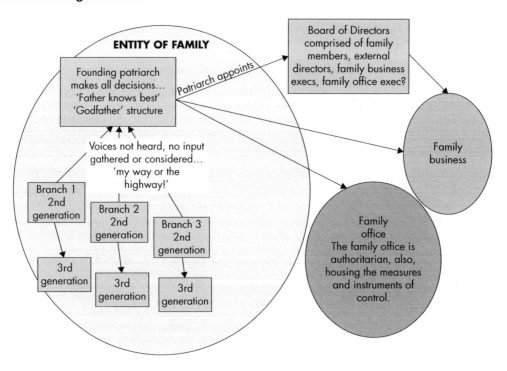

Source: graymatter Strategies LLC.

trust (the 'glue' that holds families together), may foster factions and possibly even resentment.

Authoritarian governance is the least effective, harbours the most potential for dysfunction and division, and plays right into the fulfilment of the edicts of the 'shirtsleeves to shirtsleeves in three generations' Proverb. When family members have no voice, they feel no ownership; when they feel no ownership, they feel nothing they say or do matters. This type of governance erodes the self-esteem of other family members, breeds a lack of trust, and offers little, if any, opportunity for communication and cohesion. Such an effort to rigidly control the wealth becomes an illusion which easily breaks down when new leadership takes over, either before or after the death of the founder. This form of governance is strictly an imposed linear progression which contributes to 'family combustion'. 'Iron-clad' legal structures often build resentment and divisiveness and can cause behavioural and even substance abuse problems, in some cases. Quite often, even the most 'iron-clad' structures can be circumvented in some way.

In a governance system based on pure democracy, the entire family votes on all decisions. This can sound attractive, but in practice, it can set family members up to vie to win votes for their position on a matter, fostering divisiveness. As well, the losing minority will often feel their voices were not heard or that they were basically left out. This can cause the family to divide into

Exhibit 11.5

Majority rule governance

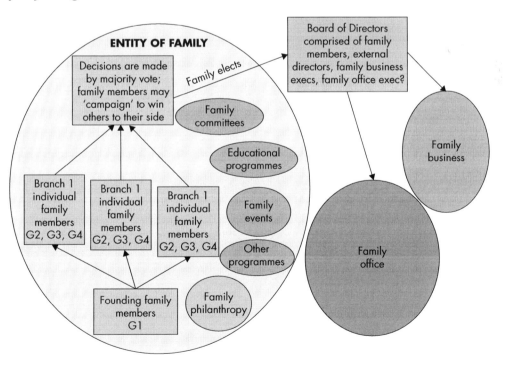

Source: graymatter Strategies LLC.

Exhibit 11.6

Representative democracy with a patriarchal overlay

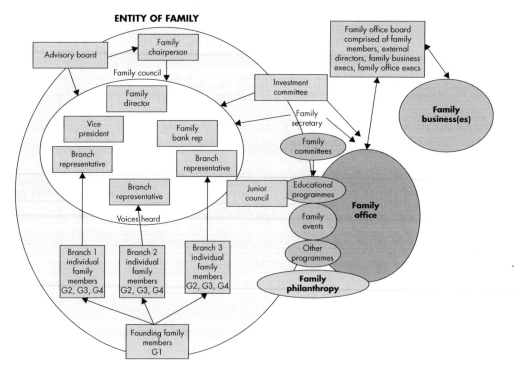

Source: graymatter Strategies LLC.

factions. Family offices attempting to serve such families can become confused about who really has authority and whose wishes they are to fulfil. Pure democracies with no checks and balances can breed anarchy; a flat governance structure ruled by majority vote can have the same effect in families.

A representative democracy that has checks and balances of authority is effective for current generations and also offers the greatest flexibility to accommodate transitions the family experiences from generation to generation. Notice this form of governance has a 'bottom-up' approach; the first two models have a 'top down' approach. All voices are heard, acknowledged, and considered in decision making. Decisions are made jointly, which may mean that the wishes of family members are made known and decisions are made by leadership in consideration of family members' desires; or that branches vote, then branch representatives vote their constituency on the council; or some other type of representative arrangement. In all cases except for the tactical management of the family business, all family members (as defined in the constitution) have a vote at some level. As well, the family office works as a service entity to the family and often works closely with family members to fulfil goals or accomplish projects. In cultural traditions where the patriarchal system remains in place and is part of the culture and heritage, this structure has the ability to strengthen the patriarch's leadership and position him as even more beloved. Family members become more willing followers if they feel their voices are heard and considered even though their particular wishes may not be directly fulfilled in the decision to be made at hand.

Knowing leadership is aware of family members' feelings and will continue to consider them in future decisions builds trust, bridges relationships, and nurtures the spirit of family so that present and future generations may contribute to the family's authentic wealth. Patriarchs who are willing to listen to new ideas may discover authentic wealth within their family structure of which they were not previously aware. One only has to look at the corporate world to find examples of this model's basic effectiveness. This is not to encourage that the family should be governed by the management of the business or even by the family office. As noted earlier, the role of family governance is different than that of either the business or the family office. Rather, it is to signify that in any organisation, people rise to the occasion when offered the opportunity to contribute.

Exhibit 11.7

Representative democracy

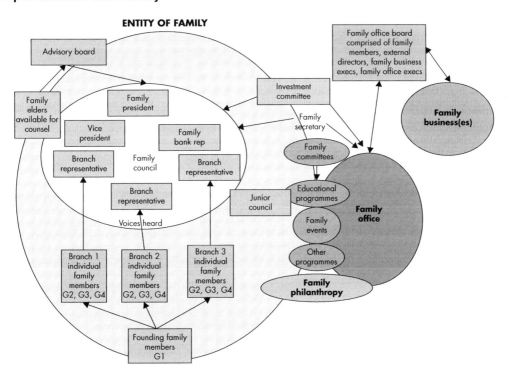

Source: graymatter Strategies LLC.

A flatter organisation such as a representative democracy still has a decision making body, although that body is comprised of multiple family representatives instead of just one person. The representative body – such as a family council or family board – may elect a president and may position the family elders as the 'judicial system' which is charged with enforcing the agreed upon tenets of the family constitution and to serve as mediators in family arbitration. The council or board itself is the 'legislative branch'; especially in larger families, this branch takes the lead in authoring the family's decision making process. The president presides over the council or board, ensures representatives are heard, and oversees the implementation of the decision making process.

Before proceeding to family business and family office governance ...

Developing a cognitive awareness of each type of governance structure and how the perspectives of the family's generations factor into it equips families to choose a structure – or a combination of structures – that best fits their needs. One generation may view a specific governance structure as effective while another generation may develop an entirely different structure. Awareness of each generation's view of the world is essential toward designing and implementing a structure through which the family's authentic wealth – and, ultimately, the tangible wealth – will thrive.

As we move on to other aspects of the family governance trilogy, we are compelled to note that no form of governance will be effective if the various bodies of authority are not empowered to use that authority. Token representation may as well be no representation at all. Often, structures that resemble representative governance become authoritarian structures in disguise! As we will see in a later discussion, this can significantly affect the family wealth's bottom line. The impact of the family's authentic wealth on the bottom line of the tangible wealth is one of the most fascinating aspects of wealth management. It is a core reason behind the mandate for a new approach.

The entire discussion of family governance points to the realisation that tangible wealth can serve two purposes; it functions within the family either as an invaluable gift which fosters unity and strength or as a plague which divides the family through irreparable dysfunction. *Understanding the impact of generational perspectives is key in determining which role wealth plays within families who are fortunate enough to have such a choice.* Successful family governance serves as the instrument through which the gift is offered to each family member from generation to generation. Such an understanding offers the ability to view governance of the business of the family and also the family office in an entirely new light. It equips the family to institute appropriate relationships between family members and the other entities of the family so that all family entities function as they should to nurture the flourishing of the family's wealth in all its forms.

---

[1] Koldyke, M. Laird, Personal interview, February 2007.

[2] Hughes, James E., Jr., Personal interview, August 2007.

[3] Hughes, J.E., Jr., *Family: a compact among generations,* (New York, NY: Bloomberg Press, 2007), pp. 35–37.

[4] Hughes, James E., Jr., Personal interview, August 2007.

[5] Ibid.

[6] Hughes, James E., Jr., Personal interview, October 2006.

[7] Rankin, M.J., President, the Rankin Group, Personal interview, November 2006.

[8] Hausner, L. and Freeman, D.K., *The Legacy Family*, (New York, NY: St. Martin's Press, 2009), p. 57.

9 Hughes notes that the most effective way for families to make decisions together is jointly rather than by consensus. Consensus is needed in order to come to joint agreement, but making decisions by consensus denotes a majority rule rather than consensual agreement resulting in joint decisions. Hughes, James E., Jr., Personal interview, August 2007.

10 Hughes, J.E., Jr., *Family: a compact among generations,* (New York, NY: Bloomberg Press, 2007), pp. 4, 10, 32, 50, 62. The four virtues of family consisting of fusion, altruism, beauty as harmony, and joy as an expression of love.

11 Ehlern, S., 'Global private wealth management: an international study on private wealth management and family office services for high net worth individuals', doctoral study (London, Zurich: Ferguson Partners Family Office, 2006–2007), pp. 276, 282, and 455 for additional notes on the definition of family.

12 Hughes, J.E., Jr., *Family: a compact among generations,* (New York, NY: Bloomberg Press, 2007), p. 144.

13 Hughes, J.E., Jr., *Family Wealth: keeping it in the family,* (New York, NY: Bloomberg Press, 2004), pp. 10 and 11.

14 Ibid.

15 Strauss, W. and Howe, N., *The Fourth Turning: an American prophecy,* (New York, NY: Broadway Books, 1997), pp. 123–38.

16 Hughes, James E., Jr., Personal email conversation, March 2 2007.

17 Hughes, J.E., Jr., *Family Wealth: keeping it in the family,* (New York, NY: Bloomberg Press, 2004), p. 113.

18 Duncan, John P.C. Principal of the law firm Duncan Associates and Counselors, P.C., personal interview, February 2007.

19 Ibid.

Chapter 12

Family business governance

'Understanding the family enterprise begins with examining the complex roles that family members may fulfill in various family ventures. In order to avoid difficulties in the enterprise and conflicts among family members, each family member must understand and clarify the specific role he or she has in the ownership and management of the family wealth.'

Dennis Jaffe[1]

It may seem a bit out of sequence to jump to business governance directly from family governance as the more logical progression might treat family office governance next. But there is reasoning behind the order of treatment. Family businesses are entities to which families are often very emotionally tied. They can serve as instruments of identity – so much so that aspects of the business invade their owners' personal lives. Trying to separate a founder's identity from the business can be damagingly difficult and can impede the business's ultimate benefit to the family if, at some point, the business needs to be sold. The business can also overshadow the governance of the family, causing the appropriate hierarchy among the three governance components to be skewed.

How important are family businesses to families? Extremely! So are the family's emotional ties to it. The business carries within it a great deal of the history of the family – it is a critical instrument within the stories of valour which are told about family ancestors, the bearer of the family colours, and an identity which lives on even if the business is eventually sold to enable future wealth generating opportunities.

However, the emotional ties to the business do not make the business an appropriate governor of the family. Whatever the business of the family happens to be – whether an operating company, a group of investments, mutually owned assets, or even the upholding of a traditional class standard such as membership in the French Foreign Legion or the ownership of a family castle – the business first and foremost is the vehicle through which the material and financial wealth came to be. The goal of this chapter is to show how the business of the family can – and should – continue to be such a vehicle from one generation to the next. *The way this can most effectively occur is to understand the authentic role of the business and to rightly position governance of the business within the triad of family governance forms.*

Family governance is essential as a first consideration since family members themselves are the source of the original financial wealth creation and any wealth which may be created in the future. We discussed early on how generational perspectives come into play from the generational cycles within our mini society of the family. We subsequently examined how those cycles affect the complexity of relationships and the roles family members perform. The communication elements which are essential to maximising the potential for those roles to be performed to their ultimate level are the subject of various chapters throughout this book. The next critical element to discuss then is the role of each family member as a dynamic stakeholder owner. This element must be firmly planted before we can effectively discuss governance of the family office.

Keeping in mind our preferred view of wealth as a gift rather than a plague of dysfunction, this chapter will show the 'Figure 8' relationship between family governance and family business governance. It will show how family governance influences the family business by preparing well-educated dynamic stakeholder owners and how some of the principles of family business governance can add structure to family governance, enhancing the way the family functions and incorporating substance over mere semantics. It will then note the characteristics of the family business and its needs and goals as a family entity, thus defining its governance requirements. This chapter will address four primary points: (i) the needs and goals of the family business entity; (ii) how family governance influences the family business; (iii) the role of the business in serving the family; and (iv) effective family business governance. A case study illustrating the importance of function over form closes the chapter.

The needs and goals of the family business entity

The following points summarise the needs and goals of the family business with the hope that the reader will keep them in mind as the chapter progresses. In essence, successful family businesses require:

- well-educated family members who are actively involved as dynamic stakeholder owners;
- savvy business management with clarity that their role is tactical rather than strategic;
- clarity on the part of family members that their role is strategic rather than tactical – and definitely not passive;
- a well-functioning governance system designed to fulfil the needs of and enhance the goals of the business; and
- monitoring of governance systems to ensure those systems foster leadership from behind.

The goal of the family business is to serve the family by providing financial capital to fuel the growth of the family's primary assets, its human, social and intellectual capacities.

The synchronised relationship of family governance with business governance

We saw chronicled in Chapter 9 the influence of generational perspectives and family dynamics upon each family member in the development of both familial roles and ownership roles. It is in the topic of this chapter – the governance of the family business – that the quality of family members' performances within those roles may be felt the most. The most important application from Chapter 9 is the fact that every family member is an owner in the sense that each person has input regarding the decisions made by the family. As such, the role each family member performs must be valued equally.[2] Consider that the family business is the materialisation of the founder's dream, his or her intellectual capital. A critical by-product of the work the second generation does is the development of a governance system which will serve family members by supporting and nurturing their individual callings for generations to come. Since the financial capital produced by the family business supports those dreams, each family member is affected by the business and, therefore, has an interest in it. In turn, the business has a responsibility toward each family member.

Some of the most common ownership roles family members may perform[3] include the following.

- Founder.
- Owner of:
  - shares of a family corporation; and
  - a general or limited partnership interest in a family partnership.
- CEO or Co-CEO.
- An employee of:
  - a family corporation;
  - a family partnership; and
  - a family foundation.
- Board member of:
  - a family corporation; and
  - a family foundation.
- Member – general or limited – of a family limited liability company.
- Trustee.
- Beneficiary.
- Benefactor.
- Entrepreneur.

In many cases, family members are not adequately educated in the responsibilities inherent in these roles; many may not realise these roles are theirs to perform nor have an awareness of the responsibilities that accompany them. Despite the religious application of the tenets of business governance to family governance by professional consultants the world over, the education of family members in their roles as dynamic stakeholder owners is still severely lacking. Much of the education afforded family members is limited to basic financial and business concepts. There is little tie-in with the fulfilment of family members' individual dreams or with the goals of the family over the span of a long human life. Instead, such education tends to focus on ripening a new field of management candidates and fulfilling short-term responsibilities to shareholders.

By contrast, the very definition of the term 'dynamic stakeholder ownership' is founded in generational cycles which rejuvenate the family and, through the role of the dynamic stakeholder owner, regenerate[4] the family business. The 'dynamic' aspect of the stakeholder owner role automatically incorporates generational cycles into all systems of governance for the family since it encourages active participation of every family member from every generation alive in the family's particular generational maze.

To this end, each role family members perform – regardless of whether ownership was inherited or chosen – carries a heavy bearing toward the success of the family business. Often the perception is present that the roles of family members managing the business are more important than those not involved in management, not employed by the family business, or family members following a pursuit of happiness not associated with the family business. Such perceived inequality causes friction and dysfunction – not only among the family, but also within the family business.

Indeed, the 'business' of the family and all of its entities is to enhance its entire portfolio of human, intellectual, social, and financial capacities, not to set up competing forces which lead to entropy. *Most critically, it is impossible for the family business to thrive unless its proper role – that of fostering the family's entire portfolio of wealth by generating financial assets – is clearly and ever present in the minds of its leaders.* Further, family leadership must not be a restricted privilege, reserved only for those formally placed in executive or management positions; leadership also must be the prerogative of any sufficiently talented and educated family member. True leadership of the family – and, by association, of the family business – comes from behind[5] with executives opening the path for new leadership from the 'lower' ranks to move forward.

How family governance influences the family business

Hughes notes that families are self-governing entities and, therefore, can benefit from the application of systems theory. Families often act like enterprises. They are complex systems which intend to be profitable by generating the greater happiness of successive generations and to that end, it is possible to measure and analyse results. As increasingly complex systems, families must organize themselves in a highly structured manner to accomplish their long-term goals.[6] Therefore, the proper application of systems theory to family governance can help families function better within the entity of family. This application creates better educated family members who may then appropriately fulfil their roles as dynamic stakeholder owners to enhance the performance of the family business.

The Williams Group survey cited in Chapter 1 showed that families of wealth attributed 25% of the fulfilment of the edicts of the Proverb to the lack of clarity on the part of family members regarding their roles and the responsibilities which accompany them. Hughes makes the connection between this lack of clarity and the family business when he says, 'the lack of education of beneficiaries as to the roles and responsibilities of stakeholder ownership as well as to the way investments and businesses work creates the greatest risks to a family's long-term success'. The translation of this lack of education into the family business looks like this.

- The next generations are caught unawares and completely unprepared for the roles and responsibilities that previous generations apparently have assumed they would become knowledgeable about simply through osmosis. Thus, they are incapable of providing leadership for the family business or any other family entity.
- Since they are unsure about their abilities to perform these roles and to fulfil the accompanying responsibilities, they develop low self-esteem – they feel they cannot measure up and that it is impossible to 'catch up' since they already are so far behind.
- Such lack of confidence translates into difficulty balancing work and family which leads to further unhappiness and an increased sense of failure.
- With such low self-esteem fuelled by an increased sense of failure, heirs do not feel confident in seeking out external resources which would help them materialise their dreams.
- Therefore, they give up on their dreams and never develop to their full potential; they have no capacity for dynamic stakeholder ownership.
- The net result? Dissipation of the wealth by any definition with the edicts of the Proverb fulfilled on schedule.

Since family members are not simply non-performing assets which can be sold at a loss, lack of an educated pool of dynamic stakeholder owners presents a significant problem for family owned businesses. The roles of management and family members become confused. The strategic nature of the roles of stakeholder owners becomes sacrificed through the tactical nature of managerial roles, making owners passive recipients of company dividends and incapable of capitalising on the opportunities the business can offer them.

Proper identification of the needs and goals of the family business may only be accomplished through the lens of family governance. Like the family office, the family business exists to serve the family. However, the role of the family business is different from that of the family office. Often, the family business is viewed merely in terms of making a financial profit to be used to provide for the family's day-to-day needs and to provide a good return to shareholders. Such a view is too limited, however, and overlooks a critical element for success – that of funding the opportunity for the fulfilment of each family member's dream. It is from these dreams that family enterprises materialise[7] and, in turn, fuel the family's livelihood. By providing financial support for the dreams of future generations, the business also plays a role in continually regenerating the wealth.

Exhibit 12.1

'Figure 8' type of flow between well-educated dynamic stakeholder owners and the family business

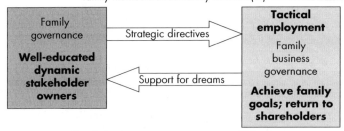

Source: graymatter Strategies LLC.

We have talked thus far about the roles of family and business governance in enhancing each family member's ability to follow his or her calling, but it is also the role of each family member to support every other family member in his or her pursuit. Recall our earlier discussion of roles. According to Hughes, this is this role that genuinely fosters the wealth of the family.[8]

The family business is positioned within this scenario as a primary tool for fulfilling that role – either directly or indirectly. If the family business is allowed to fulfil its proper role, the wealth of the family is broadly supported and spills over into the community at large. This is the family's social capital – and the business's good will – which can be channelled through philanthropic efforts, influential political activity, or active involvement on boards of other businesses or civic organisations.

In the real world, family owned businesses share many of the same problems as non-family owned businesses. Harvard Business School senior lecturer John Davis[9] notes that '... personalities, passions, and power are at the heart of any enterprise'. Accordingly, he notes the following short-sighted approaches which may be employed by management and family leaders to handle emotionally charged tensions within family owned businesses.[10]

- 'Exclusion and secrecy – keeping some family members or shareholders out of conversations and keeping too many secrets from employees, owners or family members.'
- 'Divide and conquer – relying on the support of some allies and excluding others from information and decision making.'
- 'Bribery – hiring relatives who do not deserve jobs, paying relatives more than they deserve, distributing more funds from the company than is responsible for the sake of preserving family harmony or maintaining certain individuals' power.'

These types of approaches not only embrace conflict, they promote it and encourage it to act like a poison to undermine the success of the business, the family, and everyone associated with either. But if family leaders encourage input from all family members (or employees in the case of family business managers), perceive the roles of all family members as equally important, and employ fair hiring practices, much of the fodder fuelling the problems listed above becomes practically nonexistent. This isn't to say that effective governance eliminates conflict – unfortunately, situations such as those listed above are quite common. The example of the Laird Norton family in Chapter 11 acknowledges the existence of genuine conflict within even the best governed families. But by embracing such conflict, making sure everyone's voice is genuinely heard, taking the time to discern the real concerns behind the conflict, and taking those concerns to heart, even conflicts of the most severe nature can yield positive results. Through effective family governance, well-educated stakeholder owners become significant contributors to business governance. In such a case, the family members – both those who are directly involved in the family business and those who are not – set the tone for the governance of the business and send the proper messages to employees. Thus, our discussion concludes that what happens in the family affects not only the family, but also the family business and every other entity of the family.

The role of the business in serving the family

With that backdrop, we appropriately set the stage for the business to function as an extension of and regenerator of the family wealth. If business management acknowledges the strategic role the family members play as dynamic stakeholder owners, it frees management to do what they do best – focus on the tactical management components with which they are charged.[11] The proper role of the business then becomes more clearly defined and management may function more effectively to accomplish the family's goals for the business. If the business is viewed as the primary entity of the three (family, family business, family office), family members have no way to understand how to function in the governance of the entity since the governance sequence has fallen out of proper alignment.

When family members do not function as dynamic stakeholder owners, managers must spend time away from the employment of their tactical management skills in an effort to maintain a balance in perspectives between the family, the business, and the external ownership group or the shareholders. Davis notes that family members who are owners but who do not work for the business may view the appropriate level of dividends differently than those family members who do. One group may feel the level should be higher than the other group – a justifiable position within each group. Thus, management is burdened with this extraneous role of trying to maintain balance among the family, the business, and its ownership group. More critically, this promotes the view that management's role is strategic, taking over the proper role of the stakeholder owners and making family members passive dividend receivers.

Such a view causes family members to hand over their responsibilities to management, severing family members' connection to the governance of their financial wealth which further leads to the 'entropy that befalls any absentee owner of any asset'.[12] *The role of management is to employ the tactical management skills they possess to accomplish the goals set forth by the family.* Indeed, if the family members are robustly educated as dynamic stakeholder owners, there should be no need for a 'balancing act' as each family entity knows its purpose and is appropriately governed to perform its proper role. Family members are educated and responsible participants who understand their own roles as well as the roles of other family members.

As noted earlier, the creation of financial capital supports the growth of the family's human, intellectual, and social capacities. So, the financial profit created by the business does its part in supporting Hughes' larger idea of profit relative to family enterprises as 'the greater happiness of each succeeding generation'.[13] In this light, we can describe the goals of the family business as follows.

- To support and enhance each family member's ability to pursue happiness.
- To create a profit, which results in the greater happiness of each succeeding generation.
- To support and enhance the goals of the family as a collective entity.
- To employ ethical and sound business practices.
- To return a financial profit to shareholders.
- To be a responsible citizen of the larger community.

These are 'big picture' items, the tactical implementation of which should be customised within the tenets of accepted best business practice for each family's situation by the management the family has chosen.

Exhibit 12.2 shows the proper relationship of the family business to the other entities of the family and the appropriate flow of authority from the family to the family business(es) so that the family as an entity as well as individual family members benefit and are fully equipped to reach their goals. Note that both the business entities and the family office are positioned as service entities with specific, yet quite different roles to perform in helping the family achieve its goals.

The positioning of the family business in Exhibit 12.2 shows more clearly the role the family business is to perform. The chart also illuminates what is required for the business to successfully perform its role as well as the goals management should have within the operation of the business. How does all of this work in a real-life family business setting? Is it practical to think of the flow of family governance and family business governance in this way? The best way to answer these questions is through actual example, the first of which is outlined below and the second of which is the subject matter for Chapter 14 which examines a seventh generation family who has successfully implemented these tenets. The case study at the close of this chapter adds even greater clarity.

Exhibit 12.2

Three forms of governance: delegation of authority

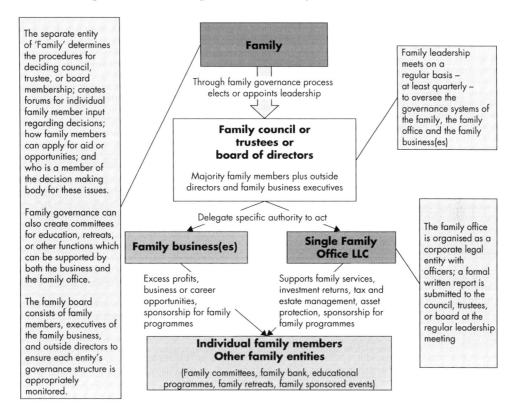

The separate entity of 'Family' determines the procedures for deciding council, trustee, or board membership; creates forums for individual family member input regarding decisions; how family members can apply for aid or opportunities; and who is a member of the decision making body for these issues.

Family governance can also create committees for education, retreats, or other functions which can be supported by both the business and the family office.

The family board consists of family members, executives of the family business, and outside directors to ensure each entity's governance structure is appropriately monitored.

Family

Through family governance process elects or appoints leadership

Family council or trustees or board of directors

Majority family members plus outside directors and family business executives

Delegate specific authority to act

Family business(es)

Excess profits, business or career opportunities, sponsorship for family programmes

Single Family Office LLC

Supports family services, investment returns, tax and estate management, asset protection, sponsorship for family programmes

Individual family members Other family entities

(Family committees, family bank, educational programmes, family retreats, family sponsored events)

Family leadership meets on a regular basis – at least quarterly – to oversee the governance systems of the family, the family office and the family business(es)

The family office is organised as a corporate legal entity with officers; a formal written report is submitted to the council, trustees, or board at the regular leadership meeting

Source: graymatter Strategies LLC, Family Office Metrics LLC.

Effective family business governance

Having identified the needs and goals of the family business, we may now address specific aspects of governance. While most readers may be familiar with the basics of corporate governance and the myriad aspects of successfully running an operating business, the distinguishing element of family ownership adds a different dimension to the realm of governance. Some – not nearly all – of the basic areas of business governance include:

- normal business operation guidelines in the form of policies and procedures;
- hiring criteria and other personnel issues;
- IT, communication, and other functions;
- business plans based on goals of the family;
- business operations and functions;
- compliance with governmental policies, publicly traded company regulation;

- company executives and officers;
- ownership matters;
- family employment matters;
- family compensation matters; and
- involvement of business leadership in certain family matters.

We have talked at length about the relationship between family and business governance – what makes each successful and how each differs from the other – and it is particularly gratifying to see the media deliver a real-life example of the effectiveness of these principles, albeit in the form of a non-family owned business. A *Wall Street Journal* article[14] described companies which were 'hamstrung by the demand from investors and analysts for immediate results' yet who wanted to change the way they operate in response to global climate change. The article identifies 'leadership from below' the 'C Suite' of CEO, COO, and CFO. It notes that, although the illusion that an 'all-powerful' CEO can change companies by sheer strength of will still reigns, in actuality, no CEO can truly change a company's direction completely on his or her own power. The article clearly outlines the benefits horizontal leadership can offer by enriching the success of the organisation at every level. This is quite a different animal than what may be called a 'flat organisation' where no one seems to be able to truly execute performance.

The 'leadership from below' concept corresponds precisely to Hughes' argument for leadership from behind. The article shows that in the corporate world, such leadership can be initiated from the occupants of the ranks below rather than waiting for an opening from the 'C Suite' above, although such an opening certainly facilitates the process. Middle managers who are capable leaders may employ calculated risk to successfully break out of the pre-determined mould of their assigned day-to-day duties. Such duties can be all-consuming, leaving no opportunity for these potential leaders to 'expand their influence'. Yet, the managers examined by the article successfully did so, enriching the entire company and expanding its profits from a much wider base.

Here are the basic points extracted from the article.[15]

1 'Make the decision to be a leader.' In every case examined by the authors, it was the decision of the middle manager to become a leader, not an appointment from the 'C Suite' to do so. These managers had to face the decision risk of realising that failure to lead once the door is truly open would create significant opportunity costs.

There were two methods successful managers used to pry the door open. The first was delegation of their daily duties in a fashion where their personal involvement became less critical to the operations and governance of their respective divisions. This provided the time needed for the leadership pursuit. It also paved the way for people working under them to contribute their own intellectual capital, something not possible with a manager who has to control everything and is completely absorbed in the duties of his or her designated position. The second method involved the managers' openness to influences outside the corporation – they paid attention to messages from the marketplace including customers, competitors, suppliers, neighbours, and the media. The managers then extracted actionable application from those messages to employ within their divisions.

2 'Focus on influence, not control.' Here, the article applies to the corporate world the point that people participate more willingly and enthusiastically in a system in which they have input and

feel that input is valued. It emphasises sharing of information rather than guarding it to boost egos or to wield power. The goal here is to work within existing systems and with existing assets to influence others – sometimes even the most disagreeable parties – to come to your side by winning their voluntary support, not dictating it.

3 'Make your mental organisational chart horizontal rather than vertical.' Traditional organisational charts reflect a hierarchy of authority which flows down from the top with no connection between peers to foster collaboration. What would be considered *objections* within a vertical structure becomes *feedback* in a horizontal one which leaders would be more inclined to consider in making decisions. Such decisions are then supported by the entire division, expanding the manager's influence and overall success.

4 'Work on your trusted advisor skills.' A trusted advisor is someone who is sought out by others for his or her expertise. Most often in corporations, managers hand down edicts rather than being asked for advice. In the best cases, managers become mentors but even then, the unwritten rule of not asking questions to which those being mentored do not already know the answers is still in play. Trusted advisors, on the contrary, ask provocative questions which encourage people to think large and long-term. The search for answers becomes a combined pursuit. Trust is built through listening and respecting others' viewpoints.

5 'Do not wait for the perfect time, just find a good time.' In the corporate world, it can be risky to broach leadership from below. Trying to time perfectly the taking of such a risk can be futile. But executive management often appreciates a forward move from middle management in areas where its own knowledge may be less than robust. The article suggests looking for areas in which corporate complacency is already being challenged. These will be the areas of least resistance to new ideas.

6 'Integrate a broad range of risks and potential impacts into your business decisions.' Encouraging leadership from those who report to you invites a more broad-based perspective and illuminates internal as well as external implications for a decision being considered.

7 'Expose yourself to a broader range of perspectives.' An atmosphere which encourages input from everyone helps managers see bigger, longer term solutions from which the steps of implementation can be identified. As Brunel often states in his presentations, 'no one has a monopoly on brains'.

8 'Create vacuums rather than imposing solutions.' It is much easier to encourage leadership among subordinates if the path is cleared for them to come forth. The article calls such openings 'vacuums' which management can provide by intentionally requesting more attention be paid to a certain issue and inspiring staff to research sources and answers for themselves.

9 'Encourage questions without answers.' This is the opposite of creating a vacuum in that executive leadership actually encourages questions to be asked for which no answers currently exist. The article points to this as the antithesis of normal mentoring form which prohibits those being mentored from asking questions to which they have not already found the answers.

10 'Ask "what if" questions.' Here, the article points to archives from the Cuban missile crisis in which President Kennedy began asking his advisors 'what if' questions in response to the advisors' proposed military action. Ultimately, the answers the advisors gave included the possibility of a nuclear exchange. Other options to solving the problem were then explored.

11 'Openly discuss values as well as value.' A common theme among business people – and wealth management professionals – today is how to extract more value from assets. But it's much more difficult to discuss the values (virtues) connected with what should be done. The article points to

leadership to open the door for comparing 'value' and 'values' in a way that encourages trade-off possibilities or perhaps even complementary solutions.

12 'Refresh your radar screen periodically.' Consistently reevaluating risks that should be taken and the impacts of decisions that are made can equip management with more prudent assessments of future requirements, expectations, and demands. As we have consistently pointed out throughout our discussions, the cyclical nature of life makes it impossible for solutions to stand the test of time completely unchanged. Only through regular review and periodic tweaks which better match current situations can well thought out solutions remain viable.

How do these points support the role of the family business? By eliminating linear thinking and subconsciously recognising the power of cyclical leadership. The ideas and talents of middle management coming up through the ranks keep the company fresh and eliminate complacency. The input encouraged from every member of the staff only makes leadership stronger and more effective. The goals of each staff member become united in the effort to allow every staff member to shine using the unique talents and abilities he or she can contribute. The tight reins of control are broken in order to allow staff to more willingly accomplish the goals of the organisation out of their own volition because they now have something personally at stake – they, in essence, *become dynamic stakeholder owners of the enterprise.*

In Exhibit 12.3, we see how the different governance systems work together in the fashion we have described. In a slight departure from our discussion, readers should note that trusts are listed on the bottom left as family members – indeed, they are the family members with the longest life span. It is my great hope that this realisation spurs significant thinking and discussion among readers. I am indebted to Jay Hughes for my own enlightenment to this fact and embrace it fully as a critical component of the various structures of family and family business governance. Recall the notion that a trust is indeed an owner, according to Hughes, as 'the representation of an act of love from one person to one or more people designed to enhance the second group of people's journeys of happiness'.[16]

In other words, the ability for family members to pursue their individual callings may lie in great part with the financial wealth inside the trust and how that trust functions as a member of the family. Properly constructed, trusts become the means by which the intellectual assets – the dreams of the family – may be materialised. Chapter 19 stresses the relationship risks inherent in advisory roles but the notion that trusts are indeed family members – the longest lived family members – sheds a completely different light on the function of family business governance. Trusts often last longer than a single human life – they definitely last longer than an elder family member's mentoring years. With such a long life span, trusts can offer continuity between the family governance and family business governance systems, enhancing the success of each.

Where Exhibit 12.2 shows the flow of delegated authority from the family through the board to the family entities, Exhibit 12.3 shows the structures through which each entity's governance structure is monitored. In many family business governance structures, trustees and their functions are relegated to the family office and trusts are considered simply the legal vehicles through which the family's financial wealth is transferred from one generation to another. But as family members, trusts are represented on the family council by trustees. As representatives of the longest lived family members, the trustees are then automatic attendees at the meeting of the dynamic stakeholders of the enterprise along with other representatives of the family. Some are also members of the Board of

Exhibit 12.3

Relationship of family governance entities

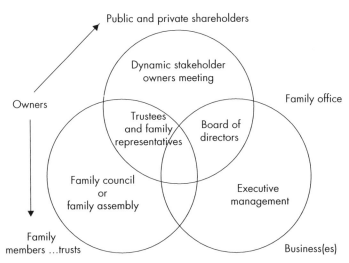

Source: graymatter Strategies LLC.

Directors. What does this mean? Significantly that the guardians of the financial wealth created by the family business are dynamically involved as stakeholder owners in monitoring the very governance system that fosters more financial wealth creation by the family business. Further, these guardians become the primary glue that binds the interests of the family business with those of the family.

Rather than use the Venn diagram structure to simply show the composition of board membership, Exhibit 12.3 employs it to show how governance flows from the family on the lower left to the representative body of the council and from there to the Board of Directors; how the governance of the family business flows through its tactical management to the Board of Directors; and how the interests of all dynamic stakeholder owners are represented on the Board of Directors. Therefore, at the stakeholder meeting, we have representatives of the family, representatives of the family business management, certain outside directors, and possibly the family office executive. Representatives from both the family and the family business converge in the meeting of dynamic stakeholder owners to discuss the family's needs, the business's needs, and how the business is supporting the goals of the family and providing good returns for external shareholders.

Even in business governance, the natural laws of cyclicality must reign. Robert I. Sutton, professor of management science and engineering at the Stanford Engineering School[17] recommends treatment of a business as an unfinished prototype. I recommend changing the word 'unfinished' to 'never-finished'. The different verbiage adds even greater depth to the concept and further opens the family business to cyclical change brought about by generational cycles which filter through over time. As a never-finished prototype, the business indeed can maintain the flexibility needed to keep pace with the vast and rapid changes occurring in the marketplace since the marketplace is also affected by generational cycles. In doing so, risks in business operation – many of which

179

are lodged within linear thinking – can be substantially mitigated.[18] The resilience and fluidity of dynamic stakeholder owners created through effective family governance spills over into the governance of the family business in the same way that middle management leadership emerged as described above. The resilience and fluidity of the family business spills over as profit for the family through a contribution to each family member's pursuit of happiness which, in turn, flows out to benefit society at large. The systems of governance produce a compounding positive effect in complementary fashion, each enhancing the other's effectiveness, compounding the benefit for future generations and also for the larger community.

A case study: form versus function[19]

Three brothers inherited a family's $40 million business after the founder's death 25 years ago. The talents of the brothers complemented each other – one was phenomenal at growing sales, another was excellent at keeping the books, and the third was particularly talented in management skills. Although they did not always agree, they had worked well together and had grown the business to $275 million. However, as the brothers grew older, their respective talents began to become liabilities because each developed his own motive for thinking his role was more important than the other two. The sales and marketing brother consistently wanted more money to conduct extravagant campaigns to attract more business; the number crunching brother more adamantly tied the purse strings; and the manager brother felt his ideas for operating the business were more important than managing the books or getting in new sales in preserving the assets they had accumulated.

As the number of employees grew, policies and procedures were designed. But exceptions were always made for employees who had worked in the business the longest and the three brothers did things they way they saw fit, paying only lip service to the policies and procedures they had set up. Later in their lives, the three brothers sought legal and other counsel since their goals were changing. They listened to what the advisors had to say and agreed to implement some of the recommendations.

But they had successfully grown a profitable business and each wanted to ensure the quality of life he had dreamed of for himself and his family in his old age. The sales and marketing brother felt the only way to accomplish this would be to pour all the effort and money he could into generating more sales – that would keep the money flowing in, keep the business growing so that everyone would benefit, and allow him to spend what he wished, both personally and to generate sales. The number crunching brother felt the way to ensure his own quality of life and that of his children was to protect what had been built by cutting back on expenditures and conservatively managing what had been accumulated. The manager brother was confident that the way to preserve what they had built would be to create greater efficiencies by upgrading their technology and also laying off employees whose performance was not ideal.

The three brothers began to resent each other; the numbers crunching brother felt threatened and uncomfortable by what he deemed to be reckless spending by the sales and marketing brother and he resented the management brother's efforts to boost efficiencies internally by spending more money for the technology upgrade and in just 'chopping off' people who had been in the company for years. Several of the underperforming employees were good friends of the family and the other two brothers wanted their friends to stay on – they felt an obligation to support them since they were getting older, too.

The sales and marketing brother resented the number crunching brother because he began saying 'no' to every request for funds, regardless of merit, and he resented the manager brother because he felt the money should be spent on more sales and marketing efforts, not better technology. The managing brother and the numbers crunching brother felt the sales and marketing brother was losing perspective and was endangering everyone's livelihood by wanting significantly more funds for marketing and to support his sales trips.

The second generation was tired of hearing the three brothers and their wives argue. One second generation member had entertained going into the business when she was younger but the opportunity for her to do so was never realised – the brothers were intent on doing things the way they had always been done so there was no upcoming designated next-generation leadership in whom the family could have confidence. The second generation began to fear there would be no money left for them to pursue their own interests. They also began to fear that, after their parents were gone, the family would split along the lines of the money. The family brought in counsellor after counsellor. The brothers would initially agree to implement the programmes they recommended, only to revert to their old practices within a few months.

The policies and procedures that had been created were inconsistently followed. Regular family meetings had been instituted but after the intergenerational blowout at the first one, everyone had lost interest. A couple of years later, each of the brothers agreed in meetings with legal and other counsel to acquiesce some of his power to a board the family would jointly elect but they never followed through with the procedures recommended for selecting board members.

Five years later, the business was liquidated for $120 million. Each of the brothers received $30 million and each of the six children received $5 million placed in trust until they were 35.

The family had 'done all the right things' – they had set up good business policies and procedures. But little had changed in the way the business actually functioned. When the brothers originally took over the business, each was performing the role of dynamic stakeholder owner but as each began to focus more on his own interests, the role of dynamic stakeholder owner was gradually abandoned. The second generation had never realised their roles, much less understood their responsibilities.

There are many universal aspects within this conglomerate family story. It is an example of a 'perfect storm' of family dysfunction and how the business can be affected by it. This chapter outlines a better way – a path family business can travel to fulfil its role in financially supporting the wealth of the family in all its various forms.

With the roles of the entity of family and the family business clearly defined and a description of how their corresponding governance systems can function effectively – as well as how they may fail to function – we turn in the next chapter to the role of the family office and the needs and goals its governance system must address.

---

[1] Jaffe, D.T., 'Stewardship in your family enterprise', (Pioneer imprints, 2010), p. 28: www.pioneerimprints.com.

[2] Hughes, J.E. Jr., 'A reflection on the roles and responsibilities of each family member as an owner of the family enterprise in a family governance system', 1999: www.jameschughes.com.

[3] This list is a combination of roles identified by the author and roles identified in Hughes, J.E., Jr., *Family: a compact among generations,* (New York, NY: Bloomberg Press, 2007).

[4] Wealth Regeneration® is a registered service mark owned by Laird Norton Tyee and is used throughout this book Laird Norton Tyee's permission.

[5] Hughes, James E. Jr., Personal interview, August 2007.

6   Ibid.

7   Hughes, James E., Jr., Personal interview, October 2006.

8   Hughes, J.E. Jr., 'A reflection on the roles and responsibilities of each family member as an owner of the family enterprise in a family governance system', 1999: www.jameschughes.com.

9   Davis, J.,'Governing the family-run business', *Working Knowledge for Business Leaders,* Harvard Business School, 2001: http://hbswk.hbs.edu/item/2469.html.

10   Ibid.

11   Hughes, J.E., Jr., *Family: a compact among generations,* (New York, NY: Bloomberg Press, 2007).

12   Ibid.

13   Ibid.

14   Kelly, J. and Nadler, S., 'Leading from below', *The Wall Street Journal*, March 3 2007, p. R4.

15   Ibid.

16   Hughes, James E., Jr., Personal interview, February 2007.

17   Pearlman, E., (2006). 'Robert I. Sutton: making a case for evidence-based management', *CIO Insight,* Ziff Davis, 6 February 2006: www.cioinsight.com/article2/0,1540,1930244,00.asp.

18   Ibid.

19   This case study represents aspects of behaviour and also categories of factual and situational information that may be common to many families. No one family was chosen to be the subject of this case study and every family will be able to find elements which seem to pertain to them. This would not be an accurate assessment from a factual or situational standpoint. All facts have been significantly changed to prevent the possibility of identification of any family the reader may think is represented here when, in fact, no family – in whole or in part – is represented in this story except as inspiration for the conglomerate and fully manufactured family story used in this case study.

Chapter 13

Family office governance

> 'The long term success of the single family office demands a clear family vision, a business mission, clarity of all participants' roles and responsibilities and a solid system of internal controls. When these governance success elements are in place the single family office will "pay for itself" and deliver to its owners a positive return on their investment.'
>
> *Jon Carroll*

Now that we have established the proper role of governance in general, the importance of family governance and family business governance in particular, and noted the pervasive impact of generational perspectives, we shift our attention to the family office and the role governance plays within that entity to support the ultimate goal of the family. In thinking of each form of governance, it is important to note that each governance system is guided by different aspects of a family's consummate portfolio of wealth – human, intellectual, and social capacities, and financial capital. Just as a prudent asset allocation design employs a different investment focus for the goals of each pool of financial assets, the design for the various governance systems must be based on the goals of the respective family entities they serve.

Although each family entity has its own goals, its particular role of its corresponding governance system must be clearly understood in helping to achieve the primary goal of the family. Just as family members contribute to the entropy of the family business if they lack clarity regarding their roles and responsibilities, so each family entity will contribute to the entropy of the various forms of the family's wealth if its governance system lacks clarity about the role it is to perform.

Since this chapter discusses the governance system of a family entity which essentially serves the other two, it first will briefly review the needs and goals of each entity. The family office has a specific role to perform; it is essential to have a clear understanding of the correct relationship between family governance and family office governance. A significant part of this chapter will discuss operational family office governance; however, I urge the reader not to become completely absorbed by the operational aspects of family office governance as they have absolutely no purpose without the application of the overriding element presented at the end of this chapter.

The purposes of the three family entities

In Chapter 11, we identified the need of the entity of family to foster the growth of the intellectual, human, and social capacities of its constituency, the family members. The role of the family entity is strategic in building trust relationships and fostering communication, gathering input from every member of its constituency, and formulating strategies and guidance designed to offer support for each member's pursuit of happiness. The goal of the entity of family is to transfer the family virtues from generation to generation, supporting all forms of the family's assets and their flourishing.

Therefore, the role of family governance is to serve as a portal through which the family's goals may be translated into a pragmatic system for achievement.

The role of the family business is to produce financial capital for the family. The need of the family business is to produce that capital as efficiently and effectively as possible while fostering the intellectual, human, and social capacities of its employees toward that purpose. The goal of the family business is to provide enough capital for the family to maintain its day-to-day functionality, to fuel other entrepreneurial or investment activities, and to support the dreams of family members from generation to generation. The role of family business governance is tactical; it is management's task to extract the greatest financial return from the business by employing the most efficient and productive business tactics to foster the transformation of the family members' dreams into a tangible form.

We have seen how the aspects of family governance and family business governance may overlap – the tenets of business governance certainly may be of use for the family and, as shown by the *Wall Street Journal* article,[1] the tenets of successful family governance also have application for business governance. But there are clear differences in their roles. Despite their overlapping nature, many families make the mistake of governing the family through the business or of applying business management practices to the family without considering the different roles each entity occupies and without considering it would be a mistake to have business management govern the family since its role is tactical rather than strategic. The strategic nature of family governance is determined by the human, intellectual, and social aspects of the family's wealth. The business's tactical role is centred on the financial capital.

Exhibit 13.1

Figure-8 flow through the family office

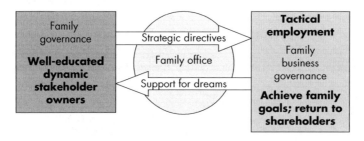

Exhibit 13.1 is a simplified view of the family office as the flow-through service entity which facilitates the figure-8 flow of strategic directives from the family governance system and support for materialising the dreams of family members from the family business governance system back to the family. Chapter 11 notes that family governance guides the governance of all other family entities. This is because other entities are, by nature, service entities to the family. Since we have freshly aligned our thinking regarding the purposes of the various family entities and the roles of

their governance systems, we can begin to consider the needs, goals, and role of the family office. We are now ready to see how the family office and its governance support the growth of both the family governance and family business governance systems as well as the flourishing of the family's entire portfolio of assets, human, intellectual, social, and financial.

Operational views of the family office

Today, families may draw from a much broader array of choices in family office services and structure. Many outsource certain services, especially those employed only on occasion. The issue of which services to outsource and which to keep in house is a significant one for many families. A family office may specialise in a certain investment strategy and may offer investment alongside the family to outside investors, in which case it more closely resembles another family business than simply a service entity. At the other end, a family may only require a few basic services to be provided in house and find it more cost effective to outsource the rest, particularly if the family's assets are not of a size which would comfortably afford the luxury of housing an entire staff of professionals.

Jon Carroll, MBA, CPA and president and CEO of Family Office Metrics LLC notes that some families delegate substantive parts of their family office management while others do not. For example, non-US based families are much less likely to outsource family office activities than American families. Although this trend seems to be shifting, non-US families currently tend to build family office functions in-house. American families have more heartily embraced the outsourcing of non-core business activities, especially the role of chief investment officer and related back-office accounting and administration. In doing so, they strive to find the best quality service providers for the lowest price. Families may delegate or not but family offices which control their affairs will 'pay for themselves' and provide a positive return on the family's investment in the family office.[2]

It might be prudent at this point to temporarily segue to a brief discussion of costs involved in both setting up and running a family office and/or a private trust company. An analogy which readily comes to mind when helping a family decide if a family office makes sense for them is the popular anecdote about John Pierpont Morgan. As the story goes, he was once asked what it costs to keep a yacht. His response is usually quoted as, 'If you have to ask, you can't afford it'. However, versions which may be truer to what was actually said include, 'You have no right to own a yacht if you have to ask that question', and 'If it makes the slightest difference to you what it costs, don't try it'.[3] Regardless, the point is sufficiently made that family offices, like yachts, are luxuries which may not be feasible for families with assets under $150 million to $200 million. Fortunately, there are family office-like structures which afford families with smaller assets access to some level of family office services. So-called virtual family offices are highly customisable and flexible and, of course, multi-family offices are a popular alternative.

Greater discussion regarding the various structures family offices may take as well as the costs related to those family office structures may be found in my first book which is listed in the Bibliography of this book. The costs of setting up an office, the annual expense of running it well, technology costs, as well as expectations regarding the costs of outsourced advisors are well treated there. For our purposes here, it is worthwhile to note that there not only are hard costs such as those mentioned above, but also the soft costs of the time spent by the family on: (a) hiring staff and advisors; (b) monitoring and coordinating outsourced advisors; and (c) educating staff on the goals of the family and ensuring a thorough understanding of how staff and advisors are expected to support the family in achieving those goals. If the right professionals are hired, their high level of expertise will make the management job more complex. Today's marketplace provides competition, as well, and some families have experienced difficulty retaining top talent. This adds to the soft costs in the extra time required to search for new talent of similar calibre. In fact, the soft costs of time and energy are the *real* costs of owning a family office and should be weighed along with the hard costs and proposed benefits the office might provide.

Some of the services a family office may provide include:

- designing and implementing family education programmes;
- providing personal family services;
- family bank processing;
- family event coordination;
- family meeting coordination;
- bill paying, chartering air and other travel, real estate investment purchases in foreign countries;
- family foundation management;
- coordinating family advisors;
- investment management;
- tax management;
- estate management;
- estate planning; and
- implementation of financial and wealth management education programmes.

The family office also must manage internal elements such as:

- internal operations, cost containment, governance implementation;
- hiring and retaining staff, and executive leadership;
- determining the roles of staff;
- setting up and maintaining a policy and procedures manual;
- overseeing compliance issues on wealth management, especially if the office becomes a multi-family office or it becomes another family business through investment management specialisation like hedge fund or private equity;
- family legal and wealth transfer structures such as Family Limited Partnerships (FLPs) and Family Limited Liability Companies (FLLCs);
- the coordination of trustees, attorneys, accountants, and other advisors; and
- providing the trust protector function (this could be a board function).

Hughes notes another critical aspect rarely considered by families setting up new family offices is the fact that a 'buy' or 'make' decision must be made regarding each family office service. This is a highly important decision, particularly in light of the soft costs an office might incur. The decision of whether to hire a corporate trustee or create a private trust company (PTC) is a perfect example. Duncan says that a private trust company can do everything a family office does and more and, if the PTC is set up right, it should cost no more than $100,000 annually over the costs of a high quality family office.[4]

A family setting up new trusts or hiring new trustees for existing trusts weighs the costs of obtaining the highest quality trust services (a 'buy' decision) against what it would cost to create its own trust company (a 'make' decision). PTCs offer many benefits, some of which include the 'right to create common trust funds to permit the pooling of individual accounts' and the ability of the PTC to be 'a repository for the family history'. A family may be willing to pay more for the high quality, 'user-friendly' services a PTC can offer if such an entity fits the governance system criteria the family has developed.[5]

The same principle applies to any service the family would provide itself through the family office. If families could come to the realisation that the soft costs are the real costs of a family office and that each service to be provided requires a 'make' or 'buy' decision, they would save themselves years of trying to 'reinvent the wheel' and could make much more efficient use of highly qualified service providers and consultants.[6]

According to Rankin, families are beginning to realise that the complexity of a family office is, in actuality, like another family business.[7] Hiring internal staff is one of the most complex aspects. Family office executives are in a unique position to serve the family. They may serve on the family council, in which case, they may be called upon to work with the family as it develops the family missions and goals and fine tunes its governance structure. They can play a pivotal role in balancing all of the aspects that are unique to the family office business.

'The family office staff is really an office of very bright professionals who help the family make better decisions about what happens with the wealth. Consequently, expectations around the types of people who should be hired into the family office and their experiences and abilities have changed – they're no longer just caretakers. There needs to be a process that builds consensus around the mission and goals for the family office and how that translates into the nature of the jobs performed and the factors that will impact job performance before conducting an in-depth search in the market place for people that have more than technical skills. Hiring only becomes a crisis when you're looking for a quick hire and the short list of candidates to place in a job,' explains Rankin. 'Family office executives need to understand how to facilitate development of family missions, goals, and governance structure' and have the patience to deal with all of the aspects that are unique to the family office business.

Linda Mack of Mack International confirms the dual role of the family office. The business of the office needs to be managed in a way that ensures the high quality and cost effective delivery of services to the family. Simultaneously, the family office executive needs to work in partnership with family leadership by bringing best practices to bear in helping the family effectively accomplish its goals. 'The family office executive should facilitate clarity, consensus, and alignment of family office services with the achievement of the family's goals. He or she should also facilitate the family's development of missions, goals, and strategic plans to create sustainability for future generations,' says Mack.

The emphasis on the facilitation role of the family office supports the notion of the family office as a service entity rather than a governing entity. This positions the office to function in its authentic role as an advisory resource which works with the family in bringing the family's goals to fruition. Exhibit 13.2 shows an example of a single family office organisation with notes outlining the reporting/accountability matrix and basic qualifications for personnel. The chart shows the positions of president and chief investment officer, financial officer, and personal assistant as in-house functions with the option of outsourcing the tax and investment pieces. Legal advisors, philanthropic advisors, estate management, and other advisors may also be outsourced. Advisors providing counsel on the sale of art collections, purchasing foreign real estate, coordinating estate management staff, the purchase or sale of a yacht, and the purchase or partial purchase of a private jet are other services which are perfect candidates for outsourced arrangements.

Exhibit 13.2

Single family office organisation

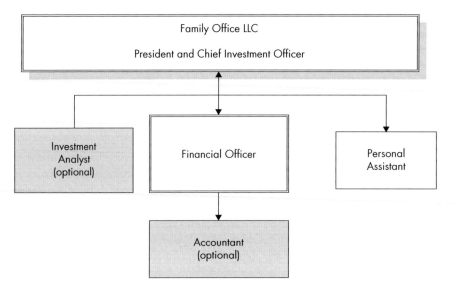

Position	Experience
President and CIO	10+ years in investment management
Financial Officer	7+ years CPA with tax background
Personal Assistant	3+ years in a professional office
Optional staff depending upon circumstances	
Accountant/tax	5+ years public accounting
Investment Analyst	3+ years in a investment business

Source: Family Office Metrics, LLC. All rights reserved. Used with permission.

Deciding which services the office should provide the family is not an easy task. Family office services involve much more than the management and transfer of the financial assets of the family. There is a fine art to managing a family's assets – both the physical assets and the intangible assets of a human, intellectual, and social nature. Astute advisors can contribute greatly to the prudent management of the family's wealth in a variety of respects. For example, Natasha Pearl[8] notes that one of the main considerations families should include in their planning is their spend rate. 'That's highly influenced by whether you purchase a plane, use fractional, use charter, or fly commercial. It's highly influenced by whether you buy your fourth house or whether you'd be content to stay in a hotel. It's highly influenced by whether you have to stay in the penthouse suite or whether you can stay in a comfortable room with a king size bed. I don't think advisors are talking enough about the spend rate and the factors that can increase or decrease it.'

Private staff is another example, says Pearl. 'You either go into homes where literally three people rush up to get your coat or, on the other hand, where there's no one there and the people are washing their own dishes. Maybe that makes them happy. On the other hand, they could be doing something more fulfilling with the time they're spending washing the dishes. There are a lot of people who feel there's still some virtue in having caretakers at each residence or a household manager at each residence while trying to be the estate manager and effectively supervise all four – that's crazy! There are people out there who have resort hotel experience who are good property managers and can take advantage of volume discount purchases so that you have consistency across your residences and don't go into one of them asking, "Where's the corkscrew? I can't find it anywhere!" It's penny wise and pound foolish not to have an estate manager.'

All of these considerations become part of the family office's operational governance structure. Which services to provide, who will provide them, how they are incorporated into the overall service mix ranging from the types of services described above to the investment and other financial wealth planning services – these all are concerns which have to be prudently governed and balanced by the family office entity for the overall benefit of the family. So, as is any enterprise, the family office is concerned with providing services in the most efficient and cost-effective manner. Outsourcing should be decided based on the quality of service obtainable relative to the price the family is willing to pay.

Family office considerations in today's marketplace

Indeed, the family office may be viewed as a simplifier or manager of complex wealth management issues. Yet each family office will reflect the dynamic composition of the family it serves. The family's generational maze determines the dynamics of the family which, in turn, determine the specific governance structure of that family along the guidelines set forth in Chapter 11. Each family office will have a different 'flavour' depending upon the generation starting it, the event which initiated its conception, and the family entity's 'differentness'.[9] The specific operational needs and goals of an office also will differ based on those factors. The dynamics of the family, born of the generational perspectives embedded in the archetypes at work in the generational cycles, have a critical bearing on the success of the family office entity. Carroll notes that generational issues are very important in governance from the standpoint of clarifying the founders' roles and the roles of the next generation as well as putting together the right board of directors. The family office CEO reports to the board or the family council and the selection of those board members or council members is influenced by generational issues which, in turn, influence the family office.

Rankin also observes that family offices change depending on the family dynamics, the generation in charge, and the needs of the family. Consequently, the governance structure has to be flexible and responsive to the evolution within the family. There may be years when a family member runs the family office. That family member will be the CEO and the employees of the family office will report to him or her. Or, if there is a family board and the office is self-sufficient, governance is going to function differently than when the patriarch played a direct role in management.

Carroll positions the family office CEO as the gatekeeper between the family and the rest of the world. The person serving the family in that position has to be able to help the family understand the issues, make plans, and execute those plans. He or she not only has to have technical skill but also has to have the ability to lead and to be a mentor.[10]

If a liquidity event has occurred, the family office may become the new 'family business', setting into motion an entirely different set of family office governance parameters. A new entity such as a limited liability company may be formed to serve as a sort of holding company for other businesses the family owns and/or partnerships in which the family is involved. In such cases, the family may wish to set up a PTC which would function as the family office for the family with the multi-family office investment firm becoming the operating business. Exhibit 13.3 shows a typically complex structure providing family services which can be enhanced by the PTC structure depicted in Exhibit 13.4.

In Exhibit 13.3, we see the disparate relationships between the various family member groups (clients) at the top, the governing bodies on the second level of the chart, the family office and other advisors in the lower levels and service providers at the bottom. Both Exhibit 13.3 and Exhibit 13.4 show the 'clients' at the top of the chart and the 'advisors' in the bottom half of the chart with the board, family office or PTC and other functional entities in the middle. Exhibit 13.4's PTC chart shows the authority given that entity to govern relationships between all levels. The clients at the top of the chart include ownership entities both inside and outside the original entity of family. Such external ownership may include other families who have been invited in to participate in the family's investment focus, making the new family business a multi-family office.

The family entities who exercise control (those who have the power to make discretionary decisions) of the owned assets are on the second level. The board acts as protector to make sure various internal trustees do their jobs. The investment and distribution committees manage the assets of the trusts and make appropriate distributions. The audit committee ensures the assets are managed prudently and that the distributions are documented correctly. On the lower half of the chart, entities in which the owners are invested are advised by investment and allocation advisors; service providers and other types of advisors are shown as support entities. A PTC enables the family to house its own trustees rather than hire corporate trustees or other individuals. The PTC as a whole is then viewed as a trustee of all the entities contained within the family office structure. PTCs set up for single families should, according to Duncan,[11] become the family office. 'For a family with significant wealth, the two should essentially be the same in order to avoid a lot of duplication. A private trust company can do everything a family office does and more.'

Duncan says an advantage of positioning a PTC as the implementation arm of the family structure is that this trustee can make decisions which are more consistent with the family's wants and needs. 'An individual or corporate trustee may make decisions they view as being consistent with the family's wants or what they've been told are the family's wants, but the decisions that a private trust company makes as trustee are informed by a governing body that's been created by the family and represents the family as a whole.'

Exhibit 13.3 shows how a PTC can effectively organise the complex functions of investment, oversight, and implementation required of a family office. The board and other functioning entities serve as internal 'checks and balances' safeguards for the family's financial assets.

Indeed, the family office entity or private trust company may serve the family as a platform

Exhibit 13.3

Typical complex family services structure

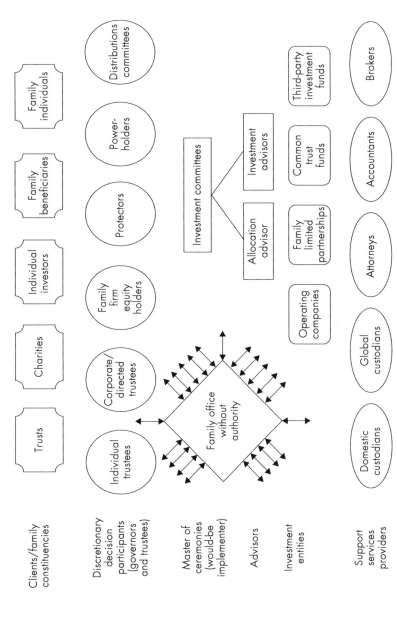

Exhibit 13.4

Private trust company organisation

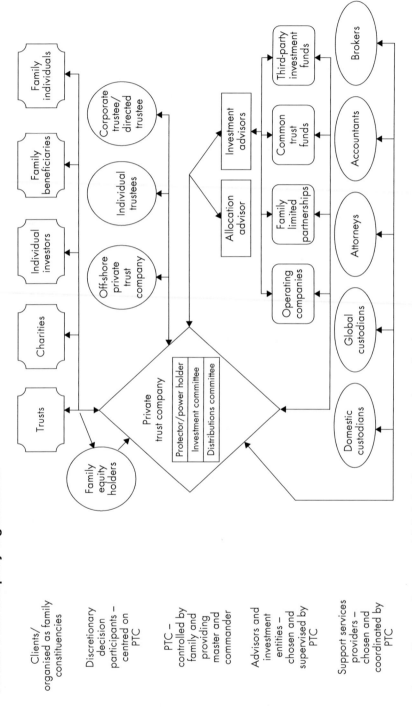

through which the portfolio of the family wealth can be managed. A PTC can actually be a vital instrument for family governance by serving, as Hughes describes, as a 'family seat or centre to which family members can look for leadership and services in their individual pursuits of happiness'. A PTC also encourages the use of protectors as an alternate source for trustee/beneficiary dispute resolution.[12] A family office or PTC can provide investment management, tax planning, estate planning, and other financial and investment management for the financial assets; it can work with family members to plan family meetings and facilitate the implementation of other family governance projects to foster the family's human capabilities and the 'spirit of family'; it can provide educational planning, set up apprenticeships, provide access to external support for entrepreneurial ventures to support the family's intellectual capacities; it can offer support for networking, the family foundation, community involvement, and political influence for the family's social capital. These activities revolve around the family and its various forms of capital; no family office activity occurs for the exclusive benefit of the family office itself. Therefore, the role of governance of the family office entity is to provide support to the governance systems of the family and the family business.

If the family experiences a liquidity event as discussed above, the family office may develop a specific investment specialty such as real estate or some type of hedging strategy. It may offer this specialty to other families.[13] The nature of the family office changes and its needs more closely resemble that of a family business – in essence because it has *become* the family business. In this case, the three separate entities do not disappear into two; but the entities of the family office and the family business combine to form a unique family entity. Exhibit 13.4 is an altered version of the Exhibit 12.2 shown in Chapter 12 where the business and the family office are shown side by side as service components within the overall governance delegation of authority.

In Exhibit 13.5, the chart reflects the shifting of the service provisions the family office entity was expected to provide into the realm of family governance with the creation of a post entitled 'family president' to oversee the functions of education and family committee activities. Recall the discussion in the Family Governance chapter of the role of a family member as 'project manager' in working with the family office in these areas. By appointing a family president, the family council effectively frees the family office of the more personalised aspects of service, allowing the multi-family office to more fully incorporate a family business governance structure designed to generate financial profits. This frees the family office to give greater attention to the needs of the business of managing the family's financial assets and maximises the relationship between family governance and governance of the family office entity.

Operational governance of the family office entity

To this point, we have examined each primary family entity and the facets of appropriate governance for each. We have seen how vital the respective support processes are to the entity being served and that none of the three entities stands completely on its own. Just as the entity of family is larger than the individual family members, the concept of governance necessarily becomes larger to enable the successful integration of all three governance systems and the ultimate support of family goals which include goals for the business as well as the family. As noted earlier, the function of the family office is to serve the family and house the tools that foster the family wealth such as investment management, tax and legal planning, estate planning and/or personal family services to support the growth of human, intellectual, social, and financial capacities.

Exhibit 13.5

Family office support flow chart

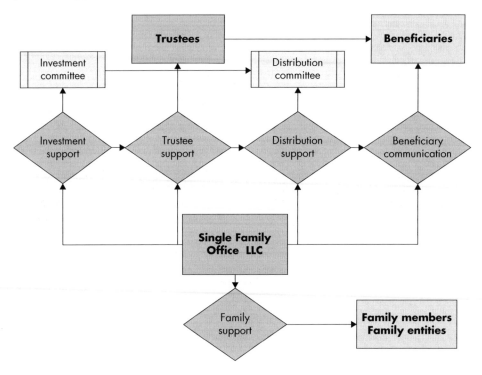

Source: Family Office Metrics, LLC. All rights reserved. Used with permission.

In Exhibit 13.6, we again see how the three governance structures work together, conceptually integrating the governance systems of each of the three entities so that decisions are made appropriately for each entity, then viewed comprehensively for the benefit of the whole. The family either votes or appoints delegates from the family and the family business to the family board. Outside directors may also be appointed as well as the family office executive. Representatives from the two primary entities, the family and the family business, serve on the board and representatives from the family office are appointed at the family's discretion, based on the family office structure. Thus, the family board is the collection of family representatives chosen by the family to guard their interests and make decisions which will both protect the family wealth and foster its development.

Exhibits 13.6 and 13.7 are a more robust illustration than Exhibit 13.1 of the implementation of governance with the family office positioned to appoint positions of authority between the family services performed, the people and advisors performing them, and the family members themselves as well as family entities such as the family operating business. It shows how the various sub-entities work together for the benefit of the other two primary entities of the family and the family business. Although the chart shows the trustees hiring the family office entity to provide support services,

Exhibit 13.6

Governance: delegation of authority

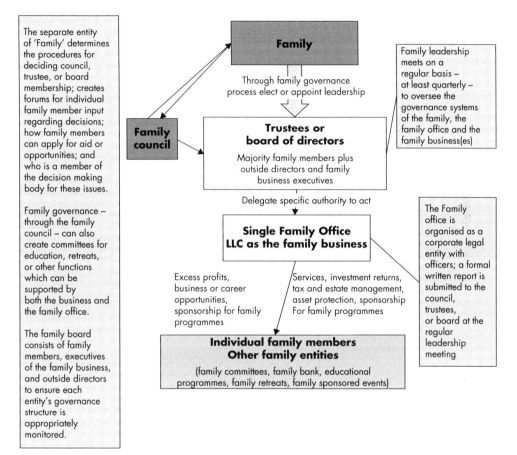

Source: graymatter Strategies LLC. Family Office Metrics LLC. Used with permission.

the trustees themselves – as well as all other family advisors – are, in some form or fashion, under the governance of the family. A trust protector may be hired to ensure trustees are indeed fulfilling their duties and should have the power to replace a trustee if that becomes necessary. Although the family office is the conduit through which multiple advisors work with the family, the unique nature of family office service includes the possibility that the family may not take the advice of its advisors. Such a decision ultimately may be to the detriment of the family, but it is, nevertheless, the family's prerogative and any resulting mistakes fall under the accountability of the family.[14] The family office has the responsibility to help the family understand possible ramifications of such a decision, but *all advisors – either in-house or outsourced – as well as family office executives and staff are deemed to be in the service of the family.*

Exhibit 13.7

Family office flow of authority and services

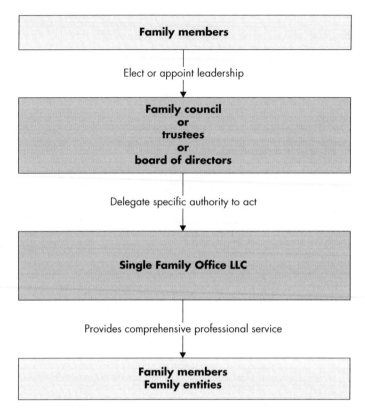

As the number of family members and family entities grows, the demands of the family office become more complex. Families may wish to establish a private trust company to better organise the management of all their concerns. Hundreds of trusts, multiple operating businesses and partnerships, multiple trustees, advisors of all types, and multiple investment pools need coordination and monitoring if the proper service level to the family and its entities is to be maintained.

The overriding element of family office governance

The family office is a unique entity with a duty to implement best practices while remaining attuned to the family and flexible enough to serve them in a manner consistent with the family's goals. The role of family governance relative to the family office is to select the services needed by the family, select the staff and advisors qualified to provide them, allow those advisors and service providers to do their best work within the guidelines the family has set forth, and replace them if the family collectively feels they are not performing as they should. In the best situations, family governance and family office governance work side by side, with overlap and direct family involvement in the areas deemed to be most appropriate. The right staff and advisors who sign on with such an arrangement take on very fulfilling professions because they are enabled to serve at the highest level.

'You want the brightest and best from the industry who have the service heart required to work with families in a close relationship and who really want to make a difference on a private basis rather than working in a public company, accounting firm, or law firm. You have to really understand the nature of the family office business and the interrelationship between family issues and business issues,' explains Rankin.[15]

Hughes notes that the core addition to a family's suite of services by affording its own office is having people who are committed to the principle that in everything they do, they will seek to educate family members on their roles in that part of the family's administration and government. One surprising result of the survey conducted by Williams and Preisser was that much greater time was devoted by family members in setting up estate planning documents than in educating their progeny to effectively manage the impact those documents would have on their lives.[16]

Indeed, according to Hughes, '*Unless the educational component is the raison d'être for the office in the first place, there is no reason to have a family office* as opposed to using out-sourced services. Outsourcing will always be more cost effective and efficient, basically because the hard costs will be less. More importantly, the family will have no soft cost of its time given to the management of the office. Family offices' only reason for existence other than the hubris of saying you have one is if they are the educational antidote of the form and function paradox.'[17]

This means that the primary focus of the family office is *qualitative*, not *quantitative*. I would add to Hughes' statement above by noting that education simply cannot be effective unless the family has developed a solid foundation of family communication and trust on which to build. The family respondents in the Williams and Priesser survey attributed 60% of the fulfilment rate of the Proverb to a lack of communication and trust among family members and 25% to heirs' lack of clarity regarding their roles and the responsibilities which accompany them.[18] *Therefore, everything we have discussed in this chapter up to this point is completely moot if an overriding concern of supporting the trust-level communication and educational roles of the family governance system are not first and foremost in the minds of family office personnel.*

This turns the dynamic of the family office completely on its head. Rather than thinking of the family office as simply a place to house trustees and advisors to manage the family's financial assets, it becomes a critical support system for the communication and educational roles of family governance. Since the support of those roles becomes the very reason for the family office's existence, it also places the family office squarely in its most proper and excellent role of serving the family in its effort to achieve its goals. Even if the family office becomes another business of the family, the service element remains. Within this new dynamic, an added dimension for hiring family office personnel emerges: *Personnes de confiance* should be hired for the key qualitative positions and *Personnes d'affaire* should be hired for the supportive quantitative functions.[19]

Examples of qualitative positions include but are not limited to:

- education of younger generations on how family systems and organisms work and their roles in making them work[20];
- family meeting support (communication, mission statements, family constitution);

- coordination and monitoring of family advisors;
- estate planning and wealth transfer structure design; and
- family bank process design.

Examples of quantitative positions include but are not limited to:

- operations and business processes;
- investment management and trustee functions;
- office management and compliance issues;
- tax management;
- family foundation management; and
- personal services management.

Conversely, a virtual office structure – one which employs outsourcing as a total solution – by its very nature cannot effectively support either the communication or educational role of the family governance system. The support of these roles comprises the soft costs of the family office. The virtual structure is designed primarily with efficiency in mind and soft costs are not part of the equation. Therefore, if a family cannot afford the luxury of a family office focused on supporting the communication and educational functions of the family governance system, the family governance structure itself will have to develop and support those programmes and outsource the hard cost functions in the most efficient manner possible.

Now, if we go back over the entire chapter with these new elements in mind, we see how the three forms of governance – family governance, family business governance, and family office governance – truly complement each other toward achieving the ultimate goal of the family entity. Chapter 11 begins the discussion of governance with that very concept in mind and the three forms of governance have now been brought together conceptually under a single umbrella to support the goals of the family – including goals of dynamic preservation of all its entire portfolio of wealth and avoidance of the Proverb's edict. As noted in Chapter 11, 'any form of family governance is designed to provide a means for the higher functioning of the joint decision making process – no more and no less'. The paradox of many governance systems today is that families are so concerned with getting a form of governance in place that the functions of governance are often overlooked, causing the governance systems to fail, the family goals to go unachieved, and the family wealth to be diminished. The combined focus of family governance and family office governance on building communication and trust among family members and educating family members to perform their roles excellently is, as Hughes so aptly states, 'the antidote of the form and function paradox'.

Chapter 14 rounds out these four chapters by illustrating through a family case study the embodiment of the principles outlined through our discussion of the three forms of governance. Most importantly, essential points of application follow these four chapters for the purpose of creating a robust integration of the complete cycle of wealth management from beginning to end – from consideration of a family's particular generational maze to a dynamic, highly customised, and successful strategic allocation of all of its forms of assets and their flourishing.

[1] Kelly, J. and Nadler, S., 'Leading from below', *The Wall Street Journal*, March 3 2007, p. R4.

[2] Carroll, Jon, MBA, CPA, President and CEO, Family Office Metrics, LLC, personal interview, January 2007.

[3] Strouse, J., *Morgan: American financier*, (New York, NY: Random House, 1999), p. 206.

[4] Hughes places the minimum asset level at $60 million in his book, *Family Wealth: keeping it in the family*, (New York, NY: Bloomberg Press, 2004), p.147; John P.C. Duncan, Principal of the law firm Duncan Associates and Counselors, P.C., places the figure between $100 million and $250 million, Personal interview, February 2007.

[5] Ibid. pp. 150–151.

[6] Hughes, James E., Jr., Personal conversation, March 2007.

[7] Rankin, MJ, President, the Rankin Group, Personal interview, November 2006.

[8] Pearl, Natasha, Founder of Aston Pearl, Personal interview, December 2006.

[9] Hughes, James E., Jr., Personal interview, October 2007.

[10] Carroll, Jon, MBA, CPA, President and CEO, Family Office Metrics, LLC, personal interview, January 2007.

[11] Duncan, John P. C., Principal of the law firm Duncan Associates Attorneys and Counselors, P.C., Personal interview, February 2007.

[12] Hughes, J.E., Jr., *Family Wealth: keeping it in the family*, (New York, NY: Bloomberg Press, 2004), pp. 152.

[13] Ehlern, S., 'Global private wealth management: an international study on private wealth management and family office services for high net worth individuals', doctoral study (London, Zurich: Ferguson Partners Family Office, 2006–2007), p. 256.

[14] Handler, Thomas J., J.D., P.C., Handler, Thayer & Duggan, September 2006.

[15] Rankin, M.J., President, the Rankin Group, Personal interview, November 2006.

[16] Williams, R. and Preisser, V., *Preparing Heirs* (San Francisco, CA: Robert D. Reed, 2003), p. 45.

[17] Hughes, James E., Jr., Personal email exchange, March 14 2007.

[18] Williams, R. and Preisser, V., *Preparing Heirs* (San Francisco, CA: Robert D. Reed, 2003), pp. 17, 36, 43.

[19] Hughes, James E., Jr., Personal email exchange, March 14 2007.

[20] Ibid.

Chapter 14

The Laird Norton family: a governance case study

Throughout the governance chapters, the Laird Norton family has been cited as an example of a successful seventh-generation family with fifth generation leadership. The family's governance structure is so effective 'that the majority of Laird Norton family members come together once each year in the spirit of family, which is an important connection point. Out of 380 family members, between 200 and 250 make it to the Annual Meetings', according to Laird Norton Company CEO Jeff Vincent, the first non-family member CEO in the family's history.[1]

I am deeply indebted to Laird Koldyke and the Laird Norton family for allowing me to share their story as the real-life application of the governance tenets which have been set forth in the previous three chapters.[2] In this case study of their family, we'll take a look at the most recent generations of the family's history showing the generational influences on the dynamics of the family and, in turn, the effects of those influences on governance. In particular, we'll see how family governance functions, how the Laird Norton Company (LNC) board supports that governance, and how the family's multiple businesses support the family's needs. The effects will be shown of the shift in generational leadership from the third generation to the critical leadership of the fifth generation on the family's communication, governance, education, and philanthropy.

We will start by briefly relating the elements of the family's history that are most relevant to our discussion. This will be followed by a glimpse into its systems of communication and education, governance, philanthropy and the different generations' perspectives on the wealth. The family's humanness makes its story that much more appealing in that it uses that pervasive attribute with which we all wrestle to make more positive decisions than negative ones. This is a story of how family wealth in all its forms may be fostered from generation to generation by developing and employing the human, intellectual, and social capacities of all family members, regardless of gender, and including new family members from birth or marriage.

The Laird Norton family: a brief history

As in all successful families, the contribution of the second generation is a vital component in laying the foundation for the family's future success. In this particular family, the majority of the second generation were women, according to former family president Chalan Colby.[3] 'Their husbands ran the business but it was the women who wanted to make sure this thing hung together and that it wasn't just a business. The family aspect of the business was just as important to them. Now, there are both men and women on our board – the first woman to sort of break the ice was one of my first cousins who became the first female board member in 1970. Today, I see no one who should be a board member but who isn't because of their gender.' In fact, three women were elected to the Laird Norton Company Board of Directors that year, one from each branch of the family. Almost two decades later, Nathalie B. Simsak became the first female president.[4]

'When Nathalie became our family president in 1988, that was a *real* change for us! And that was during the time when the positions of family president and company president were held by a single person,' explains Colby. Prior to Simsak, the presidency was a post appointed by the chairman – then Norton Clapp – not one for which application could be made.[5] 'Norton basically selected the presidents and, for the most part, they were from the Seattle area and were friends of his. So the first time he reached out to the entire family and asked, "Is anybody interested?" I submitted my application just to see what would happen,' says Simsak. She did not expect to get the job immediately and did not. But she was placed on the board – a move she sensed was an opportunity for Clapp to assess her abilities. When she got the call a couple of years later offering her the presidency, she initially turned it down saying that she had submitted her application simply to raise awareness that 50% of the family's assets were not being utilised. 'I just wanted him to wake up to the fact that there were some very smart women in this family,' explains Simsak. 'But nobody said "no" to Norton!' So, in 1988 after four generations, a female family member (also a fifth generation person) took the job of president for the first time for a three-year term; when that term was over, she was asked to serve for three more years.[6]

Simsak viewed the presidency as a full time job. 'The men who had served before had done it in addition to their regular jobs. But this was my work and I expanded the role dramatically.' The first two items on the agenda for Simsak were: (a) to find out what she should focus on as president; and (b) immediately begin looking for her successor. She asked the family whether the focus should be more on the business or on the family. The overwhelming response was 'family'.

As a trained facilitator, Simsak was adept at opening doors for involvement and inviting people to express their ideas and opinions. She was able to draw on Clapp's continued patriarchal influence in the sense that 'whatever Norton wanted, people did. Our family at that time were sort of like sheep – Norton said, "this is going to happen" and everybody trusted him and said, "fine".' With Clapp's blessing, she was able to broaden communications across the family by instituting many of the programmes that exist today which have become hallmarks of the family spirit.

Some fourth generation family members were not sure about the changes but they went along with them because Simsak had Clapp's support. Most of the children's programmes, the educational opportunities, the family forums, and the annual meetings were either instituted or significantly expanded during the six years of her leadership. 'When I was a child, there were meetings but the younger generations were only invited every five years. So there wasn't the cohesive bonding that can be built when you start with infants who play with their cousins every year,' she explains. That level of give and take had never happened in the family before. Simsak's themes became 'involvement' and 'participation'. 'I wanted to find places for people to volunteer and get involved with the company. When you're involved in something personally, it means more to you.'

Clapp recognised that incorporating the talents of spouses was also important to the family's growth. Even in cases where spouses became exes, their contribution to the family enterprise was ongoing. In these cases, the spouses had truly become part of the family through their involvement and contributions. 'Norton kept employing the talents of the ex-spouses of family members. You might divorce out of the family, but you weren't leaving!' says Colby.

'The key to our success is that we've always been very inclusive,' says Simsak. 'We don't distinguish between whether you married in or whether you were born in. If you're a part of the family, you're a part of the family. Frankly, people who have married in sometimes honor this more than those of us who have been raised here because they see what a unique thing it is. It's easier for us to become ho-hum about it, but they give us key reminders about what we have. Some families think that only blood relations matter but I want to say to them, "oh, you are losing so much!"' continues Simsak. She gives the example of a woman who married into the family who established a day care business. 'We had a program set up where the company would give money to support entrepreneurial efforts – she was actually the first woman to get such support. She created a very successful business, turned around and sold it, and now works for the acquiror.'

If we pause for a moment and consider the generational archetypes at work in society at large at the time, we can see the mirroring of generational archetypes within the smaller society of the Laird Norton family. Clapp represented the GI generational archetype (Hero) with its highly patriarchal form of leadership and Simsak issued in the influence of the first half Boomer (Prophet) birth spectrum. The Silents were represented by the family's fourth generation who, although unsure of the new changes instituted by Simsak, acquiesced to them in true Silent generation style as a result of Clapp's support of Simsak, their trust in his leadership, and the 'this is going to happen' patriarchal style. Sandwiched between the third generation and the first half of the fifth, the family's Silent generation mirrored the Silent archetype of society at large: they made no leadership imprint of their own even though they were involved and active in the family.

Clapp's prescient change in leadership style from that of governing patriarch to leader from behind opened the door for a smooth transition between the generations and gave the family a tremendous gift in the process. As the inaugural leadership of the Boomer cohort within the family, Simsak's success was significantly enhanced by the duality of Clapp's patriarchal influence over the family and his recognition for the need to embrace change. His leadership was brilliant in that he did not hubristically insist on instituting the changes himself; he was able to allow the new generation leadership – a bit radical at the time since it also was female – to lead the family in the way it needed to go. And his active incorporation of the talents of family members' spouses enhanced the family's growth of human, intellectual, and social wealth.

Simultaneously as society at large was experiencing upheaval through a significant clash of generational archetypes, the family was at a critical point in its development – the stage when the fifth generation assumed leadership. Hughes states that by the time a family reaches its fifth generation, the system it has created for long-term success overtakes sheer luck as the chief ingredient for its success.[7] At this critical point, the leadership of the Laird Norton family was able to build on the success of its previous generations by enabling the family to embrace significant change and further cement the entity of family rather than oppose it and facilitate the edicts of the Proverb. Thus, the leadership of both Clapp and Simsak were vitally important to the transition process and contributed significantly to the ongoing success of the family.

Simsak's terms were succeeded by a cousin, Tim Taylor, and Peter Evans followed Taylor. In 2001 during Evans' presidency, the role of president was split in two, creating an LNC president and CEO as well as a family president. Evans was the first to serve in the separate post of family president, serving a single term; Laurie Lucas followed as interim family president for one year until the beginning of Colby's term. Vincent has held the post of LNC president and CEO since the 2001 split.

After Simsak took the ball Clapp handed her and ran with it, Taylor's presidency continued to foster broad-based inclusiveness. Colby recalls that Dr. David Bock spoke to the family during its 1990 annual meeting. He synthesised four credos while researching the family's books in preparation for the meeting and presented them when he spoke. Simsak considers the presentation of the credos as an 'ah-ha!' moment for the family. These were credos that the family founders lived by and which have, in one way or another, been passed down through the generations.

- Our life is at the frontier.
- Do business as well as possible.
- Keep material things in perspective.
- Be brothers and sisters who care about each other.

When Taylor became president in 1994, he reintroduced the concepts so they would continue to serve the family. So, whether cloaked in former generations' mores or openly more inclusive, the family has a history of keeping the entity of family as its fulcrum.

The entity of family: communication

Communication and education provide the glue that holds even 380-member families together within the larger concept of family as a separate entity. 'I think the different generations help achieve that,' says Simsak. 'The earlier generations knew everybody in the family and they introduced their children around so the family would know each other. And now, at the family meetings, we make opportunities for my generation to talk with the younger kids. They can interview us or whatever they wish. We have a luncheon with them.' Colby gives the example of a family gathering when the teens of the family went off on a beach excursion. 'They camped out around a big bonfire. Tim Taylor, who was then our joint family and business president, went out to meet with them. He just sat around the campfire and invited them to ask him any questions they wanted. I've had sixth generation family members come to me, telling me that was a turning point in their lives – that at that point, they realized that they were part of this family and that they could play a role. You have to make them feel a part of things.'

Simsak adds, 'When we first started having annual meetings, my mother used to define people as "this is so-and-so from the X branch". But I said, "Forget this – we're all one family here!" There are some branches and individuals in the family who are wealthier than others and being inclusive breaks down barriers. If we're part of a whole, then we're all in this together. So now, when someone refers to some type of branch division, it seems foreign. This sixth generation – unless a grandparent has reminded them "from which branch they cometh" – doesn't come from a branch; they come from the Laird Norton family.'

'There are greater numbers of family members each year, so you have to come up with new methods of communication,' says Vincent. 'There are a variety of ways we maintain the family history. We have an archivist who comes in once a month to maintain the company and family archives. The archivist also goes out and interviews members of the fourth generation. We keep things on file and bring them back in different ways in the family meetings and newsletters. There are letters dating all the way back to incorporation, letters on key decisions that were made and refer to something that was done 40 years ago. We sometimes take the time and try to understand what was done 40 years ago and to figure out how we need to think about something today.'

Hughes notes that 'our family stories are how we define the specific ideas and the values and practices flowing from them that define our sense of family, our differentness. We recount these stories as a way of knowing who we are. We seek the connections and the sense of common family nature they offer'.[8] For the Laird Norton family, that connectedness is nurtured on several fronts. Under the auspices of the Family President, the family tree is updated and distributed to all family members every five years and access to the family tree is always available on the family's intranet. The family newsletter, *Woodstock*, is written by family members with articles from the company archivist and contains news about family events – births, deaths, weddings, travelogues – articles and notices about upcoming company events, family programmes, and the family's various philanthropic entities. The original newsletter dates back to 1975 when it was called *The Gazette*. From 1976–1979, it was called *The Log* and was edited by a member of the fourth generation. Two fifth generation members co-edited the inaugural issues of *Woodstock* from 1978–1980 'when the fifth generation was seeking its own voice within the family', according to the current editor.

Box 14.1
Linking generations

Woodstock
Intranet
Family Directory
Laird Norton Family Tree
Archivist

Source: www.lairdnortoncompany.com. Used with permission.

'Our family programs are extensive,' explains Koldyke.[9] 'The Laird Norton Company is a holding company that owns and manages operating businesses but it is also a company that sponsors family related programs and initiatives. We have a philosophy and a culture of involvement that permeates both the business side and the family side of our family enterprise.'

But involvement is invited, not demanded or 'expected' in the traditional sense. Koldyke states that well-run families tend to have a family leader who is, for the most part, not resolute on his or her position and is able to communicate that effectively to the family. The successful ones have a process that makes sure family members feel they have been heard, whether or not they are actively involved at the time. 'We have a culture of participation but we don't mandate it. If you don't want to get involved, that's OK. We certainly encourage people – in some cases, we recruit those who we think are particularly capable of a given opportunity but a cousin who does not participate is held in no less regard than a cousin who does.'

Regarding participation and involvement, Simsak notes the importance for family members to have the ability to ebb and flow with what's going on in their personal lives. 'If they say "this isn't working for me right now but please be open to my coming back when I'm ready" and you can hear that without making a judgment, then they *will* come back.' She acknowledges: 'There's life beyond the communal family! In some families when somebody doesn't step up to the plate when they're first asked, people think they're not interested or not capable and those people just get shut off. Our family doesn't do that.'

This strength of family as a separate entity serves as a positive influence by allowing family members to thrive within a safe environment. 'Sometimes people need to be asked and if you can value everybody and give them a safe place, their expertise will become evident,' says Simsak. 'That is one of the biggest blessings of this family. There's no way I would have ever been president of a company or chairman of the board of a major business if I hadn't been connected with this family. It shows that, given the chance, someone like me can just blossom!'

Good communication fosters family education

As outlined in Chapter 11, the influence of good family governance flows back and forth between family members and the family businesses to benefit both. According to Colby, educating the family about its businesses is an ongoing challenge. 'For a long time, it was something that people just sort of went along with but now, there's much more of a requirement to be involved and to be knowledgeable about the family's activities. So, how do we accomplish that without forcing it down their throats?' Colby asks. She feels the next generation is much more interested in the family's activities than the fifth. 'I think a lot of us in the fifth generation look at each other and say, "Thank God for the sixth generation!"'

'The real challenge in educating the younger generation is not to lecture to them,' she notes. The LNC sponsors a number of ongoing communication and educational events that provide multi-faceted support for the family knowing each other and participating as dynamic stakeholder owners. Koldyke considers one of the most important family events to be Camp Three Tree, a four-day long day camp for family members age 13 and under. 'This is a dawn-to-dusk space where cousins – no matter how loosely related they may be – come together as a family unit in Montessori-like age groups. They bond together for four days through fun and games. We try to teach the older ones specific things about Laird Norton – we're not as good at that as we should be but the important thing is that they swap stories about being at Camp Three Tree together. As a unit, as a family, they're strengthening the linkages that will allow them to work well together as adults later.'

Box 14.2
Celebrating spirit and enterprise

Laird Norton University
Family Forum
Community Service Project
Camp Three Tree

Source: www.lairdnortoncompany.com. Used with permission.

'My greatest challenge as chairman is shepherding the various and often conflicting opinions of our family – trying to understand and encourage unity within a community that brings differing opinions and positions, which we welcome,' Koldyke continues. Family communication boils down to confidence in the leadership and to a sense that everyone has a voice and is being heard. As it applies to the business, confidence and communication stem from a feeling of a family member knowing what to expect of the business and knowing how to behave in a business setting.[10] 'Within the family, knowing individual family members as people is very important. It's face to face; it's at the campfire; it's at breakfast; it's those four days together which are augmented by all the other programs. Real confidence and harmony are not built over the phone.'

Another part of really knowing each other is working through conflict, an opportunity which presents itself in the Family Forum. The Forum is essentially a block of time set aside during the Annual Meeting for family members to speak out, offer ideas, and raise questions about family issues. Simsak began the Forum before she became president expressly for the purpose of creating a safe environment where family members would feel free to express their opinions and feelings. In the days when Clapp was chairman, lists of ideas were created from the Forum and presented to the appropriate committee or the board for consideration. No names were attached so the submissions were completely anonymous. By the next Annual Meeting, if not before, the ideas, issues, and questions would have been addressed.

Over the years, the Forum has become a venue through which family members can feel free to express their ideas and feelings to leadership directly, knowing they will be genuinely heard and their issues and feelings acknowledged on the spot. Such freedom of expression can create a difficult and emotional environment; it can also be an opportunity to foster the entity of family. Koldyke says, 'You have to listen through the emotion and try to listen for the point the person is trying to make. You listen for the motivation behind what's being said and try to figure out how to validate the position of the person. If that position is diametrically opposed to where the company is or where I feel we need to go, we have to figure out how to make sure that person feels his or her voice was heard – and heard seriously – and how to validate that person's position although the ultimate decision might not support it.'

Sometimes valuable education comes in the form of experience. In the 1980s, the family invited a guest speaker to talk about inherited wealth during the family's annual gathering, the Annual Meeting (also called the Retreat or the Summit). According to Colby, one of the most important messages from that speaker was that allowing a family member to lose part of his or her inheritance could be a valuable lesson. 'You might go off and buy yourself a Ferrari and then realize – all of a sudden – there went the money! But that wasn't necessarily a bad thing because it was part of a learning opportunity. For this reason, of course, the wealth should be passed in stages rather than given to heirs all at once.'

Other LNC sponsored family programmes include an associate director programme that provides a chance to observe the boards of directors of either LNC, one of its subsidiaries, or the family foundations. They learn how a board works and gain experience on the governance side about running and operating a business. There is an associate education assistance programme where the company gives limited financial reimbursement for continuing education. The Annual Meeting, a four and a half-day gathering, includes a financial academy for younger family members that emphasises not only the language of business but also basic accounting and business practices that are relevant to the family businesses.[11]

Box 14.3
Laird Norton family enrichment programme

Intern Programme
Associate Education Assistance Programme
Associate Opportunity Fund
LNC Associate Director Programme

Source: www.lairdnortoncompany.com. Used with permission.

This is in stark contrast to the way things were done in earlier generations. 'With my parents, there was no conversation about wealth or educating us about it because not only was it not a priority, it wasn't even talked about. And educating the females was absolutely not a priority!' says Simsak. She recalls that, even though the financial wealth was her mother's, she saw her father come home and bring her mother papers to sign without any discussion about anything. 'The women were absolutely in the background. They came to meetings but they would bring their knitting with them. We used to joke about them knitting. That just doesn't happen today!' she says.

Yet another communication/education programme the company sponsors is Laird Norton University. 'Laird Norton University is a great thing!' adds Simsak. 'We get to sign up and hear our family share their personal interest – weaving, photography, whatever is of interest to the family. If someone's interested in trekking in Tibet, they come and present about trekking in Tibet. It helps you learn things about people because the family is so big, it's not easy to know the things that are meaningful to people.' According to Koldyke, the company has sponsored a new series of family events promoting travel together. The first in the series was a 2008 trip to Ireland. 'We have the courage and interest to try new things. The family has significant roots in Ireland so we thread that through it and also meet with another multi-generational family to share stories.'

Governance

All of these activities are part of the family governance system which is sponsored and supported by the LNC and the family's other businesses or foundations. The Laird Norton family clearly sees the Figure 8 connection between the family and family business governance systems and, like any large successful family, that connection supports family members on a wide variety of levels. 'By the time a family gets to the sixth generation, wealth becomes determined as much by individual family line estate planning as by the family business. So, we have family members where their Laird Norton wealth is a very, very small percentage of their overall net worth. But there could be seventh generation family members who are children today who have a significant amount of value pursuant to a generational trust of which they may be beneficiaries. Ownership is reasonably wide spread and it varies by each family member and by their estate planning,' explains Koldyke.

He points to another category of family wealth that has to do with the spiritual well being of the family. 'Although the economic well being may not be evenly spread across the family, the spiritual net worth of the family seems to be. We see evidence of this at our family meetings where the number of shares someone owns has absolutely no bearing on who can or should participate in our family enterprises, our businesses, and our programs. It has zero bearing. Ownership makes a difference in matters of major corporate governance. But relative to managing the family business and decisions made by the board, the matter of where the wealth is concentrated is rarely, if ever, taken into consideration.'

Koldyke states that well-run families tend to have a family leader who is, for the most part, not resolute on his or her position and is able to communicate that effectively to the family. The successful ones have a process that makes sure family members feel they have been heard. He notes, 'My greatest challenge as chairman is shepherding the various and often conflicting opinions of our family – trying to understand and encourage unity within community that brings differing opinions and positions, which we welcome.'

That is why, Koldyke says, the Family Forums are free of judgment and open to any comments any family member wishes to make. Family members break into small groups and will have specific questions the board wishes them to answer. The groups subsequently reconvene, the answers are listened to, and any other input is heard and considered before making a final decision.

Colby acknowledges that such a process can create a temporary chaos but that order can be found through chaos. 'There's a theory that things can't change, can't move forward if you don't go through the chaos. You can have things fly off in a hundred different directions and still be able to pull them back into some sense of order. For example, when we were considering the sale of our major asset, Lanoga, we got together, broke into small groups, and talked about various ideas. The board didn't just come to the family and say, OK, here's what we're going to do.' Colby says some family members thought they should go public, others thought the family should find a partner. 'We had all sorts of ideas coming forth. I think that's how we got 98 percent of the family to support the sale – everybody was able to speak, be heard, and have their views acknowledged.'

The family also has numerous committees created and chaired by family members. There is a nominating committee whose members are chosen by the chairman of the board and which is completely independent and autonomous from that point on. He explains, 'There are typically at any one point in time two to three LNC directors on the nominating committee out of a total of 11 members. So the nominating committee is truly representing the family's interests at every level.' Koldyke notes that in many families, such a committee can be characterized as simply a puppet of the board, 'but that is by leaps and bounds not the situation at LNC'. Each Laird Norton business has one or two associate director positions open to the family. The nominating committee nominates candidates for the LNC board and the associate director members of the board – all of whom are elected by the entire family.

The LNC board has seven family members, two outside independent directors, and Vincent and Colby as representatives of management. The Laird Norton Company CEO and family president report to the board. An important aspect of the governance structure, the Family Council Committee, is a committee of the Board and is chaired by the Family President. Eight family members serve on the committee which provides leadership of non-investment matters involving LNC and assists the Board in overseeing LNC Member programmes. So there's a family governance structure, a family office governance structure, and Vincent manages the family business governance structure.[12]

The entity of family remains an ever-present focal point. 'In an enterprise as wide as ours, you can't focus too much gravitas and importance on the business over family. The business has a crucial role but it's not the most crucial role. The crucial role is involvement. It's making people feel aligned with and part of this Laird Norton enterprise. People determine their own roles – they're encouraged to pop their heads up out of the hole and say, "It's my turn". They're encouraged to have their ideas spread widely and to have a relationship with those on the nominating committee,' explains Koldyke.

Although there are continuing threads of the entity of family throughout this family's history, the normal variations in focus between family and business which have the potential to undermine the preeminence of family governance have occurred throughout the generations. Colby notes the differing views of her 91-year-old mother and her own daughter. 'Although my mother appreciates the "family", she basically believes this is a business. My daughter, on the other hand, thinks that we're predominantly a family. Yes, it's nice that we have a business because that pays for the family things, but the really important thing about us is the family.'

Good family governance includes checks and balances to ensure input and bolster participation from all family members during the times when focus gets off track. Simsak adds, 'When the presidency was a single post, only family members held it and the emphasis was more on family. Jeff came not knowing about the LNC family, not knowing about *this* family, and the focus became business. And, of course, Laird is very focused on business,' referring to current chairman Koldyke. Simsak attributes the incident described earlier where family members felt they had not been properly consulted regarding proposed changes sent out by the board to this temporary shift back to the business focus. 'It seemed leadership had veered off in its own direction. There were six of us who said, "Excuse, me. Stop! You work for *us* and don't forget it!" We reminded the shareholders that their power was in voting this board. It was a reminder for the family leaders to slow down and remember the values. It's the value system that says "family is important and business supports that sense of family" that keeps this family together. Everything had seemed to become more secretive at that point and people didn't like that,' she explains. From the concerted efforts by leadership over the last few years to foster greater communication and participation, the lessons from that incident, obviously, have been well learned.

Koldyke adds, 'Today, there is an evolving view of the Laird Norton Company as a responsible steward over the preservation and growth of both the family's spiritual and economic wealth. The family is realizing that strong leadership, responsible governance, and professional management at the Laird Norton Company is of significant value as we build for the seventh and eighth generations.'

Good family governance provides wealth protection

'Success can be defined in two ways,' says Colby, 'business success or success as a family. We've gone through different stages of success and have developed different types of businesses over the history of the family. One element for success is patience. Another is the lack of pressure to continue paying dividends no matter what happens to the business. For many families, the sole source of their income is the family business so they may end up taking more risk than they should because of everyone's need for dividends. We've considered it better to put a lot of the growth back into the businesses instead of trying to get as much out of them as we can.'

As a non-family member – a closely involved 'outsider' looking in – Vincent describes his observations on the success of the family. 'To say that the Laird Norton family might not continue on would border on heresy! The family does a very good job of bringing the kids together, the cousins together at family retreats. It's really a childhood bonding exercise that will, hopefully, carry you on into your 20s or 30s. So there's the expectation of continuance, the things we do together to develop the relationships, and the bonds that make people want to come together.'

No family can be successful without a strong desire on the part of family members to be so. Vincent notes that family success is difficult to define. 'The Laird Norton family has a desire to keep going for an indefinite period of time. At the same time, it maintains a business partnership that is based on its financial success and a set of common values. In looking at this family and the reasons it is successful, there's a sense of community that's very important to them – a sense of something special and unique that's hard to find any other place in life. It's those dynamics and knowing how to make the difficult trade-offs and prioritizations. Sometimes you even have to emphasize the individual more than the broader family based on what's happened over a 20 or 30-year period of time.'

In advising families who are creating new wealth and thinking about governance issues, Vincent says, 'There are three things that are essential. One, individual family members have to have a sense of something beyond themselves to give them purpose. The family has to realize the value in keeping people together – that the sum is greater than the individual parts. Two, you have to understand that there are trade-offs. There are going to be points in time where you will have to make tough decisions involving trade-offs between the individual versus the family versus business. Those are conscious decisions that will have to be made.' Vincent also points to the danger of taking the financial wealth for granted in making those tough decisions. 'If you believe you can just do everything, there will come a critical point where the resources needed to address a critical need simply won't be there. And third, you have to have a culture that embraces change, which is something we've really had to work on. You've got to remain flexible because the business is going to change – we're not in the same businesses we were 150 years ago or just 10 years ago.'

Clapp was the first to encourage a more active investment approach.[13] Today, the family businesses and investments no longer hinge on the fact that the family's financial wealth originally came from the lumber industry. It has significant investments in the financial services, real estate, and private equity sectors. Vincent speaks of a 'generational harvest' where a business or other asset may be sold to provide liquidity needed as a safety net for the family. That helps to balance the needs of the individual members, the broader family, and the family business. The Lanoga sale was such a harvest. Not only did the sale help the family fund new opportunities, but it freed capital for developing a new philanthropic entity within the family as described below.

From a family office perspective, Laird Norton Tyee serves some of the family in the area of wealth management but is separate from all other family programs and businesses. Laird Norton Tyee is a multi-generational office which is used by approximately one third of family members. It was set up approximately 40 years ago and is majority owned by LNC but also serves third party clients.

Attitudes of the generations

Attitudes toward the wealth, including issues of privacy, are reflected differently over the past few generations. For members of the GI and Silent generations, the topic of the family wealth was sequestered – simply not open for discussion. 'You just never would have spoken about it,' says current family president Chalan Colby. 'There are some funny stories about how, at age 21, family members would be taken down to visit the family attorney who would say, "Well, here. You've inherited this", and they'd never have known a thing about it!'

'My husband and I felt we were stewards and it was our responsibility to pass our wealth along to other generations,' notes Simsak. 'Our generation felt like we almost couldn't use it for us but my children are not that way. They think more in terms of "I have this gift, how can I use it?" It's a balance between a global perspective and a personal benefit. One of my sons is a practicing artist and he can do that because of his resources. For my generation, it was "we have to earn our own way" and save what was given to us to pass on to the next generation.'

In the age of the internet and websites such as MySpace, Facebook, Del.icio.us, and Digg this, families' efforts to protect their wealth and their privacy are becoming more challenging. Since the fourth generation, the family has gone from not speaking about the wealth to facing the facts that with the Echo generation – and younger Gen-Xers – that privacy in the traditional sense is disappearing. Family president Colby notes, 'As I was writing the most recent letter to the family, a newspaper article came out which caused a great deal of concern among our family members because it contained names and pictures of some of our family members and we just don't do that as a family!' says Colby. But in looking at the situation, 'we realized we just can't fly under the radar anymore. We can limit [the exposure], but that's as far as we can go.'

Philanthropy

In looking at future generations and the ingredients for continued family success, Vincent notes, 'This family has always been very socially conscious and it's definitely present in the sixth generation. What they're doing through philanthropy reemphasizes that consciousness – its part of what keeps this family together going forward. During my first three years here, Peter Evans educated me on the importance of philanthropy to this family. It was one of his major areas of focus during his period as family president.' The first family foundation was formed in 1940. That foundation, now called the Laird Norton Foundation, has since had many iterations, focusing mainly on environmental issues. Its current focus is watershed sustainability. The Winona Foundation was created in 1982 and those were the only two family foundations for many years.

Box 14.4
Broad philanthropic goals

Laird Norton Foundation
Winona Foundation
Laird Norton Family Foundation
Member Suggested Charitable Contributions Programme
Sixth Sense Committee

Source: www.lairdnortoncompany.com. Used with permission.

The area of philanthropy has been one of the first to experience some of the benefits of the bonding that occurs among the younger generations at Camp Three Tree. 'Camp Three Tree is roughly 16 years old, so we have yet to really know the benefits. But the early returns are great! About five years ago, the sixth generation started their own committee and called themselves the Sixth Sense. They have been very influential in asking for and receiving philanthropic allocations from the family and they've been very helpful to us in thinking about amendments to the annual retreat agenda,' says Koldyke.

Colby agrees that philanthropy is an important focus for the family, especially with the younger generation. She says the sixth generation established the Sixth Sense as they entered their teens and twenties because they felt left out of the family's existing philanthropic venues and wanted to establish a group of their own. Monies are given to them each year and they decide what organisations to fund. But even that group does not offer opportunities for all family members on as wide a scale as Colby and the rest of the family leadership had hoped. 'We set aside part of the money from the Lanoga sale for a new philanthropy. Last fall, 85 family members came to Seattle to talk about what's important for our family in that regard and, as you can imagine, we got all kinds of ideas. But, believe it or not, in about a day and a half we were able to agree upon four directions and say, "OK, who wants to sign up for these and work on the committees to decide where we're going to go from here?" About two weeks ago, the 40 who volunteered got together to plan next steps. The recent gatherings which formed this fourth philanthropic arm of the family are bringing both the fifth and sixth generations together in a much more significant way.'

Simsak sees the philanthropic focus of these next generations as different from the philanthropic efforts of the past. 'Earlier generations were definitely philanthropic but it was more of a case of "this is what you do". This new generation thinks more globally. It's much larger than self, or family, or *this* family. It's more like, "how can we change the planet?" It's built into them somehow.'

This latest example of the family's governance system at work continues to show the power the family has unleashed through prudent fostering of the family wealth. Are there challenges to the growth of the family's wealth going forward? How could there not be? Like many families of wealth today, the Laird Norton family faces larger numbers of family members than ever before and a completely new and different generation which is educating themselves to assume leadership in a globalised world where opportunity is robustly accessible and the concept of privacy is being completely redefined. But the multi-generational pulse of this family holds much promise for the future. 'Never in my wildest dreams did I expect to become president of this company,' reflects Simsak. 'I expected to shake things up (with leadership) enough so they might consider my daughter at some point! But that's no longer a barrier and, today, younger family members believe they can do anything. There's a self confidence and self worth in this new generation that we somehow didn't get.' If leadership continues to successfully apply the tenets of generational wealth management, it can look forward to benefiting from its many forms of wealth for multiple generations to come.

---

[1] Vincent, Jeff, CEO, Laird Norton Company. All quotes from and attributions to Vincent throughout this chapter are from personal interview, December 2006.

[2] Leadership, Laird Norton Family. 2007. The entire contents of this chapter including all quotes and attributions as well as the author's comparisons to and conclusions from her generational wealth management premises and tenets have been examined and approved by the leadership of the Laird Norton Family.

[3] Colby, Chalan, Family President, Laird Norton Family. All quotes from and attributions to Colby throughout this chapter are from personal interview, February 2007.

[4] Colby, Chalan, Family President, Laird Norton Family, personal email exchange, April 2007.

[5] Colby, Chalan, and Simsak, Nathalie B., Family President, Laird Norton Family; Former president and CEO, Laird Norton Family and the Laird Norton Company. All references to and descriptions of the leadership of Norton Clapp and Tim Taylor are from personal interviews, February and March 2007, respectively.

[6] Simsak, Nathalie B., Former president and CEO, Laird Norton Family and the Laird Norton Company. All quotes from and attributions to Simsak throughout this chapter are from personal interview, March 2007.

[7] Hughes, J.E., Jr., *Family: a compact among generations,* (New York, NY: Bloomberg Press, 2007).

[8] Ibid.

[9] Koldyke, M. Laird, Chairman, Laird Norton Company. All quotes from and attributions to Koldyke throughout this chapter are from personal interview, December 2006.

[10] Koldyke, M. Laird, Chairman, Laird Norton Company, personal interview, December 2006.

[11] Koldyke, M. Laird, Chairman, Laird Norton Company, personal interview, December 2006.

[12] Vincent, Jeff, President and CEO, Laird Norton Company, personal interview, December 2006.

[13] Laird Norton Company website, 2007. 'About LNC; History; Third era, 1950': www.lairdnorton.com/about/history.htm.

Part 2 summary: the triangular relationship in family governance

Now that we have come full circle on the issue of family governance, we can view the Family Governance Triangle[SM] from a relational perspective. What are the appropriate relationships between the three?

Exhibit PS.1 shows the progressive order of development of the entire family governance system. In this summary, we address the fuzzy edges that overlap between the three forms of governance as well as the boundaries that separate them. We also drill deeper into the common needs of all families of wealth from a governance perspective and what makes the governance systems of large families different than those of small and medium size ones.

Exhibit PS.1

Progressive order of family governance

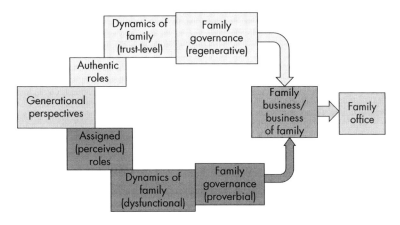

Exhibit PS.1 shows family governance development from its roots. At the point of handoff in the Generational Wealth Management Continuum[SM] from Step 1: Family systems to Step 2: Family governance, the family governance component assumes the hierarchical role. Stuart Lucas and David Lansky say it quite well: 'Family should come before business, even if it means you don't work in the family business.'[1]

One of the most striking things in working with families of wealth is the idea that, simply because a family has less than 20 members, its members do not need an organised way of interacting with each other. They look at the diagrams of governance structures in Chapter 11 and say, 'Those are for much larger families. We don't need such a complex organization'. Great complexities are often found in families of 40 members, 20 members or less. The Bancroft family, one of the families featured in the Preamble of six family stories, is a perfect example. There were only 40 of them at the time their company, Dow Jones, was sold; still, they could not effectively make a decision together regarding the sale. Instead, it was decided for them through a take-over bid. The decision was forced upon them against the will of quite a few of their members.

Families who institute governance systems which educate their members, keep them informed, and invite their input on major decisions are able to make such decisions in a much timelier manner, enabling other opportunities which may benefit the family more and which also benefit the family business and the people who work in it. It means the difference in selling a company whose value may have been suffering and, therefore, has diminished the wealth of the family, the company's shareholders, and perhaps even employees, and selling a company which has increased in value, enabling that value to continue increasing under the new ownership for the benefit of all shareholders.

Here are common governance needs of all families of wealth, regardless of size.

- A support system for nurturing the development of the family's authentic wealth.
- An organised format or structure through which to make decisions together, even if it is recorded on a single sheet of paper.
- A mutually agreed upon guide for interacting together which ensures that trust-level communication is fostered, all voices are heard, and the family truths remain the conduits for the intergenerational transfer of family values.
- A monitoring system for keeping the family's focus on its authentic wealth as the source of all material and financial wealth.
- A mutually agreed upon system for managing the paradoxical[2] relationship between family members, the business, and the family office or family office entity (which can simply be a set of external advisors and/or trustees).
- Education of family members on their authentic wealth and what it means to be a dynamic stakeholder owner; what wealth can mean to their lives; business, financial, and investment education; philanthropic and other areas.
- External professionals or staff to assist the family with tasks it cannot – or chooses not to – accomplish on its own.
- A monitoring system to keep the family on track with achieving its goals – all types, not just investment, financial, and business goals.

Families with 20 members or less can be in the fourth generation with third generation leadership. They can have family units which have gone separate ways, yet who wish to develop a greater spirit of family as an entity. They can have dysfunctional dynamics to the point of disrupting the family's ability to make decisions together. They need to know appropriate ways to interact with family advisors and other professionals who serve them. Whether 20 members or 600, the same four virtues of family are present or not; the dynamics of the family – the way they interact with each other – come from the same source, the family's generational maze and the resulting roles family members occupy. Families of all sizes need to understand the plans for wealth transfer and existing trust documents and to develop responsible and workable relationships between trustees and beneficiaries.

In larger families, the creation of a constitution may involve an initial draft by a consultant working with the family council which is then put before the rest of the family for comment. An objective third party adds a 'step away' view for the family so that all of the family's needs may be adequately and fairly addressed. In smaller families, the consultant may work directly with all family members.

Families with fewer numbers may still find it beneficial to establish a small family council. This is a different type of body than the family board. The family council must be empowered and must have representation on the board; however, representatives for the family at large should be members of the family council rather than the family board. The advantage of developing a council in smaller families especially as the third chronological generation is coming into leadership is the establishment of a structure just as the family is growing into the need for greater organisation than the single sheet of paper. It is much better to establish governing bodies as the family is growing into the need for them than to go back after serious problems have developed and try to institute better ways of functioning. The former method is preemptive; the latter tends toward focusing on the problem that is making the most 'noise' for the family at the time rather than addressing the source of the issue. Often, by doing so, the design of the governance system becomes centred on managing that particular problem rather than instituting fair and workable guidelines through which the family can effectively function. Other long term issues may remain overlooked until they, too, become a 'family event'.

Relationships between the three forms of governance

By educating family members about the appropriate roles and functions of each form of governance, the family can manage issues between the family and the family business preemptively. This puts employees at greater ease and frees business management to accomplish its most important task of generating higher profits to benefit the family, the employees of the business, and all owners.

Separating the governance components also makes it much easier for families to address their needs and to identify sources for support in achieving their goals. Monitoring the family, the family business, and the family office for possible issues becomes much easier through a three-faceted system. Imagine a family who spends the time, effort, and money to develop a governance system for the family and sets up the family office after the family governance system is in place rather than the other way around. What better insight into their authentic needs might they have! What greater knowledge of the types of advisors they need, of the services they need to provide in house, which can be outsourced, and what will be expected of each advisor, executive or staff member. Think of the time and money saved and the higher quality of service the family will experience as a result.

The separation of governance structures also enables a family to manage its emotional connection to the business in a more beneficial way. It allows a founder to see that the identity to which he is so closely tied will always be there for him, regardless of a decision to sell the business. What he built for the family will always distinguish the family. It will live on through the stories that are told – the history of generations past told by the generations who are living – and it will continue to add meaning to the lives of generations who follow.

Throughout the discussion of governance of the various family entities, the common denominator has been the empowerment of family members as dynamic stakeholder owners. The ability of the family to act together for the benefit of the family in making decisions – especially difficult ones – inspires the family spirit, recreates the family identity, and makes the family a stalwart entity.

Part 1 introduced governance not as an onerous and oppressive set of rules and regulations, but as a service element which enables the family's authentic wealth to flourish. By educating each family member to their roles and responsibilities – and the privileges that their input affords them – the family has a bevy of qualified people who are well incented to work together to make the most beneficial decisions for all. It also serves as an effective 'checks and balances' system to keep the flexibility the family needs as it experiences inevitable growth and change. A win for the family; a win for the business of the family; and a win for those serving the family through the family office.

Now, we are ready to look at family roles in a different light; we are ready to see how they influence the goals which are set which guide the investment policy for the management of the by-products of the family's authentic wealth, the material and financial wealth.

---

[1] Lucas, S.E. and Lansky, D., 'Managing paradox', *Family Business,* Spring 2010, pp. 68–70.
[2] Ibid.

Part 3:

A. Translating individual and family goals into financial and investment goals

B. Prioritisation, risk level assessment, and investment policy

'Multi-generation wealth management involves a lot more than simply generating the highest possible return … Getting to know needs is equally important, particularly when these needs are expressed in … strictly subjective terms.'

Jean L.P. Brunel*

---

* Brunel, J.L.P., *Integrated Wealth Management: the new direction for portfolio managers*, 2nd edition, (London: Euromoney Books, 2006), p. 20.

Chapter 15

Family roles: how they shape family wealth management goals

'Families who see themselves linked by affinity act from a philosophical base that has the greatest possibility of successfully enhancing the individual development and growth of their members and thus dynamically preserving themselves for at least five generations. Families who only see themselves linked by blood will rarely survive much less overcome the proverb. Family is what we leave to individuate and where we return to tell the stories of our lives to those most willing to listen.'

James E. Hughes, Jr.

The aging of generations connects the 'rhythms of the past' to the 'rhythms of the future'. It explains why each generation is not only *shaped by* history but also *shapes* later history.[1] In this way, the goals of one generation make preparation for the goals of the next. The goals that are formed are shaped by the needs of the family. The family's needs are assessed from the roles – either perceived or authentic – that family members perform. Roles are defined by generational perspectives. Therefore, each generation has fundamental impact on the goals that are set and the strategies designed to achieve them.

The process families go through in setting their goals is not even known to them in any cognitive fashion. They come up with a stated goal either from a desire to accomplish something based on their own ideas of how things should be done or in response to an upcoming meeting with an advisor where they know they are going to be asked, 'What are your goals?' This advisor may be an attorney, an accountant, or an investment or other type of wealth management advisor. The greatest influences on the answers families give to that question are the underlying factors which were present when the goals were identified. These influences have a direct yet clandestine type of impact on the goals clients set and, subsequently, all forms of wealth management decisions they make.

It is at this point where personal goals get lost in translation within the family client-advisory relationship. We are crossing over from the 'warmer' issues to the more 'solid' issues of traditional investment management. To date, these two types of issues are still treated almost completely separately. Each is robustly discussed within the confines of its individual silo. But rarely, if ever, are the two consciously and methodically connected in any meaningful way. Yet, the influence of the one upon the other is unquestionable.

One of the great failings of the wealth management industry in serving families of wealth has been the lack of recognition that these two components are indeed intricately connected. The disconnect that exists between family clients and their advisors of all types points to a huge chasm in the understanding of both clients and advisors of the consummate family wealth portfolio[SM2] and of the authentic assets that are such critical components of it.

The significance of understanding the stealth influence of generational perspectives, the impact of cyclical and linear time measurement, and the generational archetypes present within the family maze – all topics discussed at length throughout this book – lies in the impact each of these components ultimately has on the management of the family wealth.

This is a convenient point in our journey for us to bring these concepts together in a way that points to the underlying concern of families of wealth, that of fostering the family wealth beyond the reach of the three generations proverb. So we enter the next phase of our journey along the Generational Wealth Management Continuum^{SM}, that of preparing ourselves to cross over from one side to the other and, in doing so, to bridge a critical gap in the client-advisor relationship which significantly contributes to the fulfilment of the Proverb's edicts right on schedule.

This chapter and the next will prepare us to cross this great divide. In doing so, we will identify the process within the continuum through which goals are set for achievement by the family. The individual segments of the continuum flow either cognitively or subconsciously within the family process as follows.

- The influence of generational biases and prejudices on role assignment.
- Identification of needs based on family members' roles and the motivation to satisfy them.
- The manner in which goals are set for achievement.
- The connection to wealth management decisions, particularly goal-based asset allocation,[3] asset location issues, and investment selections.

By exploring the impact that roles make on goal formation, we take the wealth management process to a much higher level. Authentic goals of the family and its individual members can be more directly addressed. Advisors see their roles with much greater clarity within the wealth management continuum. We begin by briefly examining the various elements of the goal formation continuum^{SM} listed above and their influence on decision making. A case study offering two scenarios based on the application of these elements within a family will finalise our preparation.

Generational biases and prejudices toward role assignment

Clearly from our examination of the generational archetypical templates we can see that there are biases and prejudices grounded in generational perspectives which influence family members' perceptions of the roles other family members perform. Although these biases and prejudices often are subconscious, they are real and have great impact on the ability of the family wealth to regenerate itself. Such perceptions colour a person's view of a role, causing decisions to be made based on information or criteria which may be merely assumed.

Families who identify their needs based on role perceptions as opposed to authentic roles may set goals that do not match the authentic needs of the family entity or of individual family members. This potentially throws the entire wealth management mechanism off kilter, causing every investment strategy built upon the stated goals to become at best unsuccessful and at worst completely irrelevant.

By noting the differences in outcomes when family members operate within the family system in certain capacities,[4] we can readily see that roles not only are critical components in needs identification as discussed in Chapter 9, but they are also critical components in goal setting. When goals are set that match the family's authentic needs, effective strategies can be designed for successful achievement. Employment of the generational wealth management continuum[SM] brings attention to these elements and the flow of goal setting and decision making processes. When families, individuals, and their advisors become aware of the underlying forces which influence the formation of their goals, they can be more proactive in the overall wealth management process and have greater confidence that their goals will indeed be reached.

The influence of generational viewpoints on the roles family members perform cannot be ignored. Family roles may be unwittingly 'assigned' by older generations leading the family or may be assumed by the family member as a result of the set of dynamics through which the family functions. Each family member's performance of his or her roles is judged (or pre-judged) by every other family member according to his or her generational frame of reference or generational template. These roles, either accurately identified or inaccurately imposed, are foundational components in the process of identifying goals for every aspect of wealth management for the family.

Since the foundation from which these goals are formulated is comprised of perceptions grounded in generational biases, the resulting goals may or may not serve the family on the path to optimality.[5] Whatever the generational frame of reference of family leadership, it will colour leadership's perception of the roles family members should perform. In turn, each family member's generational template will shape his or her own role perception. As leadership imposes its own template by consciously or subconsciously assigning roles to family members, the manner in which family members interact with each other also is determined. Hidden rules become part of the family's framework or 'personality'. The degree of openness and communication among family members is determined. These dynamics are the framework through which roles – either authentic or imposed – are assigned based on generational perceptions. Once assigned, needs required to fulfil the role are identified and motivation enters in to satisfy them.

Needs-based motivation for satisfaction

We saw in the black sheep example in Chapter 9 the manner in which needs manifest themselves based on the roles (or perceived roles) performed by family members. The concept that need inspires motivation to set a goal follows two modes of thought which are illustrated in Maslow's Need Hierarchy Theory and Alderfer's ERG Theory, the latter of which was a revision of the former. To review, Maslow's theory is dependent upon the satisfaction of a hierarchy of five levels of need, each of which must be met in succession. The five levels are depicted in a pyramid as shown in Exhibit 15.1.

The first three levels are further categorised as deficiency needs and the top two as growth needs. Growth needs belong to a higher order which people attempt to satisfy after their deficiency needs have been met. The theory states that deficiency needs provide motivation as long as they remain unmet; once they are met, growth needs inspire the greatest motivation for fulfilment. There is no reverting back to the deficiency levels.

Alderfer's approach employs a simpler structure which has received greater empirical support.[6] As shown in Exhibit 15.2, Alderfer's ERG theory is also based on a hierarchy of three types of needs: existence (the combination of Maslow's physiological and safety levels), relational (Maslow's social level), and growth (combining Maslow's esteem and self-actualisation levels). Unlike Maslow's model, Alderfer's theory recognises that the fulfilment of different levels of needs may be pursued simultaneously. It also recognises that the order of fulfilment may be different for different people.

Exhibit 15.1

Maslow's hierarchy of needs

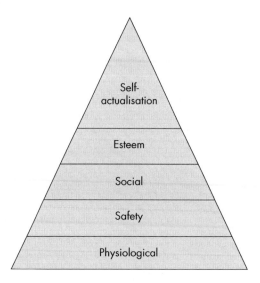

Source: www.abraham_maslow.com/m_motivation/Hierarchy_of_Needs.asp

Exhibit 15.2

Alderfer's ERG theory pyramid

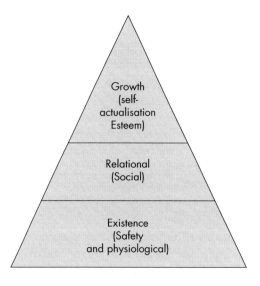

Source: www.12manage.com/methods_alderfer_erg_theory.html

People may 'regress' from a higher level need to fulfil a lower level need to which an easier solution may be found.[7]

This coincides with Brunel's[8] observation that individuals have multiple goals with a different risk level for each, the achievement of which may be pursued simultaneously although with different priorities. He points to Meir Statman's observation that people who buy insurance may also buy lottery tickets and, therefore, be risk averse when buying insurance and risk seeking when buying lottery tickets.[9] This means that investors may identify multiple needs, yet their true concerns may be less obvious. In the second case study cited by Brunel and Gray,[10] the key to unlocking the authentic needs of the family hinged on the fact that the patriarch was performing a role that was inappropriate for his stage of life. Therefore, his need to continue building the wealth within the perceived CEO role he was carrying over to the family office was an inauthentic, inaccurately identified one.

His underlying concern was that the three pools of wealth within the family would spoil his grandchildren. This concern was masked by his focus on performing the CEO/build wealth role as head of the family office. Through the process of education employed by the advisor, the patriarch's acceptance of his new and more appropriate role of educator and mentor allowed the identification of the family's authentic needs, subsequently enabling joint decision making by the family and a workable goal-based allocation to be designed. In the process, he was able to move beyond his generational biases to see the authentic roles of his children and to give their needs the validation which had long been withheld.

Needs – and the goals formulated by the motivation to satisfy them – are identified through the family governance system during the process of analysing the family's current situation, the heritage of its ancestors, and the contributions being made to the family wealth by living family members. When clients and their advisors begin in the middle of the goal-based asset allocation continuum, this vital component is completely left out.

Setting of goals

As often as clients come to advisors at the point of setting a goal – as in the situation of the black sheep – advisors must incorporate the ability to find the source of the goal to determine if its formulation is indeed based on the authentic needs of the family or if it is based on assumptions presented through the lens of generational biases. Brunel speaks of 'defeasing each goal in a way that makes sense to the investor'. How better to defease goals in a way that addresses investors' concerns 'where they live' than to match them directly to the fulfilment of accurately identified needs?

In describing the roles of family members and how they may affect the family's future, Williams and Preisser[11] state that: 'The careful assessment of an heir's *interests,* and the proper match-up with the family's *needs,* is important to the heir's long-term satisfaction and performance in the job. In addition, where heirs 'bought in' to their roles, the necessary preparations, and the heir's active participation in developing their own competencies seemed to follow.' This implies that heirs are aware of their roles and that those roles match the talents, passions, and stage of life of family members, serving as a solid foundation from which needs are identified and effective goals may be set. The work of L.W. Porter and E.E. Lawler[12] notes that motivation is not the only force behind 'performance in the job' and cites the relevance of individual abilities, traits, and perceptions of roles.[13]

The ultimate role for every family member, according to Hughes[14] is that of dynamic stakeholder owner. Every family member performs the role of an active owner of the wealth with a personal stake at risk. This personal stake, in fact, looms larger than a single person since the combined energy of a family of dynamic stakeholder owners is much greater than the energy of any single family member.[15] Such an owner is aware of the roles he or she should be performing, accepts the responsibility of carrying out his or her respective performance, and voluntarily contributes to the regeneration[16] of the wealth over multiple generations by helping the family form goals which are aligned with the needs, values, and desires of the family as a collective entity as well as of each individual family member. This indicates a level of relationship among the family's goals which allows individual family member's goals to be realised without jeopardising the ultimate goals of the family. It also points to the necessity for all advisors to the family to be fully aware of these goals and to have them uppermost in mind to facilitate relevant and meaningful service.

Thus, the roles family members perform have a direct bearing on the investment goals the family develops. If the roles being performed indeed are not well suited to the family member's talents and passions or to the appropriate function within the family, they can cause the formation of the family's goals to be faulty. This can lead to a misunderstanding of the true risks the family faces. Hughes[17] notes that 'no family can manage risk of any kind – financial, personal, or familial – if it can't manage the risks of its own life. If family members don't understand fundamentally who they are, how can they answer the questions about how much risk to take?' Further, if the family perceives its risks to be of one nature when, in fact, its true risks lie in less obvious areas, the risk parameters accompanying the multiple goals of the family become impossible to effectively manage.

The generational perceptions of the roles other family members perform or should perform along with the family members' perceptions of their own roles feed into the formation of goals which are brought to the advisor at the commencement of the advisor-client relationship. By educating families to the possibilities of their own generational biases, we can create awareness of the authentic roles family members should be performing by employing the concept of dynamic stakeholder ownership. A robust understanding of what makes a stakeholder an owner and the difference in a stakeholder who is dynamic and one who is not enables families and their advisors to understand family and individual needs. This enables the family to understand its goals more clearly within the current maze of generations alive in the family as well as for future ones.

Goals set by family members who understand their roles as dynamic stakeholder owners inspire themselves with further motivation for achievement by setting meaningful goals. Vroom's Expectancy Theory[18] tells us that once a goal has been set, the likelihood of satisfactory achievement is linked to effort, performance, and motivation, expressed as three variables of valence, expectancy, and instrumentality. Valence has to do with the level of importance placed on an expected reward or result; expectancy operates on the notion that the greater effort extended, the better the performance; instrumentality is connected with the belief that a valued outcome will be received if a high level of performance is expended.

Therefore, individuals change the level of effort they put toward achieving a goal according to the value placed on the outcome they expect to receive and the satisfaction they get from achievement. Dynamic stakeholder owners have a clear concept of their roles, the needs those roles present to be fulfilled, and the rewards that achieving the goals set for that fulfilment will provide. So if the original motivation is created by the identification of needs based on the authentic roles family members perform, appropriate goals are set, and the goals themselves subsequently reinforce the motivation for achievement. This translates into sound joint decisions made by the family for the management of its wealth.

It logically follows that investment strategies may be formulated with the objective of achieving goals based upon fulfilling the needs of roles or perceptions of roles. Family members and/or advisors to the family are then charged with implementing these strategies and are assigned actions of strategic execution.

When the family and its advisors fully understand the components of the continuum and how they influence each other, matching the goals to authentic needs clarifies the amount of risk required to achieve the goal. This level of understanding also equips both the family and its advisors in understanding and educating against the influences of behavioural biases. Behavioural finance may be used as a tool with which to gauge the authenticity of a goal, enabling the advisor to open the door to an examination of the roles family members are performing and the resulting needs which the goals were identified to fulfil. For instance, the founder of the family in the black sheep example may carry his fears of the risks he perceives relevant to the black sheep over to a decision to invest a disproportionate percentage of assets in the capital preservation bucket. As in the example cited in Brunel's book in the chapter on goal-based allocation,[19] he may view real estate as a capital preservation asset and, in our example, become overly concentrated in real estate as a 'safe haven' from the 'recklessness' of the black sheep. The risks of short-term fluctuations in the real estate market are completely overlooked and the ability to satisfy the founder's need for income may be compromised.

An advisor well educated in the effects that perceived roles can have on goal-setting would be able to ask appropriately diagnostic questions to uncover the founder's real concerns and also to open channels of communication within the family which may overcome generational biases. In this manner, behavioural finance serves to translate the family's goals into a financial language[20] which may ultimately be utilised to correctly position the family's authentic goals within Brunel's goal-based allocation model. Not only may goals then be appropriately categorised within a goal-based investment framework, but the appropriate risk tolerance for each goal can be readily measured and the assets located in appropriate ownership vehicles.

Family case study

To see how this might work in real life, we can use the case of a family which presents opportunities to discover authentic roles, authentic goals, asset protection and risk management considerations, as well as wealth transfer issues. We will take a look at them first to identify perceived and authentic roles and how those views affect the wealth of this particular family. We will do this through a revolving door type of view that enables two different outcomes. Chapter 18 will refer back to this family to discuss in detail the inherent risks in this family's situation as well as asset protection solutions to diffuse them.

Consider the Skee family.[21] Mariel, an engineering major, and John, an architectural design major, met during their graduate studies. Both had a passion for skiing. Together, they developed a line of ski equipment preferred by champion athletes and built a company recently with revenues over $2 billion[22] and multiple global outlets.

Exhibit 15.3

Global locations of Skee International*

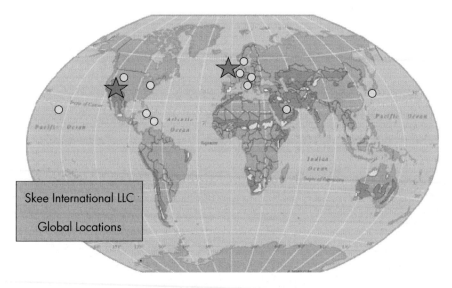

Skee International LLC

Global Locations

    * Skee International is a fictitious company and has been
    fabricated for the use of this case study illustration.

Source: graymatter Strategies LLC. All rights reserved.

Susan, age 35 and the oldest of their three children, and her husband Omar manage one region of the firm located in an oil-rich area of the world. Michel, age 33 and the only son, is expected to take over the business in five years when Mariel and John plan to substantially scale back their involvement. Michel is engaged to Swiss-born Zia, a top-line fashion model. He likes the attention he gets when Zia is with him and loves the prestige of representing the company at significant social events around the globe. Anna, age 22, spends most of her time jetting from city to city to meet up with her friends.

The family own the majority of the company's shares and also have extensive real estate holdings along with their homes in Aspen, Carmel, and London.

Generational role perspectives

Mariel and John are workaholic baby boomers who value work ethic and immediate results above all else. They view Michel as the logical choice to lead the company because of his visibility which garners new business from each major event he attends. They feel he 'knows' the business and will quite capably lead the firm to the next level. Susan and her husband Omar are viewed as steady workers who are reliable, yet with little business acumen and not tremendously resourceful. Both genuinely have a passion for the business, have extraordinary talent, and are driven to succeed.

As Gen-Xers, they are independent thinkers and like to pose what-if scenarios to present ideas for growth. Mariel and John listen but rarely go beyond complimenting them for their ingenuity and subsequently discounting their ideas.

Anna is viewed as the black sheep of the family with little interest in anything but keeping up with her friends and spending uncontrollably. Her exploits are reported in the media on a regular basis.

Susan is a Gen-Xer who has always sought to please her parents and has intentionally wanted them to view her as reliable so that they would feel comfortable handing her the reins at some point. With Michel slated to lead the company, Susan and Omar are frustrated that their real talents have never been recognised or appreciated. The fact that they have doubled sales in the Middle Eastern, African and European region receives little recognition and is primarily attributed to the growth of luxury spending in the oil-rich countries.

Michel, another Gen-Xer, is essentially a playboy who revels in the limelight and enjoys doling out favours to his friends with little real basis for doing so. Zia has exerted her influence as a top fashion model to obtain invitations for him to exclusive gatherings attended by important ski enthusiasts. She has asked for shares in the company as a wedding gift.

Anna, a member of the Echo generation, would love to contribute but she feels no one really cares what she does. She figures the money will always be there and that she will start a business of her own one day and wants to spend time having fun with her friends while she can. Her secret desire is to become an aquatic microbiologist. Anna wants to make an impact and wishes to contribute to the family but she is given little information about the business and her efforts to be involved are consistently patronised. She constantly texts Mariel and John asking how eco-friendly the business is and submitting ideas she has researched for going green.

Because of generational biases, Mariel and John have been too busy building the company to spend much time genuinely listening to their children. They assume Michel and Susan, having 'grown up in the business', know as much as they need to know about the company and also about managing wealth. Susan and Michel felt abandoned as children since Mariel and John were away quite often building and growing the company and have pursued their own interests in their own way with little coordination or input from their parents.

Obviously, little real communication occurs within this family. Trust among the family members is shaky at best and, although family members may be involved in the business, their potentially dynamic involvement is inhibited by the roles imposed upon them. Other family members are simply passive recipients of dividends with little opportunity for involvement of any kind.

Perceived goals

As a result of Mariel and John's perceptions of the roles their children should play within the family and the family business enterprises, they have identified a number of goals they wish the family to pursue and they have expressed these goals in meetings with their advisors. Mariel and John are obviously in leadership roles but they have never examined the quality or effectiveness of their leadership. They have never been good delegators yet their perception of Michel's qualifications as designated heir of the business has made them feel confident in their ability to scale down over the next few years.

They want the wealth they have created to last for seven generations and they have set up trusts that own company stock with their grandchildren as beneficiaries. Their primary goal is to secure the lifestyle they wish to maintain after they retire at age 60, hand over the business to Michel, and pursue their dream of conquering the most challenging ski terrain across the globe before they reach age 70. They also are concerned about protecting the family's assets from Anna and Zia whom they see as the largest threats to the wealth they have built. As certain as they are that they are placing Michel in the proper role of CEO, they are equally comfortable keeping Susan and her husband in their supporting leadership roles over the Middle Eastern, African and European region. Their goal is for Susan and Omar to create and lead a second headquarters there and report to Michel. They want the bulk of the company stock to remain in the family so that the family will always have majority control.

Mariel's family recently left her $75 million. After having set up generous trusts for their grandchildren, Mariel has decided she would like to leave more wealth to her children; however, she would rather have them receive the money at an age when she feels they will be more responsible. She decides to place her entire inheritance in a trust with distributions to be made to her three children as each reaches age 50.

Scenario 1: results of perceived roles and perceived goals

Mariel and John retire and manipulate board approval of Michel as the new CEO. Susan and Omar become increasingly frustrated that Michel has been given control; they sell their shares of the family business and build a rival company with a competing and substantially different line of ski equipment which they designed and patented. Meanwhile, Michel revels in the prestige that his CEO position offers; he cares primarily about maintaining that prestige regardless of its effects on the company's profitability or employee morale. He succeeds in damaging shareholder confidence and, on top of inept leadership, the family business begins to lose market share to its new rival. Zia leaves Michel after having sold the shares she received after their wedding to invest in Susan's and Omar's new company. She uses another part of the money to start the fashion design company of her dreams.

Most of the family's money is tied up in the company stock and other illiquid partnerships owned by the trusts. The value of those assets plummets to half the value the shares commanded at the offering and the family is virtually powerless to do anything but watch. Lawsuits begin to mount. Continually on the sidelines, Anna becomes increasingly depressed because she feels her life has little meaning. She gives up on her dreams of becoming a microbiologist.

Meanwhile, Susan turns 50 and receives her distribution from the trust Mariel set up with her own inheritance. Two years later, Michel turns 50 and receives his distribution which is larger than Susan's since the money has had two more years to grow. Susan fumes that this is unfair but her complaints fall on deaf ears. Increased discontent can be imagined regarding the size of Anna's distribution when she turns 50 ten years later.

Family meetings become non-existent; even less communication exists between family members because of ill feelings on several levels.

The asset allocation Mariel and John set up based on the perceived goals they identified works against them. By locking up most of their assets in the company and long-term, illiquid investments, they have no access to the small amount of funds that are left. Their retirement lifestyle plans become moot and their multi-generational aspirations disappear altogether. They eventually divorce. John takes his portion of the assets that are left and invests in a new venture. It fails and John becomes homeless.

Scenario 2: results of authentic roles and goals

If the family's governance process had correctly identified the roles of the family members and the goals for the wealth, and if the strategic allocations for achieving them had been based on those authentic roles, the results could have been quite different.

In this case, Susan and Omar's ideas are heard and considered. Some are implemented on a trial basis; others are kept for later consideration. Many prove beneficial, adding to the company's profits and enhancing value for both the family and public shareholders. When Mariel and John retire, Susan and Omar are recommended and subsequently elected by the board to lead the company. Since Michel has consistently made less than wise decisions over his area of the company, his role is reevaluated. He becomes media and public relations head. He thrives in this role, manages the company's image and investor relations segments brilliantly, and loves the prestige of talking with media types and being recognised for his frequent interviews on investment news shows.

Susan and Omar improve upon the company's original ski design which is successfully tested by world ski champions and proclaimed, 'the ultimate ski for ultimate athletes'. Profits for the new line soar. Meanwhile, having found ready listeners in her parents, Anna verbalises and subsequently realises her dream of becoming an aquatic microbiologist. Zia, realising her beauty will one day fade, expresses her desire to become a major fashion designer. She and Anna team up to design an eco-friendly line of ski apparel, adding an entirely new stream of revenue for the company. Mariel and John make headlines as they conquer the most challenging slopes around the world, breaking records in their age bracket.

Implications

Although the two outcomes are a bit overreaching, they illustrate how various family members' perspectives on the roles they and other family members perform directly affect the management of the family's wealth and the ultimate success of the family. By understanding the source of individual and family goals and not simply taking them for face value, advisors can offer a more robust form of integrated wealth management. The wealth management continuum basically connects the 'warmer' issues of family wealth to the investment component in a way that makes sense and that also speaks to the client's deepest level of concern. This creates a new model of service that consummately integrates both sides of the spectrum, within which particular areas of expertise may be more effectively applied.

This new model of service is the Generational Wealth Management Continuum[SM] laid out in Chapter 1. Such an approach creates efficiencies in the management of all forms of family wealth, the ultimate objective of which is goal achievement. The next step is to effectively convert the information gained in the goal formation process so that it can be utilised in the decisions that are made about the investment, legal, and other traditional wealth management pieces. For this translation to occur without introducing undue risk to the portfolio, a foundation of trust-level communication must be laid. This foundation will span all family members and all advisors who serve the family. Such a foundation guards against the abandonment of the goals identified through the family governance system in order to follow traditional investment management tenets.

1 Strauss, W. and Howe, N., *The Fourth Turning: an American prophecy,* (New York, NY: Broadway Books, 1997), p. 62.

2 The 'consummate family wealth portfolio' is the service marked property of graymatter Strategies LLC.

3 Any references to goal-based allocation throughout this chapter are based on Brunel's goal-based asset allocation model which identifies four basic goal buckets with which investors identify in their daily lives: income, liquidity, capital preservation, and growth. Other buckets may also be identified as opportunistic investments or trades, operating businesses, and collectibles.

4 Brunel, J.L.P. and Gray, L., 'Integrating family dynamics and governance into strategic asset allocation,' *The Journal of Wealth Management,* Winter 2005, pp. 37–47.

5 In his book, *Integrated Wealth Management: the new direction for portfolio managers,* 2nd edition, Brunel notes that 'individual investors will travel on the road to optimality rather than reach it in one fell swoop.' He speaks to the need of individuals to learn and gain experience with markets and specific strategies over a sufficient period of time, focusing on their 'individual needs, goals, aspirations, fears, constraints, and preferences.' It is the responsibility of advisors to guide individual and family clients along the path that will lead to what may be considered an optimal strategy based on their particular goals, both as individuals and for the family as a separate, distinct entity.

6 Kanov, J.M., Teaching notes for University of Michigan Business School course, 'OBHRM 501: human behavior and organizations', Class 6, May 19 2003, taught by Jane E. Dutton.

7 These comparisons are sourced from 'ERG Theory,' a publicised comparison with implications for business management at www.netmba.com/mgmt/ob/motivation/erg.

8 Brunel, J.L.P. and Gray, L.P., 'integrating family dynamics and governance in strategic asset allocation,' *The Journal of Wealth Management,* Winter 2005, pp. 37–47.

9 Brunel, J.L.P., *Integrated Wealth Management: the new direction for portfolio managers,* 2nd edition (London: Euromoney Books, 2006), p. 7.

10 Brunel, J.L.P. and Gray, L.P., 'integrating family dynamics and governance in strategic asset allocation,' *The Journal of Wealth Management,* Winter 2005, pp. 37-47.

11 Williams, R. and Preisser, V., *Preparing Heirs,* (San Francisco, CA: Robert D. Reid, 2003), p.66.

12 Niklos, R. 'Commentary: succession planning creates business continuum', *Daily Journal of Commerce,* March 4 2008, p. 2.

13 Chartered Management Institute, 'Victor H. Vroom: motivation and leadership decision making, *Thinkers,* March 1 2002; www.accessmylibrary.com/coms2/summary_0286-25331792_ITM describes the work of Porter and Lawler as an extension of Vroom's Expectancy Theory.

14 Hughes, J.E., Jr., *Family: a compact among generations,* (New York, NY: Bloomberg Press, 2007), p. 24.

15 Ibid.

16 Wealth Regeneration® is a registered service mark owned by Laird Norton Tyee and is used throughout this book Laird Norton Tyee's permission.

17 Hughes, J.E., Jr., *Family: a compact among generations,* (New York, NY: Bloomberg Press, 2007), p. 24.

18 Vroom, V.H., *Work and Motivation,* (Somerset, NJ: John Wiley & Sons, 1964), p. 207.

19 This section of Brunel's book illustrates how goal buckets may interact and cites an example using the income and capital preservation buckets. In this example, the investor viewed real estate as a capital preservation instrument. The point of the illustration is that, although different assets or structures may be used to satisfy multiple goals, it is important to keep the goal buckets separate in the view of the investor in order to keep him 'on track'.

20 The author is indebted to Jean L.P. Brunel for the insight into the role that behavioural finance plays within the goal-setting continuum and its utility in translating personal family and individual goals into a language which may then be used by the advisor to develop a valid and effective goal-based allocation.

21 Although based on a conglomeration of real life family cases, the names, monetary values, and descriptions of business enterprises, professions, and ideas in this case study illustration are completely fictitious and have no intended or non-intended reference to real life persons, regardless of any similarity of situation or name.

22 The Skee family, the company Skee International and any public events involving the company and any details about the family are used for illustrative purposes and are completely fictitious. No such public company exists and no such offering has occurred in the public marketplace.

Chapter 16

Trust-level communication

'Trust brings out the best in people and literally changes the dynamics of interaction. While it is true that a few abuse this trust, the vast, vast majority of people do not abuse it but respond amazingly well to it. And when they do, they don't need external supervision, control, or the 'carrot and stick' approach to motivation. They are inspired. They run with the trust they were extended. They want to live up to it. They want to give back.'

Stephen M.R. Covey, The Speed of Trust

Trust is an essential ingredient in the successful management of any form of wealth. As one of the critical elements of family success, communication which establishes and continues to earn trust involves much more than learning a skill set. It demands a working knowledge of the family's particular generational maze which comprises the 'family culture'.

Today, the development of effective communication is often viewed as a skill. Communication specialists conduct exercises with participants to learn how to listen better, phrase things differently, read body language, and frame what they are hearing and saying within the context of the way they process information. These skills are all valuable and work quite well with people external to the family. Within family, however, communication absolutely must go deeper. Whatever communication skills we acquire, *nothing can take the place of genuine interest.*

It is quite easy for people to tell if we are genuinely interested in them. Any effort at multitasking while 'communicating' is a dead giveaway that they do not have our full attention! Trust-level communication requires more than just understanding what people are saying. It requires baselevel knowledge of the person and the way they may interpret what is said to them in response. Communication skills can be useful in this endeavour but genuine interest is felt when another person wants to know about the things that interest *us* rather than only the things that interest them. Genuine, altruistic interest within families can point the future of a family toward an entirely different direction.

This is the perfect point at which to address trust-level communication. We've laid the groundwork by looking at the source of family dynamics – the perspectives of archetypical and chronological generations, the roles that family members occupy within the family's generational maze, and the goals that they set. Now that we're aware of these determinant influences, the institution of trust-level communication among the family becomes the cohesive element for their effective management.

How to earn trust through communication is a three-pronged study. It involves delving into the nature of trust-level communication, the generationally shaped culture of the family which either fosters or prohibits its dynamic presence, and the responsibility of leadership to sustain it and transition authentic wealth preservation from one generation to the next. A theme woven throughout the entire discussion as appropriate is the development of trust-level communication with children. Younger generations are critical to the rejuvenation of the family wealth. Ideally, trust-level communication begins the day a child is born and is carried throughout a lifetime. Since younger generations determine the future of the family wealth in all its forms, this chapter will address all three areas of study and will close with a case study illustrating the multiple effects of trust-level communication on family wealth.

The difference trust-level communication can make

With such busy lives – especially if you are a wealth creator or a proactive contributor to the family wealth – taking the time to develop genuine interest in other family members may seem to be unproductive. When placed within the context of the impact family dynamics have on the family's material and financial bottom line, such time may prove to be productive indeed. A surprising amount of joy may also be discovered.

It is common knowledge that two people can hear the same words and come away with entirely different interpretations of what was said. Not only can two people hear the same words and think two different meanings, what is said may unwittingly trigger a memory from the past to which a family member of another generation associates negative feelings. Or the family member may associate the comment with an incident where he or she felt wronged by another family member. Even though the family member making the comment had no intention of 'opening old wounds', the association of the comment with the person's memory may be unavoidable. With adult children, a wayward word from a parent can still spark intense emotions and feelings of unworthiness, inferiority, and judgment from the past.[1]

The memory triggered also may have nothing to do with the two parties involved. It may be related to an experience one family member had before the other family member was born. Just as past generations shape history as well as the future,[2] so do generational perspectives shape the way we communicate with family members. The subconscious imprint frames what has been said within the context of our formative experiences. For two family members who have not explored the differences in their generational lenses, misinterpretation of what is said can occur quite easily.

It is through relationships with family that we learn to individuate. Trust-level communication is the vehicle through which our initial sense of being valued by others is delivered.[3] Low self esteem and the resulting lack of confidence has been cited as the primary causative factor shared by drug, alcohol and other addicts. It also renders them unlikely to have the confidence they need to realise their authentic wealth.[4] Addiction is not a requirement for a family member's failure to realise his or her authentic wealth; failure to recognise authentic wealth can happen in much more subtle fashion and its effects do not have to lead to addiction in order to be impactful. In *Children of Paradise*, Lee Hausner notes that children with low self esteem have difficulty facing challenges. They are sick more often, miss more classes, and may not ask for help when they need it. Their resulting underperformance only confirms their low self opinion. Translated into adulthood, this leads to a life of dependence which denies self-fulfilment and stifles creativity needed to solve problems and assume leadership.[5] It is not uncommon for a single unfulfilled family member to disruptively control what goes on in almost every aspect of family wealth management.

Fostering an atmosphere within the family where trust-level communication can thrive is the responsibility of family leadership. Individual family members may be proactive in their individual efforts but the breadth of trust-level communication across family units or branches as well as within each is vital to the family's wealth sustaining health. This certainly does not mean that leadership hands down a mandate! One cannot mandate trust, respect, or understanding; that is the quickest way to break them down. Trust and respect must be continually earned, even if they are initially offered voluntarily.

Understanding the other person's frame of reference and the past experiences which are closely accessible to the present are a good first step toward developing heartfelt interest in those who mean the most to us, our family members. Both archetypical and chronological generational perspectives are excellent tools for developing understanding but care must be taken not to label or stereotype. Each generation is fascinating in its own way. Knowledge of each generation's common characteristics can open the path toward an exploration of how individual family members view themselves and the influences that shaped who they are. I am convinced that our family members are the people we often know the least, even if we have been living with them for years.

Understanding comes from proactive altruism, one of the four family virtues.[6] Broad-based trust-level communication comes from the innate virtues of fusion and altruism present within each family member. It is subconsciously written into the framework of the family virtues. Families whose members come together as a whole to recognise that trust-based communication is part of their identity will become forces to behold. The spirit that binds them will be unbreakable and will provide the haven that everyone seeks in safety from the world of multiple risks – either external or internal – in which we live.

The nature of trust-level communication

In his book, *The Speed of Trust*, Stephen M.R. Covey says relationship trust is all about consistent behaviour, that is, words followed through with action. We either interact with people in ways that build trust or destroy it. The speed at which either occurs is astounding. Although trust can easily be broken, the backdrop against which the breach occurs may allow for quicker restoration of trust. If the relationship history is not favourable, trust may still be speedily restored through an authentic change in behaviour that consistently matches actions with words. The words one chooses signals the behaviour the listener may expect, then that expectation is either followed through by supportive action … or not.

Although the words we choose, the tone of voice we use, and the body language we observe are all important aspects of communication, nothing is a greater saboteur of communication than someone saying one thing and doing another or presenting one 'face' to one family member and another face to others. This is the litmus test of authenticity. Perceived roles are those roles which seem appropriate but which indeed are not. They are hidden beneath a delusional veil and recognised primarily during times of crisis when much of the damage has already been done. So it is with the relationship between communication and trust. What may seem to be effective communication proves shallow without trust to back it up. The perception of roles sets up the dynamics (culture, personality) of the family. This is the portal through which trust-level communication either thrives or is thwarted.

In *Preparing Heirs*, Williams and Priesser note three elements of trust.

1 Reliability (follow through).
2 Sincerity (someone's 'inner story' matching up with his or her 'outer story').
3 Competence (having the capacity to accomplish the task at hand).

They use the example of a business executive's history of either being late or not being there at all for meetings he had set with his children. Feeling he was building the company for them and that they should appreciate and understand the gift he was giving them, he was inadvertently sending them the message that they were not important to him – that he cared nothing about participating in their lives. This eroded his children's self esteem despite the fact that they loved him. This father was operating within his own lens of what he thought would show his love for his children, completely oblivious to their interpretation of his actions. After three years of rigorous recordkeeping to rectify his communication problem with his children, his ability to become more trustworthy to them ironically also enhanced his relationships with his six corporate presidents![7] This is a perfect example of how something which seems counterintuitive can actually have greater impact, be more efficient, and cement the relationships which are most important to us.

In line with these three elements, Covey notes there are 13 behaviours that people of high trust exhibit. Covey's book is written primarily for business and professional relationships, although a few personal relationship applications are made. From a generational wealth management view, we can extrapolate a meaningful translation of the 13 high-trust behaviours for building trust-level communication within families.

13 high-trust behaviours[8] for families

1. *Talk straight:* tell the truth; do not 'hedge' but be tactful, keeping in mind the family member's likely receptivity; tell the whole story, not just the part that's expedient at the time.

There's a saying, 'the truth hurts'. Normally, it should not. This attitude is not about trust building; it is about ego building. Usually, when someone uses 'the truth hurts' in conversation with another family member, it is to drive the point home that the one telling the 'truth' is in the right and the one hearing it is in the wrong. This is a different motive than 'leaving the right impression' as noted in Covey's original list. As well, respect is not something which can be commanded in authoritarian fashion. For example, if a child asks why a parent wishes him or her to do something, the answer 'because I said so' can feel demeaning, hubristic, and hollow.

Children as well as other family members deserve the respect of being given an answer that is explanatory in an age appropriate way, even if it needs to be brief. The 'because I said so' answer makes *any* person (especially a child) feel worthless in the parent's or family member's eyes; the explanatory answer instils personal worth and value – a prized attribute that can circumvent addiction problems, depression, behavioural issues, and the seeking of celebrity status in social media. Every person wants to be valued. Especially during their formative years, children will seek and follow whatever source they can find to give themselves a sense of worth and that they are valued by others.[9] Receiving this sense from family is how we learn to value ourselves enough to be responsible, dynamic, stakeholder owners and helps children deal effectively with peer pressure; although this applies to all family members, the foundational opportunity for this level of trust between parent and child cannot be ignored.

2. *Demonstrate respect:* become familiar with each family member's generational lens and how that lens may cause him or her to misinterpret the meaning behind the words you use and the context within which you use them.

This also shows respect for other people – not from an authoritarian view but from an apprecia-tion of who the family member is as a person. Positions of authority – either outside the family or inside – indeed deserve an initial vote of respect. Great leaders go on to earn that respect over and over and over again by offering it first to those they serve. Taking time to understand another family member's generational lens fosters respect and acceptance – two critical ingredients for fostering authentic wealth.

3. *Create transparency:* do not assume a family member does not have the expertise to understand what you are saying; do not assume the family member will be against what you are proposing.

Lack of transparency within the family structure is a fear-based attempt to control. Leadership believes its particular view is unequivocally correct or a family member has ulterior motives and hopes to manipulate other family members' views in his or her favour. Transparency in issues that affect family members' lives should be open and complete. Lack of transparency breeds deception rather than truth. Decisions based on deceptions can cause almost irreparable rifts in relationships over time.

4. *Right wrongs:* do not be afraid to say you are sorry, especially to your children; do what is possible (without overpromising) to rectify the outcome.

None of us is perfect. We make promises we cannot keep; we tend to tell only part of the story when we fear a negative outcome; we fail to see others' perspectives as legitimate, alternative views. When we do these things, offering an apology is a sign of strength. It bolsters the feeling of value on the part of the person who was wronged. It is a bridge for healing. Especially in relationships with children, the ability for an adult to offer a sincere apology and admit mistakes is powerful in building and maintaining trust.

We receive our initial self concept from our parents. If our needs are met and we receive loving acceptance, the self concept is healthy. Healthy self-esteem does not lead to entitlement. Entitlement is hubristic and ego driven, not the result of a healthy sense of self. Praising children for everything they do and teaching them that they deserve whatever they want based simply on 'who they are' leads to a lower valuation of self worth.[10] Allowing a family member to experience the natural consequences of their actions within a loving environment and supporting him or her in finding a solution builds self esteem and also relationships.

A healthy self-concept leads to responsibility and the capacity to nurture the self concepts of others. It allows the virtue of altruism to be present. If self-confidence and a feeling of self worth are to continue to develop, we must be given the gift of trust on the front end. An opportunity to research the data needed to make a decision and then, to be allowed to make that decision based on the research and reasoning powers we have available are age appropriate ways to confirm parents' trust and value in children's eyes. Being able to see that parents make mistakes, too, and that the relationship between parent and child is valuable enough in the parents' eyes to yield an apology when one is due adds to the sense of self worth and builds communication patterns of trust in this most critical relationship.

5. *Show loyalty:* give credit for achievement or a task well done freely and without favouritism;

do not send messages to family members through other family members; talk directly to the family member about the issue; do not disclose what the family member said to another family member without the disclosing family member's permission.

Favouritism, family gossip, and the breaching of confidences all eat away at trust. Family secrets are at the heart of family gossip and feed the dysfunctional family approaches noted in Chapter 1 that become ruinous to families and, ultimately, to the family business. Speaking directly to family members who are involved in issues which need resolving offers respect, value, and continues to build trust. Keeping secrets erodes trust. Respecting confidences and allowing family members to disclose information about themselves also builds trust; disclosing it for them does the opposite.

6. *Deliver results:* be consistent, self-motivated, and proactive.

Successful families have members who are confident, self-motivated, and willing to occupy their authentic roles. Trust-level communication builds a safe space in which family members develop these traits and are willing to take informed risks. Educated risk taking is essential to the development of any form of family wealth.

7. *Get better:* get feedback and learn from your mistakes; one sign of a great family leader is one who regularly asks for feedback from constituents (family members!), makes physical note of it, and considers it in current and/or future decision making.

As an evolving entity, the building of trust can only improve if family members feel free to make comments or to register their feelings about family matters that affect them. Even if a family members feeling or suggestion will not alter a current decision being made, it should be acknowledged, recorded in the minutes of the family meeting, and given assurance that it will be considered the next time such a decision comes up.

8. *Confront reality:* tackle issues head on, even the 'undiscussables'; encourage new ideas; do not avoid sensitive issues; be the voice of calm, comfort, and impartiality.

Avoidance breeds suspicion; suspicion erodes trust. A willingness to talk about any issue makes family members feel there is no hidden agenda or manipulative behaviour afoot. In many cases, not saying anything is much worse than not knowing quite how to broach the subject.
    The contribution of new ideas, especially from younger generations and new family members by marriage or recognised partnership, is a wonderful way to make them feel included. It also injects fresh approaches into the family organisation to ensure it matches the family's needs. Knowing that new ideas will be heard and not discounted builds trust through this type of communication.

9. *Clarify expectations:* understand the authentic roles family members occupy; make sure your expectations match their capabilities.

As with many other behaviours, this particularly has to do with the way the family governs itself. It all goes back to understanding generational perspectives, the roles family members occupy, and the resulting dynamics of the family. If each family member is occupying authentic roles and those roles are recognised, expectations will be realistic and contributions will be reliable. Communication will be enhanced and misconceptions will be minimised. People will not be afraid to ask questions, express opinions, or offer new ideas. There will be no need for 'unspoken rules' which can unravel the communication tapestry of any family.

10. *Practice accountability:* take responsibility for the consequences of what you say and how you say it.

None of us is exempt from saying things that will be misunderstood or misinterpreted. Taking responsibility for clearing up such misunderstandings – directly between the people involved – goes a long way toward developing trust-level communication.

11. *Listen completely:* do not interrupt the family member or finish their sentences for them. Do not begin talking until you are sure the family member is finished with what he or she has to say.

Interrupting is the height of hubristic trust erosion. We all feel that what we have to say is important. Interruptions occur easily with family members who may be reticent to express their feelings based on how they have been treated in the past. Listening completely is an excellent way to make family members feel that what they have to say and what they feel is valued and that their contribution matters. This can be particularly difficult to do if one or more family members has difficulty finding a place to stop talking. This, actually, is another form of hubris. As hard as it may seem to put into practice, simply allowing that person to finish completely and allowing complete silence afterward may send an effective message. Hopefully, the person will realise he or she has been monopolising the conversation and also needs to extend the courtesy of listening completely to other family members.

12. *Keep commitments:* do not make promises you cannot keep; do not make promises just to placate another family member, especially if that family member is a child.

This is one of the fastest ways to either build or erode trust. If a commitment cannot be kept, notification should be given as soon as the realisation occurs. People may forgive lack of follow through on a commitment once, but it will still create a heightened awareness about trustworthiness. If someone is trying to improve a habit of breaking commitments, it will take much longer and some family members may always carry suspicions about the ability for this family member to be true to the commitments he or she makes.

13. *Extend trust:* do not withhold trust because there is risk involved, even with your children; extend trust on the front end without making family members have to prove their trustworthiness first.

This may seem counterintuitive to many families but extending trust on the front end breeds confidence and responsibility. Just as the quote at the beginning of this chapter states, people want to be trustworthy. The authentic wealth of all family members thrives when trust is extended in advance. Children especially thrive when given the gift of trust before they have to prove it, especially from their parents. They should not be 'set up' to become untrustworthy; they should have a genuine vote of confidence. It encourages them to make age-appropriate decisions and to learn from their mistakes.

Parents who care enough to support their children in earning that trust over and above the pressure to belong exerted by their peers are engaged in trust-level communication. So often, parents view their children through their own generational lens, expecting them to be just like they were at their children's ages. Understanding how their children perceive the world – especially the world of the 'next great generation' – and understanding their generational communication styles can build a foundation for solid family leadership in the future.

Educating children on what it means to be trustworthy and what can happen when trust is broken can have an impact on their self-esteem. In *Children of Paradise*, Hausner says that open communication is key to a child's sense of self-worth and sense of competency – both extremely contributory to success later in life.[11] She notes that children must be heard at the time when issues are in the midst of their excitement or trauma over what may seem to parents to be 'nothing important'. However, whatever is of pressing interest to the child at the time is vitally important in his or her eyes; communication with children does not happen 'on demand'. Parents lose precious opportunities for communicating messages of love, trust, and acceptance at one of the most vital times of children's lives by neglecting to take just a few minutes to listen to their children at a time of seeming 'crisis' or particular excitement in their children's lives.

Overlooking such opportunities is particularly easy in the lives of families of wealth. Wealth creators have 'driven' personalities and occupy roles in business which may not translate effectively in personal relationships with family members. Although they may practice listening skills with their employees, other executives, or business partners, they often fail to practice those skills at home. The issue of parents and children not talking to each other more often than not has to do with parents not taking time to be available to their children when they have important things to tell them.[12]

Having had personal experience with this, I can vouch for the success of trust-level communication during the formative years. My own child began coming downstairs to talk to me before bed each night when she was in middle school. I remember telling her once early on that I had to be at the office early the next morning and that I was tired and needed to go to sleep. As soon as the words came out of my mouth, I realised that this might be my only opportunity to establish good communication with her. She was going to be a teenager soon and if I did not establish it then, I might lose the opportunity at a later and more critical time in her life for her to know that she could trust me with whatever she had to say. So I turned over and asked her what was on her mind.

From that night on, she came down for our 'talk' every night before going to bed. These nightly conversations and the interest and trust she felt from me gave her confidence to tell me whatever was bothering her or to come to me when she had difficult decisions to make. Years later, when she left for university, those were the times that I missed the most. She is now 31 years old. The trust that we developed during those years was a critical factor as she became a beautiful, responsible young woman and the responsible spouse, mother, and businesswoman she is today. I am not the perfect parent by any means. But this one thing – the cultivation of trust-level communication – has been a solid foundation for our relationship to this day.

Where we spend our time sends clear messages to family members. We often take for granted that family members of any age know that we love them. If we do not back up our declarations of love for family with action, time taken to be present, and an empathetic understanding of generational views, the declarations seem empty and false. The three elements of trust that Williams and Priesser identify are woven through the 13 behaviours Covey lists. They apply to all family members, not just the adults.

So we find that trust-level communication drills down to a deeper level. Communication skills without trust prove empty when tested during family crises. The dynamics of family provide the environment in which trust-level communication either thrives or is thwarted. Perceived or authentic roles create the dynamics of the family. And generational perspectives offer the lenses through which each family member interprets words, body language, and action in his or her own particular way. The generational lens is the interpretive factor which determines the trustworthiness of other family members in each family member's eyes. To develop trust-level communication, we must understand the foundation of family dynamics, the roles family members occupy, and the lenses through which we interpret the world.

The generational trust factor

Often after a presentation on generational perspectives, people often make comments like, 'I never realised it before, but what you said perfectly describes my father. I always thought he was against me. Now, I realise that's just the way he thinks'. In working with families on wealth issues that affect their relationships, the generational lens factor becomes an immediate portal for trust-level communication. Is it possible to imagine that taking away the supposed ill intent on the part of the father from this son's eyes would make him more open to what his father says? And is it also possible that eliminating the impression expressed as 'I don't understand why my son so enjoys doing exactly the opposite of what I told him' would enable the father to actually hear what his son was trying to say and understand his meaning from the son's perspectives?

Communicating has much more to do with the words being uttered. It has to do with getting to the heart of relationship. Getting to the heart of relationship builds and continues to earn trust. It causes people – even children and parents – to spend time with each other so each person's authenticity can enrich the other. Particularly for families of wealth, leadership's role in fostering such communication is an imperative.

Communication styles are important 'common language' facilitators; they are the doors through which effective communication can enter. But they are just that – doorways. Anyone who has learned a second language understands that unless we also grasp the cultural background and many of the common expressions used in that language, we still will not go far in successful communication. Generational perspectives serve as the entry point into a person's individual cultural background. Real understanding comes from listening in such a way that the listener becomes aware of the other person's perspective. Only then can understanding and empathy translate into acceptance, even if there is disagreement. Communication and trust does not mean that everyone agrees in perfect utopian harmony. The harmony spoken of in the four virtues of family is based on the ability of family members to be aware of and accept each other's perspectives.

When acceptance and empathy come into relationship, we can take down the walls that make us feel that a family member is against us. If we realise that a family member – especially one of another generation – is impacted by his or her particular view of the world, we have a utilisable tool with which to work in bridging differences. This, in turn, clears the path for joint decision making as described in the chapter on family governance. It enables dynamic stakeholder ownership[13] and the identification of authentic roles. It makes it possible to nurture and support others in their authentic pursuits, realising that whatever they are pursuing will be a unique and wonderful contribution to the family wealth.

Effective communication and trust are inseparable. The two walk hand in hand with understanding cross-generational styles. Reflecting the perspectives of various generations, Jeremy Stoltz observes that, when communicating with Silents, respect is the core psychological need in communication. He offers a useful breakdown of generational communication styles.

Box 16.1
Generational communication styles[14]

Generation	Core Psychological Need	Top Communication Keys
Silent	Respect	*Words* Reluctance to share thoughts Be clear and to the point Face to face or written is best Use formal titles and schedule connections Feedback: no news is good news
Boomer	Build rapport	*Body language* Speak openly, directly, without controlling Want detailed answers Welcome flexibility of responses Feedback: once a year is enough
Gen-X	Life balance	*Email* Short, concise conversations Offer and solicit feedback Informal communication style Feedback: sorry to interrupt but how am I doing?
Echoes	Confidence	*Equal opportunity* Resents being talked down to Communicate by email Constant feedback exchange Do not take yourself too seriously

Words of wisdom:
- Silents have had experiences that offer lessons for future growth
- Boomers are passionate and value competition, change, hard work, and inclusion
- Gen-Xers value diversity, efficiency, personal development, independence, fun, and most importantly, life balance.

Source: Jeremy Stoltz.

Ana Alvarez-Holmberg, MA, PMP, also notes generationally based communication styles. Silents or Veterans have a practical outlook, dedicated work ethic, and an aversion to vulgar talk. Boomers are into optimism and political correctness; Gen-Xers are more balanced, do not appreciate stereotypes, and are naturally more skeptical. Echoes (or Millennials) also have a hopeful outlook and strong work ethic.[15]

Most information available about communication between generations seems to apply to the workplace. If we apply generational communication styles to family members, a new level of relationship and trust may become develop. Busy entrepreneurs often interpret everything in their lives in terms of the business. This is a natural and logical progression in a life completely absorbed in the wealth building process of running a successful enterprise. However, it only more deeply entrenches the distorted order of governance noted in the governance chapters of this book. It also functions from the definition of wealth as material and financial.

Case study[16]

As we have noted, there are layers through which the development of trust-level communication must drill down. It is often easier to see how principles work within a story based on real life relationships. Expanding on a case study previously cited for the patriarch's transference of his CEO role to the family office, we look at the experience of an advisor who is hired to work with this particular family and, in the process, discovers that it is impossible to gain consensus, although the family seem to be very loving. It highlights the dysfunctional dynamics of the family which completely prohibits effective communication based on both chronological and archetypical generational perspectives.

Let us imagine a family currently comprising three generations. The first generation (G1), which created the wealth, is led by an iron-willed patriarch who just retired as the CEO of the company he started. His son succeeded him in that post, and achieved that position entirely on merit, being recognised by the rest of the management team as a fabulous organiser and an inspired leader. The patriarch's other two children, two daughters, both married individuals who have proven to be equally unusually successful in different business ventures. Thus, though the first generation currently holds the bulk of the family's $250 million wealth, the members of the second generation do not really feel they need any of that wealth, having become independently wealthy in their own rights. Upon retiring from the family business, the patriarch appointed himself the head of the newly created family office and set out to achieve prudent diversification and foster further growth in the family's already substantial wealth.

When confronted with the situation, the advisor the family originally hired was somewhat puzzled by the surprising dichotomy he found in the family. At one level, the family appeared very loving and well-adjusted, while it seemed totally dysfunctional when it came to financial conversations. Helping the group formulate a strategic asset allocation for its assets proved virtually impossible, as there was a conflict between a seemingly all-powerful patriarch who could very effectively organise his thoughts and goals and worked well with the male members of the family, and an inability to achieve any sort of consensus among the whole group as to needs, issues and even areas of focus.

In the end, the most critical issue seemed to be the advisor's inability to reconcile the various roles each of the members of the family were actually playing with the roles they would need to play to have a constructive process. In particular, the patriarch was running the family office just as he had run the company, assuming that financial success was the only reasonable goal for all members of the family and that nothing short of total commitment to that cause on the part of all would be acceptable. By contrast, several of the members of the family, feeling that they did not need most of that wealth, were in fact hoping that the money could be used primarily for philanthropic purposes – rather than for the accumulation of more wealth – and thinking that their primary duties were related to their own, more narrowly-defined households, with a particular focus on the education of their children.

Imagine how different the scenario might have been if the advisor had been able to get the patriarch, who was in fact genuinely concerned for the welfare of his grandchildren, to define a different role for himself. Could he have been convinced that he could serve as a role model, as the keeper and transferor of the family's Midwestern values or as a leader of the family's philanthropic endeavours? Could the disaffected members of the family have been convinced to play an active role in the process if at least some of the wealth had been dedicated to their concerns, that is, philanthropy? Should there have been a more active discussion as to the need to create permanent wealth transfer structures to allow each of the branches of the second generation to begin to associate more directly with the wealth?

A diagnosis of the generational perspectives at work in this family reveals a much stronger GI influence on the founder patriarch and completely ignores the patriarch's spouse, since her voice is basically without consideration by the patriarch and has no influence on wealth management decisions. The two daughters' voices, however, do carry some weight, although comparatively little relative to their respective husbands'. Using proprietary tools,[17] this assessment can be made by noting the weight of the types of roles played by the husbands from a business standpoint (the roles of greatest import from the patriarch's perspective) compared to the 'lesser weighted' roles of Spouse, Sibling, Parent, and so on, played by the daughters. Keep in mind these roles are perceived roles which have been assigned by the patriarch. In practise, the daughters are active in their authentic roles but not in a way that is recognised by the patriarch. This lack of recognition inhibits the daughters' ability to fully develop their authentic roles and diminishes the contribution they could make to the family wealth by raising the social influence the family might be able to have for the philanthropic cause in which they have interest.

The patriarch – acknowledging in his own mind a need in these 'modern times' to involve his daughters more – indeed wishes they would show more interest in the family wealth and share his goals of financial success, but his strong GI perspective automatically causes him to defer to their husbands, who have gained the patriarch's respect by creating substantial wealth on their own. In addition, the patriarch's chronological G1 perspective as the wealth creator leads him to continue in a role that is no longer appropriate for him, that of wealth builder as a result of the CEO role he used to occupy within the family business which he founded. Further diagnosis uncovers the roles the various family members play, who makes the decisions regarding the various pockets of wealth, and each person's personal values and objectives. Knowing this information would be critical for this family and would reveal the mismatch between their authentic goals and objectives and the ones presenting themselves on the surface. In the process of analysis, a clearer picture would emerge, offering better defined and more reliable information with which to work.

Immediately, two important implications can be gleaned from analysing this family's situation. The first is that both the founder and the son are both noted as CEOs, not from a realistic standpoint, but from their individual points of view. In actuality, the son is now the CEO of the original family business, but the implicit transference of the patriarch's CEO-level authority to the family office shades the goals he lists in the analysis. The CEO role the patriarch has unwittingly transferred to the newly created family office must be redefined if real progress for this family is to be made. Facilitating the redefinition of that role is extremely tricky, but it can be done – and done well.

The second implication of import is the assignment of roles to the daughters, both from an archetypical view that they are Boomer children and the chronological view that they are members of the second generation, G2, from the original wealth creator. The daughters feel their opinions have little value in their father's eyes. Their desires to funnel the family funds into philanthropic channels simply do not register with the patriarch. Thus, having concluded that all communication to that end is hopelessly at loggerheads, they spend their time in social activities, shopping, and various volunteer efforts.

The patriarch views both daughters as spendthrifts because they do not share his all-encompassing goal of financial success and also because of his lack of appreciation for volunteer social activities. Because these activities do not generate revenue, he views them as totally useless. He feels his daughters' time could be used much more productively if they worked in the family office assisting him in serving the family's needs and organising the day to day activities of the office.

This fuels the patriarch's concerns about the spoiling of his grandchildren, setting up a vicious circle of misjudgements and frustrations on the part of all family members. In fact, the daughters wish to use their time and the family money to create a family legacy of philanthropy and view their social networking and volunteer work as 'laying the groundwork' for that purpose as well

Exhibit 16.1

Broken communication based on perceived roles

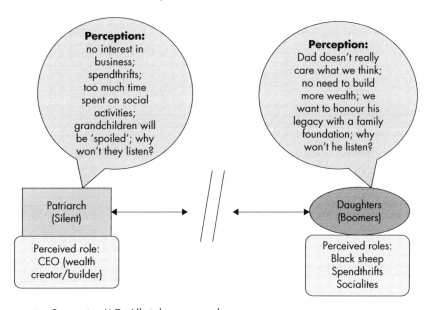

Source: graymatter Strategies LLC. All rights reserved.

as for the education of their children through participation in the family philanthropic entity. But they feel stymied in their quest due to the patriarch's deference to their husbands and brother in discussions about the family wealth and his misjudgement of the way they spend their time. These family dynamics easily set up the dichotomy of loving relationships but total financial dysfunction as a family.

It is at this point that greater opportunity presents itself for this family. Let us suppose the advisor asks the patriarch what concerns he has, what 'keeps him up at night'. The patriarch's eyes get misty and he indicates his deep concern regarding the effects of three significant pools of wealth on his grandchildren's value system and the ultimate effect on their happiness as individuals. With appropriate guidance over time, the patriarch sees that the role of CEO is no longer authentic for him. The more appropriate roles of educator and mentor as a family elder and also of benefactor through dedicating a large portion, if not all, of the family wealth to a family foundation offer him authentic avenues through which to develop trust-level communication with his daughters, simultaneously easing tensions for his son who had inadvertently been placed in the middle between his father and his sisters.

Exhibit 16.2

Support for trust-level communication among family members

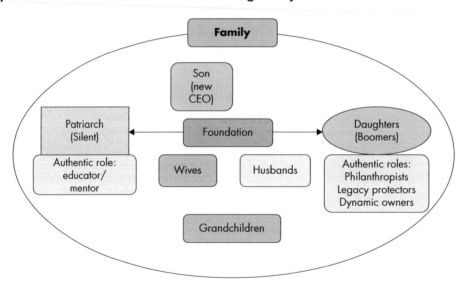

At the same time, the inauthentic, generationally assigned role of spendthrift is no longer applied to the daughters, enabling them to freely develop their authentic wealth and use their newly recognised roles to foster trust-level communication from their side.

The new role of benefactor serves the dual purpose of opening communications with his daughters who already share his new philanthropic goal and creating cohesion among family members that previously did not exist. The virtues of fusion and altruism now have the opportunity to actively work within this family, creating harmony and much greater joy in this family's relationships, their family spirit, and their identity as a corporate and philanthropic citizen. The trust and family continuity enabled by the clearing away of perceived roles and the new dynamics facilitated by trust-level communication also create a family story to which each successive generation may make a meaningful contribution.

Conclusion

So far in our journey, we have examined the impact of generational perspectives on the roles of family members, the dynamics of the family, and the goals that are set for achievement. We have equipped ourselves well with the knowledge of three forms of family governance and trust-level communication.

Now we are ready to cross the divide through Step 3 of the Continuum to manage the material and financial assets in a way that will protect and nurture the flourishing of the family's entire wealth portfolio.

---

[1] Hausner, L., *Children of Paradise: successful parenting for prosperous families*, (Los Angeles, CA: Tarcher, 1990), pp. 178–82.

[2] Strauss, W. and Howe, N., *The Fourth Turning: an American prophecy,* (New York, NY: Broadway Books, 1997), p. 62.

[3] Hausner, L., *Children of Paradise: successful parenting for prosperous families*, (Los Angeles, CA: Tarcher, 1990), pp. 35.

[4] Rubino, J., 'The importance of self esteem in the treatment of drug, alcohol, and other addictions,' Treatment Centers, March 2010: www.treatment-centers.net/self-esteem.html.

[5] Hausner, L., *Children of Paradise: successful parenting for prosperous families*, (Los Angeles, CA: Tarcher, 1990), pp. 50.

[6] Hughes, J.E., Jr., *Family: a compact among generations,* (New York, NY: Bloomberg Press, 2007), p. xxiv.

[7] Williams, R. and Peisser, V., *Preparing Heirs,* (San Francisco, CA: Robert D. Reed, 2003), pp. 36–39.

[8] Covey, S.M.R., *The Speed of Trust,* (New York, NY: Simon and Schuster, 2006), pp. 136–229.

[9] Focus Adolescent Services, 'Your teen's friends: peer influence and peer relationships': www.focusas.com/PeerInfluence.html.

[10] Seltzer, L.F., 'Child entitlement abuse: how parents inadvertently harm their children, Part I,' *Psychology Today*, September 2009: www.psychologytoday.com/blog/evolution-the-self/200909/child-entitlement-abuse-how-parents-inadvertently-harm-their-children.

[11] Hausner, L., *Children of Paradise: successful parenting for prosperous families*, (Los Angeles, CA: Tarcher, 1990), pp. 150–152.

[12] Ibid.

[13] As in other chapters, the terms 'joint decision making' and 'dynamic stakeholder owner' are used with permission from James E. Hughes, Jr.

[14] Stoltz, J., 'Communication key to cross-generational relationships', *The Business Ledger,* September 2008: www.thebusinessledger.com/Home/Archives/CommentaryViewpoints/tabid/86/newsid415/478/Communication-key-to-cross-generational-relationships/Default.aspx.

[15] Alvarez-Holmberg, A., 'Using generational perspectives at work,' Media Communications Association International, Minnesota: www.mcai-mn.org/resources/articles_generations_0412.html.

[16] Actual case study and part of the analysis were taken from a pre-published article. Brunel, J.L.P. and Gray, L.P., 'Integrating family dynamics and governance in strategic asset allocation,' *Journal of Wealth Management,* Winter 2005, pp. 39–46.

[17] The tools mentioned here refer to tools and processes which have been developed by graymatter Strategies LLC in its work with families of wealth and their advisors.

Chapter 17

The behavioural finance overlay and goal-based asset allocation

'... people are always functioning within a portion of their possibilities. There are many possibilities, only some of which are elicited or constrained by the contextual structure. Therefore, breaking or expanding contexts can allow new possibilities to emerge.'

Family therapy techniques[1]

When we established that generational perspectives have the greatest fundamental impact on wealth management decisions, we began by identifying cyclical elements in society at large. We got expert opinions. We noted the impact of linear versus cyclical time measurement and the corrective powers inherent in the 'turnings'[2] of larger society. We then applied critical elements from our research to the smaller society of family. Through this process, we established that the true wealth of the family is its intellectual, human, and social capacities and the relationships that nurture them. We recognised that for these assets to flourish, we must understand a family's generational maze, the roles family members occupy, and the essential nature of trust-level communication. From that point, we were able to set goals that are directly aligned with the needs of the family's authentic wealth. The wealth flourishes into a tangible form, then flows back to the family to foster the materialization of more authentic wealth, establishing a rejuvenating cycle.

Two questions now arise: 'Is this all we need to do to ensure the family's authentic wealth will flourish in a way that will defeat the Proverb?' and 'How do we translate the individual and family goals we set into a language which our advisors will understand and in a way in which our goals will remain directly aligned with the family's authentic needs?'

The first question can be turned around to ponder what could sabotage the strategic plan we have designed for this purpose. The danger lies in imposing a linear path – a path which would squelch the cyclical rejuvenation of the family's authentic wealth and steer the family directly into the throes of the three generations Proverb.

This is the juncture where the conversations about generational perspectives, roles, family dynamics, and governance begin to translate into the management of the material and financial wealth of the family. Within the Generational Wealth Management Continuum^{SM}, Steps 1 and 2 (family systems and family governance) create a strategic plan through the family governance system. This plan guides the creation of an investment policy to steer the management of investments and financial capital in Steps 4 and 5 (goal-based asset allocation and monitoring) through the family office or family office entity. Step 3 (translation of goals) serves as the bridge point; it crosses the divide from the family's authentic assets to the material and financial assets they have produced. It is the critical point where the strategic plan can most easily become derailed – we tend to leave the cyclical nature of our authentic wealth behind as we begin to focus on managing the investment and financial wealth it created. It is also the door through which a linear path may be imposed.

The weakness of linear time measurement, as noted earlier, separates people from the grounding force that gives life its meaning. When we consider our social destiny to be ultimately within our own control and the direction of our lives to be self-determined, we deny ourselves the rich experience of participation 'in a collective myth that is larger than ourselves'.[3] Our linear way of thinking 'flattens' the natural ebb and flow of cyclicality – but only to a certain point. This flattening prevents the normal clearing away of the old to make way for the new. The longer the old continues to collect, the more forcefully it will demand its eventual release. In larger society, this occurs as some societal or economic catastrophe – what Strauss and Howe call a Great Event. In families, it erupts as a crisis or series of crises which can permanently sever relationships – and dissipate whatever forms of wealth were present.

Since this is the largest single threat to the invaluable work done up to Step 3, there must be indications at this critical juncture which could serve as warning signals before things stray off course and away from achieving the family's goals. A key to these indications is human behaviour. As human beings, we are subject to our own human natures. At times and as the result of various stimuli, we become emotional and irrational; our thought processes pick and choose what they want to pay attention to and what they do not. In reality, we are not looking at all the facts; we are not making fully informed decisions. These tendencies show that we are subject to biases grounded in emotion (the way we feel) and cognition (the way we think). This limits our ability to step back and see the cyclical view which fosters a more informed decision. Emotional and cognitive biases cloud our judgment. When dealing with investment management, these biases are components of what is called 'behavioural finance'.

The work of Strauss and Howe connected the cyclical measurement of time to the definition of archetypical generations of larger society. The discussion in Chapter 3 tied the cyclical measurement of time to family generations (chronological) and the proverbial dissipation of the wealth. As the archetypical generations in larger society 'lend balance and self-correction to the continuing story'[4] of the peoples of our world, the turnover of generations within the family lend 'balance and self-correction' to the Family Story. These connections enable families and their advisors to use common behavioural biases as data points[5] to alert us to what Brunel calls 'decision risk' or 'the risk of changing horses in mid-race' [6] which amounts to sabotaging the strategic plan we so carefully created.

Applying behavioural finance as an overlay to generational attitudes toward wealth, we will make the case that behavioural biases invite a more linear path, undermining the cyclical nature of a family's generations and derailing families from their focus on nurturing their authentic wealth.

Understanding and using the terms that have been developed over the years in the identification of behavioural biases also can serve as a translator of personal goals – both individual and family – into a financial language which may then be used to identify investment goals within a goal-based asset allocation model.[7] Goal-based asset allocation more directly fits the way investors think and, therefore, serves as an invaluable tool with which advisors may provide optimal service to families of wealth.[8]

Therefore, this chapter will explore two functions of behavioural biases within the Generational Wealth Management Continuum[SM].

1 Using behavioural biases as data points which can be monitored to help families stay on course.
2 Using behavioural biases to translate individual and family goals into a financial language which can then be used to structure a goal-based asset allocation.

Behavioural finance encompasses much more than these two functions. Statman defines behavioural finance as simply finance populated by normal people.[9] This, obviously, refers to any aspect of finance and investments in which individuals and families are involved, which encompasses a broad scope. Our utilisation of behavioural finance does not seek to limit its scope; rather, it simply employs behavioural finance as a tool to accomplish the two objectives stated above.

The role of behavioural biases

To best utilise behavioural finance for our purposes, we have to understand the position of behavioural forces within the cyclical continuum. Each new generation's rising prevents the previous generation's persona from holding sway for too long a time. In this way, cyclicality is renewed within the turnings of the four generational seasons over the span of a long human life, making each saeculum complete.[10] Each generation thinks and functions within its own characteristics. If allowed to govern continually, these characteristics would take on a linear quality and would become constraints on the ability of society to change and complete the cycle.[11]

When we become young adults, it is no longer beneficial to function as we did in childhood. If we continue in our childhood ways, we become inept and perhaps even dangerous in our roles as adults. We have no choice about our physical growth into adulthood; and we must make the correct choice to leave the vestiges of childhood behind in order to flourish in our new role. So it is throughout our lifetime. We make the required adjustments in our roles through the way we behave.

Just as new life phases require us to function differently, each generation faces a time when it must give way to the next generation's response to the social and economic forces with which it was imprinted.[12] As we move from one stage of life to another, our behavioural response to each stage is coloured by our generational lens.[13] Each generation is defined by the years during which it shares a common socio-economic experience.

This is why the unchallenged imposition of the elder generation's mores over upcoming generations invites the imposition of linear time and causes roles to become perceived rather than authentic. Any linear imposition corrects itself through realignment with the cyclical forces of nature. These corrections can be significant and they can be abrupt and harsh. In larger society, Strauss and Howe call these corrections Great Events. In families, they are corrected through family dysfunction, rebellion, and severed relationships – otherwise known as family crises. The attempt to force the elder generation's behavioural mores onto upcoming generations rather than encouraging the free reinterpretation of them stifles the development of the family's authentic wealth and causes the entire family wealth portfolio to suffer. We saw examples of this in Stories 1 and 2 in the Preamble.

Just as our behaviour signals our stage of life and the roles we occupy, the way we behave also affects the way we invest. For example, Statman[14] notes that investors tend to think of their stock purchases individually rather than as part of an overall portfolio. We readily take 'paper' gains in individual positions and we put off taking 'paper' losses, even if we 'know' intellectually that taking a small loss will ultimately result in less pain than if we hold on to a losing position. Through our mental way of accounting, we do not consider 'paper' losses to be real unless we sell the position and 'realise' the loss. We may also mentally reframe the stock's value as an 'unrealised' loss at one point and as a tax deduction at another. Ultimately, after holding on to our 'unrealised' losses in hopes that the stock will rebound at some point, we often end up 'throwing in the towel' (selling or 'realising the loss') at the bottom of the market. Then we feel regret as we look back and see 'obvious' signs in hindsight that we made a mistake and we extrapolate from our perfect hindsight vision that we should have been able to see what was happening in foresight.[15]

Statman says that such behaviour means that we are normal and that we are sometimes normal 'smart' and at other times, we are normal 'stupid'. 'The trick is,' he says, 'to learn to increase our ratio of smart behavior to stupid. And since we cannot (thank goodness) turn ourselves into computer-like people, we need to find tools to help us act smart even when our thinking and feeling tempt us to be stupid.'[16]

Families are also normal and sometimes act normal smart and at other times, act normal stupid. The danger in the advisor-family client relationship presents itself when advisors treat family clients as institutions, which they are not even though they may have the asset level and investment sophistication to *participate as* institutions.

Statman points out that traders are also normal but that, knowing their weaknesses, they establish tools which force them to be normal 'smart' more often, even when they realise they may still feel regret after the fact.[17] If traders can establish a system to serve as markers that they are about to be normal 'stupid,' why could we not establish a system that would serve the same purpose for families? Like the traders Statman mentions, the goal is to establish customised monitoring systems that reflect behaviour and, therefore which really do work.

This is the key to keeping linear forces at bay and adhering to the larger view behind the strategic plan we created to foster the family's authentic wealth. It is also the key to the successful translation of individual and family goals to a language investment advisors can use to design a goal-based portfolio which is directly aligned with the needs of a family's authentic wealth.

The behavioural bias-linear time connection

How can we use our awareness of behavioural biases to alert us to mistakes we are about to make? First we must realise that succumbing to these biases invites linear views into our thinking. Behavioural finance is not linear in and of itself; however, it invites us to think in linear fashion and we eventually find ourselves travelling a path which does not feel comfortable. Thus it is easy to make the connection between mistakes which occur when we are being normal 'stupid' and the subsequent participation in linear thinking.

The benefit we enjoy from the linear time track is a sense of progress.[18] Behavioural biases steer us onto the linear pathway. As human beings, it is the feeling of achievement which drives us forward. That's why a linear progression feels so good, even though it is artificially imposed! The longer the progression goes uninterrupted, the more subject we inevitably become to a violent re-entry of the cyclical force of nature, seemingly at its own whim. The event seems to be a shock and awe type of experience. We get caught up in the momentum of the linear progression and we become surprised more than 'normal'[19] when the inevitable Great Event occurs.

This is how behavioural forces lure us into the adoption of linear time. We do not naturally follow a linear pathway. The fact that we are born, make our marks on the world, and then we die completes a cycle of life which is replenished by the lives of our children so that they may make their own marks. Brunel adds the illustrative point that the Japanese language and culture also do not naturally follow a linear progress. Probably because of the historical precedent of Samurai powers, language and culture tend to follow concentric processes where one can judge the reaction of the 'other' party before proceeding to the next step.[20]

Behavioural biases offer us the seeming opportunity to continue making 'progress' when there are subjugating forces at work to which we should pay attention. After the fact, we try to go back and realign what actually happened to match the way we think things should have occurred. According to Howe, it's probably true that we correct for past mistakes in our behaviour by assuming linear time. This type of correction bias underlies the turning methodology discussed above that he and Strauss outline in their work on generations.[21]

Viewing time through a linear progression narrows the lens through which we can absorb our day to day experiences. Like money, it is an invention of humankind. It limits our view to the subject of our current attention, supports our desire to find a solution as quickly as possible, and gives us a sense of satisfaction that we have progressed by the simple fact of having made a decision.

As behavioural biases support our linear sense of progress, they expose us to risks we choose not to see; therefore, we experience consequences we did not anticipate. Instead of working with the cyclical tools nature has provided to ensure long-term success, we tend to frame things like we want them to be, gaining a short-term desire without going through the more prudent process, only to regret these mistakes after the fact.

As Chapter 7 noted in its discussion of Modernisation, all linear progressions are a dually-phased process. After its initial phase of success, the progression begins to experience a cyclical turn in which the societal push increases momentum even as the cyclical tide begins to expose travellers of the linear path to more and more risk. In the process, expectations for progress become harder to meet, requiring more and more resources to keep the momentum going. Finally, as resources dry up, continuation along the linear path becomes threatened by conflicting interests.

Exhibit 17.1

Similarities between Modernisation and linear time effects

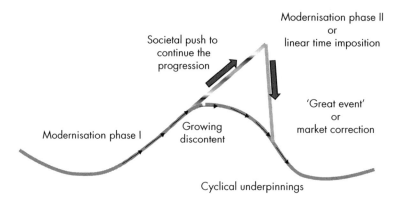

Source: graymatter Strategies LLC. All rights reserved.

For example, after a significant market move, money begins to flow out of stocks and into bonds or commodities when the returns in those markets become more attractive than the returns yet to be had by continuing to hold stocks. We may then experience a stock market crash which corrects the values of equities to match their appropriate valuation in the market cycle against the existing economic backdrop. Behavioural biases cause us to frame our decisions in a way that goes along with the situational pressures to invest, inviting us to ignore the cyclical undercurrent already underway.

Stephen Greenspan cites the situational pressures to invest, causing even intelligent and educated investors like him to ignore the warnings of clearer headed minds.[22] Economist Robert Schiller calls this the 'feedback loop theory of investor bubbles'.[23] It causes us to employ selective evidence or support from a view we consider to be fact. Because people we know are doing well in a certain investment, we begin to feel a sense of safety and confidence regarding it. We frame the decision (a cognitive bias called mental accounting)[24] to invest through other people's experiences, deciding to take the plunge without doing the proper due diligence and considering the cyclical view. We ignore the data points which, in hindsight, look so obvious. We think that just because we can see them after the fact, that we should have been able to see them when they were still in the future.[25] On the other hand, things are not obvious if we choose to not see them.

The behavioural finance overlay for individuals and families

Families are comprised of normal human beings with significant wealth locked inside their intellectual, human, and social capacities. Emotional and cognitive human tendencies make people behave irrationally even after they have carefully developed a wealth management programme directly aligned with the goals our authentic wealth needs to flourish.

Advisors are also human. Like other human beings, they tend to focus on their own expertise, working within that expertise to create an optimal solution for clients. What is optimal in their view often is optimal within the constraints of their expertise.[26] What is optimal for families of wealth is alignment of all family services – including investment management, tax, and legal services – with the authentic goals the family has set. Again, two critical needs are identified here. First, to understand the behavioural forces which can temporarily distort rationality, making families 'normal' human beings; and second, to effectively communicate family goals to their advisors so that their expertise can be applied in a way which will support the flourishing of the family's authentic wealth rather than confine it to the predetermined parameters of their professional world.

The most pragmatic way to do this is to overlay generational attitudes toward wealth with common behavioural biases. By looking at probable goals based on these generational attitudes, we can see how behavioural biases can sabotage their achievement.

Using behavioural biases as data points for monitoring risk

In this section, we look at three common behavioural biases and the generational perspectives which may lie beneath them.[27]

1 Overconfidence.
2 Hindsight.
3 Mental accounting.

We can actually use the behavioural biases as data points or signals that we are in danger of behaving normal 'stupid'. Earlier, we spoke of the difference in two generations of entrepreneurs and noted their common personality traits which overlay their different generational perspectives. In like fashion, we note that similar behavioural biases are common to all generations; *the danger in the translation of individual and family goals is that advisors – and individuals and families themselves – look at the behavioural characteristics and never do the work to uncover the generational outlook.* This perpetuates the linear path the investor has already been invited to join and, thus, the entire family-advisor relationship becomes based on a distortion rather than a reality.

In his first book, *Behavioral Finance and Wealth Management*, investment consultant and author Michael Pompian developed tests appropriate to the various behavioural biases which help advisors – and families – diagnose behavioural tendencies. He breaks emotional and cognitive biases into 20 different behaviours, listing a case study example and diagnostic test method for each.[28] For example, overconfidence (a cognitive bias) is described as 'unwarranted faith in one's intuitive reasoning, judgments, and cognitive abilities', especially in one's ability to predict the future of the markets. In this case, investors narrow the range of expected gains, predicting a range of say, 10% either way, when historical standard deviations reveal a different story. Test questions include asking the investor to give high and low estimates for the average weight of an adult sperm whale, the distance to the moon in miles, and then, their estimated returns for their own stock portfolio. Responses which offer too narrow a range of possibilities to either question (10–20 tons versus 20–100 tons for the first question and 100,000–200,000 miles rather than 100,000–500,000 miles for the second) are a tipoff that the investor is subject to overconfidence bias.[29]

Brunel cites a trivia test employed by Hersh Shefrin[30] which includes asking how old Martin Luther King was when he died and how long, in days, is the gestation period of an Asian elephant.

Although these questions may seem farfetched, they serve a pragmatic purpose and can help investors laugh at themselves while getting the point that they may be overestimating their actual abilities to predict future returns of the position that seems such an imperative addition to the portfolio.

What we discover is that it is not enough to ask, 'What are your goals?' Answers to this question during the initial meeting between individuals and families and their advisors – including tax and legal advisors – are often accepted as real goals when they are actually based on behavioural biases. This completely gets the investment process off kilter from the very beginning. Everything that is built from this point becomes an assumption which can easily break down when market and economic crises hit. The authentic goals which lie beneath are grounded in the family's generational maze of perspectives, the roles family members occupy, and the dynamics at work within the family – all the components of Steps 1 and 2.

This realisation clears the way for us to see the generational wealth attitudes underneath. Since behavioural biases are common to all generations and, actually, serve to mask the vital information underlying, it is appropriate to start with the biases themselves and work down to the authentic goals of the family.

Here is how the process could work.

In June 2008, an individual family member says that he wishes to invest heavily in the stock of General Motors because it is beginning to make new highs and it has just announced the closing of four plants.[31] It is a solid 'blue chip' company that the government would never let 'go under'. The family member feels the closings indicate GM is becoming more fiscally responsible and that the rising stock price is evidence of its certainty to continue going up. He feels the position would be a good long-term addition to the family's portfolio which would also be more conservative. He feels the family has taken too much risk in the portfolio in years past.

This person happens to be an elder generation member – a Silent patriarch – who feels that investing in 'America' is the way to ensure a good investment future and was disappointed that the stock position which was inherited from his father was sold in the late 1990s to make room for a position in Amazon. The value of GM stock in June 2008 was approximately $35; by June 2009, the company had filed for bankruptcy protection.[32]

This gentleman was subject to overconfidence, framing bias, and hindsight. He was certain of the investment prospects of GM and he was looking at the 'facts' he wished to see to support his confidence, making a judgment based upon them, and ignoring important other facts – such as the condition of GM's pension plans, the sales records of some of its brands, and other pertinent data – that could have helped him make a more informed decision. In hindsight, he viewed the selling of the former GM position as a mistake even though the Amazon investment had done well. Amazon was a company with a business model – internet commerce – he could not understand and with which he could not identify. He was also using hindsight to see the mistakes of those who had invested in other .com companies during the late 1990s and was lumping Amazon into the same group, despite the fact that Amazon had been one of the few with a business model that has survived.

The advisor working with this gentleman could have asked some questions to help the man become aware of his biases, although this would have to be done very carefully. Asking some of the test questions listed above at the first meeting might have insulted the patriarch rather than helped him to see that he was picking and choosing a stock which, at one time, was legitimately viewed as a stalwart investment and which symbolised the fortitude of America during World War II – a war in which his father had fought – as well as the economic prosperity after the war. The confidence bias questions listed above most certainly could be asked after the establishment of trust-level communication, something that applies to the advisor-client relationship as well as to relationships among family members, but might have caused the patriarch to view them as insulting initially.

Brunel notes that investors are path dependent. This means that the decision processes we employ are unduly influenced by the path we have taken to get to the decision point! Thus, two investors, both with $100 a year ago and $110 now, might have different behaviours if one went from $100 up to $115, and then down to $110, while the other went steadily up from $100 to $110.[33]

The biases the patriarch held were inviting him to continue on a linear path based on: (a) his particular view of the value of GM stock based on the path he knew regarding GM; (b) the ignoring of facts pertinent to his decision; and (c) his definition of what constituted a prudent investment. Becoming aware of these biases would free the patriarch to look at the investment from a larger view, seeing the cyclical forces underlying GM's stock price at the time as well as the momentum that seemed to be building.

After having brought the patriarch's biases to light, further questions could be asked to understand this man's perspectives from a generational view. For example, it could be discovered that, as a member of the Silent generation, this man was afraid of running out of money despite the fact that he had consistently lived below his means and had a very healthy net worth. He wanted someone to listen to him, unlike his family had when they sold the original position and bought the Amazon stock. He felt his Boomer children were greedy, were taking too much risk in the portfolio, and that they wanted excess returns to support what he considered to be an extravagant lifestyle. He wanted to put the GM position in a trust he had set up which would benefit his children upon his death but which would keep his children from gaining access to the funds until then.

His feelings about his father, America, and the war are clues about the values and also the hopes he holds for his children, grandchildren, and his legacy. His fear of running out of money could also translate into fears he has about his children's and grandchildren's future after he is gone. There is much which can be unearthed simply by understanding the different levels of influences on decision making, signals to indicate which influences are at work and in what ways, and how authentic goals get lost in the translation between the family governance system and the investment piece.

We can also view generational perspectives as a contributor toward path dependency – again, an invitation to a linear time view. This is because our particular view of the world guides us over our entire life and we line things up to match that view. Unless we become aware of and try to understand the perspectives of other generational perspectives in our families, we tend to close ourselves to our own generational lens and continue on a path that introduces dysfunction – and eventually destruction – to our family relationships. A clear example is when family leadership tries to push through something about which he or they feel there will be disagreement and ultimate rejection. Feeling that they 'know best', they prevent the introduction of ideas which may serve the family's needs even better, destroying the desire for wealth fostering participation by other family members, and significantly harming family relationships in the process.

In similar fashion, behavioural biases distort our goals in a way that may lead us – and our advisors – toward mistakes that we later regret. In this way, both behavioural biases and generational biases can function as data points which alert family members and their advisors to impending mistakes in judgment and preference. A solid level of understanding is required for the detection of each in a way that will benefit the flourishing of the family's authentic wealth. Behavioural biases are usually present in the first point of contact and are universal – people of all generations are subject to them. Awareness of behavioural biases can be used to drill down to generational biases and to uncover the authentic needs and goals of the family. We must keep in mind that this approach is based on a larger society generational persona and that individuals inside families will have their own particular way of relating or dealing with that persona. So our process mandates that we begin with a larger society view, then customise it to fit the needs of a particular family's generational maze.

Other generational perspectives and multi-cultural perspectives

Although we used the American Silent generation perspective in the example, similar behaviours are detected in other generations as well as in other cultures. Statman notes that, although 'people are the same all over the world ... not only in physical features but also in cognition and emotions', cultural (and generational!) perspectives affect expectations, cognitions, and emotions.[34] Wherever people are, they 'import norms from the culture they know into their new surroundings'. He gives examples of the number of parking tickets incurred by diplomats from a variety of countries, noticing that diplomats from countries where corruption levels are higher also incurred higher numbers of parking violations. People from different countries also view insider trading differently. Fifty-six percent of people in Turkey rated insider trading by financial professionals as fair or acceptable; 16% of people in Italy and Australia thought it was fair; and only 5% of people in the Netherlands and the United States.[35]

The level of trust among cultures also varies – people from countries where levels of trust are high are more likely to invest in stocks. China, Norway, Finland, and Sweden are among the highest and France, Italy, Mexico, and the West Indies are among the lowest.[36]

Brunel gives the example of a family office executive in Singapore who viewed the investment manager's skills unfavourably because of the wealth owner benchmarked the performance to the best performing strategy during the most recent period even though the executive knew that a few objective benchmarks would have provided a much fairer evaluation.[37]

The younger generations in various cultures will be farther removed from the mores of the older generations and peeling back their behavioural biases will uncover the different perspectives of their generations. Understanding that a post-war Japanese patriarch (similar time period to the American Silent) will be much more concerned about family relationships than the Dankai (similar to the Boomers) who became 'company men' will make a marked difference in the way their behavioural biases may peel back against the perspectives of their respective generations.

The behavioural biases of a Middle Eastern male family member will peel back quite differently against those of a Middle Eastern woman. And those of a European family member who values the heritage of the family castle will peel back quite differently against younger generations more interested in philanthropy.

The fact remains that families are also normal investors rather than rational ones which further means that, as human beings, we all have emotional and cognitive weaknesses that can derail any long-term planning we may do. A long term plan may look fine from a far-away view of things, but place investors in the day to day throes of a September 2008 or even a May 6 2010 and emotional reactions will lead to decision risk which readily invites the linear path to interfere. We only have to think back to the example in Chapter 9 where the family council was created but not empowered to realise the significance of the potential consequences to the family's bottom line.

Goal-based asset allocation

It is useful to introduce here the utility of behavioural biases in translating individual and family goals into investment and financial goals – one of the two main points of this chapter.

Behavioural finance lends itself to this purpose quite easily. In contrasting standard finance or what is more commonly known as modern portfolio theory, with behavioural finance, Statman notes that behavioural portfolio theory is a goal-based theory, reflecting the fact that 'individuals divide their money into many layers of a portfolio pyramid corresponding to many goals such as secure retirement, college education, or having the means to hop on a cruise ship whenever they please'.[38]

He states, 'A central theory in behavioural portfolio theory is the observation that investors view their portfolios not as a whole, as prescribed by mean-variance portfolio theory, but as distinct layers in a portfolio of assets, where layers are associated with particular goals and where attitudes toward risk vary across layers'.[39] He cites that one layer might be designed to protect people from becoming poor, another might be to offer the opportunity to become rich, noting that people may accept higher levels of risk after achieving their aspirations and lower levels of risk before having achieved them.

Brunel has fashioned a goal-based asset allocation model which categorises goals into financial terms investors use every day such as income, liquidity, capital preservation, and growth as well as opportunities.[40] He creates buckets into which goals similar to those Statman iterates can be prioritised and to which a risk level can be assigned. From this, a more detailed allocation can be developed and, after the consideration of asset location issues, specific securities or investment strategies chosen.

Statman created a pyramid which categorises the goals people have in layers, with the layers protecting from becoming poor at the bottom and the layers offering the opportunity to become rich at the top.

Exhibit 17.2

Behavioural finance goal-based portfolio pyramid

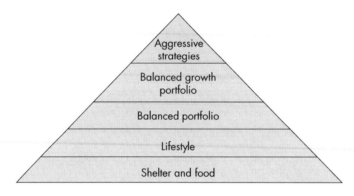

Source: Statman and Brunel.[41]

We can expand this progression of goals to include the authentic individual and family goals that are identified through the family governance system and which are designed to flourish the family's authentic wealth.

Box 17.1 illustrates one way that individual and family goals may be translated into a goal-based allocation using a behavioural bias overlay. There are, obviously, multiple ways the translation could occur, all of which could be correct based on the level of trust-level communication between family client and advisor. This is the point at which a highly customised level of expertise is required. No single translation – even when inputting the same variables – will be the right prescription for every family. Each individual within the family will also have his or her own translations. For example, one does not always require immediate liquidity to become rich; becoming rich will eventually require liquidity and being illiquid for several years prior could actually aid the process.

Obviously, the desire to enhance one's lifestyle may cause an investor to be more aggressive and may also lead to overconfidence and optimism if the investor has experienced recent success in the market. If this investor is a member of a Boomer era generation, he or she may be spending at a rate which may preclude such enhancement, thinking that there is more in the mental account for that category than is actually available and framing decisions based on that accounting. Gen-X era investors may also be overconfident, thinking that the money will always be there. A Silent

Box 17.1

Authentic goals	Behavioural overlay	Investment goals
Enhance lifestyle (buy a yacht)	Become rich (optimism – aggressive)	Opportunistic (eventual liquidity)
Philanthropic	Value Function (risk aversion – balanced growth)	Capital preservation
Educate grandchildren	Generation skipping trust (endowment bias – balanced growth)	Growth
Support daily family needs	Invest in high interest rate bonds (overconfidence – lifestyle)	Income liquidity
Preserve lifestyle in retirement	Fear of running out of money (mental accounting – shelter and food)	Capital preservation

Source: Gray, Statman, Brunel.[41]

era investor may also employ mental accounting from a fear of running out of money but in a different way than the Boomer. The Silent investor also may carry a loss-aversion bias which Brunel categorises as a value function, which denotes the different levels of satisfaction resulting from the same outcome.[42] In the earlier example, the family imposed the sale of GM on the Silent patriarch because it viewed having money enabled them to take more risk where the Silent patriarch was still afraid of running out of money, even after the Amazon position became a success.

Starting with the behavioural bias and drilling down, we may discover that the desire to enhance one's lifestyle encompasses more than just having more money; it also may include the desire to paint or to pursue a musical interest that was suppressed in earlier years. Of course, these pursuits also require more money. The desire to educate grandchildren may result in a generation skipping trust out of fear that the next generation does not have the skills to manage the money. It also may reflect an endowment bias causing the investor to hold a stock position for too long or in too concentrated a fashion thinking that, like the Silent patriarch thought about GM, it would be around forever.

As we think about specific examples, it becomes easier to see that behavioural finance can help discover authentic goals by translating the specific investment behaviour to discover what families and individual investors are really trying to accomplish. Needless to say, the strategies designed based on each would be quite different! By understanding the family's real needs and also the behavioural biases at work, goals can effectively be translated, prioritised, and investment and risk management strategies can be designed which more directly support the flourishing of the authentic wealth.

The data point monitoring system

Any tool or mechanism which positively and effectively 'catch' early warning signals which can alert us to impending difficulties before they reach the point of crisis is one which enables us to step back and take a more objective view of what may prevent significant damage to portfolios, investment strategies, quality of life, and most importantly, family trust in relationships. If one thinks that trust in relationships is separate and apart from the way the money is managed, it would be wise to think again! This is the spot at which we discover the real level – or lack, thereof – of trust within the family. In fact, there is hardly a clearer indicator.

Unlike one's generational imprint, behaviour can be changed, although it may be difficult and requires a great deal of conscious and determined practice. When we become aware of the biases present in our decisions, we can set up systems to monitor those biases and guide us to alter our behaviour accordingly. Such a system must be customised based on each family's particular biases (and the biases of individual family members within it) and then constructed so that it can be monitored through both the investment review and the family governance system. Maintaining this connection to the family governance piece is essential. By using the monitoring system to connect both sides of the consummate family portfolio, we stand a much better chance of being able to catch warning signals in time to make a difference in the outcome.

Although this is guaranteed not to be consistently perfect, the ratio of improvement would most certainly be substantial. It requires knowing ourselves and it requires our advisors to also know us at a level they may not previously have ventured to go.

This chapter, along with the two following, outlines the advisory relationship in a new way, enabling families to use their advisors – of all types – in ways that support the flourishing of all forms of their wealth.

---

[1] Minuchin, S. and Fishman, H.C., 'Family therapy techniques,' President and fellows of Harvard College, 1981 and 1996, p. 15.

[2] Strauss, W. and Howe, N., *The Fourth Turning: an American prophecy,* (New York, NY: Broadway Books, 1997), p. 3.

[3] Ibid, p. 11.

[4] Strauss, W. and Howe, N., *The Fourth Turning: an American prophecy,* (New York, NY: Broadway Books, 1997), p. 98.

[5] The author is grateful to Jean L.P. Brunel for permissioned use of his term 'data points' in the development of a monitoring system which could alert families and investors to certain data and events to which they might not normally pay attention.

[6] Brunel, J.L.P., *Integrated Wealth Management: the new direction for portfolio managers*, 2nd edition (London: Euromoney Books, 2006), p. 11.

[7] In a personal discussion with Brunel, he positioned behavioural finance within the context of the Generational Wealth Management Continuum^{SM} as a translator of a family's personal goals into a financial language which then facilitates the development of a goal-based asset allocation. The author is greatly indebted to him for this insight as it holds the key to bridging goals from the first two steps of the Continuum^{SM} to the last two.

[8] Brunel, J.L.P., *Integrated Wealth Management: the new direction for portfolio managers*, 2nd edition (London: Euromoney Books, 2006), p. 203

[9] Statman, M., 'What is behavioral finance', in: Fabozi, F., editor, *The Handbook of Finance*, (Hoboken, NJ: John Wiley & Sons, 2008).

[10] Strauss, W. and Howe, N., *The Fourth Turning: an American prophecy,* (New York, NY: Broadway Books, 1997), p. 31.

[11] Ibid, p. 62.

[12] Ibid, p. 33.

[13] Strauss and Howe note the different behavioural responses of each generation to a Great Event. They illustrate how each generation reflects its generational characteristics in the behaviour exhibited through the roles it occupies in response to the

Event. A Great Event is identified as an event which serves as a 'crystallising moment' according to Mannheim and which holds such social consequence that all society's members respond differently based on their stage of life when it occurs. Strauss, W. and Howe, N., *The Fourth Turning: an American prophecy,* (New York, NY: Broadway Books, 1997), p. 58.

[14] Dr. Statman is the Glenn Klimek Professor of Finance at Santa Clara University in Santa Clara, CA and is a specialist in the study of behavioural finance.

[15] Statman, M., 'What is behavioral finance', in: Fabozi, F., editor, *The Handbook of Finance*, (Hoboken, NJ: John Wiley & Sons, 2008).

[16] Statman, M., 'The mistakes we make – and why we make them', *The Wall Street Journal,'* August 24 2009.

[17] Statman, M., 'What is behavioral finance', in: Fabozi, F., editor, *The Handbook of Finance*, (Hoboken, NJ: John Wiley & Sons, 2008).

[18] Strauss, William, and Howe, Neil, (1997). *The Fourth Turning: An American Prophecy,* Broadway Books, a division of Bantam Doubleday Dell Publishing Group, New York, NY, p. 62.

[19] Statman, M., 'What is behavioral finance', in: Fabozi, F., editor, *The Handbook of Finance*, (Hoboken, NJ: John Wiley & Sons, 2008).

[20] Brunel, Jean L.P., Personal email exchange, June 2010.

[21] Howe, Neil, Personal interview, June 2010.

[22] Greenspan, S., 'Fooled by Ponzi (and Madoff): how Bernard Madoff made off with my money', *eSkeptic*, the email newsletter of the Skeptics Society, December 23 2008: www.skeptic.com/eskeptic/08-12-23.

[23] Ibid.

[24] Statman, M., 'What is behavioral finance', in: Fabozi, F., editor, *The Handbook of Finance*, (Hoboken, NJ: John Wiley & Sons, 2008).

[25] Ibid.

[26] Brunel, J.L.P., 'How suboptimal – if at all – is goal-based asset allocation?' *The Journal of Wealth Management,* Fall 2006, pp. 19–34. Brunel notes that what is considered optimal for the portfolio may or may not be optimal for the client.

[27] Both Statman and Pompian note two broad categories of behavioural biases: cognitive and emotional.

[28] Pompian, M.M., *Behavioral Finance and Wealth Management*, (Hoboken, NJ: John Wiley and Sons, 2006), Chapters 4–23.

[29] Ibid. Overconfidence bias case study example, pp. 51–61.

[30] Brunel, J.L.P., *Integrated Wealth Management: the new direction for portfolio managers*, 2nd edition (London: Euromoney Books, 2006), p. 39.

[31] 'GM to close Janesville assembly plant by 2010', Channel3000, Janesville, WI, June 4 2010. www.channel3000.com/news/16464398/detail.html.

[32] http://bigcharts.marketwatch.com/advchart/frames/frames.asp?symb=&time=&freq; Wikipedia, History of General Motors: http://en.wikipedia.org/wiki/History_of_General_Motors.

[33] Brunel, J.L.P., *Integrated Wealth Management: the new direction for portfolio managers*, 2nd edition (London: Euromoney Books, 2006), p. 7.

[34] Statman, M., 'Countries and culture in behavioral finance,' *CFA Institute,* September 2008, p. 38: www.cfapubs.org.

[35] Ibid, p. 39.

[36] Statman, M. and Weng, J.A., 'Investments across cultures: financial attitudes of Chinese-Americans', Santa Clara University Research, November 2009, p. 2: www.scu.edu/business/finance/research/statman_research.cfm.

[37] Brunel, J.L.P., *Integrated Wealth Management: the new direction for portfolio managers*, 2nd edition (London: Euromoney Books, 2006), p. 6.

[38] Statman, M., 'What is behavioral finance', in: Fabozi, F., editor, *The Handbook of Finance*, (Hoboken, NJ: John Wiley & Sons, 2008).

[39] Ibid.

[40] Brunel, J.L.P., *Integrated Wealth Management: the new direction for portfolio managers*, 2nd edition (London: Euromoney Books, 2006), pp. 205, 206.

[41] Source material for this chart is from Brunel, J.L.P., 'How suboptimal – if at all – is goal-based asset allocation?' *The Journal of Wealth Management,* Fall 2006, pp. 19–34, which includes Statman's behavioural pyramid work from which the middle column of the chart was formulated. Brunel's goal-based asset allocation model was used for the far right column.

[42] Brunel, J.L.P., *Integrated Wealth Management: the new direction for portfolio managers*, 2nd edition (London: Euromoney Books, 2006), p. 42.

Chapter 18

Authentic risk management and asset protection

'You go to the market and bring home a beautiful flowering plant on Saturday. You go out of town for a week. You come home and find that the plant has died ... you get frustrated that you spent a lot of money on a plant that was supposed to bloom and be beautiful but in the absence of food, water, and light, the plant cannot flourish. It's the same for families. In order to flourish, grow, and regenerate human, intellectual, and social capabilities, families need to provide education, empowerment, and ongoing coaching of family members, beginning from childhood.'

Linda Mack

In her book, *The Soul of Money*, Lynn Twist[1] tells the story about a group of primitive people and their first experience with money. They had watched other groups in their region become moneyed societies. They had observed as those groups misused the money because they did not understand its true utility and did not understand its power. In their enthusiasm to exchange their most valuable assets for a commodity which became depleted after a very short period of time, the other groups had 'lost their land, their homes, their way of life, and the heritage that had been theirs for all time before'.[2] This people were determined not to follow the same path as their neighbours. They realised this new relationship with money must have its roots in the things that were most important to them, the virtues they held dear and those aspects of life which commanded their highest level of commitment. The people realised that this relationship with money would constantly challenge the relationships that were most important to them as well as the 'ancient communal principles of their culture'.[3]

The dynamics of the family are the waters through which effective communication has to navigate and through which trust relationships among family members are either built or broken. As our modern society becomes more deeply embedded in the elements of linear time, we find ourselves struggling to keep alive the ancient communal principles of our culture and to protect and nurture the relationships which are most important to us. We find ourselves increasingly ruled by sound bites, the demands of the workplace, and the 'rush' to get in on the best performing markets. We are constantly trying to balance the effects of this linear invention called money against the preservation of our cyclical family. Efforts at trust-level communication become lost in the busy-ness of life and daily concerns with the business of the family.

The beginning chapter of this book noted that every material wealth creating business starts with an idea (intellectual capacities). In it, we also concluded that the authentic assets of family members – the intellectual, social, and human capacities – should indeed be regarded as assets and, as such, should be considered components of a Consummate Family Portfolio[SM] which need to be effectively managed. When considering the vital elements of asset protection and risk management relative to that portfolio, the authentic assets of the family tend to receive the least attention. Yet they are the first level where risk threatens the family's ability to defy the Proverb and to keep alive the communal principles of the Family Story.

Our journey, which began by examining the influence of generational perspectives on wealth management decisions, has inherently implicated multiple risk factors along the path which can impede family success in defying the Proverb by regenerating[4] the family wealth. This is the chapter where those multiple risk factors are brought together 'under one roof', so to speak. It is also the chapter where we outline protective measures to monitor and manage those risks. The fact is that dynamic stakeholder owners[5] do not simply sprout up on their own! The seeds and affinity of authentic family wealth ownership must be watered and nurtured and fed starting early in each family member's life and continuing throughout.

In light of the natures of the two types of family wealth, the question must be asked, 'which is the more important to protect?' Could it be that protecting the assets from which the material and financial wealth originate might also serve to protect the material and financial wealth they create? Yet, our typical focus completely misses that mark. By utilising a tool which addresses a family's full range of assets – the Generational Wealth Management Continuum[SM] – we identify five levels of risk to the Consummate Family Portfolio.

They match the five components of the Continuum[SM] as follows.

1 Relationship Risk[SM6] measured by the dynamics of the family. The family's generational maze[SM] of perspectives which assign roles family members occupy and form the dynamics within which those roles function (Step 1: the Family System).
2 The robustness of education and the governance structure through which all types of family education flows (Step 2: Family Governance).
3 Behavioural influences – internal threats – and the miscommunication mismatch with advisors – another type of relationship risk (Step 3: Translation to investment piece).
4 Healthcare, personal protection and other external threats (Step 4: Implementation).
5 A different look at traditional risk management and asset protection tools set up through the family office (Step 5: Monitoring and review).

The work of this chapter is to take a look at each area, outline the risk factors within, and identify ways to most effectively protect the family's entire portfolio of assets against them. In doing so, we will address the consummate family portfolio which includes both authentic and traditional assets.

Relationship Risk[SM] within the family system

Rarely are families as focused on risk than during a significant economic crisis. The Family System holds the greatest risk of any other part of the continuum; it is the point of emanation for the most dangerous types of threats – those which are often hidden and which come from within the family's ranks. As we saw with the credit crisis of 2008, the capital markets can wipe out 40% to 50% of financial and material wealth in a very short time period. In families where prudent risk management and protection of the authentic assets (over the material and financial assets) is a consistent focus, the extent of the damage may be mitigated or may be avoided completely. More importantly, the source of the material and financial wealth lives on to recreate and revitalise the material and financial wealth, enabling the family not only to survive, but to thrive for many other days.

Failing to know and understand the generational perspectives within the family serves as an open invitation for the Proverb to be fulfilled. Without continual vigilance to maintain trust-level communication, differences in these perspectives create a backdrop of dynamics in which the seeds of dysfunction quickly become established and grow. The dynamics of the family are the greatest harbingers of threat to the family wealth. The absence of the four virtues[7] creates a void in which disagreements can thrive and we end up with a family of traditional assets with little else to tie them together rather than with a family of affinity[8] whose wealth continues to revitalise itself through its innate cyclicality.

The case study of the Skee family is illustrative of the range of risks families can face and the range of results each situation can yield. Although each proposed outcome is an extreme within which infinite realities exist for any family, different combinations of this family's risk elements actually occur in more families than we would like to admit. A family's particular generational maze is a vital tool that equips families to counterbalance these risks – *it enables a family to know itself as a family entity rather than a group of individuals.*

What are the risks inherent in the family systems phase?

Box 18.1
Risks in the family system

Family risk factors:

- rank of family on the hierarchy of priorities
- presence or absence of trust-level communication
- level of knowledge of the family's generational maze
- perceived (assigned) roles versus authentic roles
- quality of time spent with family members
- level, amount, and frequency of interaction among family members
- attention when needed from leadership's view rather than the family member's view
- moral support and assistance based on leadership's definition rather than the family member's
- lack of education as dynamic stakeholder owners
- lack of transparency
- financial capital used as a carrot or method of control.

These risks stem from the degree of trust-level communication within the family. Without this critical element, it is impossible to know and understand the family's generational maze or to discover the scope of its authentic assets. The family follows the linear time track until the point of crisis and they attempt to manage the fallout after the fact.

As illustrated in the Skee[9] family, a significant contributor to this risk grows out of the roles that are assigned (perceived) by other generations, including but not exclusive to leadership and the dynamics that are set up from those role expectations. From those interactions we can measure what I call 'relationship risk'[SM]. Relationship risk applies to families in dual fashion; it has to do with the relationships among family members and it also has to do with relationships between the family and its advisors.

There are a number of other risks born from relationship risk.

• The risk that each governing generation will follow its own linear path, expecting generations who follow after to do things exactly as the governing generation has done before them.
• The effort to 'control' what happens to the material and financial wealth after the governing generation has died, putting into place traditional asset protection mechanisms designed to continue the linear pathway by 'controlling from the grave'.
• The use by the governing generation of roles it has assigned – as well as those others have assigned – as a basis for 'protecting' succeeding generations against ruin. (An example is the role of black sheep where a family member is viewed as a spendthrift or as not responsible with money, which may or may not be the case. Trusts are often set up to keep the money from the family member until he or she is of a 'responsible' age or to provide a moderate income over the life of the person. Roles assigned on the basis of gender, perceived aptitude and or interest may also be used to 'protect.')
• The lack of transparency which denies succeeding generations the education they so desperately need about their authentic roles and the responsibilities and privileges that accompany them.
• The setting of goals based on perceived rather than authentic roles which are taken to family advisors and around which are structured investment, tax, legal, estate planning, and other strategies.

This is where it all starts. The risks at this level are virtually hidden. No one assigns roles at a conscious level; that is how generational perspectives become such a stealth influence on wealth management decisions. The claim these risks make on the family's authentic wealth eventually becomes so entrenched that the risks become difficult to manage. In fact, they often cannot be reversed; but they can be countered. The risks here are so critical in nature because *the risks at every other level of the Continuum[SM] spring from them.*

Assessing Relationship Risk©

The fostering of authenticity requires consciousness. It also requires transparency and the willingness to trust. One of the best definitions of trust is, 'The willingness of a party to be vulnerable to the actions of another party based on the expectation that the other will perform a particular action important to the trustor, irrespective of the ability to monitor or control that other party'.[10] Such vulnerability is the essence of trust-level communication and opens the door to understanding and acceptance of the different perspectives within the generational maze. For this level of trust to develop, each family member must have a level of commitment that keeps 'family' at the top of the hierarchical tree of priorities. When 'family' occupies any other space, family functions are misaligned; everything flows from whatever that priority happens to be and becomes misaligned along with them.

We obviously cannot always begin at the point of a family's forming. It is possible, however, to diagnose relationship risk beginning with the following data.

Box 18.2
Data available in family members' authentic assets

- Voluntary input from family members.
- Awareness of the areas of family members' talents and passions.
- The level of education as dynamic stakeholder owners.
- Family members' willingness and comfort with sharing ideas.
- The regularity and nature of conflict within the family.
- Each person's generational biases.
- Each person's behavioural biases.

The example of the Skee family enables us to see the risks inherent at every level of the Continuum[SM]. Applying the tools of analysis listed above, we can utilise their experience to illuminate the multiple risks present in their situation. We discussed this family at the end of Chapter 15 to illustrate how families set their goals based on the needs they identify from the roles family members occupy.

To briefly recap their story, there are three generations of family members who own a ski design company – John and Mariel who founded the company and their three children, Susan, Michel, and Anna. This is a loving family who generally have a good time when they get together, although such get togethers tend to happen infrequently. When they do occur, it is usually around a holiday or family celebration.

We will pick up the story where Michel, age 33, is slated to take over the business despite his serious lack of business acumen. John and Mariel, the parents and founders of the business, have decided they would like to follow other pursuits in their golden years and have chosen Michel to run the company, in their mind by merit. Although, Susan, age 35, and her husband Omar really have the talent and passion for the business, they are relegated to heading a support team for Michel and continuing to manage – in superb fashion – the Middle Eastern, African and European region for the company. The youngest child Anna, age 22, is busy finishing university and jet-setting across the globe to meet up with her friends. Michel is engaged to Swiss-born Zia who is a fashion model with ideas of her own. As it turns out, she is also quite a good businesswoman; unfortunately, this is no real saving grace for Michel.

The dynamics of this family show the influence of the different generational perspectives both within the relationships of the family and in the decisions that are made.

- John and Mariel are workaholic Boomers who value work ethic and immediate results above all else.
- Susan and Michel are Gen-Xers who basically grew up by themselves with a nanny to keep them out of harm's way.
- Anna is an Echo who is excited about her world and wants to contribute to it. She feels a responsibility toward the family and toward the business but has no real outlet for either.
- Zia is also an Echo – she is 28 and was born in the early years of the Echo birth spectrum. She realises that, unless she has the fortune of Kate Moss's good looks as she ages, her days are numbered as a top fashion model.

The family's interactions also show the roles which have been assigned and which roles are authentic to the family members.

- Mariel and John view Michel as the logical candidate to run the business because he 'lives and breathes it' like they do, despite the fact that his business acumen is sorely lacking and what they assume is good judgment of character has yet to be proven.
- Susan and Omar are viewed as the 'steady Eddies' they have always been – reliable, thorough, and time sensitive in their work.
- Mariel and John view Anna as a kid growing up with nothing better to do; they cannot seem to find anything she is interested in. She also is viewed as a liability because of the public nature of her activities and the way she spends money.
- They view Zia as a nice addition to the family, yet as a liability from multiple perspectives.

We can also get a good sense of this family's authentic wealth from the Family Systems stage – note the generational imprints filtering through.

- John and Mariel are truly entrepreneurs and have two pools of intellectual talent that are difficult to match. They have loyal employees and have done a good job of managing the company at each level of growth. They have a natural passion for their respective architectural and engineering skills as well as for skiing and this passion spills over into everything they do.
- Susan and Michel have grown up around this passion. Susan has seen how hard her parents have worked all their lives and she respects their hard work, yet she wants more to her life than just work. She learns to work smarter to free time to be with her husband and their young family. Working with her in the business, Susan's husband Omar balances her out both in the business and at home. They both feel that they are building something different than Susan's parents, although they respect what John and Mariel have accomplished and appreciate the resulting material wealth of which they are beneficiaries.
- Michel is passionate about being in the limelight and enjoying the prestige it affords him. He felt neglected growing up and he enjoys the attention he gets from the media and also in the social settings he and Zia enjoy. He is actually quite shy in closer corners and Zia, although much quieter in public, has a natural way of interacting and networking with people – something for which Michel has less talent.
- Anna has a brilliant mind much like her parents' and has a fascination with microbiology, specifically aquatic microbiology. She has been around bodies of water all of her life and is fascinated with the organisms that are in them.

As for the family dynamics themselves.

- John and Mariel feel they have done a good job as parents, have offered their children a good example, and have provided everything they could possibly have needed, although they do wish they had had more time to enjoy their children growing up. They hope that what they have built together has meant something to the children.
- Michel becomes extremely anxious just thinking about the time when control of the company will be his. As much as he enjoys talking with the media and being featured on global news

magazines, he really does not know much about business and he is so afraid of telling this to his parents that he takes extreme measures to avoid talking about company matters. Whenever his parents talk to him about it, he says very little and just listens as much as possible, although he is not always sure he understands what they are saying.

- Susan and Omar resent her parents' choice of Michel to take over leadership because it completely ignores the authentic wealth they have – the critical authentic wealth the family needs to rejuvenate the material and financial wealth.
- Anna grows despondent at times. She feels her life is rather empty although she has a great time with her friends and enjoys being able to go wherever she wants whenever she wants and to buy whatever she wants. She feels her parents do not value her as she would wish. She feels she has some really good ideas that would help the company and might bridge the gap in their relationship but her parents either ignore her text messages or do not know how to text back. Since she cannot fathom the latter, she chooses to believe the former.
- Zia likes the family very much but senses that it will take a long time to develop rapport with them. She feels very much the outsider and becomes frustrated by repeatedly having to educate the family about Swiss customs and family life.

Risk analysis

Voluntary input: although the family offers to hear voluntary input, there is no mutually recognised forum for doing so and whatever is offered tends to fall on deaf ears. The older generations are not 'into' the same ways of communicating as the younger generations which makes Anna's texting annoying in Mariel's view. John does look at her texts occasionally and intends to respond but rarely does so in a meaningful way. Susan and Omar have difficulty pinning John and Mariel down for a meeting about anything other than the business so there is little opportunity for them to share their passions.

Awareness of passions and talents: it is quite clear that the authentic wealth of this family's members is completely under its radar. The degree of trust-level communication is low although John and Mariel feel it is quite good. They feel communication is particularly good with Michel (because he is always listening) and they feel if Susan and Omar had any real issues they would come to them voluntarily. No one asks Anna about her passions and wishes for her life. Since she feels no one really cares, she does not volunteer any information. She feels the rest of the family are busy and like having her out of the way, so to speak.

Level of education as dynamic stakeholder owners: business and financial education have been offered by the trust advisors to this family on each child's 21st birthday. Since Susan and Michel have been involved in the business for most of their adult lives, John and Mariel feel their education is reinforced on a daily basis. They feel they see evidence of this during the monthly and quarterly business meetings. However, education regarding other roles and responsibilities such as learning about the family ancestral history, knowing the story of the family business and how the wealth was created, and understanding the appropriate relationship between the family, the board, and the business has never occurred at any meaningful level.

Since communication is largely business focused and little effort has been made to discover the real desires of family members, John and Mariel are the only family members who feel they have a stake in the business. Susan and Omar feel increasingly frustrated that their deliberate and well organised contributions seem to go unappreciated and that they are to be relegated to a support team. The 'pat on the back' for their division's profits leading the rest of the company seems hollow thanks for the dedication and loyalty they have given. Anna feels little connection to the business. The entire family is beginning to feel less connected and that there is less of a stake for each of them in keeping the family together.

Willingness and comfort to share ideas: John and Mariel share their ideas freely; the children attempt to submit ideas but feel they go nowhere. If there were a forum where they know their ideas would be listened to, discussed, and evaluated, they would be more forthcoming. At this point, it seems to be a futile effort. Susan, Omar and Michel discuss things among themselves but Susan and Omar worry when they hear some of Michel's business thinking. Anna does share some ideas with her siblings but has never really felt they take her seriously. With the addition of Zia to the family, she hopes that will change.

Regularity and nature of family conflict: conflict is rarely overt in this family; rather, it is kept under the surface. Underneath it all, frustration and feelings of lack of appreciation are brewing on all fronts. John and Mariel are disappointed that their children do not seem to appreciate what they have built for them as much as they would like and that they do not seem to be 'taking it and running with it' as they had hoped. They worry about Anna and what she will do with her life; they also worry about Zia's influence on Michel, especially since she has asked for shares of the company as a wedding gift.

Zia truly likes the family and hopes to become close to them; however, she feels the discontent bubbling underneath and has asked for the shares as an insurance policy against whatever might happen in the future. She realises her modelling career will not last forever and she hopes to use the shares to fund a clothing design company she wishes to launch in a few years. Anna does not like conflict and just tries to stay out of any uncomfortable discussions among the siblings and Zia.

Generational biases: most of the roles the family members occupy are assigned and, therefore, perceived rather than authentic. Michel's expected role is most obviously assigned – it does not fit his innate talents and passions at all. He is not well suited – nor does he really have the desire – to run the company, yet Mariel and John see only what they wish to see out of their preconceived notions. They like that he 'works all the time' when, in reality, Michel goes to party after party, is in the media often, and does little more than keep up with what he needs to know to be a good spokesperson. He enjoys doing research and keeping up with the sports equipment marketplace.

Susan's role is also perceived since she has been assigned as a subordinate team player. She is, in fact, very entrepreneurial and has wonderful ideas for a new ski design. Omar has similar talent. Susan and Omar view John and Mariel as workaholics and misinterpret John and Muriel's sharing of their passions about the business as being able to 'only talk about business,' even at family gatherings.

Anna's role of black sheep is blatantly a perceived role rather than authentic since her brilliance is completely masked by her youth and seeming disinterest. Her occupation of the role of 'black sheep' seems to grow more comfortable as time goes by.

Behavioural biases: John and Mariel are employing framing bias in their choice of Michel to take over the company. They are paying attention to the aspects they wish to see and are not even seeing them clearly, as they are in reality. Michel is going with the momentum of their decision as it gains ground through unofficial conversations with board members and other company executives, conversations which eventually will become official. He is confirming the choice in his own mind (confirmation bias), convincing himself that he is fitted for the job and will somehow rise to the occasion and fulfil the role which is expected of him.

Susan and Omar are employing hindsight, thinking that they should have been able to figure out much earlier that John and Mariel were grooming Michel for the CEO spot. Instead of putting all their time, energy, and money into the family business, they could have started a business of their own a long time ago. They should have seen it coming.

Anna is experiencing an illusion of control over her own life when she is ill-equipped to manage her life, thinking that she can 'grow up' at some point in the future when she feels some reason or expectation to do so. She feels the money will always be available to do what she wishes so she has plenty of time to act responsibly later.

Some of the risk factors which can be readily identified for the Skee family are shown in Box 18.3.

Box 18.3
Risk Factors for the Skee Family

1 Trust-level communication is impeded by generationally disparate modes of contact.

2 Absorption of leadership in their own generational view.

3 Misinterpretation of trust-level communication as listening skills.

4 Failure to show interest in family members' personal lives.

5 The view of every function of the family in terms of the business.

6 Misunderstanding the full scope of educational needs.

7 The lack of contribution of new ideas to keep the family spirit alive and the business concept fresh and evolving.

8 Building pressures of underlying conflict, not knowing when or to what degree they will erupt.

9 The invitation to linear time thinking by generational biases which expect the next generation to lead the business and the family in the same way as the previous generation.

10 The invitation to linear time thinking through behavioural biases including framing, correcting through confirmation bias, and correcting through hindsight.

Conclusion

It is easy to see from this analysis how factors which seemed normal and fairly benign at first began to build, then resulted in the tragic consequences outlined in the first result of the case study in Chapter 15. We can compare the two outcomes in the case study to see the wealth this family lost and also the wealth it could have had if it had seen these risk factors and been able to either diffuse them or counter them in some way. None of these tragic consequences developed overnight.

The lack of trust-level communication made it impossible for the various generational views to be aired, much less understood and accepted. It also squelched the input of new ideas and prevented the discovery of the family's authentic roles and the authentic wealth it needed to revitalise the family and the company. The failure to show interest in personal lives of the family members or to give them a personal stake in keeping the family together or in what happens with the business contributed to Susan and Omar's decision to break off and form their own company, taking enough of the family's intellectual capacities with them to create a ski design just beyond the reach of patent infringement laws.

The assignment of roles placed the wrong people into leadership and drove the right people away. What could have been an infusion of product line and new financial capital for the business and the family was never allowed cognisance much less a chance to develop. When Zia left Michel, she took part of the ownership of the company with her as well as the authentic assets she had to contribute by joining with Anna in creating the eco-friendly ski apparel line in the second outcome of the case study.

By identifying the factors which place the family's authentic assets at risk, we simultaneously identify hidden risk factors for the family business and may also discover risk factors present in the operations of the family office. A complete and foundational risk scenario can be assembled just from looking at this initial segment of the Generational Wealth Management Continuum[SM]. From such a scenario, risk factors in other segments may be identified and added to the master from which the risk monitoring system is created.

Education through family governance

In the family governance chapter, we saw that there are many types of education family members need to fulfil their privileges as dynamic stakeholder owners.[11] Since we offered such a thorough treatise of governance over the course of six chapters in Part 2 of this book, there is no need to reiterate here. The risk factors present in the governance segment are also mentioned in Part 2 but in a woven fashion throughout the course of the chapters. To bring those risk factors into context, a list of the most predominant ones has been created below.

- Viewing the family through the lens of the business.
- Handing off the task of creating family governance to the family office.
- Representing each family branch on the family board rather than on the family council.
- Enabling conformity through the family office.
- Thinking that families with smaller numbers do not have similar basic needs as larger families from a governance and organisational perspective.
- Giving business managers the task of also managing family members.
- Assigning roles to family entities which are not authentic to them and which go against their original nature.
- Misalignment of the hierarchy of governance.
- Prohibiting input from all family members when creating the family governance structure.
- Confusing the purpose and roles of each form of governance.

- Failing to empower the governing bodies of the family governance system.
- Lack of clarity on the part of family office executives, staff, and advisors on their roles and the service objectives they have in supporting the family in reaching its goals.
- Handing off the full educational responsibility to the family office without guidance from the family or family governing bodies.
- Choosing family office executives, staff, and advisors who do not have sufficient commitment to serve the family in flourishing its authentic wealth.

Identification of each of these risks through analysis creates opportunities for education, including the following.

- Clarity regarding the responsibilities of family members as dynamic stakeholder owners.
- Family members' relationships with the business and the family office.
- The purpose of the business and the family office.
- Education through participating on a committee or heading a committee which includes family office staff as well as family members in carrying out a family project.
- How to manage material and financial wealth through participation on the board of the family foundation.
- How to make decisions together through participation on a junior board.
- Education about what it takes to manage a family of wealth, its members and all its holdings.
- What wealth can mean to the lives of family members and also to those whom the family employs.
- How to develop sound judgment regarding people as well as investments and business matters.
- Hands-on education through decision making on smaller issues or practicing 'what-if' scenarios.

The reason for instituting a governance system in the first place is to put into place a mechanism to guide the family along the path it has chosen for itself and to offer the flexibility within that path for individual family members to be empowered and live happy, fulfilling, and productive lives. The only purpose for governance is to support the family in achieving the flourishing of its authentic wealth. Education in all aspects of dynamic stakeholder ownership is essential to that purpose.

In fact, Chapter 13 illuminates that the only reason for a family office to exist is for the roles of supporting the family's development of trust-level communication and educating the family.[12] The family office shines in these most proper roles and handily pays for itself, both from soft and hard cost perspectives.

Advisors can be excellent advocates for such education. However, care must be taken that family members do not abdicate their educational roles. Advisors who are aware of the family's authentic wealth and who also understand the family's authentic goals can be part of a remarkable system of support and monitoring which alerts the family to above average risk levels. They may be able to alert the family if a monitoring data point has been triggered, even if the action required is a review to see if more serious action needs to be taken. Advisory expertise can lend a ready hand to this type of support, educating against harmful risks in the process.

Education of family members of all ages, not just younger generations, is an ongoing process. Guidelines for the scope and design of this education may be found in Part 2 in Chapter 11.

The behavioural influence and Relationship Risk© with advisors

When discussing behavioural biases, we noted that families are also normal and, at times, act normal smart and at others, normal stupid. Families are not institutions and they are not operating companies although they may be quite closely associated with them – even emotionally so. Although a family may have enough material and financial assets to act like an institution in the marketplace, they are still a family, not an institution. Advisors who treat them as institutions run the relationship risk of applying standard finance rather than behavioural and generational elements which more closely match the way families function. A family who is not well versed in a prudent advisor selection process will experience an advisory relationship which will be less than optimal[13] for both.

Other risks which can be present in the advisory relationship include the following.

- *The advisors' own generational biases:* these biases can cause certain family members to be left out of conversations or to not receive the level of transparency that is appropriate. They can also filter into other types of relationship risks with advisors.
- *The advisor's own behavioural biases:* this can result in an imposition of the advisor's value function over that of the family's.[14] Brunel cites the example of an advisor imposing his or her own comfort level or preferences for certain investment strategies. An advisor who has greater comfort with risky strategies than the family client may lead the client on a path which is not optimal for the authentic wealth; conversely, a family may have greater comfort – based on prudent criteria – with risky strategies than the advisor may allow. Advisors are also human and must take care to not impose their particular biases on their family clients.
- An advisor's unwillingness to offer support for a task that the client must do to the point that the task is never accomplished.[15]
- Failure by the family to design an advisor selection process that emanates from the needs of the family governance system.
- Failure to design an advisor selection process which includes sufficient due diligence as well as different criteria for different types of advisors.
- Failure to educate family members on the intelligent use of advisors.

Inherent in each of the above sections outlining risk factors for families are also ways to protect the assets from those risks. As we travel from the Family Systems and Governance components through the behavioural and advisory relationship risk segment, we shift from identifying risks and lifting asset protection strategies from those elements to identifying asset protection strategies which guard against risk. This shift will allow us to maintain our focus on aligning all risk management and asset protection components to support the flourishing of the family wealth in all its forms.

Healthcare and personal protection

Two increasingly important risk areas for family wealth today include healthcare and personal protection as well as other external threats to the family. Family leadership may travel globally on a consistent basis; families may vacation in countries with high kidnapping rates; busy wealth creators may overlook the need to manage their own healthcare. Even with families who have the wherewithal to have the best care at their service on a moment's notice, there are many gaps which are regularly overlooked, opening the family to risks that may turn into devastating family crises.

The generational sea change occurring as I write is affecting the way healthcare is accessed as well as delivered, even to family members of wealth. This filters down into the doctor-patient relationship from a generational standpoint, as well. Older generations were accustomed to a more personal relationship with the physician and also accepted diagnoses without question. This level of physician care is quickly disappearing. According to Dan Carlin, M.D. founder and CEO of WorldClinic: 'The World War II guys are not well served because their belief system's in a previous age, and now the Boomers want to work in tandem with the physician. They want full information and that's not happening because of the time limitation of the doctor. So they're going away frustrated.'

Carlin adds that younger generations are beginning to understand what it means to have good healthcare regarding transferring the wealth. They understand that healthcare is a vital protection mechanism for the family's authentic wealth. It can serve as a critical lens through which to protect the family's authentic assets, the family business, and the strength of each family unit.

'How do we get this message to the Baby Boomers that healthcare is vital to protecting the wealth for future generations?' Carlin asks. 'We already have a fairly broken primary care system. The Boomers will be the first generation in more than 50 years to put down cash for private medical care and be willing to pay a premium to have physicians pay attention to their care.'

He says globalisation of healthcare is in its infancy. Some of the major academic centres in the US are beginning to form overseas partnerships. For example, Pacific Medical Center has a partnership in Italy and the Mayo Clinic is active in the Middle East. He predicts the global branding of certain American and European medical institutions. 'We're building in-home private medical care space for three primary purposes: urgent immediate care, video linked-in space where you can actually talk to the doctor, and guided rehabilitation with physical therapists by video.' Carlin notes there's more sophisticated care happening in-home through sophisticated technology. He feels this is just a glimpse into the future of healthcare for families of wealth.[16]

Of course, the best and least expensive form of healthcare is prevention. Regular exercise and healthful lifestyle habits contribute significantly to the quality of life as people age. A recent article in *The Wall Street Journal* noted that a healthy lifestyle is frontline armour in the battle to live well into old age. People over 85 are the fastest growing population segment across the globe as of this writing. This segment of the population is still the Silent generation, not the Boomer generation so the numbers and speed of growth are only beginning. As the Boomer generation ages and longevity continues to increase through the cessation of smoking, elimination of many childhood diseases, and a fall in cardiovascular disease, quality of life may compete for the desire to live to a ripe old age. The more proactive people become in caring for their health, the greater the propensity for the authentic wealth of the family to flourish. The longer elders are alive to mentor and educate, the greater the benefit to the younger generations, the rest of the family, and the family business.

The research cited in *The Wall Street Journal* article advises 'getting control of a combination of risk factors – including blood pressure, blood sugar, cholesterol, smoking and diet – is emerging as an especially effective way to improve health and extend healthy longevity'. One physician said that regular exercise lowers blood pressure and blood sugar and helps control cholesterol and 'is an especially potent weapon against disease'.[17]

Personal protection goes hand in hand with healthcare in protecting the family's authentic assets and, again, prevention is key. Chris Falkenberg, president of Insite Security, Inc., notes that there are two types of risk families of wealth face. 'The first is a standard risk that everybody has – if someone is waiting in an alley to attack you, it makes no difference whether you have $100,000 net worth or $1 billion. That's not an issue.' The second kind of risk is specific to a particular crime that is premeditated. These are very well planned home invasions, robberies, and kidnappings – crimes that specifically target wealthy families because they are most likely to have assets.[18]

Social networks, the *Forbes* list, and *Alpha Magazine*'s list of the wealthiest people are common sources Falkenberg cites. More striking is the information gleaned by people who serve the family on a daily basis such as housekeepers, nannies, landscapers, pool and other maintenance workers. 'When you think of a wealthy family you see a family that has a lot of moving parts,' notes Falkenberg. 'They may have multiple homes, multiple staff members taking care of those homes, they may take private aircraft, they vacation a lot, they have a whole series of support staff – tutors for the children, caterers for social events, private massage, private trainers. All these folks are permitted at varying levels to work in close proximity to the family. They see the number of children, they can identify the children, they know when the kids go to school and when they come back, when the husband and wife arrive and depart – all this information is essential in planning a crime.'

Carlin and Falkenberg agree that prevention is the most effective approach and effective prevention requires strategic planning. If families consider all the different ways information may be leaked to potential perpetrators, they can take proactive steps to limit the information flow. Falkenberg and Carlin often work together to devise as robust a plan for emergency prevention and response as possible. Especially on the internet, children should be supervised at all times. 'You shouldn't allow your children to do in the virtual world what you wouldn't allow them to do in the physical world. It's no different than what our parents did before computers came around,' Falkenberg adds.

Personal protection is vital for the development of the family's authentic assets as well as for their preservation. Many families – as well as family businesses – are thrown into turmoil when family leadership experiences a sudden life threatening or disabling event, either from a health risk or a personal risk. Personal risks may also threaten the financial assets in the form of lawsuits, ransoms for kidnappings, or physical damage to property. The damage to authentic assets is usually much deeper.

Therefore, an essential component of strategic planning is in striking the right balance between prevention, protection, and living a normal life. The appropriate balance will vary for each family. The most effective strategic plan will include five things.

1 Awareness of the risks by all family members, even children to the extent of their comprehension – an amazing degree of comprehension is present as early as two years old.
2 Transparency and open discussion about the issues and how they can affect every day family life.
3 Input from family members about ways to protect everyone in the family. Children should offer input, as well.
4 Regular review of preventive guidelines.
5 Consistent integration of the guidelines into the lives of all adult family members; this, like any other set of guidelines, will mean nothing if there is not active implementation.

Other external threats

From a traditional risk management perspective, the litigious nature of society, the seizure of assets by creditors, and the division of assets through divorce settlements are increasing threats. Tom Handler of Handler Thayer LLP notes that the asset protection piece on the list of family priorities is moving up. 'People are becoming more cognizant of it. Every time you open a paper you see the increasing magnitude of money damages and the increasing scope of liability. Simultaneously, the property and casualty insurance markets have contracted so people are becoming pretty nervous. For many clients, asset protection is now the primary objective and estate planning or tax planning is secondary.'

Handler says he has been surprised at the lack of traction (the asset protection) theme has got over time. 'Unless they've actually witnessed a horrific event, they don't take it as seriously. Someone who's seen a friend go bankrupt, lose 80% of their assets in a divorce, or lose 100% in a class action gets a whole new sense of what can happen.' Even more devastating is the inability to revitalise the material or financial wealth after such an event.

He notes that patriarchal generations can become unwittingly vulnerable through 'doing things the way they've always been done'. 'The critical nature of this doesn't resonate with them because it's not what they're used to. The environment in which businesses are built today is quite different from the environment in which they built their businesses. Asset protection is no longer a luxury: if you don't do it, it's simply imprudent. We've had the second or third generations hire us on behalf of the older generations because the older generations didn't view it as a priority and neither did their attorneys who are also older.'

As catastrophic as these events quite often are, the most effective protection against their devastation begins with the risks inherent in the family system. If traditional mechanisms are used as tools to support that foundational system, a family can build a mighty fortress, indeed.

The emphasis on education of family members as dynamic stakeholder owners cannot be too great. Especially for younger family members for whom education has been postponed until adulthood, the risk scenarios are all too well known. 'The minute they get control of the money you see the typical symptoms – overspending, poor investments, not the high level of discipline it takes to maintain wealth. If you don't appreciate how difficult it was to create the wealth in the first place, it's unlikely you'll understand the steps required to keep it from going by the wayside. So it's likely to dissipate significantly and by the time it gets to the third generation there's very little left. Even if there's something left, the children haven't learned what they need to know because their teachers were people who never understood those things, either,' notes Handler.

Those steps begin with an assessment of the risks inherent in the family system and designing governance systems to support their management. The addition of traditional asset protection and risk management tools in a way that custom fits the family's needs can round out a comprehensive strategic plan. Traditional 'asset protection, premarital planning, and very sophisticated risk matrices that combine the right allocation and diversification with the right ownership structures, tax minimization, insurance policies, and proper planning,' according to Handler, can support the foundational strategies necessary to carry the family through.

The consummate family portfolio

When a family becomes vulnerable to any one or a number of the risks cited above, a portfolio of authentic assets which has been prudently managed could make the difference in the family's very survival. For example, a small portion of a successful author's profits could help to carry the family while the capital markets investments or other sources of wealth were rebuilt; a new business from a younger family member also could fill that role or add to it; the empowerment of family committees could mitigate damage before it occurred and help the financial segment of the portfolio better weather the economic anomaly, whatever its source. I have seen many families pool either part or even substantial amounts of their resources to offer entrepreneurial opportunities, to make investments together, for educational purposes, to provide support for indigent family members, and for many others purposes.

From a risk management standpoint, employing the family's financial wealth to support the transforming of family members' visions into a tangible form may create something much greater than relegating family progeny to become familiar with struggle and hardship for the sake of experiencing struggle and hardship. In observing families of wealth in general as well as families of wealth with whom I consult, I am not at all sure that taking away the access to privilege builds as much character as it does resentment.

Education in the beneficial use of money as well as education on how to enjoy its use in a way that brings fulfilment rather than misery would seem to be a better path. Enjoyment of money for enjoyment's sake is a right and a privilege; education on how that privilege can be an enriching experience becomes a true and love-filled gift. One of the best ways to provide such education is through participation in a family board or family council – two components of family governance which filter through to the risk management and asset protection scenario.

Family boards and other governing bodies

The last risk we will discuss is what I call empowerment risk. Consider this recipe.

Take these ingredients:

Family mission and/or vision statement
Family council, board, or other governing body
Family representatives
Family committees and their members
Family foundation

Get input from family members on the creation of each, hire consultants to help develop each ingredient. Mix well into a family constitution. Bake in the family meeting oven and, 1st alternative: when decisions arise to be made – especially in areas that affect family members' lives – have leadership or the family office make all the decisions. Or, 2nd alternative: educate, give the authority to act, and institute that line of authority as appropriate throughout the family's system of entities.

We have seen through various examples the importance of empowering family members within the family governance system in whatever capacity they serve. Of course, term limits and guidelines can be excellent risk management tools but they are most effective when used to support educated family members. One of the best educational tools is the junior family board. Such a board may have members in age from as young as eight up to 35 or so. Empowering such a board to use the education it receives can add enormously to the family's authentic wealth.

Junior board members may be effectively groomed from junior councils. A large family may develop a system of junior councils where younger family members within groups of family units

may learn to make decisions, be in charge of researching family archives, researching possible investments for the family, researching and recommending grantees for the family foundation, helping to
plan family events, and creating their own educational curriculum.[19]

Family members of whatever age who are empowered as they seek to make their own contributions to the family's authentic wealth – whether through the development of their personal wealth
or through their involvement in family governance – become walking risk management and asset
protection mechanisms. When they come together through a body such as the family council or a
junior board, their power is balanced by every other family member on the committee or board.
Add trust-level communication to the mix and we have risk management and asset protection which
is practically impermeable.

The family meeting: the quintessential risk management and asset protection tool

We have attempted to address risks from all corners of the consummate family wealth portfolio
within the word count of this chapter – no small task, indeed. The one place where all elements
of risk management and asset protection come together on a regular basis for the family is the
family meeting.

As with family boards, families rarely think of their meetings as an asset protection and risk
management tool. However, regular family meetings can be a primary element in binding the family
together. Marie Mentor, current Laird Norton family president notes, 'Once a family grows to the
size of Laird Norton – nearly four hundred this year – it is essential that they meet annually to
celebrate their success and family legacy. It takes our family a whole year to plan this gathering,
and it's not inexpensive. But ultimately, it's worth every penny.' Not every family has to plan
as extensively for its family meetings, although planning for an annual meeting of as few as 15
members can take a minimum of six months.

There are essential ingredients which can make the family meeting the primary source for
nurturing the family spirit and for implementing a monitoring system for risk management and asset
protection needs. Clarity of purpose and attention to planning details makes everyone feel that the
meeting will be an enjoyable experience. They will know what to expect and will look forward to
the activities planned, even if some activities introduce the possibility of disagreement. If there are
issues to be discussed, it is imperative to speak with family members beforehand to see what their
feelings are about the issues and to determine if educational planning needs to done so that the
issues may be discussed at the meeting in an informed manner. A venue through which open yet
organised discussion may be entertained about the issues is a mandate for the agenda.

A cyclical process between leadership and family members as preparation for the meeting
takes place ensures that all items that should be on the agenda indeed are included and that all
family members have the opportunity to make their feelings and opinions known at some point
in the process. The family meeting process is an excellent tool for leadership to get to know its
constituency. Care must be taken to ensure that every aspect of the meeting is designed to support
the authentic wealth of each family member. This, in turn, strengthens family leadership by creating
willing and contributory family participants!

The family meeting can be a place where family members have time to visit and learn more
about what is happening in each person's life. It is an event where family members can share with

the entire family the lessons they have learned and the things they have accomplished. It is an event where family rituals can be celebrated and where new family members can be welcomed into the fold.

Most of all, it is an opportunity to create a safe space where family members can gather together, get the family nourishment they need, the education they require as dynamic and responsible family members, and where the cycles of regeneration can flourish. In this place of safety, preventive risk management that is put into active practice by the adults in the family will integrate preventive risk management into children's lives as they grow up. It will become a natural, lifelong practice.

With all the moving parts to effective risk management and asset protection, the insights offered in this chapter are designed to bring them together under a thoughtful yet pragmatic system which can be custom designed to flourish each family's unique portfolio of authentic and traditional assets.

1 Twist, L., *The Soul of Money*, (New York, NY: W.W. Norton & Co, 2006), p.116.

2 Ibid.

3 Ibid.

4 Wealth Regeneration® is a registered service mark owned by Laird Norton Tyee and is used throughout this book Laird Norton Tyee's permission.

5 The term 'dynamic stakeholder ownership' belongs to James E. Hughes, Jr. and is used throughout this book with his permission.

6 The term 'Relationship Risk' used throughout this book is the service marked property of graymatter Strategies LLC.

7 Hughes, J.E., Jr., *Family: a compact among generations*, (New York, NY: Bloomberg Press, 2007), pp. 88, 89.

8 Ibid, p. 3.

9 The Skee family, the company Skee International and any public events involving the company and any details about the family are used for illustrative purposes and are completely fictitious. No such public company exists and no such offering has occurred in the public marketplace.

10 Brockner, J., Siegel, P.A., Daly, J.P., Martin, C., Tyler, T., 'When trust matters: the moderating effect of outcome favorability', *Administrative Science Quarterly*, September 1997: http://findarticles.com/p/articles/mi_m4035/is_n3_v42/ai_20345588/.

11 The term 'dynamic stakeholder ownership' belongs to James E. Hughes, Jr. and is used with his permission.

12 In Chapter 13, Hughes notes the only raison d'être for a family office is for education. The author also included the support of the family's goals to build communication and trust among its members as a primary role of the office.

13 Brunel, J.L.P., 'How suboptimal – if at all – is goal-based asset allocation?' *The Journal of Wealth Management*, Fall 2006, pp. 19–34.

14 Brunel, J.L.P., *Integrated Wealth Management: the new direction for portfolio managers*, 2nd edition (London: Euromoney Books, 2006), p. 42.

15 Hughes, J.E., Jr., *Family: a compact among generations*, (New York, NY: Bloomberg Press, 2007), pp. 247–64.

16 Carlin, Daniel, M.D., Personal interview, April 2010.

17 Winslow, R., 'To double the odds of seeing 85, get a move on,' *The Wall Street Journal*, July 1 2010.

18 Falkenberg, Christopher, Personal interview, April 2010.

19 Hauser, B.R., 'Family governance: using junior boards for the successful continuation of family businesses in the Gulf Region,' *Arab News*, February 2010.

Part 3 summary: a treacherous juncture

Prepare

This section of the book prepared us to cross the Great Divide of family wealth management, then led us ever-so-carefully through it to the investment management component and many of the traditional components which surround it. The second bookend of the roles discussion leads us to the point of setting goals which are based on the needs family members have to flourish the authentic wealth of the family. Those goals are authenticated by the application of trust-level communication which serves as the oil by which the consummate family wealth portfolio is continually lubricated.

Then, an interesting thing happens. Typically, those goals – as formulated by the family – get lost in translation as the family cross the Great Divide into the traditional Netherlands of wealth management. They seemingly get left behind as soon as the family client enters the advisor's office door with only vestiges remaining in their wake. A clandestine transformation occurs as what were once well-thought-out and carefully formulated family goals turn into investment management, legal, and tax goals with a set of risk parameters whose real meanings are largely foreign to most individual and family clients.

So it becomes necessary to find a reliable tool to help prevent that distortion. We find such a tool in behavioural finance and, in the process, we find a customised, very personal set of data points which can be used in a well-designed monitoring system to alert us when either we or our advisors are about to let the distortion creep in once again. With these tools by our side, we successfully navigate our way through to effect a translation of our goals rather than a transformation. This translation is a vital aid to the ability of advisors to serve families at an optimal level – a level defined by the family client rather than the advisor.

Proceed

This makes it possible to formulate an asset allocation designed to achieve those original family goals which were formulated in a way that satisfies the family client's definition of success. A win-win-win relationship is then set up which enables external support in the form of genuinely interested advisors who can and are willing to help the family remain on the path it has chosen for all forms of its wealth.

A team of such advisors may be selected to serve the family at all levels of need through the well organized family governance system set up through Step 2 of the Generational Wealth Management Continuum[SM]. Outlining the process for selecting these wise advisors is one of the tasks of Part 4.

Protect

The family discovers quickly that there are risks along the way. We recognise the need and the desire to protect the assets contained within the consummate family wealth portfolio from harm, or dissipation, or misuse. Through thorough analysis, we discover the bulk of these risks within the

Family System and the tools which have been gathered all along the journey are now utilised to monitor and protect the assets against those risks.

This frees the family to select the kinds of advisors it requires to support its risk management and asset protection needs and desires. In the process of unmasking hidden risks within the family system and translating its goals into a financial language, it has also unearthed risks of which it was not previously aware in its advisory relationships.

Finally, armed with specific educational needs which also serve to protect the consummate portfolio of assets as well as with processes and tools to satisfy them, we are ready to take the final steps of our journey – the steps which will keep us on the path with the greatest possibility of taking us where we wish to go.

Part 4:

Ongoing monitoring and review

'Parents often talk about the younger generation as if they didn't have anything to do with it.'

Dr. Haim Ginott*

---

* http://thinkexist.com/quotations/generations/3.html.

Chapter 19

Family leadership and the advisory component

'It's an opportunity to get children, grandchildren, or great grandchildren on boards with accomplished people in finance and business or law or accounting. That's a critically important thing – to have a resource or a role model to talk to. The education itself and the connections developed with those people are extremely valuable. You can lose all the money but having access to talented, motivated, good people who have both business experience and the right educational background can help the family live to fight another day.'

Tom Handler

The Generational Wealth Management Continuum^{SM} positions all forms of the family's assets within two 'sides' of the consummate family wealth portfolio^{SM}. The family wealth management industry refers to the left side as the 'family issues' side and the right side as the 'private wealth management' side, as shown in Exhibit 19.1.

Exhibit 19.1

Two 'sides' of the continuum

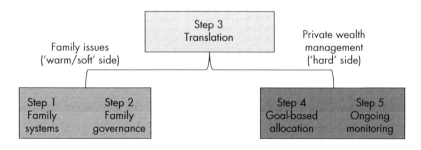

The ability of the private wealth management model to adequately serve families and individuals of wealth is a work in progress. Brunel's integrated wealth management paradigm has contributed exponentially to the improvements in the model by distinguishing between the natures and needs of institutional and individual investors. The primary differences between the two are that individual investors have multiple goals, have to pay taxes, and are subject to behavioural biases which can steer them off course from their investment policy. Institutions have a single mandate (goal), do not have to pay taxes, and have the ability to hold fast over a specified time period based on their belief that actuarial assumptions for achieving the mandate will prove to be true.[1]

Pompian makes a further distinction between individuals and families, noting that families have to deal with personality differences among their members. He also notes that the money family advisors are working with is the family's; institutional advisors are working with funds which do not belong to those institutions.[2]

According to Brunel, private wealth management (family and individual clients) includes three issues which investment management (institutional clients) does not.

1 A focus on after-tax wealth accumulation.
2 A sharper look at time horizons.
3 A different way of measuring performance.

Translated into real life, he shows a critical difference: two institutions with similar goals will likely have similar portfolios; two families or individuals who have similar goals will not only have portfolios that are different, but the differences in their portfolios are likely to increase over time despite the fact that the goals of both are quite similar.[3]

If we bring generational perspectives, the roles family members occupy, and the resulting dynamics of the family into play, we get an even more robust picture. The rising of the Echo generation makes this picture even more profound. Yet, these foundational influences are usually left almost completely out of the private wealth management equation.

The generational wealth management model expands beyond the private wealth management model to acknowledge the source of family and individual investors' goals as well as the influences at work when families and individuals are forming their goals. In the private wealth management model, behavioural biases become key tools with which family and individual investors and their advisors can create data points to guard against decision risk[4] stemming from emotional and cognitive biases. In the generational wealth management model, generational biases go beyond behavioural biases to enable investors and their advisors to create data points which would help them understand how they arrived at their goals (or to help them articulate them in the first place), to identify a broader scope of risks to which the family may become subject, and to subsequently align the private wealth management components in a more directly related fashion. The generational wealth management continuum layers the behavioural elements of the private wealth management model over the generational elements which create awareness of the family's authentic assets and the relationship dynamics surrounding them.

Exhibit 19.2

Broader scope of the generational wealth management model

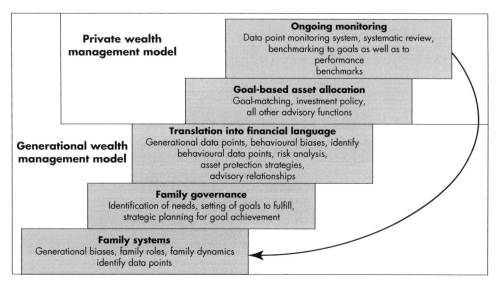

This shows a clear difference in the scope and utility of generational wealth management – a scope that fully encompasses the integrated management of all forms of the family's assets, authentic as well as material and financial. This integration requires a lubricant with which generational differences may successfully flow together toward achievement of the family's goals, mitigating relationship risk. Communication is the 'oil' which facilitates the flourishing of all forms of family wealth; generational biases alert families and their advisors to relationship risk at all levels.

Not only does generational wealth management offer a more robust integration of asset management, it also imbues the private wealth management model with the flexibility of Alderfer's ERG theory (see Chapters 1 and 15) which more closely matches the way families deal with wealth management issues.

Chapters 17 and 18 began our transition from the Family Issues side to the Private Wealth Management side through Step 3, the translation element.

In my view, such a transition consists of three distinct components.

1 Assessing the influence of a family's generational and behavioural biases in the formation of their goals.
2 Based on that assessment, becoming aware of the broadened scope of risks to be managed and, in the process, designing effective methods of protecting all assets of the consummate family wealth portfolio including authentic as well as material and financial assets.
3 Examining the relationships between the family and its team of advisors, specifically the relationship between the advisory team (private wealth management) and family leadership (family governance).

In rounding out the translation process which occurs in Step 3, this chapter brings the three components listed above together in a way which will lift the quality of relationship between families and their advisors to an entirely new level. In achieving this new level of relationship, both families and their advisors may take a significant step back and expand their views, increasing the ability of the family to make informed decisions and creating a more direct link between the family's authentic goals and the components of the private wealth management process. This linkage is brought to bear by the family governance system through which the elements of the family system flow.

Therefore, the focus of this chapter is three-fold.

1 To firmly establish the relationship between family governance and the private wealth management process.
2 To bring the family governance process fully into the advisory relationship.
3 To expand what the family-advisor relationship should look like and how its built-in flexibility may serve multiple generations of the family.

Approaching wealth management from the family's perspective

In consulting with families of wealth and in working with advisors who serve them, I have observed a significant gap that exists in the advisory relationship which greatly inhibits the ability for family clients to be effectively guided toward their own paths to optimality.[5] Brunel points to the fact that investors do not arrive at an optimal private wealth management solution 'in one fell swoop'. Rather, they travel an experiential road on which they learn about markets and strategies, establish a greater comfort level with them[6] and, in the process, learn more about themselves and their authentic needs and goals.

This brings to light an immensely important realisation: *individual and family goals which are formulated on the family issues side get lost in the translation to the private wealth management side within the family leadership-advisory team relationship.*

Exhibit 19.3

The disconnect

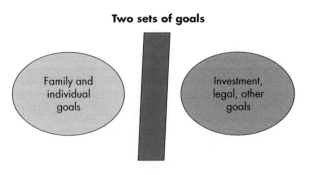

This is why the three aspects of Step 3 are so critical. A subsequent realisation is that the practices inherent in private wealth management do not fully reflect the path that families and individual investors travel. When considering the consummate family wealth portfolio, the description of the family or individual investor's path to optimality within the confines of the private wealth management process becomes insufficient. It must be expanded and tied all the way back to the Family Systems component in order to consider all aspects of a family's journey toward a wealth management philosophy that is uniquely optimal for them. Particularly in bridging the gaps between leadership generations and the Echo generation now coming into its own, this component holds the keys to family success beyond the third generation. It is critical for today's generations to learn each others' languages – both in family relationships as well as those between the family and its advisors – so that the goals the family sets authentically serve all family members and, once set, do not become lost in the translation to the private wealth management component.

This is the point where private wealth management typically fails family and individual clients since it only considers assets to be material and financial, failing to include authentic wealth as additional assets to the family wealth portfolio. *Inherently, there is a disconnect between the solutions designed within the private wealth management paradigm and the solutions which more closely fit family and individual client needs.*

Exhibit 19.4

Family governance and private wealth management

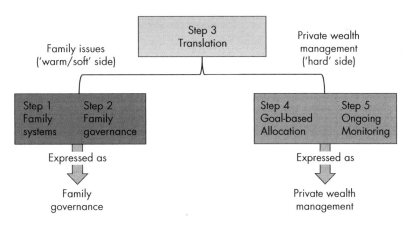

In the first few paragraphs of this book, we spoke of the need to come to the wealth management process beginning with the family and leading to its wealth rather than from the current trajectory which views the family from a business and wealth management perspective to find applications for organising the family. This applies not only to the organisation of the family but also to the management of the family wealth.[7] If we dig a little deeper, we see the need to alter the view of advisors from a primary focus on their particular expertise to viewing the services they offer based on that expertise from the family's perspective and the meaning a particular family may associate with 'success'.

Since family and individual clients often describe goals which reflect their generational and behavioural biases and may not even understand what their authentic goals are, the Family Systems and Family Governance components of the Continuum become essential elements of wealth management process. It would be useful to develop some sort of structure through which these data points could be monitored and compared against the broader cyclical view. This is what family governance accomplishes in its purest form, a structure through which the family's needs are monitored so that sound strategies may be developed to fulfil them. The family governance structure then serves as the data point monitoring system for the family.

In addition to Brunel's contribution, there are other strides the private wealth management model is making toward better family client service. These include the move from the application of standard finance (also known as modern portfolio theory), the institutional client-based approach which employs the Capital Asset Pricing Model (CAPM), toward behavioural finance (or behavioural portfolio theory) and Hersch Shefrin and Meir Statman's Behavioural Asset Pricing Model (BAPM). According to Statman, standard finance is expanding CAPM to include market capitalisation and book-to-market ratio along with beta as characteristics which determine stock price. This is called the three-factor model of standard finance. Rather than taking them at face value, BAPM reflects individuals' interpretation of these characteristics through their emotional and cognitive biases, noting that people tend to associate good stocks with good companies and bad stocks with bad companies. For example, value stocks are viewed as stocks of bad companies. This pushes the prices of these stocks lower, creating higher expected returns in the process. The opposite view – that good stocks are associated with good companies – pushes the stock prices of 'good' companies ever higher, decreasing their expected returns as their prices increase.[8]

More recently, Das, Markowitz, Sheid, and Statman have shown that there is a mathematical equivalence between modern portfolio theory and mental accounting.[9] This further validates the goals-based asset allocation model which the generational wealth management piece plugs into so appropriately to create a more direct link from the family governance side to the private wealth management component.

The expansion of standard finance into behavioural finance through the BAPM model becomes the perfect overlay within the generational wealth management model because it comes into play just at the point where the advisory relationship enters the generational wealth management picture. Rarely does the application of the generational wealth management process begin with the Family System. Instead, the family or individual waits to the point of discomfort or pain before seeking help from an external source. The relationship between family client and advisor most often begins at the point of an issue with which the family is grappling and has decided it does not have the expertise or the time to deal with the issue on its own.

It makes sense that families and individuals come to advisors with a predetermined set of goals based on needs they perceive as critical at the time. If the markets are going down 40%, that circumstance will create a point of pain where the family will come to the advisor to try to keep further damage from happening to the portfolio. At this point, the portfolio they are referring to is the private wealth management portfolio rather than the consummate family wealth portfolio.

Or, the family may be experiencing a change in leadership or life stages of its members. Current leadership may be entering the elder/mentor stage of their lives and may wish to abdicate some of the more active forms of leadership in favour of a consulting or educational type of role to the family.

Let us imagine a family who is in the midst of the first scenario and, employing hindsight and thinking their current advisor 'should have seen this coming', have decided to find a new advisor. A recommendation is obtained from a friend, a call is made, and a meeting is set. To this point in the dialogue between client and advisor – even before the first meeting – an underlying protocol has emerged. Once a meeting is set between the family or individual and the advisor, all parties who will be involved in the meeting begin to anticipate that the conversation will be about investment and other wealth management matters. They will develop a set of expectations regarding topics to be discussed as well as answers to be delivered to the questions which will be asked. The family expects the conversation to be about investments. They also expect to have to answer questions about their goals, risk tolerance, the plans they have for their retirement, and a plethora of other questions listed on questionnaires that advisors typically use. Exhibit 19.5 shows a few of the thoughts which might be running through this family's mind in anticipation of the meeting.

Exhibit 19.5

Expectations...

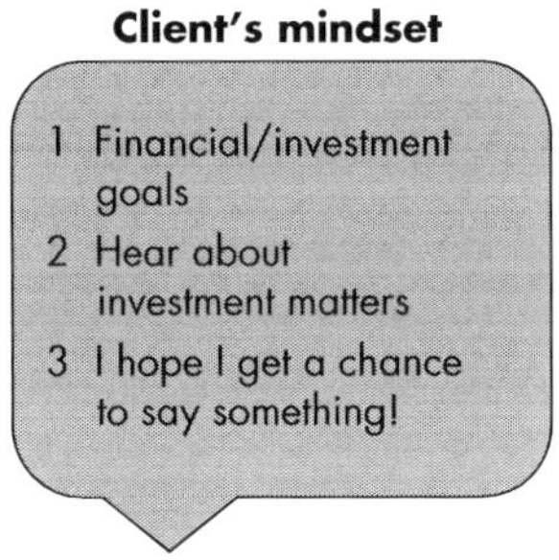
Client's mindset
1 Financial/investment goals
2 Hear about investment matters
3 I hope I get a chance to say something!

Source: graymatter Strategies LLC. All rights reserved.

The language the advisor speaks in his or her head tends to vary significantly from the language the family or individual client speaks in his or hers.

Exhibit 19.6

Expectations...

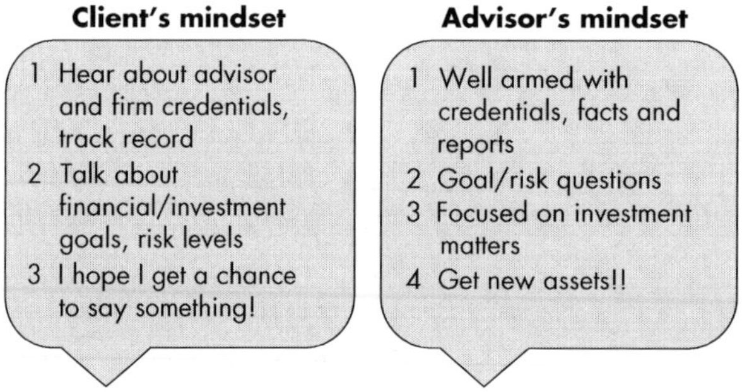

Client's mindset	Advisor's mindset
1 Hear about advisor and firm credentials, track record 2 Talk about financial/investment goals, risk levels 3 I hope I get a chance to say something!	1 Well armed with credentials, facts and reports 2 Goal/risk questions 3 Focused on investment matters 4 Get new assets!!

Now, let us imagine the same scenario, only this time, we have a different approach from the advisor – this advisor has a different mindset.

Exhibit 19.7

Expectations...

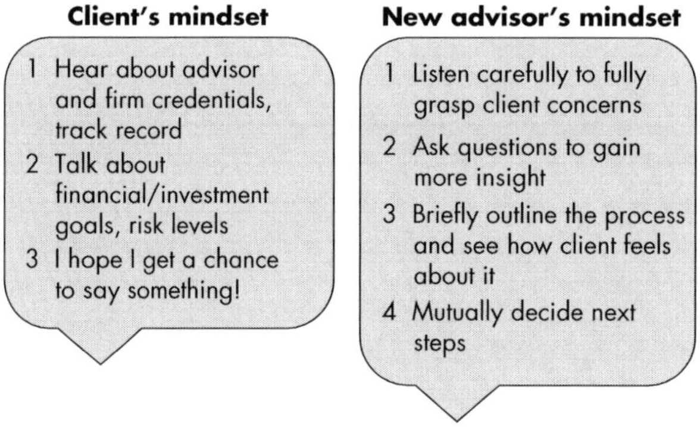

Client's mindset	New advisor's mindset
1 Hear about advisor and firm credentials, track record 2 Talk about financial/investment goals, risk levels 3 I hope I get a chance to say something!	1 Listen carefully to fully grasp client concerns 2 Ask questions to gain more insight 3 Briefly outline the process and see how client feels about it 4 Mutually decide next steps

In this case, the family or individual client is likely to come away from the meeting pleasantly surprised, thinking how refreshing the meeting was and hoping that this is an indication that this advisor is genuinely interested in their family, not how many assets he or she can gather. And all the advisor really did was to listen first to the client's needs before explaining anything about his or her firm, credentials, track record, or anything else. After all, if the advisor and the firm did not have good credentials and the desired level of expertise, the chances that the family would be meeting with the advisor are quite small.

This changes the dynamic of the expected relationship altogether from the very first meeting. It is likely, then, that the client's mindset will also change, and there will be more openness toward the advisor as he or she steers the client toward a deeper exploration of the family's needs. In the case that the family had done the work to develop an advisor selection process, the two mindsets might look something like that shown in Exhibit 19.8.

Exhibit 19.8

The new client / advisor relationship

Client's mindset	New advisor's mindset
1 Get input from family council on what type of advisor(s) is needed	1 Listen carefully to fully grasp client concerns
2 Develop criteria based on needs and advisor type	2 Ask questions to gain more insight
3 Measure questions advisor asks against quality scale	3 Briefly outline the process and see how client feels about it
	4 Mutually decide next steps

Source: graymatter Strategies LLC. All rights reserved.

It is not likely that these two mindsets would come together before an initial meeting between family client and advisor. It would only be the result of a family client who had done the work necessary to develop an effective advisor selection process and was preparing to gather information to take back to the family for discussion. The new mindset on the advisor side would be rare. More likely, the advisor would have a predetermined goal of some type, even if it were to get the client's approval for developing a version of the process he or she outlined, fully customised for the client. Of course, it would be impossible to customise the process in any meaningful way from the information gathered at a first meeting. Any family representative who had been well educated in the advisor selection process the family developed would take such a request as a sign that this advisor might not be the best fit for the family.

The fact that this latest scenario is likely to never happen points to the reality that it is perfectly all right for family clients to come to advisors with a specific and/or pressing need, seeking assistance with that need, although the point of contact is in the middle of the generational wealth management process, not at the beginning. This is where clients live. And their most pressing needs should be addressed first. It may not be necessary to resolve the issue right away, but it is absolutely essential for the advisor to focus on the need the client presented and either help the client think through and resolve the matter or to introduce several reasonable options for taking care of the issue.

Regardless of the pressing nature of the issue, clients most often simply want someone to care enough to acknowledge their concern and to give them an actionable piece of advice which will allow them to feel a solution is on its way. The flexibility of the generational wealth management model enables the advisor to address the family or individual's immediate concern(s), then over time, work back through to the issues present within the family system. With the help of a well assembled team of family advisors, the family may discover their generational biases, the roles family members occupy, and the bearing the dynamics of the family are having on the goal-setting process.

Private wealth management, meet family governance

Now is the time to introduce the two parts of the consummate family wealth portfolio to each other within the generational wealth management process. Many advisors think that family governance has nothing to do with the services they provide for the family. When we look at the Family Systems component of the process and realise that the family governance system is the facilitator for discovering the authentic needs of the family and for helping it set appropriate goals to satisfy those needs, we begin to realise just how much influence family governance has over the services advisors provide families. This influence increases significantly when the family has done the work to develop an advisor selection system.

To rightly position family governance as an influence on private wealth management functions is to understand how the family makes decisions, who makes those decisions, and who or what factors influence their outcome. It also is a tremendous aid to the family. How much more manageable is the family wealth when all the moving parts are recognised, their needs for flourishing assessed, and their utilisation well integrated and monitored!

The same factors that govern the degree of trust-level communication among family members also govern the degree of trust-level communication with advisors. The assignment of roles – resulting in perceived roles rather than authentic ones – contributes to a relationship between client and advisor that is based on assumptions rather than authentic roles and authentic goals. When roles are misunderstood, communication and trust break down among family members and they have problems identifying with and contributing to the achievement of the goals that are set. This results in an inability of the family to make decisions around wealth management which everyone supports and, in turn, makes it impossible for advisors to have an effective relationship with the family client. Any effort to design a workable allocation strategy becomes unsuccessful.

Needs identified based on role perceptions rather than authentic roles may result in the setting of goals that do not match the actual needs of the family or of the individuals within. This potentially throws the entire goal-based asset allocation mechanism off kilter, causing every investment strategy built upon the goals to become at best unsuccessful and at worst completely irrelevant. These elements also filter into the investment policy, spreading the contagion throughout the entire family wealth portfolio. Because of generational and behavioural biases, this is done in clandestine fashion with the result that the family has no idea things are breaking down until a crisis has ensued and damage – sometimes irreparable – has been done. Whatever path the family travels toward achieving its goals goes off the mark. It is certainly not the path toward optimality.

For this reason, it becomes essential for the family to do the work to become aware of its authentic wealth, the related needs presented by the roles family members occupy, and the influences those needs have on the goals that are set. An advisor who is educated in the generational wealth management process can help guide the family in identifying each person's authentic wealth. A family who is educated in the process becomes an intelligent selector of advisors to the family. Families can assemble an entire team of advisors who are functioning as personnes de confiance[10] whose services together with a focus on meeting the needs of the family is first and foremost in their minds and hearts.

The most accurate identification of family goals can only occur by considering generational perspectives and the family dynamics which result. Stopping anywhere short of this origination point allows assumptions – at least in some part – to be used as a foundation for managing the wealth. But how do we get there? By establishing a framework for families and advisors to work within, we must acknowledge that the continuum is inconsistent with real life application. Families do not normally think of their intellectual, social, and human capacities as assets. An advisor who leads the family to this type of awareness is functioning at the highest level of service.

It is the role of advisors to slow down the client acquisition process and to give full attention to uncovering the authentic needs family and individual clients bring to them.[11]

Every wealth creator wishes his or her progeny to benefit from the family's good fortune.

If a wealth advisor can do no more than to help succeeding generations of family clients gain some understanding of the basis for certain decisions, opportunity may arise for understanding the underlying love and care in those decisions. Within the new model, this level of service can be extended to every form of the family's wealth.

The advisory selection process

Families of wealth are best served by a team of well-vetted advisors who are willing to take the time to fully understand their needs and to understand the family's goal setting process sufficiently to support the family in achieving those goals. Such a team can be difficult to assemble. If the family is not clear on why it needs an advisor, what they realistically hope the advisor will do for them, or what the boundaries of that advisor's expertise may be, they may be setting themselves up for a less than satisfying experience.

Advisors should be willing to take the time with family clients to fully understand their issues and their needs. Particularly in times of emotional stress or reaction to certain types of events, the right advisor can help families think clearly and make good decisions even during times of distress.

The establishment of a process to guide the family through intelligent advisor selection should be part of setting up family governance, although the process can certainly be developed and instituted at any time. The important point is for the family to have a strategic plan which it can follow, checking off due diligence activities and rechecking important points which were listed at the time of decision to find an advisor.

For such a process to adequately serve the needs of the family, both now and in the future, the advisor selection process must begin at the family governance level. The process can become part of the family governance system so that reviewing and selecting advisors can becomes a venue for education and involvement of family members.

The advisor selection process should be well designed, clearly delineated, and well integrated into the family governance system. This is another aspect of risk management families often overlook.

The most dangerous risk factor in a family-advisor relationship is the propensity of the advisor to become immersed in his or her own expertise at the expense of offering optimal service from the client's perspective.[12]

There are seven basic steps families should incorporate into the advisor selection process.

1 Determine the needs and goals of the family through the family governance process.

Once the family has done the work to recognise its authentic wealth, the roles family members are occupying will become clear. The family will also be able to confirm which roles are authentic and which are perceived (assigned through generational biases). This applies to individual roles as well as to roles family members occupy from a family entity perspective. As we saw in Chapter 9, there are roles that have to do with the interactions of family members with each other and for the family entity as a whole and there are other roles that each individual family member occupies which attest to each family member's authentic assets.

By doing this work, the family gains revelation about its authentic assets. It unveils an entire set of assets which were not previously recognised. The family can see how the authentic roles of each person contribute to the family as a whole from the roles each occupies within the family governance system. As well, it can take an inventory, of sorts, of the authentic talents and passions of each family member so the family may accurately assess its needs. Once the authentic roles have been identified, the needs of those family members can be used to set the family's goals. The monitoring system alerts the family to new needs which spring up as well as to the satisfaction of current needs. This process builds in the flexibility to accommodate the fresh capacities of new generations which add to the family's pool of authentic assets and which present specific needs for apprenticeship as future family leaders. In this fashion, the monitoring system can keep the family and its advisors abreast of areas which may need attention as family life stages change.

2 Decide what types of advisors are needed to help the family achieve those goals.

Selecting the right advisor for the right purpose is essential. The identification of the family's authentic needs can help determine if an advisor needs to be hired full time or in-house and whether those services can be effectively outsourced without compromising the quality of service. This also involves a clear understanding of the scope of the advisor's expertise. One of the prime ingredients in a disappointing advisor-client relationship is the set of expectations the family or individual may have for that advisor's performance. Getting a candid sense of the advisor's scope of expertise and how far he or she may be willing to stretch beyond that expertise will set the relationship up in a straightforward manner from the beginning. Managing expectations on the front end is easier and much more comfortable than employing hindsight in an effort to deal with the inevitable regret.

3 Create a list of criteria specifically designed to vet the type of advisor the family is seeking.

This is a job for the entire family. In addition to the due diligence a family should normally do in selecting an advisor, this list should include items specifically tailored to the needs of the family's authentic wealth. This added list is much more important than the usual list of manager due diligence criteria. This list vets the advisors who are going to help the family flourish its authentic wealth, the source of all the material and financial wealth it now enjoys and which has the power to replenish the material and financial wealth if it is managed as part of the consummate family wealth portfolio.

For example, the family in the case study in Chapter 9 should include advisors who know something about fashion design and the needs required to succeed within that industry. The advisors should be willing to work with a young woman in a way that makes her feel her aspirations are being taken seriously, and they also should be able to proactively support the family in communicating better about its wealth, despite the history of secrecy within the family.

Advisors should welcome such a list of criteria. It guides them in knowing just how to serve the family so that the relationship can be as much of a win-win as possible. Knowing that the entire family created the list enables the advisor to understand the things that are important to each generation of the family's generational maze.

4 Conduct the due diligence required, using the list of criteria as a guideline.

This is an excellent way to get family members involved in dynamic stakeholder ownership. For family members who are not involved in the family business, this is another very important educational as well as functional role for them to occupy. Family members may be sent out to interview advisors, armed with the list of criteria, checking things off as they proceed. It is a wonderful educational tool for family members of almost any age. I highly recommend taking young children to the interview process and having them prepare a question or two before the meeting. Especially if a junior board exists, this activity could be on the list of educational milestones. The most important thing is follow through; if the child prepares a question, he or she needs to be given the opportunity to ask it. This is also another litmus test for the advisor. Any advisor who seems annoyed at entertaining any family member's question – of any age or gender – should be avoided.

The list of criteria the family has put together can also be used within the family monitoring system to facilitate regular evaluation of advisors and the family's happiness with their service. Responsible criteria should be developed so that advisors are not fired for reasons that cannot be substantiated. These criteria should be shown to the advisor at the beginning of the relationship to ensure fairness and to give the advisor important information on what the family expects and how to serve them. A solid relationship with a responsible advisor who has your best interests first and foremost in his or her mind is too valuable to dismiss on a whim. Even more importantly, an advisor who does not have the family's best interests above his or her own is too expensive to keep for *any* length of time.

5 Write an objective report on all advisors interviewed and submit it to the family council.

The family scouts should bring their findings together, compare notes, and write a report to be sent to all family members. Family members can and should collaborate when possible on this task so that a thorough report can be presented to the family. The report does not have to be perfect. Going over the report is also a wonderful educational opportunity, especially with younger family members but also with family members who have not worked with advisors before. The top scoring advisors should be interviewed personally by family leadership after leadership has heard the reports from the family scouts and discussed the findings with the family council.

6 Discuss the report and recommend two top choices.

Final advisor candidates are then chosen and a final interview is given. In this interview, it is important to make sure both the advisor and the family or individual client fully understand what to expect from each other and how they would like to work together. The family should indicate how much communication they would like to receive as well as in what form. If the family uses its advisors and consultants to help educate family members – a practice I highly recommend – educational guidelines should be outlined, particularly in areas regarding the wishes of various family units for disclosure of information to minor children. Obviously, confidences between individuals and advisors must be maintained under all circumstances. A confidence is different than a family secret.[13] The subject of confidentiality is a must on the list of items to discuss with advisors. The difference between confidences and secrets is this: confidences are a factor in trust-level communication; secrets are born out of fear and distrust and only breed more fear and distrust. The right type of advisor will alert family members if he or she feels the family member is keeping a secret which could prove to be harmful to the family's well-being. In no case may the advisor break confidence; but an advisor who is willing to bring dangerous matters to the attention of family members is a prized relationship.

7 Once hired, enrol the advisor in the data point monitoring system created through the risk analysis component.

The monitoring system set up through the family governance system should encompass all assets of the family wealth portfolio as well as advisors. The family can set up different components which are designed to monitor different types of assets as well as to log the minutes from family meetings. Advisors have generational and behavioural biases, too. Data points to monitor the biases of advisors should also be included as part of the family's data point monitoring system. This system should also include benchmarks used to monitor the performance of all assets, including authentic ones. Benchmarking should be done against appropriate indexes including customised benchmarks, and against the achievement of the family's goals across all goal buckets. Overall performance should also be monitored and attribution analysis should extend to the authentic assets which support the dynamic stakeholder ownership of family members as well as to support the flourishing of those assets.

Intelligent use of advisors

Once the advisors have been selected, families must understand how to follow through with the relationship and utilise advisory relationships in a manner which creates a win-win-win result. The weaving of wealth management influences into wealth management practices shows the effect of the family's authentic wealth on the material wealth's 'bottom line'. Chapter 16 illustrated just how much the bottom line can be affected by the lack of trust-level communication. This applies to trust-level communication between the family and advisors, as well.

Family members must be educated about advisor relationships and also about relationships with the family board, the family council, and the family office. Every family member should have a clear understanding and knowledge of the family governance system so that each member feels confident to be dynamic in his or her ownership of the family wealth. This also ensures a responsible relationship between family members and family office staff and executives. Advisors should not have to spend time trying to deal with an unruly family member or a family member who is trying to take advantage of the relationship.

Advisory roles are: (a) to support the family in achieving its goals of developing trust-level communication; and (b) education of family members as dynamic stakeholder owners. Family governance guidelines should be straightforward. This is why it is so vitally important for all family members to have input when designing them. Family input serves as a built-in check point for family relationships as well as for relationships between family members and family advisors including trustees, attorneys, and other advisors.

Guidelines should also be delineated for treatment of in-house family staff and service people. Creating a wonderful work atmosphere for any person who provides a service to the family elicits the best quality service and enables the family to preempt crises, if possible, and to better manage crises if and when they do occur. Even a Family Event (comparable to a Great Event in larger society) is much more manageable when the family governance system is well designed and every family member is functioning as a dynamic stakeholder owner.[14]

Advisors must also be aware of the hierarchy of the family governance system so that he or she may support the hierarchy and, thus, support the family's achievement of its goals. The most important goals of any family are to develop trust-level communication among its members and its vital relationships and to educate each family member to be a dynamic stakeholder owner. *All other goals are subordinated to those two.* And any advisor, regardless of role or service provision, must keep these two goals preeminent in their minds when performing any type of family service.

Family members as advisors

How do these criteria apply to family members who wish to also be advisors? Often, family members are investment managers, attorneys, or other advisors and work for the family in managing the family's material and financial assets. Family members who become advisors to the family can be a wonderful gift for the family – especially when they are cognisant of the family's authentic assets – or they can become nightmarish relationship dividers. Great care should be taken when a family member serves the family in this or any other type of capacity. Conversations should take place which outline expectations for the relationship, just as they would with a non-family member advisor.

Family members who are also family advisors have an even greater responsibility as dynamic stakeholder owners since they not only hold their own stake in the management of the consummate family wealth portfolio, but they also are caretakers for the stakes of other family members. It is quite easy for a family member who is an advisor to feel that his or her contribution is greater than those of other family members or to feel the need for greater recognition than other family members' contributions. In fact, each family member's contribution – regardless of scope or nature – is equally important. Here is where leadership must be vigilant in guarding against such unequal measurement of contributions. This is a situation where the family virtues must be readily evident and trust-level communication must be guarded most preciously.

Family boards

Members of the family board, whether family members or non-family members, must also be well educated in the three forms of governance so that their roles will be clearly understood and for board members to accurately and fully grasp the appropriate natures of their roles. Family members who are on the board have the additional responsibility for seeing that this education is provided to non-family members and provision should be made within the family governance monitoring system.

Of utmost importance to any family board, including philanthropic boards, is to tie board activities to supporting the achievement of the goals of the family as delineated by the family governance system. Any board member or advisor who does not wish to support the achievement of the family's top two goals – the development and maintenance of trust-level communication and the education of members as dynamic stakeholder owners – should be dismissed immediately.

Boards can be amazing gifts to families in managing the family business, monitoring best practices for the business, and for monitoring the relationships between family members, the business, and the family board. They can provide the family with a quality of advice not found in other advisory roles. However, if they are the primary governing body, they must take great care not to confuse the roles of the three forms of governance. One of the roles board members can and should occupy is that of helping the family maintain the appropriate governance hierarchy within the family governance system. This will require education of board members of a type they have never before received and the family should obtain a commitment from each board member that he or she will uphold the family governance hierarchy and support the family in achieving its two primary goals.

Junior boards

There are so many 'books within a book' housed in this volume and the subject of junior boards is one of them. Junior boards with second generation family members are particularly important since the second generation is such a vital component of the family's wealth. The last chapter of this book will offer much greater insight into the second generation's roles, privileges, and responsibilities.

For this mention, I will say that the junior board is a vital training ground in any number of areas, not just in philanthropic training or to learn material and financial wealth management. Philanthropy is instilled by example and from an early age. So also are the various educational components of dynamic stakeholder ownership. Dynamic stakeholder owners are bred; they are not born. Although the foundation and desire are there, dynamic stakeholder ownership must be nurtured from early childhood. Junior family councils are wonderful training grounds for the greater responsibilities of junior board membership. Junior board membership is a wonderful time for regular inclusion in certain family council and family board meetings. Of even greater value is when juniors are offered the opportunity to express opinions, share ideas, and ask questions. What a rich experience across the entire generational maze!

The best advice I can give regarding junior boards is to not limit their roles too severely while offering the ability to make mistakes safely. The clearest support for this advice I can offer is when my daughter learned to drive a car. The year she had her learner's permit, she was asked to drive at every possible opportunity, under every possible weather and road condition, and over a wide variety of driving distances. Any possible situation I could imagine that she might encounter, she drove during her apprenticeship with me in the car. When she passed her driver's test, both she and I felt much more comfortable in her ability to navigate the car on her own and to be a responsible driver.

This is true with all apprentices of whatever age. The more opportunities we can give them, the more education we can impart, the more 'trial decision making' we can allow them to do, the more mistakes they can make under our watch, and the more we can lovingly turn those mistakes into learning experiences, the greater the future leadership of the family will be. This is also the reason I urge parents to educate their children early about the family money. Keeping this education from them is like putting a new driver on a slick, rainy road all by themselves with no preparation at all, going the wrong way on a one-way street.

Apprenticeship is a wonderful time for junior council members and junior board members. It offers the easiest opportunity for establishing trust-level communication and for discovering the authentic assets of new generations. Families should take full advantage of the opportunity to educate the younger generations and to discover their authentic assets early on so that full flourishing of those assets may occur.

Generational wealth management: the new approach to flourishing family wealth

The beauty of going through an organized process like the Generational Wealth Management Continuum[SM] is the assistance the process offers families in understanding all aspects of family wealth management across the entire family wealth portfolio. These three chapters have offered a three-faceted approach to effectively translating the elements of the family governance side of the generational wealth management process to the private wealth management side, making the entire process flow within a step-by-step continuum which protects the family's entire portfolio of assets while enabling them to flourish freely.

The process also enables families and their advisors to take a critical step back and broaden their horizons regarding the family wealth. Inclusion of the family's authentic assets within the management of the consummate family wealth portfolio is essential to the family's success – and to the successful advisory relationships offering guidance along the way.

It can be difficult for families to look at their portfolios as a whole rather than to view components in silo fashion relative to the goals they have set. Brunel and Statman both make the point that individuals keep mental accounts and, therefore, frame their decisions based on a selective view.[15] Families and individuals can become emotionally attached to a projected outcome they hope will benefit them by the achievement of certain goals. The generational wealth management process provides tools to help families and their advisors step back from those attachments to see the broader picture to make better, more informed decisions together.

---

[1] Brunel, J.L.P., *Integrated Wealth Management: the new direction for portfolio managers*, 2nd edition (London: Euromoney Books, 2006), p. 7.

[2] Pompian, M.M., *Advising Ultra-Affluent Clients and Family Offices*, (Hokoben, NJ: John Wiley & Sons, 2009), p. 76.

[3] Brunel, J.L.P., *Integrated Wealth Management: the new direction for portfolio managers*, 2nd edition (London: Euromoney Books, 2006), pp. 8, 9.

[4] Ibid, p. 11.

[5] In his book, *Integrated Wealth Management: the new direction for portfolio managers*, Brunel suggests that investors out 'to travel on the road to optimality', p. 203.

[6] Brunel, J.L.P., *Integrated Wealth Management: the new direction for portfolio managers*, 2nd edition (London: Euromoney Books, 2006), p. 11.

[7] Ibid, p. 35. Brunel notes that 'advisors need to take the time to understand what issues and problems clients bring to the table. Then advisor's job is to develop the best possible solutions to their problems ...' and further, 'from an advisor's perspective, an investor's choice of investment strategies may seem to make no sense'.

[8] Statman, M., 'What is behavioral finance', in: Fabozi, F., editor, *The Handbook of Finance*, (Hoboken, NJ: John Wiley & Sons, 2008).

[9] Das, S., Markowitz, H., Scheid, J., Statman, M., 'Portfolio optimization with mental accounts,' *Journal of Financial and Quantitative Analysis,* Vol. 45, No. 2, April 2010.

[10] Hughes describes personnes de confiance as 'the people of confidence families trust to offer a window through which privacy-conscious families can see out into the larger world'. Hughes, J.E., Jr., *Family Wealth: keeping it in the family*, (New York, NY: Bloomberg Press, 2004), p. 233. The author interprets personnes de confiance as advisors whom families trust to be the windows to their intellectual, human, and social capacities – the family's authentic wealth.

[11] Brunel, J.L.P., *Integrated Wealth Management: the new direction for portfolio managers*, 2nd edition (London: Euromoney Books, 2006), p. 35.

[12] Ibid, p. 35.

[13] Hughes, J.E., Jr., *Family Wealth: keeping it in the family*, (New York, NY: Bloomberg Press, 2004), p. 45.

[14] The term 'dynamic stakeholder owner' is used with permission from James E. Hughes, Jr.

[15] Brunel, J.L.P., *Integrated Wealth Management: the new direction for portfolio managers*, 2nd edition (London: Euromoney Books, 2006), p. 44; also Statman, M., 'What is behavioral finance', in: Fabozi, F., editor, *The Handbook of Finance*, (Hoboken, NJ: John Wiley & Sons, 2008).

Chapter 20

The tales of two families

'Money is not a product of nature … Money is an invention … Somewhere along the way, the power we gave money outstripped its original utilitarian role.'

Lynn Twist, The Soul of Money[1]

Nothing makes as great an impact as seeing theory actually being put into practice. In this penultimate chapter, it seems appropriate to come back to the reason we began this journey in the first place. Before we can be beneficially prescriptive, we must understand the concepts behind the prescription and we must also see evidence of those concepts put into practice. We must also be vitally aware that the prescription will not be exact; rather, it will be a principle-based guide to elicit thinking from families and their advisors on the flourishing of authentic assets. In some instances, this will mean that the authentic wealth becomes material or financial in form; in others, it may not. Some of the family's authentic wealth may translate into good will in the community, break-through research, or becoming the first woman to walk on the moon. In whatever form, the flourishing of each family member's authentic wealth will contribute to the authentic assets of the family as an entity, empowering it to benefit the family and the community in extraordinary ways.

We saw in Chapter 14 how the seven-generation Laird Norton family has effectively implemented a governance system based on their authentic wealth rather than their net worth.[2] It is their story and, although their specific governance structure may not work for everyone, the principles on which it was designed are universal. As well, the European family whose story is told below fosters its authentic wealth in a different, yet very effective way, still based on the principles outlined in this book. Both are valuable examples and aspects of each family's system may be appropriate for other families to adopt.

The second family's story proves to be just as valuable. Theirs is the story of five generations with less than 20 family members currently living. It is a story of love overcoming feelings of unfairness and distrust within relationships. For that reason, its lessons are as powerful as the two success stories with hundreds of family members.

Chapter 21 outlines a critical path for rejuvenating the family wealth and, in essence, recreating the second generation over and over again rather than subconsciously succumbing to the edicts of the three generations Proverb.

The stories of the two families in this chapter steer us toward that purpose. In a never-ending search for ways families of wealth can enrich their experience and foster all forms of their wealth, the examples of these two families are a meaningful contribution to what I hope will become an ongoing discussion. That would make the work, and certainly the reading of this book, most worthwhile.

The journey we have travelled has been an exploratory one which will lead families of wealth to a fountainhead of new life – not only of their material and financial wealth but of their family spirit. For what other reason do we accumulate material and financial wealth? We can say that it is to enjoy a particular lifestyle, to experience the fulfilment of our own success (at which point, it ceases to be exclusively ours), to provide a future for our families, to feel secure that our needs will be taken care of for the rest of our lives, and to feel confident that the needs of our families will be taken care of for multiple generations. Whatever the stated reason for the creation of material and financial wealth, it all traces back to a desire for the wealth to be a benefit to those whose lives are affected by it. Even wealthy individuals who 'have no family' are often interested in benefiting others in some way. Most often, those individuals are also part of a family – with nieces, nephews, and other relatives if not children of their own.

The questions this brief chapter poses are, 'What practices do large, multi-generational families of wealth employ which afford them the ability to function well together for the benefit of the larger family entity as well as for the benefit of their individual members?' and 'What can be learned from these successful, larger families to steer families with fewer members along their own path to success?'

By looking at two real-life examples and contrasting the dynamics of these two families, we can get a better sense of the challenging realities of wealth combined with the spirit of family. These examples are quite different, both in nature and in circumstance. The first family is European and offers a view of family spirit within wealth management for a family with hundreds of members. Much like the Laird Norton family featured in Chapter 14, this family has created a wonderful network which emphasizes the spirit of family as the glue which enables the effective and beneficial management of the tangible and financial wealth. The second family brings this view down to the current generation and shows us some of the challenges faced by a fifth generation family up close and rather personal. I am hugely indebted to both families and especially the John R[3] family for their candidness and gracious permission to share their story.

The Mulliez Family[4]

This is the story of a family with 603 members, each of whom is an accredited investor according a strict, definitive standard. The family are majority shareholders of 90 business units, all within various private companies in numerous retail sectors under '10 different pole-metiers' through the Mulliez Family Partnership.

Regis Mulliez is a third generation member of the clan of 1,111 living family's members. The family is in its sixth generation. Mulliez participates in industry think tanks and new developments in the patrimonial pattern[5] as an outsider to the retailers' core businesses.

A European example of joint decision making, this family's glue comes from the view that it is impossible to effectively manage the family wealth unless a strong relational network which holds a 'win-win' type of benefit for each family member has been established. The family epitomises the four virtues outlined in Chapter 8, extending the virtue of 'beauty as harmony' to the relationship between the family and its business endeavours.

One of the things I find fascinating in working with families of wealth all over the world is that, often, larger families in their fifth generations and later seem to have figured out the recipe for maintaining the spirit of family while making the money work for them, both as a family entity and for its individual members. Yet, each family with hundreds of members started out as a two people who came together and had children. As these families grew through their multiple generations, there was an ingredient which helped them foster their authentic wealth in a way that allowed them to work together to keep the material and financial wealth working for the benefit of all, simultaneously keeping the material wealth from ruling their relationships.

In the case of the Mulliez family, what is good for the family is also good for the family partnership. The 'win-win' extends to the employees of the private companies in which the partnership invests by means of 'workpeople sharing and stock options conventions'.

For a family with so many members, the investment stakes are significant and investment success is heavily dependent upon the family's ability to stay in relationship with one another, even though it is impossible to be close individually with hundreds of family members. The family stays in contact by means of numerous workshops each year and through educational teams.

Mulliez refers to the family structure as a relational network which offers its members communication, understanding, and mutual aid. These ingredients are listed as essential for the effective management of the material and financial wealth.

One thing that distinguishes families whose wealth flourishes to survive well beyond the proverbial third generation is the realisation that their view of the wealth must be broader than a single lifetime. A family network has a mandate to live through time, whereas individual networks may not even survive the course of one life. The cycles of each generation must share this view. It requires a different type of approach. The virtues of family are carried from one generation to the next, with each generation's contribution flourishing the wealth in all its forms. Although not all family members' contributions to the flourishing will be equal, each family member's contribution is equally important.

Mulliez speaks of an intangible asset which must be passed from one generation to the next through moral duty and a mutual respect for both elders and youth. This is a bridge across generations which enables the upward progression of generational cyclicality; it allows progression through strength and confidence born from the family's knowledge and understanding of its particular identity – its 'differentness'.[6]

This protects the family against the linear forces at work in the families represented in the six stories of the Preamble. These forces show up in family life as resistance to new ideas and sticking to what 'has always worked' in the past; the seeming need to conform to the assignment of roles despite the consequence to the family's authentic wealth; the expectation that younger generations will learn to be responsible stewards simply through osmosis; and the attempt of one generation to make decisions for succeeding generations either out of an effort to 'control' the wealth or simply not trusting next generations to make wise decisions.

For the Mulliez family, each member invests over 90% of his or her personal holdings in the family partnership. Along with the transition of the material wealth, succeeding generations are also heirs to the family's heritage. 'We do not simply pass on the value of a portfolio of participations; we pass on companies with their human capital, their clientele, their products, their personality, their life,' says Mulliez.

The responsibility is also passed on to steward the holdings so that the 365,000 people employed within the companies in which the family invest may also benefit. Whatever relationships family members have – whether shareholders, professional, friendships, or romantic relationships – the emphasis is on creating a 'win' for all involved.

Along with the normal risks to family wealth, the Mulliez family view group conformity as an enemy to their wealth. They cite the tendency of many families to 'agree' to a decision or an action simply because they think other family members want the decision to go a certain way or wish to take the proposed action.

Most families view disagreement and conflict as primary enemies to healthy family relationships. However, group conformity is as great a threat; it springs from individual family members acting in perceived roles and denying the authentic contributions individuals are capable of making. Sometimes an effort to remain involved with the group or the belief that any action is better than no action inadvertently turns into a conforming type of inertia; the act of conforming causes a paralysis in decision making which neither satisfies nor benefits anyone – or the group as a whole.

Those who embrace their roles as dynamic stakeholder owners most fully will guard against such inertia which is the enemy of the virtue of fusion. The concept of joint decision making[7] implies activity rather than conformity.

The John R. family

John R, a fourth generation family businessman did what he could to keep the family business thriving. Started in 1866 by his immigrant great-grandfather, John R's grandfather turned the company into the largest paving brick manufacturer in the world. Then the Great Depression hit and paving streets was no longer a pressing concern. John R's father battled confiscatory tax rates and a hostile board. Fourth generation John R took over the reins of a struggling business in the 1970s, shutting down old and inefficient plants and introducing new split tile manufacturing technology. Money generated by the sale of his wife's family's business in the late 1960s helped to fund the children's educations and provided access to patient capital when John R took the company private in 1990. As the business grew, the family experienced a comfortable lifestyle and were able to offer each of the children an excellent education as well as a distribution of funds at age 21 to start lives of their own.

While the children were growing up, the family lived comfortably from profits generated by the tile business as well as the income from trusts created for John's wife by her parents. John R's wife had worked with her father in their family business for a time and showed great aptitude for it but opportunities in senior management were rarely made available to women in the 1960s. John R's father-in-law at one point extended a job offer, but John R chose to keep his focus on the brick and tile business. When John R's wife's father chose to sell his business following his wife's death and his remarriage, John R's wife and her brother both felt frustrated that they had not been given the opportunity to take over the business. Because John R recognised how close his family had come to losing the brick and tile business after World War II, and because his wife did lose hers through sale, the couple set up trusts to plan the distribution of the family's assets.

According to two of the three children, John R did a wonderful job of structuring ownership of the family company and of setting up generation skipping trusts; so well that they felt at times that everything was tied up and spoken for since the trusts directed assets all the way to their children. Yet, the siblings have been expected to manage the family assets well, sometimes causing the John R children to feel, 'You sure can't use any of this, but boy, it's all your responsibility'.

Each of the three children used their distributions in different ways. The daughter used her distribution to pay for law school. The older son used his to fund a much more extended undergraduate career, as well as a masters' degree in education. The younger son funded business school. All three applied some of the funds to down payments on their first houses, though their forays into real estate were not equally successful.

In 1990, the brick and tile business was stable but John R was suffering from a severe auto-immune disorder. With no clear management succession in place and his sons in graduate school, John R asked his daughter to join him in the tile business. She moved back to her hometown in Ohio and learned the business from her father. Later, her younger brother would join her. The younger son really had the passion for the business so he took over when his sister returned to the law in 2003. He 'breathed his vision into the business and brought the business to even greater success,' says John R. The middle brother became a teacher, yet wanted to maintain a lifestyle similar to the one the siblings experienced growing up. With his teacher's salary, he was not able to replace the money he was spending, so his share of the first distribution was depleted.

John R has been adamant about treating all three siblings equally regarding distributions of money. 'That message was communicated to each of us growing up. But when we grew up and our propensity to either save or waste money was demonstrated, the message began to change dramatically,' explains the younger son. 'So if everyone's good, everyone's happy and successful. But if one is bad, the other two also get punished.' The conclusion is that if the middle brother receives any more distributions, he will just blow it. For that reason, few distributions were made to the younger son or to the daughter, either, regardless of their demonstrated responsibility. John R and his wife chose to increase the amount of their estates that would pass to charity.

The children sense that, although their parents were not corrupted by the money, for some reason, the parents felt it would corrupt and ruin their children; that they would not treat the money with respect and would not fulfil their responsibilities by having it. 'We've been expected to live up to the lifestyle and expectations of my parents while they've not had to walk the talk they're now passing on to us,' says the younger son. The things the siblings enjoyed growing up are things that they now have a difficult time providing on their own as adults – in large part, a consequence of the three-way division of their mother's inheritance.

The family focus from John R's side was to provide each child with equal opportunity, not equal outcome. The edict that the children would have to go out and earn their own wealth despite the fact that their mother inherited the bulk of hers sometimes felt like a double standard in the perspective of the children who are now grown with families of their own. The daughter feels that the sense of a double standard is based on the perception by their father that the middle brother is considered to be the 'money pit' of the family.

Both the younger son and the daughter have chosen to focus on their family's dynamics with a positive view; they feel the experience has taught them to be responsible for themselves and not to depend on money from the prior generation. It has forced them to be better savers. This view has helped them overcome the challenges of feeling a sense of distrust in family relationships.

John R's observation of the heirs of other wealthy families may have factored into his decisions regarding distributions. 'People who have great wealth generally know how to generate it but they tend to not be very good at leaving their children with a balanced system about how to deal with it. It tends to be more about the money and not what the money can do,' he says. He also notes that 'Great wealth is not the great end of the business of living. There's nothing wrong with it and, certainly, no one's going to throw it away but it's only a piece of the whole puzzle'.

Although the younger son and the daughter respect their father's decisions and appreciate the lessons they learned through being forced to save and to depend on their own efforts, the distribution of the wealth was designed without their input. If the wealth had been given to them outright as originally planned, rather than in trust, would it indeed have compromised their work ethic and marginalised their lives as the previous generation feared?

The younger son recognises that the family business is a tremendous asset with huge potential. After five generations, he is not about to let the business deteriorate on his watch. 'Looking back at the history of the business, it was at one time a major provider of materials as well as wealth. It may not be tremendous at this point, but it has demonstrated that it can be and it must be treated with respect.'

Wealth is not ruinous to heirs; lack of education and breakdowns in communication and trust are. Decisions made based on the generational assignment of roles introduces resentment and ill feelings. Families who love each other can overcome these feelings and still feel a sense of appreciation as shown in the John R. family. However, the challenges posed are great and may never completely be overcome. The risk to relationship – and to the family wealth – is too great for such decisions to be based on perceived roles rather than authentic ones. Both archetypical and chronological generational perspectives feed into the proverbial dissipation of the wealth unless family members' authentic roles are recognised and nurtured to offer the 'win-win'.

John R's daughter plans to establish a family bank so that a pool of money will be available to her children when they need it and pay it back 'when they're flush' so that the same availability will benefit future generations, even if the time frame between borrowing and payback is 30 years. 'Having access to available credit will get you a very long way if you have a good education and are reasonably ambitious,' she says.

Postscript: following the death of John R's wife in 2007, the three children received a portion of their mother's estate in trust. When the tile business faced severe pressure from its lenders in the recent recession, the children opted to lend a portion of their inheritance to the business to enable it to retire its line of credit.

The take-away

In our efforts to defeat the Proverb's power, we must remember that the Proverb addresses family wealth, not individual wealth. This reminds us yet again that no one creates material or financial wealth completely on his or her own and once created, every family member whose life the wealth touches becomes an owner. Thus is born the inherent responsibility of dynamic stakeholder ownership.[8]

Views of what may or may not be fair will differ with each generation. Since generations are by nature juxtaposed in such a fashion that breeds misunderstanding, trust-level communication becomes that much more vital to the family's success. Transparency, trust-level communication, and the invitation for input from all family members before significant decisions are made which affect them are essential components for understanding and acceptance. Anything less introduces the risks that family members may choose to contest decisions at best or break off from the family at worst rather than overcome fairness and trust issues with love. Although generations naturally oppose each other as next generations struggle to define themselves, these are risks no family can afford to take.

Neither can families afford the stealth risk that inertia introduces. 'Dynamism' in the sense of dynamic stakeholder ownership is a lovely word. Within it, used within this context, are packed enthusiasm, responsibility, free expression of authenticity, and joy. There is no room for the fear inherent in feelings of unfairness and distrust.

The growing focus on entrepreneurial stewardship in the family wealth industry today is a useful tool for developing dynamic stakeholder ownership. The concept of entrepreneurial steward-ship can be very helpful in realising the paradoxes present in the process of managing the material and financial wealth, such as the level of risk second and later generations must take to keep the material wealth serving the needs of multiple generations of family compared to the level of risk required to initially create the wealth.[9] However, the focus on entrepreneurial stewardship must not overshadow the flourishing of non-entrepreneurial wealth which can add as much to the family's authentic assets as the entrepreneurial efforts which result in greater financial wealth.

Once again, concepts which flow from the view of the family business (or the business of the family) must be supportive to the flourishing of the family's authentic assets – of whatever nature those assets may be. Not every family member can authentically be an entrepreneur. Every family member can and should be a dynamic stakeholder owner. That is the single common authentic role of each. Dynamic stakeholder ownership is tied directly to the four virtues of family. *The travesty of the three generations Proverb is not that the third generation has to go to work; it is that the spirit of family which is vital to the flourishing of the family's authentic assets disintegrates into oblivion.*

It is the spirit of family which elicits the commitment to do the work necessary to foster the development of the family's authentic assets through understanding the family's generational maze of perspectives and moving through the Generational Wealth Management Continuum[SM] through a 'family first' view. For this, we have outlined a process which will ensure that authentic roles are recognised and that the family sets goals to satisfy the needs of its most valuable assets. Within this process, the relationships between the family, the business of the family, and the family office are properly aligned and the tasks of the second generation will bear fruit.

---

[1] Twist, L., *The Soul of Money*, (New York, NY: W.W. Norton & Co., 2006), p. 116.

[2] This focus on 'wealth' rather than 'worth' is a stated focus of the Laird Norton family.

[3] We call this family the John R family out of respect for the family's privacy as well as in gratitude for the sharing of their story, which is a significant contribution to this book.

[4] Jadot, M., '*Là où tissu familial et réseau d'affaires se conjuguent*', *L'Echo Réseaux,* December 2008 , p. 38; also, Mulliez, R., Personal interview, May 2010.

[5] Phang, S. E., *Roman military service: ideologies of discipline in the Late Republic and Early Principate*, (New York, NY: Cambridge University Press, 2008), p. 28. Patrimonial authority in Roman society was that of a patron to his client; an overseer of the client's interests. In the Roman military, it emphasised the personal relationship the emperor had with his soldiers as a leader, material provider, and grantor of privileges. The emperor, in effect, viewed his soldiers as 'clients'.

[6] Hughes speaks of a family's differentness as its identity which is developed through the bonds of affinity in his definition of 'family.' Hughes, J.E., Jr., *Family: a compact among generations,* (New York, NY: Bloomberg Press, 2007), p. xix.

[7] As in other chapters, the use of the term 'joint decision making' is used here with the permission of James E. Hughes, Jr.

[8] The term 'dynamic stakeholder ownership' belongs to James E. Hughes, Jr. and is used with his permission.

[9] Lucas, S. and Lansky, D., 'Managing paradox,' *Family Business,* Spring 2010, p. 68.

Chapter 21

Second Gen^{SM}: the sea change opportunity in generational rebirth

'Families today are trying to find some common thread that will allow their families to stay together from generation to generation so there will be a sense of "family". More people are trying to inaugurate that sense that generations have ties and it's important to keep those ties intact. It's not just about "my" generation; it's about future generations. What are we doing for the kids? How are we teaching them? What are we willing to sacrifice so the generations coming down the line won't have problems?'

Anonymous source, family member

If one asks a family of wealth in its early generations how responsible the second generation is for determining their family's ultimate success, they will answer, 'not very'. Few speak of the power of the second generation. Even in the linear sequence of the Proverb, the second generation has no real identity. It essentially has no voice.[1] When the Proverb is on its way to fulfilment, the effect of what occurs on the second generation's watch may be clandestine and without aplomb. Whatever the second generation may wish to accomplish is most often overshadowed by the majestic accomplishments of the first, the creators of the mechanism called the family business which was once just an idea but was brought into material form.

By nature, the chronological second generation is a shadow generation. Archetypically, its purpose is to effect change and to individuate and differentiate from the first; chronologically, its assigned role, but almost never a role it would choose if asked, is to carry on the dream of the first. If the second generation has no desire or ability to carry on the founding generation's dream it will be expected by others, often who have a self interest in their doing so, to steward it. Regardless of others' goals for it, the second generation's reality is that it is incapable of effectively stewarding the first generation's dream until it has successfully stewarded its own.[2] Any effort to mandate such stewardship confines the second generation to a lifetime of occupation of a perceived role rather than a role that is authentic to the individual's true nature. I am grateful to Jay Hughes for the insight of stewarding another's dream as it so poignantly illustrates the effects a perceived role can have on the life of a family member and the ramifications it holds for the family for the generations who follow ever after. There is nothing the second generation can do within such a role to prevent the fulfilment of the three generations Proverb.

The crisis of 2008 brought heightened awareness of the statistical odds that the third generation will no longer benefit from the hard work and good fortune of the first, that it will no longer have the opportunity to live life as well. The Proverb is a universal truism. Ninety percent of families will see their wealth dissipate over the course of three generations. By the time the second generation begins handing leadership to the third, 60% will have already succumbed. The Proverb, in any language, does its work to subvert family legacies across the globe.

As we reach the point in our journey where the Continuum comes full circle, we have one vital task left to accomplish: to understand the import of the second generation's role in the family's ultimate ability to beat the statistical odds.

The role the second generation occupies within the Generational Wealth Management Continuum^{SM} becomes the cornerstone of the family system. The quality of this role is paramount. The success of the family for generations to come rests on whether the second generation succumbs to the mandate to steward something someone else created.

This final chapter will explore the role of the second generation thoroughly. First, we must find solid evidence of the unique importance of Second Gen^{SM}.[3] Second, we must fully understand the role the second generation occupies in determining the family's success; and third, we must examine how that role augments or depreciates aspects of the flourishing of the family's authentic wealth both during its lifetime and for the generations thereafter. It is time we got to know Second Gen.

Why Second Gen is so important

The second generation is proverbially a transient generation from the creation of the material wealth to its dissipation. Left to the Proverb's entropic devices, the view of the second generation is that of a silent carrier of doom whose role seemingly cannot be altered. As noted above, statistical odds of the Proverb's fulfilment are significant. With the second generation, however, we have a couple of unique opportunities. One is the opportunity to prevent the progression from ever reaching the third generation; in other words, to eliminate the proverbial third generation from the linear progression and to keep reinventing the second generation for generations to come. Another is the opportunity to discover a more authentic role for the second generation which will set the pattern for its own reinvention.[4]

The second generation is well positioned to accomplish this most authentic role. Second Gen is vitally important in the following ways.

- It is in the second generation that the chronological and archetypical generational perspectives come together for the first time. Without G2, there really is not a G1. If a material wealth creator has no children, there is no second generation growing up with the money or within the family dynamics the patriarch and matriarch have created through their coming together and forming a family.
- The birth of the second generation establishes a heritage for the first time. G1 may have an ancestral heritage but G2 is the only generation which will have a material wealth creation heritage as well as an ancestral one.
- Through the second generation comes the first establishment of cousin relationships. The relationship among siblings of the second generation will determine the relationship among cousins. If siblings are in disagreement, their children will tend to side with their parents, sometimes to the point of denying their true personal feelings.
- The establishment of the first family branches comes through the second generation.
- During the leadership of the second generation is the optimal time to establish the foundation for a family governance system.
- The second generation is the first generation to inherit the virtues of family or the family truths.

- The second generation offers the first opportunity for the family to adopt a shared vision across generations.
- The second generation is also the generation which creates what Stuart Lucas has described as the five paradoxes each business family faces.[5]

As we can see, the establishment of the entire Family System is completed in the second generation. It is through the Family System that the family's authentic roles are identified and the authentic wealth is recognised; it is also the Family System which houses the bulk of the inherent risks the family must manage over the course of its existence.

Steward versus dynamic stakeholder owner[6]

Stewardship: the careful and responsible management of something entrusted to one's care.[7]

Founding material wealth creators expect the second generation to steward the wealth so that generations after them may enjoy benefit from it. Usually implicit in such stewardship is also the stewardship of the family business. Especially in Asian cultures where it is difficult to separate business from the family, this is indeed the case.

One reason I find Hughes' term 'dynamic stakeholder owner' so compelling is that its verbiage has little direct connection to the family business. The 'stakeholder' aspect he speaks of has to do with the input family members have in making decisions on aspects of the family wealth which affect their lives. He speaks of dynamic stakeholder owners as owners of the family wealth rather than of the family business. When we correctly define wealth as the family's authentic assets, its intellectual, human, and social capacities and the relationships that nurture them, we more accurately understand the implications of dynamic stakeholder ownership. Dynamic stakeholder ownership is not necessarily entrepreneurial. And it is different than stewardship.

Exhibit 21.1 shows the proverbial progression of the three generations Proverb with the assigned role of the second generation doing its part.

Exhibit 21.1

Three generations proverbial progression

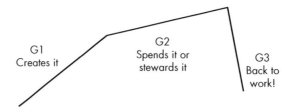

Source: graymatter Strategies LLC. All rights reserved.

310

As we can see, there are two expected roles of the second generation, either to steward the wealth or to spend it. Notice in this diagram that whichever role Second Gen chooses, the wealth continues to dissipate. This is because, by nature, the proverbial progression is subject to entropic properties. As more people are born into the family, the original pool of wealth becomes segmented into more and more pieces, eventually taxing the original pool of wealth to the point of dissipation. If the second generation spends the material wealth, the third generation is most certain to inherit the proverbial working privilege. If the second generation chooses to steward the wealth – and only steward it – the wealth may last for one or two more, postponing the work sentence until G3 or G4. Neither spending nor stewardship is a product of dynamic ownership.

If, however, Second Gen were given a third option, the possibilities of doing away with the proverbial third generation might become more realistic. This option is dynamic ownership. I often talk with second generation family members who feel they have no right to use the material or financial wealth they inherited from G1 because they did not create it. Genspring director Kirby Rosplock[8] shares this experience, noting, 'Sometimes the second generation doesn't feel like it owns the wealth. When you don't feel like you own something, you don't feel like you deserve it because it wasn't really yours to begin with'.

'The second generation is guilty of doing what their parents did, saying 'we didn't have that growing up so it doesn't feel right to me to have that,' adds Natasha Pearl, CEO and founder of Aston • Pearl. The first generation is more likely to leave money to the second generation because they grew up without money and they do not want that for their children or grandchildren.

Instead of ownership, second generations feel a heavy responsibility to steward the wealth so that it will hold some benefit for future generations. This may prevent Second Gen from using the wealth to flourish its own authentic assets – much less the authentic assets of subsequent generations – or even to enjoy a comfortable life.

If the second generation were empowered by the first to 'own' the wealth after being educated in all facets of dynamic stakeholder ownership, Second Gen would feel confident to employ the material wealth so that the authentic assets of every second generation member might flourish, contributing to the overall wealth of the family and establishing a precedent of generational revitalisation to offset the entropic forces wielded by the Proverb.

To revitalise means 'to give new life or vigour to'.[9] Synonyms for revitalise include: revive, reactivate, rebirth, renaissance, renascence, renewal, and resurgence.[10] When educated as dynamic stakeholder owners and offered the opportunity to appropriately employ the material wealth created by G1, Second Gen has the capacity to give new life to the family wealth just as new life is given to the family with each generation who is born or each new family member who enters by marriage or life partnership.

In this way, the second generation begins the precedent of grooming dynamic owners within each generation following so that their authentic wealth may flourish, adding to the consummate family portfolio in the process. Each generation is, therefore, freed to become what Hughes calls dynamic steward-conservators.[11] He cites what he calls the yin/yang problem of the second generation – the dilemma set upon it from the sacrifice of its own dreams to become caretakers for the dreams of the previous generation. This is a role the second generation was never meant to occupy; it is a role which only becomes assigned within families of significant wealth.

The assignment of this role by the first generation to the second limits the education of the second generation to those areas necessary for affirmatively answering the founding generation's

Exhibit 21.2

Second generation dynamic ownership

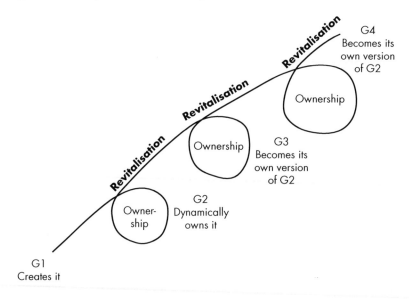

expectation,[12] eliminating any possibility that Second Gen would be sufficiently equipped for the successful materialisation of its own authentic wealth as well as eliminating any contribution it might eventually make to the authentic wealth of the family entity. This educational limitation feeds into the deterioration of self-esteem and confidence, resulting in 'confirmation' of the previous generation's assessment that the next generation would not be responsible with the wealth, even if given the chance. Exhibit 21.3 shows the typical chronological generational views of G1 toward Second Gen and of Second Gen toward G1.

The cycle of prejudgment and assigned roles which are in conflict with the authentic wealth predisposing failure which 'confirms' the generational prejudgment can be overt or well hidden. Either way, its effects are undesirable.

Families limit education of next generations by viewing the family's needs from the lens of the family business rather than from the correct hierarchical order of the family. This becomes another application of behavioural bias, framing the educational needs of the family by relying on the selective data seen as necessary to support the business and the financial and material wealth. As we have seen, this amounts to putting the cart before the horse, defeating the intended purpose by inviting the linear progression of the Proverb's fulfilment. Education in business and financial matters is a critical need. Limiting education of family members to those areas or placing priority on those areas over other areas of dynamic stakeholder owner education screens out the possibility of fulfilling other educational needs of authentic wealth holders with different capacities.

Such educational limits also filter into the design of the family governance system which serves as the primary support mechanism for the flourishing of the family's authentic wealth for generations

Exhibit 21.3

Chronological generational biases of first and second generations

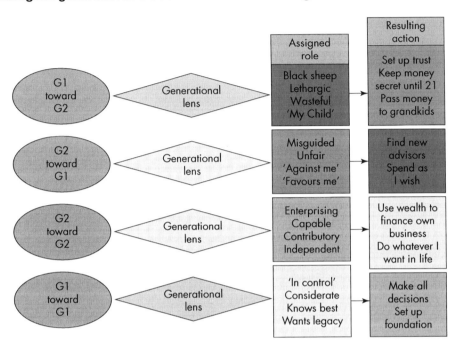

to come. When education of the second generation follows this path, it tends to stay on the same path for generations to come. Such education may support the stewarding of the wealth but it falls far short of revitalising it.

The plight of Second Gen

Until a second generation is born, there is no identification of the founding generation as 'G1'. As Second Gen grows closer to adulthood, the G1 and G2 identities become more pronounced although education of Second Gen should begin as early as possible, preferably with basic concepts in early childhood.

Second generation adults find themselves either facing the yin/yang dilemma (stewarding the founder's dream) mentioned earlier or eagerly pursuing the flourishing of their own authentic wealth.

In either case, the situations of the first and second generations are quite different. Lucas notes the founding generation only had one task: that of materialising his or her intellectual, human, and social capacities. The only other responsibilities it carried were to care for a spouse (or partner) and children. The second generation may have fiduciary responsibilities toward siblings and cousins in addition to responsibilities of their own family units and to the family business. They have less experience than the founding generation simply as a result of their location in time. And they have more at stake both financially and psychologically than the founding generation. Entrepreneurial risk has a different meaning for second and subsequent generations than it did for the first.[13]

Kennedy Wilson, Inc.'s Don Herrema says the second or third generation person may feel like the money has always been there and there's always going to be enough, whether there is or is not. So they may feel they should be able to live and travel and spend a certain way. A first generation wealth person is often more careful, certainly early in the wealth generation when there may not be the lifestyle and wealth infrastructure that exists with the second and third generations.

Family focus alignment

The most important aspect of the Second Gen role is to properly align the family's focus, positioning the family as predominant and the business as a supporting secondary. Once this alignment gets off kilter, the roles of the two entities (family and business) become confused and the family marches full face into the linear progression of the Proverb's fulfilment.

We made the case for dynamic stakeholder ownership over the concept of entrepreneurial stewardship in Chapter 20. The weakness of the concept of entrepreneurial stewardship is in its origination. Although the concept can be a useful tool, the origin of the first word is from a business mindset and the origin of the second is in the misprision we just discussed – that of stewardship over revitalisation. The goal in combining the two terms is to recreate the first generation's entrepreneurial mindset so that the material wealth will be preserved to benefit multiple generations. Entrepreneurship and stewardship can be wonderful tools for flourishing the family's authentic wealth when subordinated to the concept of dynamic stakeholder ownership. The latter supports the appropriate hierarchy of viewing the family wealth as a family who happens to have a business rather than a business with a family attached.

Where I find the concept to be most useful is in the application of team entrepreneurship within the family. Lucas and co-author David Lansky note that 'enlightened leaders' in the family 'must encourage family members to turn their focus from what has brought them much attention and gratification ([that is,] the active creation of [material] wealth) to … enhancing well-being, nurturing creativity, and cultivating the skills of individual family members'.[14] I agree with this notion and the first recipients of such attention must be the Second Gen. Second Gen leadership then has the responsibility of nurturing team entrepreneurship as one of the educational components of dynamic ownership.

For example, one family member's authentic role may be an idea generator. This family member may have significant intellectual capacities but may have very little social capacity. He or she may have a more introverted personality. He or she may be an academic or a great teacher. In such a case, the authentic goal for this family member may be to conduct research which may become groundbreaking; or it may be simply to become the best quality teacher possible, raising the standards of teaching in his or her small part of the world.

This can translate into the successful flourishing of the family's authentic assets in multiple ways that would be significant. For one, enabling a teacher to enjoy a lifestyle which could not be supported on a teacher's salary may allow that teacher to pursue other endeavours within that profession. In my view, dynamic ownership education for this family member would be education about roles and responsibilities as a family wealth owner – of all forms of family wealth – and also education regarding ways he or she may responsibly use the family's material and financial assets to pursue his or her ultimate goals for life fulfilling achievement.

To add necessary entrepreneurial components, other family members who are more authentically entrepreneurial may be able and willing to supply those aspects which may contribute to the development of the non-entrepreneurial family member's authentic wealth but which are not authentic talents – or passions – of the family member. The authentic talents of artists, musicians, and writers also lie, appropriately, in areas not traditionally considered entrepreneurial. And the talents of entrepreneurial family members rarely are as strong in artistic areas! Even entrepreneurs who are strong visionaries and less fiscally inclined may wish to hand off the business aspects of their pursuits to other people. Having a family member who is suitable for those roles can enhance the authentic wealth of both family members as well as that of the family entity.

Team entrepreneurship is particularly relevant to our focus since it no longer limits the family's view to the single, original pool of wealth which, by nature, will dissipate through the sheer numbers of people it eventually must support. It also is in line with our concept of each generation making a contribution to the wealth. Whether that contribution is large, small, or of a non-monetary nature, beginning with a focus on dynamic ownership may make the tool of entrepreneurial stewardship more effective in flourishing the authentic wealth of the family. Without question, it aligns the family's focus with the happiness and fulfilment of family members and maintains the Figure 8 relationship identified in Chapter 12 so that the roles of all family entities are in alignment with flourishing the authentic wealth.

Exhibit 21.4

Cyclical revitalisation of family wealth in all its forms

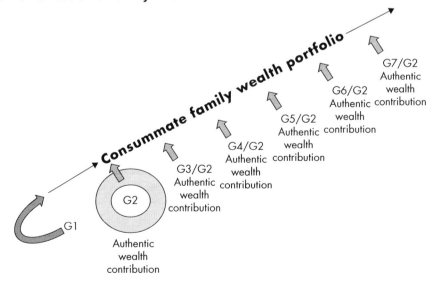

Whatever a family member's authentic roles and goals are, entrepreneurial stewardship, like any other family focus, should be applied in a way that supports the family member's authenticity rather than in a way which inadvertently suppresses it or limits its educational opportunities.

Since the situations of the two generations are different, a reinvention of the second generation with consultation from G1 rather than the recreation of the G1 mindset might be more suitable. Since the second generation sets precedent for so many aspects of generational wealth management, it can also set a precedent for managing the different situation in which it finds itself so that subsequent generations – who will find themselves facing similar issues – will have a roadmap to follow rather than trying to recreate the mindset of a generation, G1, who never experienced some of the issues or situations they face. As Second Gen hands over leadership to G3, it can most appropriately serve in the role of elders to mentor G3 into its own reinterpretation of the Second Gen phenomenon. This is in keeping with the role trilogy of apprentice, leader, and elder/mentor as outlined by Hughes.

Without the education or opportunity to become dynamic stakeholder owners, the second generation most certainly never will be! Dynamic owner education of family members with assigned roles such as black sheep just doesn't occur. Family business heirs apparent only receive education in those areas leadership feels are necessary for that role. The educational oversight occurs in much more subtle fashion with family members who have different interests or who are in families with older generation leadership. Silent and even some Boomer family leaders may still inadvertently discount the authentic wealth of women. They also may covertly discount the capacities of an entire generation based on its archetypical role. This has certainly happened with the Gen-X generation. Left to grow up basically on their own, many Gen-Xers did not receive the type of education they needed to be dynamic stakeholder owners. Instead, the mantra of larger society work-a-holic Boomers became 'fix our children' before childhood once again became desirable and older Boomers who had put careers first suddenly clamoured to become parents.

Clinical psychologist Richard L. Luscomb,[15] assesses the situation, 'There are families we all know who have learned to be managers of wealth from generation to generation. They have an understanding – almost a responsibility – toward the wealth. It seems to be their station in life. Then there's the other group where the second generation built up massive wealth and lorded it over their kids and the next generation. Now, they're trying to transfer it and they realise they never instilled any sense of responsibility or stewardship. They realise if they transfer that wealth, it's gone.'

Second Gen leadership: where generational perspectives collide

Each person alive is a member of an archetypical generation. Chronological generations are unique to families of wealth. Second Gen by definition is a chronological generation; all members of Second Gen are also members of an archetypical generational persona.

The archetypical generation of which Second Gen is a member makes a difference in its outlook toward education, open conversations, and support of authentic roles and responsibilities. This outlook translates to the family governance system which guides the family for generations to come. Let's take a look at the effects of Second Gen leadership in the different archetypical cohorts either in adulthood or reaching adulthood as of this writing.

Second Gen leadership from the Silent generation may be feeling the rejection of mores from the Gen-X generation two-generations down. They may have been disappointed that their Boomer or Gen-X children did not want to continue the family business or that they wanted to sell the

Exhibit 21.5

Silent generation as Second Gen

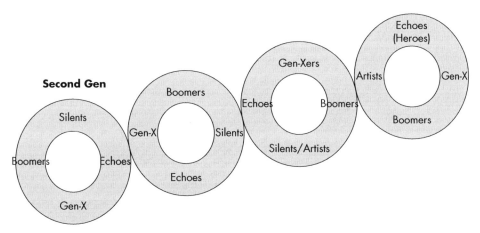

business to provide more liquid wealth or to invest in different types of businesses. They tend to live well below their means and may not disclose how much money the family really has. This is frustrating to younger generations who would like to know how to plan their lives based on any inheritances they might receive.

The children view this knowledge as good estate and investment planning; Second Gen's view is that the children are trying to get money the Silent generation needs to live on (although there is much more than enough). They may have set up generation skipping trusts for fear of spoiling the children with large inheritances. They may also feel their children were greedy or needed to learn the value of hard work and may not have distributed the wealth until the children were in their fifties or sixties. Women may have male siblings who are in charge of their trust distributions despite the fact that they are successful businesswomen of their own making. Second Gen may have kept doing what always worked for them, causing the business to fall behind market trends and the assets to diminish as in one of the stories in the Preamble.

Silent Second Gen's mentoring of younger generations may be difficult as their ideas of individualism and introspection may be the opposite of the younger generations' interests in teamwork and networking, especially through social media. They may feel their values are dying out with them.[16]

Some Boomer Second Gen leadership may have been trust recipients and less responsible than their siblings might have wished. There may be resentment on the part of more responsible Boomers to their leadership. Other less responsible Boomer Second Gens may have trustees who are more in control of their funds than they would wish.

Boomers are busy redefining retirement life and are still active at a much older age than their parents were. They are still self-indulgent and may not spend as much time with grandchildren as their parents spent with their children. Some may realise they have failed to adequately educate their children as wealth owners and may leave the bulk of their money to charity. Boomers always felt

Exhibit 21.6

Boomer generation as Second Gen

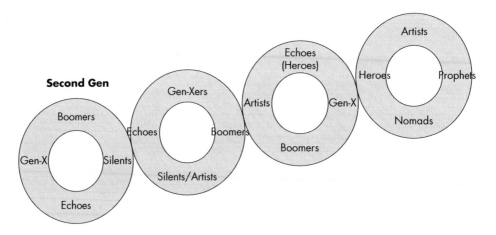

their GI and Silent parents could take care of any crises that arose. This makes them a bit reckless in their leadership. Since they serve to guide the upcoming Hero generation (the Echoes), they have the potential to either lead extremely well or to make huge mistakes. The economic crises which have hit family portfolios and are now under Second Gen Boomer leadership may reflect the future of family fortunes – all types of assets – depending on the quality of current leadership's guidance.[17]

Exhibit 21.7

Gen-X generation as Second Gen

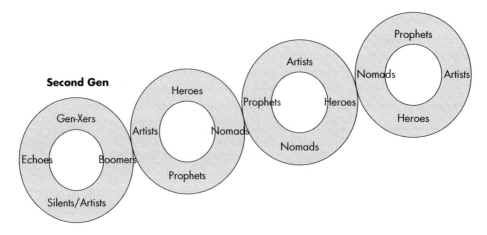

Gen-Xers who are Second Gen leaders have the skills to help the family wealth survive the current crises and to rebuild the institution of family and community rituals which have been abandoned by older generations.[18]

'The first generation made the money by being very careful with it,' according to Pearl. 'But once there's been a liquidity event, that can change. We've seen the second generation become very nervous about their parents' spending!' This would be a typical scenario between a Boomer first generation and a Gen-X Second Gen.

As the fixers and repairers of messes left by the Silent and Boomer generations before them, these Second Gen leaders will quietly restore societal order in which the new Hero generation will thrive. Their job is to balance out the recklessness of the Boomers and to ensure young Echoes are sufficiently educated and do not take over before their time.

Exhibit 21.8

Echo generation as Second Gen

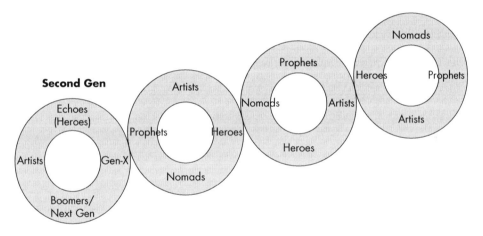

In the future, when there is Echo generation Second Gen leadership, it will be reminiscent of the GI generation's take-charge teamwork. This generation will mobilise family forces to work together for the good of the family entity. Though just coming into adulthood at the time of this writing, Echo Second Gens should bide their time and take full advantage of their apprenticeships. This will better prepare them for the great things they will accomplish in their time as leaders of family and in society at large.

As archetypical and chronological generational perspectives collide, attitudes about wealth will vary according to the archetypical perspectives of the Second Gen leading the family. These influences will impact the dynamics of the family for generations to come. They will determine the amount of transparency that is allowed, the degree of trust-level communication, the support for the flourishing of authentic wealth of all family members or of only those with a business and stewardship mindset, and the feeling of safety and inclusion each member feels within the smaller society of family.

Family governance build-out from Second Gen

Through the process of surviving difficult environments, individual civilisations are born. The struggles for survival and establishment develop the great strength which fosters the civilisation's continuance. Similarly, the difficulties experienced during the establishment of the society of family are the 'tempering of a family's steel needed for long-term success'. These difficulties evolve into the family legends which are later regaled by the aging establishing generations and handed down by those who follow.[19]

The second generation is very important because they move from the first generation into decision making at the family level. Leadership is critical at that juncture and if the family cannot agree on leadership or if real leadership does not emerge, even in the form of outside counsel, the family's success may be jeopardised.[20]

Second Gen completes the initial generational maze and gives a family its identity. Imagine children who are born and grow up in a family which has in place an educational system where each member is taught the history and characteristics of the family's generational maze of perspectives, how to appreciate the differences among the family's generations, and how those differences can educate new generations in furthering the upward spiral of cyclical progression. The recognition of each family member's authentic roles would be an ongoing process. There would be a constant feed of authentic wealth from generation to generation. Simultaneously, a pathway would be carved for new contributions from each generation to revitalise the family spirit – and, inadvertently, the family's material and financial wealth. This can all be introduced to the Family System by the Second Gen. As G1 assumes the role of elder, Second Gen can foster the transition of G1's role from leader to elder and mentor.

Elders foster the continuation of the family from one generation to the next. As elders tell their stories, family members feel a sense of belonging and want to hear more. As younger family members turn into elders, they tell the stories they heard from their ancestors and add their own stories to them. In much the same way, each person adds his or her authentic wealth as a dynamic stakeholder owner to enrich the family's pool of flourishing authentic wealth. If trust-level communication does not exist, the cyclical flow is flattened and the wealth of the family goes in different directions. Depending on which archetypical generation is in the Second Gen leadership role, the flavour of the family's governance system will be set in all of these areas.

Second Gen can also fall prey to its own generational biases. It has been my observation that even families with excellent representative governance systems which have benefited them for decades can become too comfortable in their roles and begin to focus more on their archetypical tendencies than on maintaining the systems they know to be tried and true. Silent or Boomer Second Gen leadership at the helm, may have worked in past years to acquiesce to what the family at large wants. Now, they may be making decisions in different ways than the family agreed and not inviting as much input on decisions as they should. Although we make mistakes and try to learn from them, we tend to revert to our own generational imprints as we become more accustomed to being in charge. Our generational biases invite us back on the linear pathway. The Boomer archetypical cohort, in particular is in danger of trying to lead in its own way, which can end up being reckless abandon of the principles they know to be true in their efforts to leave their mark on the life stage they occupy at the time. Many times there are significant traces of archetypical generational characteristics within family leadership which leadership is too close to the situation to see but which other family members can see – and do.

Whatever the result of that leadership, Gen-X Second Gens will be there to clean up the aftermath and will have the chance to prove themselves in leadership positions they have longed for and from which they have been held back.[21] This will pave the way for stronger Hero leadership in the generations after them.

Silent elders as Second Gens are in their elder roles, and as Strauss and Howe note, 'liberated from the grinding burdens of work and family, many elders are able to step back and provide the strategic wisdom every society needs'.[22] The small society of family is the place where the elder role matters the most.

An understanding of the archetypical generational perspective of Second Gen is critical. This is because Second Gen holds the keys to the multi-generational success or failure of the family to effectively postpone the fulfilment of the edicts of the Proverb. Knowing this truth positions family governance in an entirely different light. It helps families begin to monitor their need for governance as a preemptive risk management and asset protection tool.

Monitoring the system

Since governance becomes the primary monitoring system for the risks discovered within the Family System, the flavour of family governance based on the archetypical generational perspectives of Second Gen leadership are all the more important. Governance systems set up during Second Gen leadership will impact the family for generations to come. The attitudes toward wealth, the willingness to do the work necessary to identify the family's authentic assets, and the roles family members occupy all will be determined by the generational perspectives of family leadership.

John Benevides, President of Family Office Exchange, notes that the third generation receives conflicting messages from the first and second generations. 'The first generation is telling the second generation to work hard yet at the same time not to be so hard on the third generation. So the third generation receives an interesting message that says, "Be your own person, pursue your own happiness, yet we want you to be financial stewards so you can carry this on to the next generation." So you get conflict and tension. The second generation definitely has a responsibility but the first generation also has a responsibility since they can heavily influence the third generation. When all of this happens consciously, good things can happen. When it happens unconsciously, good things *might* happen; unfortunately more often than not, they don't.'

If leadership is currently G3, it will still be dealing with the effects of Second Gen views on governance and the way governance was set up during Second Gen leadership. Pearl observes, 'The second generation is more focused on not spoiling their kids than the third generation. You see a very conscious attempt to role model the behavior they want their kids to take on'.

The key is to develop a monitoring system based on an understanding of the perspectives held during the creation of the governance system so that new risks will not be overlooked within the confines of a system designed before those risks ever existed. Monitoring systems within governance with Boomer or Gen-X Second Gens may be more complex with the greater number of risks to monitor but they will be more flexible, as well.

Setting up the monitoring system can become a family-wide project or the project of a voluntary committee with the aid of a professional consultant. Involving the family in identifying risks can be a joint educational effort with professionals and would also be a project that could involve junior boards. This would be an excellent way to get family members actively working together and to deliver vital education through a venue that would be well received.

What is different this time

Despite the economic backdrop at the time of this writing, the numbers of the wealthy continue to increase. The innovative opportunities for starting wealth-generating enterprises are growing exponentially. A generational sea change is underway. The next Greatest Generation is growing up in the midst of this vast opportunity. They are growing up speaking its language. They are eager to learn and eager to please. In the midst of a Fourth Turning, time is of the essence to teach them what they need to know to be good family leaders.

Current Second Gen leadership is uniquely positioned to foster the flourishing of the entire family wealth portfolio. Handler agrees that the second generation is absolutely pivotal in the long-term success of the family. 'The businesses are no longer fledgling; the family now has large portfolios, and the steps they take can either turbo charge everything in the right direction or send it abysmally down the sink. Often this newfound wealth is a huge opportunity because it's probably the first time anyone in the family has had enough capital to either make a mess or to do things very well. Generally, it takes a certain critical amount of capital to responsibly take the sort of risks that can build large estates. They have the opportunity and the time, they likely attended the best schools, and they can afford the best professional advisors. So, yes, they are absolutely pivotal.'

The beginning chapter of this book sets forth the dilemma each second generation faces in stewarding the founder's dream or in pursuing their own dreams. Hughes notes that the first generation's efforts to impose its own dreams on the lives of its children is based not on the first generation's understanding of the child's dream but on the first generation's desire to live out the remainder of its dreams through the lives of its children. This comes at the expense of bringing the personal dream to life of that human being. The authentic role of the parents, regardless of the chronological generation of the child, is to help the spirits of their children 'emerge into their own journeys'.[23] The journey being spoken of is the path toward the child's authentic wealth.

Now that we have established the importance of the second generation, we go back to ask another question: Who is responsible for preparing the second generation for this extremely pivotal role? When history is viewed as a cyclical progression of generations, each generation can link itself to ancestors who have gone before and to heirs who will follow after. Each generation will discover its own path across time. Whatever our archetypical persona – Silent, Boomer, Gen-X, or Echo – 'we can locate our rendezvous with destiny, seize our script, make of it what we can, and evaluate our performance against the legendary myths and traditional standards of civilization. The seasons of time offer no guarantees'.[24] The script of Second Gen becomes the script of the entire family. It becomes what we make of it, discovering our authentic role and using our authentic wealth within the supportive safety net of family or succumbing to the assigned role of stewarding another's dream in a space that is never really comfortable.

Thus, the task of ensuring the health of a family's generations falls to the first generation – the creators of the material wealth that now dominates every aspect of family life. It is the task of the first generation to do something even more generative than it did in creating this material wealth. Its task now is to turn around and say to its children, 'What is your dream and how can I enhance its coming to life?'[25]

The ability of parents to do this requires a base level understanding of the journey their children must travel to the fruition of their authentic wealth. The generational archetypes offer us the opportunity to obtain this understanding. Becoming well versed in the archetypes of larger society will enable us to see how they are playing out in our smaller society of family. We can then overlay the chronological generational perspectives, beginning with the Second Gen, to guide us in educating heirs about the responsibilities that go along with their roles without imposing our own ideas of what they should be doing with their lives.

Are Second Gens different across cultures?

The second generation is expected to carry on the founders' dream, more so in some cultures than in others, as we have seen. But there are families in all cultures for which this is still an entrenched and unquestioned Second Gen yin/yang phenomenon. In Asian and other very patriarchal cultures, it is a great departure from their cultural traditions to consider stewarding the child's dream. The expectation is deeply entrenched that the eldest son, in particular, will follow the dream of the father and take over after the father is gone.

In some traditionally patriarchal cultures, however, this dynamic seems to be changing, although at different rates. As we noted in Chapters 6 and 7, Latin American and Middle Eastern countries are experiencing a shift, depending upon the specific country's adoption of modern ways of life. The greatest changes seem to be in the ability for second generation women to be the stewards of the father's dream rather than the sons! Although this is probably true for only a small portion of families, more women have the freedom to start businesses of their own completely separate from the family business and to be involved in business matters in some way. Although most are still kept out of traditional leadership roles, many are being allowed greater involvement in leadership roles which are below those of the patriarch.

Hughes says Hispanic and Islamic cultures actually think deeply about the question of their children's dreams. The culturalisation from their fathers and grandfathers was about stewarding the father's and grandfather's dreams regardless of any financial wealth. The greatest problem in Asian families is when the patriarch tries to maintain power for himself by creating a competitive environment among his children so that their dreams are never even considered.[26]

The impact of the Second Gen is felt in different ways within families of wealth of all cultures. Its influence is coloured by its archetypical perspectives as well as its position on the chronological generational progression. Regardless of culture, the impact of the Echo generation is being felt across the globe. They are the most connected generation in history. Therefore, their vast numbers increase their collective power exponentially. They are better educated, more ethnically diverse, and have greater wealth. They have recast the image of global youth into an upbeat and engaged group of young people.[27] Early birth spectrum members of this generation are now in their mid to late twenties. They have the power to heroically lead us out of the Fourth Turning crisis and into a new High. They also have the ability to become trapped by conformity and by the group think that revolves around their attraction to teams, networking, and their constant access to technology. In less than another generation's time, the first Echoes will begin assuming leadership in families of wealth.

I believe we are in the beginning of an unprecedented transition to a different dynamic in families of wealth. It is being led by the Echo generation. Its reach will be far greater than the Boomer's reach after World War II. Paving the way are their Gen-X generation predecessors who will exhibit leadership qualities which will be surprising to many.

Understanding the critical nature of Second Gen archetypical perspectives will offer families great insight into how they can tap into the tremendous authentic wealth rising before their eyes. Whatever the archetypical generational persona of the Second Gen, understanding the views of Second Gen leadership – either current, or in generations past – will equip families with the tools they need to greet this sea change enthusiastically and to more fully understand its impact on their futures. The Generational Wealth Management Continuum^{SM} provides a robust system which is fully customisable for any family's generational maze of perspectives. These perspectives open the door to awareness and recognition of an entirely new level of family wealth. Trust-level communication offers every family member the privileges of dynamic stakeholder ownership. The family virtues carry the family values across the threshold of generation after generation after generation.

With great power comes great responsibility. A wide swath of dynamic stakeholder owners within the ranks of a family of wealth could give families of wealth the heroic army they need to lead them through some of the greatest social and economic upheaval in history. Much more than that, the opportunity to witness a vast unfolding of authentic wealth across the family entity offers unprecedented opportunity to infuse the family spirit with new life, fostering the flourishing of the consummate family wealth portfolio across the globe.

---

[1] Hughes, James E., Jr., Personal interview, November 2007.

[2] Hughes, James E. Jr., Personal interview, November 2007. Hughes says that each of us has our own dreams and that it is impossible to adopt someone else's dream exactly as they did. We can choose to adopt their dream but we will reinterpret it in our own way. For more on stewarding another's dream, see 'Family: a compact among generations, (New York, NY: Bloomberg Press, 2007) pp. 192.

[3] 'Second Gen' is the service marked property of graymatter Strategies LLC.

[4] Hughes, James E., Jr., Personal interview, November 2007. In this conversation, the author and Hughes discussed the possibility of eliminating the proverbial third generation altogether. Hughes associates this possibility with the more authentic role of G1 to remember the child's spirit by 'helping that spirit emerge in its own journeys'. The author picks up on that theme here.

[5] Lucas, S.E. and Lansky, D., 'Managing Paradox,' *Family Business,* Spring 2010, pp. 68–70. Lucas delineates five paradoxes business families must face if they are to successfully inspire entrepreneurial stewardship.

    1 Values, skills, and attitudes of first generation to transfer power stand in sharp contrast to the skills they relied on to create the wealth in the first place.

    2 Family success ultimately resides in the hands of descendants and beneficiaries, not in the hands of the founding entrepreneur.

    3 To stay wealthy, each generation must become risk takers and wealth creators.

    4 Spending capacity demonstrates power in the short run; savings capacity sustains it in the long run.

    5 To keep a family together, it's best to set its members free.

[6] Dynamic stakeholder ownership is a term created by James E. Hughes, Jr. and is used throughout this book with his permission.

[7] Merriam-Webster Online Dictionary: www.merriam-webster.com/dictionary/stewardship

[8] Rosplock, Kirby, Ph.D., Personal interview, April 2007.

[9] Merriam-Webster Online Dictionary: http://mw4.merriam-webster.com/dictionary/revitalize

[10] Answers.com: www.answers.com/topic/revitalization.

[11] Hughes, J.E., Jr., *Family: a compact among generations,* (New York, NY: Bloomberg Press, 2007), p. 193.

[12] Ibid, p. 191.

[13] Lucas, S.E. and Lansky, D., 'Managing Paradox,' *Family Business,* Spring 2010, pp. 68–70.

[14] Ibid.

[15] Luscomb, Richard L. Ph.D, Clinical psychologist, Germantown Psychological Associates, P.C., Personal interview, February 2007.

[16] Strauss, W. and Howe, N., *The Fourth Turning: an American prophecy,* (New York, NY: Broadway Books, 1997), p. 324.

[17] Ibid, p. 325.

[18] Strauss, W. and Howe, N., *The Fourth Turning: an American prophecy,* (New York, NY: Broadway Books, 1997), p. 326.

[19] Hughes, J.E., Jr., *Family: a compact among generations,* (New York, NY: Bloomberg Press, 2007), p. 93.

[20] Ussery, Teddie, president, Family Matters LLC, Personal interview, November 2006.

[21] Strauss, William, and Howe, Neil, (1997). *The Fourth Turning: An American Prophecy,* Broadway Books, a division of Bantam Doubleday Dell Publishing Group, New York, NY, p. 326.

[22] Strauss, W. and Howe, N., *The Fourth Turning: an American prophecy,* (New York, NY: Broadway Books, 1997).

[23] Hughes, James E., Jr., Personal interview, November 2007.

[24] Ibid, p. 332.

[25] Hughes, James E., Jr., Personal interview, November 2007.

[26] Hughes, James E., Jr., Personal interview, August 2007.

[27] Strauss, W. and Howe, N., *Millennials Rising: the next Great Generation*, (New York, NY: Vintage, 2000), pp. 4, 5.

Epilogue

> 'What happens to each generation separately is only part of the picture; of more importance to history is what happens to generations together. They overlap like tiles on a roof, overlapping in time, corrective in purpose, complementary in effect, altering every aspect of society from government and the economy to culture and family life.'
>
> *William Strauss and Neil Howe*[1]

We began this journey with various translations of the famed Proverb that every family across the globe has come to know too well. If there is a single insight to be gained from the journey through this book, it would be the following: *the travesty of the Proverb is not that the third chronological generation has to go to work; it is that the spirit of family which is vital to the flourishing of the family's authentic assets disintegrates into oblivion.*

What would happen, I wonder, if we turned the edicts of the proverb around and learned to work with the laws of nature rather than against them? Would that prevent the material wealth we have worked so hard to accumulate from going through the proverbial black hole, leaving our third generation progeny to fend for themselves? Would it change our focus so that the spirit of family would replenish itself – and the material wealth – with the addition of each new generation to the family?

A black hole is commonly perceived as the place where matter diminishes into oblivion – in family wealth, we interpret this as the fulfilment of the edicts of The Proverb. But scientists are discovering that black holes are much more than 'trash incinerators' for dead stars.[2] In fact, black holes have been discovered to be a natural and necessary part of the regeneration process of the galaxies which make up our universe. Each galaxy has a black hole in its centre. As matter is drawn into the black hole, significant portions of the matter may be released in the form of energy. This energy enables the creation of new stars by expelling dust and gas out of the galaxy. The process of entropy creates cold clouds of gas, a prime ingredient in the creation of new stars through fusion.[3]

Hughes notes that entropy, the process described above, applies to all life. He refers to the second law of thermodynamics in stating that energy goes through a continuous cycle of transforming itself into matter through fusion, then back to pure energy through the deterioration of the bonds holding the atoms of matter together, or entropy. In applying this to families, he notes that the law of entropy 'dictates that the long-term preservation of any form of matter is impossible'. We can apply this to the fulfilment rate of the edicts of the Proverb. Left to follow its natural course with no purposeful direction, the fulfilment rate among families of wealth (the complete decomposition of the materialisation of dreams) will continue to be high. This realisation would seem to imply that families have no recourse, no hope of success.

But like the black hole, the Proverb assumes that there is an underlying force that connects each generation and, like gravity, pulls subsequent generations down towards demolition, thereby erasing any form of wealth the family once had. In this way, a family's destiny indeed can be compared to a black hole. Black holes have such strong gravitational force that, once close enough to the edge, the surrounding matter has no choice but to be mercilessly drawn into the centre of the abyss. What is particularly interesting about this analogy is, while this image forces us to contemplate impending doom, the element of choice is present and can introduce quite a different result.

Revitalisation of the family wealth

We begin to see the possibilities by examining what really happens when matter enters a black hole. Once the matter is drawn in, it is reconfigured and 'recycled' to create a massive force of energy that is beneficial to the galaxy in which it lives. In applying the analogy to families, we can then ask the questions, 'Are we powerless to avoid the effects of entropy or can we indeed work with them?' and 'Is there a possibility that the familial "black hole" will spit us out the other side to become newer, brighter stars?'

The answer to the second question is a resounding 'Yes!' Just as the energy from the decomposition of old stars is not lost, neither is the energy which diminishes in families through the law of entropy; it simply changes form. It follows the cycles of nature, which are often fought against in the name of 'progress' (linear, of course). Instead of fighting a battle we can never really win, we could accept the laws of nature, make them friends instead of enemies, and put them to advantageous use through the implementation of our knowledge about the generational maze.

Hughes further states, 'If we look at entropy as simply a natural law of this universe, then it really is neither positive nor negative. It's just true'.[4] This means that, like the seasons, entropy is neither 'good' nor 'bad'; it is a normative transformation. This realisation means that families *have a choice about which form the entropy in their family system takes.* Families can either allow the unguided course toward proverbial fulfilment or they can use the laws of entropy to their advantage by embracing each generational maze as the conduit to the fusion of relationships through altruistic communication and trust. This book is a call for families to discover the power they have within their own cycles of generations to work *with* the entropic laws of nature – not against them – to consciously make choices that foster regeneration and the reenergising of the family story.

I hope you have found the journey to be an interesting, productive, and enjoyable one. Most of all, I hope you will not let the journey end. And perhaps, one day, we will meet and share the stories of our experiences along the way.

---

[1] Strauss, W. and Howe, N., *The Fourth Turning: an American prophecy,* (New York, NY: Broadway Books, 1997), p. 99.

[2] O'Hanlon, L., 'Black hole simulation breaks ground,' *Discovery News,* July 2007.

[3] Ibid.

[4] Hughes, James E., Jr., Personal conversation, August 2007.

Appendix: generational attitudes of philanthropy

Philanthropy is a singular topic which can span the entire Generational Wealth Management Continuum[SM] or which can be absent from the management of the consummate family wealth portfolio. Not all families of wealth are philanthropic. Some families have mixed interest in philanthropy – some family members, including entire family units, may have more interest in philanthropy than others.

Philanthropy may be more pervasive in certain cultures than in others. For example, Europeans have not traditionally had the incentive for philanthropy through tax breaks and, depending on the country, it may be difficult for families to create a philanthropic foundation. As well, as we saw in Chapter 6, Europeans tend to be less vocal about their wealth for tax and other reasons. However, that trend may be changing. Some European bank customers are demanding assistance with their philanthropic planning and certain European governments may be considering a change in their laws to better support charitable giving in Europe. Some critics, especially in Germany, attribute the change with new efforts by families to protect the family business. However, more and more European families are taking a strategic approach to their philanthropic efforts.[1]

Although family foundations are predominant in the US, philanthropy is part of the family business in other cultures such as Latin America and Asia. According to Credit Suisse, family foundations in the US tend to give to environmental causes, animal welfare, health, religion, and social sciences and give less support to the arts, education, human services, and international and public affairs.[2]

Either family or corporate foundations offer families the opportunity to explore family history through the perspectives of each generation as well as the opportunity to foster trust-level communication. Regardless of the conduit, trust-level communication has to be a conscious objective of each family member so that generational differences may be appreciated and accepted for what they are rather than used as a tool to promote dysfunction.

In working with families of wealth, it is important to note that each family member's roles are as valuable to the family as another's. Regardless of the number and types of roles identified – even if those roles seem to be a negative influence on the family at the time – the roles each family member occupies become powerful tools by which the family can unify itself and foster trust-level communication.

A philanthropic focus holds the possibility for families to view these roles differently. It may provide a 'step-away' view which may not be quite as emotionally obstructed; then, again, it may not! Generational views on philanthropy can be as staunchly imprinted as any other generational view. Since the foundation will have a separate governance structure – particularly if it is a family foundation – it may offer an initial stepping stone for families who are not yet ready to adopt the three forms of governance structure laid out in this book. Through guided adoption of a more inclusive and egalitarian governance structure in the foundation, families may be able to 'try out' a more representative governance structure to see how it may work for them. If the foundation is part of the operating business, the three forms of governance structure can be applied to the differences in structure between the foundation and the business enterprise.

Depending on the success found within the philanthropic foundation, either family or corporate, the family may then wish to segue that success to the governance of the family, noting its conceptual separation from the business and family office governance systems.

Regardless, the recommendation for the three forms of governance structure is strong. If it is not something which is adaptable with the current family dynamics, it may prove to be an optimal path for the family to pursue over time. The natural generational shift will support this process. As we have seen in the earlier chapters of this book, cyclical change is a force which is present in our lives, whether or not it is recognised as such. Recognising, understanding, and cognitively choosing to work with the forces of nature rather than against them in linear fashion sets a family towards successful defeat of the famed Proverb.

Philanthropy as a generational education and communications tool

One reason foundations are such wonderful tools for families is the ease with which younger generations can become involved, gain hands-on experience, and develop valuable skills through a true apprenticeship under family leadership. They are also a structure through which younger generation family members have the opportunity to make decisions on their own, depending on the structural set-up the family has chosen. Families are not limited to a single philanthropic structure. They may have a family foundation which was set up by the original founders (GI) which G1 may use as a conduit for future generations to carry on the values they hold dear. In this case, it may be wise to set up other foundations either generationally based or individually based. These satellite foundations may be used as a testing ground for involvement in the larger family foundation.

Family use of foundations has become extremely flexible. I believe this is a result of the desire for families to include next generations in the process. Families fear a lack of interest by younger generations and the cyclical generational climate is such that strategies are forced to change in order to foster and keep younger generation interest. As a result, interest by families in employing foundations as educational tools and opportunities for skills and communication development has increased. The innovation with which families are using the foundation – either family or corporate – is a result of generational change.

Perspectives of American generations on philanthropy

A glimpse at the different perspectives of each generation toward philanthropy will serve to clarify differences and also to illuminate other generational changes that may be occurring within the family. This process innately fosters ways to address those differences in satisfactory fashion. Another factor in the evolution of philanthropy in America – also across the globe – has to do with the economic backdrop affecting each generation. The crisis of 2008 saw many charities lose their funding and disappear as a result. As we know, generational imprints are the result of both social and economic backdrop of the times in which people within the same generational birth spectrum come of age. Attitudes toward philanthropy are, therefore, also directly impacted by generational perspectives. Below are the comments from William Strauss on the economic backdrop for each generation.[3]

'There are two things happening now. One is that never in the history of America have we had so much relative wealth accumulated in the 60s and 70s brackets. People don't focus on the Silent generation enough. The Silents really are a generation – they were children once, too. But they have had a very lucky economic ride throughout their lives. They had no student loans and they were able to ride the wave of the GI Bill housing benefits. By the time they reached age 30, the vast majority of the males had already earned more than their own fathers ever had. They were the meteoric American Dream generation in terms of economics. They were there at the right time historically to do well and they have. So a lot of the accumulated assets in our country are theirs. Really, a larger number of them have done well than the GI generation, who is now in its 80s and 90s. Many of the GIs are dying and many of those estates have been become smaller than expected because of healthcare or other factors. But it's the Silents in their 60s and 70s who have the major legator money now.

'Boomers came along at a time when they could take large personal risks. They had the idea that the basic infrastructure of the economy was so solid, they could do their head tripping years and their rock band years and motorcycle across Mexico, then come back and at any point say, "Yeah, ok, now we'll get a job, now we'll get a house". There was always this feeling that everything was solid enough for them to come back to that at a later time.

'They still were only very lightly debt impacted. Around the Boomer rubric of choice and individualism and markets and institutional distrust and so on, we began developing the ethos which has led in large part to the spreading of economic outcomes among families. So now, you have a much larger percentage than ever of those who are in the top five percentile or the top half of one percentile. Those numbers are unusually high compared to other generations. What's key from a wealth management standpoint is the fact that our society has never before seen such a vast array of decadent millionaires. These aren't numbers which have been adjusted for inflation; it's more than Boomers searching for meaning in their lives. Much of the wealth was accumulated through real estate or financial management or through a variety of ways. However they try to justify it, it's still feels a little artificial to them. It's not like with other generations who say, "I've reached the end of my life, what did I do?" For Boomers, it's, "Well, I have all these commas and zeros ...."'

The philanthropic efforts of older generations such as the GIs and Silents often consisted of writing a cheque, particularly to a university or hospital – something on which their name could be affixed. Eileen Heisman, president and CEO of National Philanthropic Trust[4] observes that: 'The GI generation – the "Greatest Generation" that Tom Brokaw wrote about – didn't graduate from college until they got back from serving in World War II. They liked to give to big institutions which created their own sense of community within the communities in which they lived. So they gave to hospitals, universities, and churches. They loved brick-and-mortar campaigns.'

This coincides with the generational turnings identified by Strauss and Howe, noting that Hero generations favour institutions since they have been the reorganisers of established society. Artist archetypes are in leadership while that institutional focus is predominant and as its appeal begins to wane. By the time the Prophet archetype comes of age and gets involved, we see a very different attitude toward society and the institutions which were established by the Hero generation, most recently, the GI generation.

As a philanthropic professional, Heisman's observations confirm this development. '(The GI) generation gave birth to the Baby Boomers who are not brick-and-mortar oriented at all. They're very culturally oriented. They are willing to fund smaller, more cause-related organisations like Save the Whales, Planned Parenthood, and all the environmental organisations like Sierra Club and Hug A Tree and all of the women's organisations. They have supported more grass roots organisations, they didn't really care whether they saw a building built in their community. They wanted to see the impact of their gift – to right a wrong. It's very value driven as opposed to building a building.

'Now the Boomers are getting older and many are gravitating more to brick-and-mortar giving. But if you look at the Gates Foundation, he's not really building buildings. He's trying to eradicate diseases in developing countries – a very typical Boomer gift. They haven't been shy about starting non-profits. If they saw a cause, they'd start a non-profit for it.'

Strauss noted, 'Boomers are a little older than people think and their philanthropy is definitely different. They're asking "How do I make sure that it makes sense to give this and that it's not going to just disappear – that if I send it off to Tsunami aid, it won't just go off into some scandal or overhead?" So there's a quest for the personally discovered charity and often it's a matter of the Boomer having to be an individual entrepreneur in that regard. I think this is different from the Silents. The Silents are still institutional givers. They're still throwing money at these outrageously endowed universities and foundations and stuff. The Boomers are more reluctant to do that.'

He also noted that Boomer philanthropy is very personal. The Boomer generation has a greater tendency to adopt a personal cause. Older Boomers may be looking for meaningful ways to contribute in later life when they have more discretionary use of their time. By this time in their lives, they have built networks and skill sets which could support a personal philanthropic focus in addition to a family or corporate foundation in which they may also be involved. They begin to wonder about letting go of their money-making tasks and the impact they might be able to have – do they still have enough time at this age to make a difference?[5]

When it comes to younger generations, Heisman notes that, 'Gen-Xers are just now coming into their own. They're civic minded and they are having bigger families than the Boomer generation did. And as people are in their family-raising years, they don't really have time to volunteer. This is their most disengaged period. When you get out of that phase, you begin to have more discretionary income.

'The Echoes who grew up with Boomer parents have lived with these idealistic people. So far, their views look and feel more like their parents'. There are a lot of community service programs tapping into the Echoes but giving for that group isn't really clear at this point. They also are very willing to start non-profits. They define philanthropy differently – some of it is more social, some of it is more altruistic. You have a sense that the Echoes and the Boomers are more altruistic and the Gen-Xers (the group in the middle) are a little more social in their giving.'

New ways of giving foster generational collaboration

Foundations offer families the opportunity to unite around common ethics and values-based goals. From a generational standpoint, the question arises, 'What happens when all family members do not share those goals?' Kirby Rosplock, Ph.D. and director of research and development in Genspring's Innovation & Learning Center, notes, 'We're often times coming from such different frames of reference, it's no wonder our values and viewpoints are so divergent. Things just don't translate generation to generation'.

The governance system of a previously established foundation can offer younger generations a connection to their family's history. It can foster a sense of identity and purpose and guide them in developing their own philanthropic focus.[6] Generational perspectives can become a vital tool for the family in facilitating the development of philanthropic interest among younger generations. Particularly if younger generations are encouraged and enabled to reinterpret the values they have seen in their ancestors for themselves.

We discussed throughout the body of the book that a set of dynamics in the family which ignores this need for reinterpretation by each generation sets the family on a linear path which is directly aligned with the fulfilment of the Proverb. Recognition of these forces and a conscious decision to work with them rather than against them can have multiple ramifications throughout the consummate family wealth portfolio. Philanthropy can serve as a tool through which families can better come to terms with this cyclical realisation.

The fact that younger generations will not interpret the family values in the same way as older generations is not a threat to the value systems of older generations. Often, family generational lens of family leadership assigns this result when it is, in fact, their perception rather than reality. As in any other aspect of family wealth management, fresh ideas and views of younger generations may actually keep the philanthropic legacy alive, injecting new life and giving the value system greater meaning. This can also offer solidarity to the family unit.

Families across the globe are developing innovative solutions to addressing the issue of either developing or keeping younger generations' interest in philanthropy for the purpose of continuing a philanthropic legacy or for the purpose of continuing a tradition of giving, regardless of the focus. The family may develop individual philanthropic entities as well as the established family foundation. This can bring the family together for strategic planning purposes[7] to coordinate the development of these foundations with financial support dedicated to philanthropic purposes.

Such planning acts as a venue for clarifying responsibilities of dynamic stakeholder owners,[8] including the development of negotiating skills, financial management, working together as a team, and developing a common ground for trust-level communication to occur. Since philanthropy often is a common goal among generations, it naturally serves as a common area of interest through which trust-level communication can develop and subsequently spread to other areas of family interaction, most specifically joint decision making[9] around wealth management issues.

According to Credit Suisse, 'As each generation grows up with different experiences of the world, each can engage with the family's history in its own way'. They also note that younger generations have grown up in a cross-culture society where differences in race, sexual orientation, and culture are not a consideration. Their involvement in the world crosses global boundaries, giving them a broader skill set from which they ask different types of questions.

The new backdrop of the Echo generation, in particular, allows them to operate in more of a peer-to-peer environment rather than a parent-child environment, encouraging the development of their skills right before their parents' eyes and within the safety of a family values focused enterprise.[10] Both family and corporate foundations can serve as other outlets for family members who are not involved in the family business.[11] Along with the committees developed through the family governance system as outlined in Chapter 11, philanthropic entities can augment the achievement of the family's goals. When coordinated within the Generational Wealth Management process, they can serve as vital tools in guiding families toward the discovery of an optimal path through which their wealth of all forms may flourish from generation to generation to generation.

Philanthropic generational perspectives of women

Women have always been involved in philanthropy through volunteering their time as well as in giving monetarily. In this time of rapid and seismic generational change, women's giving is impacting philanthropy like never before. Genspring's 2006 Women and Wealth study[12] showed that women allocate 20% of their wealth to philanthropy compared to a 4% allocation by men although both genders ranked philanthropic giving as a critically important. It also showed that 42% of women participants inherited their wealth while another 29% had become wealthy through their spouse's employment.[13]

Generational attitudes toward giving have seen a significant shift over recent generations. Women who were members of earlier generations grew up in a time when money simply was not a topic for discussion. Wealthy women in the 19th century volunteered for organisations aiding soldiers in times of war or providing assistance to widows and children. As the 20th century drew closer, organisations were created specifically to address women's causes. Being a volunteer during this era was an acceptable role for women. Later, women's voluntarism began to be viewed with less esteem.[14] A carryover from this view was part of the case study example in Chapter 16.

Today, women of inherited wealth as well as women entrepreneurs are significant donors to philanthropic causes. Their influence is rising as not only as their wealth increases and they give to philanthropic causes, but also because more women are board members and directors, directors of fund raising activities, and managers of nonprofit organisations.

Gifting from women, especially in older generations, tends to be done under the radar. Heisman notes, 'For example, a woman who died ten years ago was a secretary, yet she left a $1 million bequest to an art museum. These are the quiet people – sometimes the charities don't even know who they are.'

Older generation women also grew up in a time when women in the workplace were a rarity. In earlier generations, many women did volunteer work along with raising their children and caring for their homes. 'The [Silents] had a different lens – there was a different mentality about everything from the conventions of marriage to how the family system was supposed to operate to roles and responsibilities. And all of that plays into the way a family views these issues regardless of the level of wealth,' says Rosplock.

According to a 2007 study,[15] philanthropic giving through a family foundation doubled in the Boomer and Gen-X generations over previous generations. The study indicates that both genders are more philanthropically minded than earlier generations. Rosplock's study noted that the family foundation has grown as the vehicle of choice based on the tax benefits foundations offer and the growing trend of families to give as an entity. Since more women in the study grew up in upper-middle class homes where charitable giving was more common, more women than men regard the families in which they grew up as philanthropic. Referring to the results found in her 2006 study, Rosplock observes: 'The quantitative piece I thought was interesting was just how much more information is being exchanged now in families versus how more closed women indicated their families were. The bulk of these women were in the Boomer generation so the majority of data is probably reflecting the attitudes of a [Silent] family of origin.'

Another study cites the fact that the economic and social position of a woman used to be determined by her husband's wealth. Often, philanthropic gifts were made to protect the class status of the family through gifts to universities and art museums.[16]

As new generations of women have come into their own, philanthropy has felt the result. Female participants in the 2007 study were significantly more likely to leave a philanthropic legacy through their estates than men. Men indicated they prefer giving to individuals or organisations with which they are familiar rather than a less specific cause or pool of money. The propensity to serve on community boards was similar to that of previous generations.

In conclusion

As with so many other topics within the pages of this book, philanthropy is a topic which easily commands much more lengthy treatment. With that in mind, I would leave you with the following thoughts.

Philanthropy can be an even more powerful tool for family success when employed within the philosophies set forth in the Generational Wealth Management process. The process also does not mandate a philanthropic focus to be a successful guide on its own merit. Rather, it offers families the opportunity to choose effective methods of fostering all forms of their wealth and philanthropy is simply one of the tools which lend themselves to that purpose.

Whatever path a family chooses, it is vital to realise the nature of the cyclical generational forces at work. In today's turbulent times, generational forces have particular relevance. Strauss notes this 'has a great deal to do with what we wrote about with the Fourth Turning. You have to understand where the societal mood is going and what is it that you can do to provide meaning in a world in which order and security are paramount over free expression. Family counts more and reputation counts more; there may be more anxiety about global events; there may be more sacrifice but other things happen. You look at some of the behavioral characteristics of Americans over the past 20 years, how they do less outdoor activities, visit national parks less, they throw baseballs less, they bicycle less because they're all busy doing their individual thing. And in a Fourth Turning environment, the sense of community and infrastructure and team and civic purpose and traditional values – honor, loyalty, service – these things resurrect'.

I personally do not think that these values are restricted to American society. As the influence of the Echo generation is being felt across the globe, so are the responses of and toward the Echo generation. Families in all cultures have felt the effects of the latest crisis of 2008. Some economic experts have cited this crisis as ushering in a new economic structure – certainly a confirming 'great event' to the ushering in of the Fourth Turning through 9/11. Philanthropy can be a wonderful tool with which to prepare the next Heroes – the Echo generation – to impact family wealth success within such an environment.

Strauss expresses this concern: 'So how does this prepare our Millennial [Echo] heroes to perform their role and save us all? We educate them well, we have confidence in them, try to not burden them so much with debt so they're able to express themselves. Try to not have them splinter into haves and have nots which is happening. It's not so much haves and have nots, it's the very affluent versus the working class. If you look at what's happened to Gen X for example, it's not that the bottom quartile has done that badly, it's the two middle courses – the shrinking of the middle class.'

Heisman adds, 'There are a lot of people with very big hearts who want to make the world a better place. Anyone who understands social problems realises that if you ignore the have-nots and pretend they're not there, you're going to pay for it sometime – in taxes, crime, and depressed housing. If people aren't educated and they can't work, they find unpleasant ways of supporting themselves or they do drugs. So you pay for it in social programs. It's a very smart investment to try to bridge those gaps – it's brilliant, really. So in some ways, they're taking their excess capital and investing it very wisely. A lot of the folks doing this are young.'

Families of wealth are well positioned to enjoy the benefits of all forms of their wealth. Some families may find philanthropy to be a wealth management tool which serves them well from multiple perspectives including personal fulfilment, carrying forward a family legacy and values system, giving back to society, and as a unifying venue across the family's generational maze.

Heisman concludes, 'If you think of the things that make you feel really, really good, one of those things, obviously, is providing for your family. But making the world better does make you feel really good. Philanthropy is never going to go away from wealthy families – it's here to stay. They know they will be richer for it and that it's also better for the family and for the community at large. Philanthropy has been part of American life since America was founded and it's only going to increase. It's fascinating to watch.'

The spread of philanthropy across the globe and the impact of the Echo generation upon it is fascinating indeed. Perhaps its influence on family wealth success through the bringing together of the generational perspectives of each family's generational maze will be a topic for a future treatise.

---

[1] Bishop, M., 'Giving: Europe gets the bug', *The Economist, Intelligent Life* magazine, August 2008: http://moreintelligentlife. com/story/giving-europe-gets-the-bug.

[2] 'Funding as a family: engaging the next generation in family philanthropy'. Research conducted by Institute for Philanthropy for Credit Suisse, 2010.

[3] The next four paragraphs are directly taken from a personal interview with William Strauss, October 2007.

[4] Heisman, Eileen, Personal interview, February 2007.

[5] Strauss, William, Personal interview, October 2007.

[6] 'Funding as a family: engaging the next generation in family philanthropy'. Research conducted by Institute for Philanthropy for Credit Suisse, 2010, p. 8.

[7] Ibid, p. 11.

[8] Dynamic Stakeholder Ownership is a term created by James E. Hughes, Jr. and is used throughout this book with his permission.

[9] The term 'joint decision making' was created by James E. Hughes, Jr. and is used throughout this book with his permission.

[10] 'Funding as a family: engaging the next generation in family philanthropy'. Research conducted by Institute for Philanthropy for Credit Suisse, 2010, p. 14.

[11] Ibid, p. 20.

[12] Rosplock, K.,'Women and wealth,' Genspring Family Offices LLC, 2006.

[13] Tomson, T., 'Women and philanthropy,' *The League,* Center on Philanthropy, Indiana University, Women's Philanthropy Institute: www.women-philanthropy.org. This paper was developed by a student taking a Philanthropic Studies course taught at the Center on Philanthropy at Indiana University. It is offered by *Learning To Give* and the Center on Philanthropy at Indiana University: http://learningtogive.org/papers/paper69.html.

[14] Ibid.

[15] Rosplock, K., 'Wealth alignment study,' GenSpring Family Offices LLC, 2008.

[16] Davidson, E., 'Women's philanthropy in the United States: trends and developments,' City University of New York, 1999.

Acknowledgements

Writing a book is a very fulfilling and humbling experience. Like the family businesses which have created the wealth that is its inspiration, this book could never have been written without the generous contributions of many others. After making so many requests of them and after unfailing responses not only with what I needed but when I needed it, I attempt now to thank you all.

The process of expressing gratitude becomes quite challenging when one considers the magnitude of what has been given. How do I begin to thank Jay Hughes and Jean Brunel who have so generously shared their work and so graciously shared their time, their invaluable guidance, expertise, and experience as well as immense patience, wisdom, and encouragement all along the way? They have travelled a long journey with me in the writing of this book!

I would like to express special gratitude to the late William Strauss and his co-author Neil Howe who together have given us the tremendous gift of generational awareness through their many books and writings on generations and the common personas which infiltrate every aspect of their members' lives. I was honoured to interview Bill a couple of months before he passed away and I am immensely grateful to Neil for his feedback and guidance on the generational portions of the work.

To the families who have openly shared their stories – the Laird Norton family, the Mulliez family, and particularly, the John R. family – in hopes of inspiring other families in their efforts to make wealth of all forms the gift that it was meant to be, I thank you immensely. It is a particular honour when families offer the lessons of their mistakes as well as of their incredible successes. The contributions of other family members and advisors who wish to remain anonymous receive a special thank you for their insights, without which the book could never offer as robust a view.

To my many colleagues – my wonderful professional friends – who shared their time, expertise, and guidance with me through interviews and conversations and by putting me in contact with excellent resources to make my research more complete – there are so many of you! Jean and Jay are again included in this group along with Meir Statman, Barbara Hauser, Kirby Rosplock, May Makhzoumi, M.J. Rankin, Linda Mack, Tom Handler, Jon Carroll, Teddie Ussery, Phyllis Tickle, Laird Koldyke, Jeff Vincent, Chalan Colby, Nathalie Simsak, Regis Mulliez, Roy Williams, Richard L. Luscomb, Eileen Heisman, Salim Omar, John Sandwick, Michael Gassner, John Benevides, Joline Godfrey, Don Herrema, Joshua Pianko, Natasha Pearl, Pierre-Alain Wavre, Vera Boissier, Grégoire Imfeld, Patricia Angus, John P.C. Duncan, Dr. Dan Carlin, Christopher Falkenberg, Joe Field, Kristin Ogdon, Michael Pompian, and Mark Blumenthal. Thank you, all.

Nothing can match the patience and forbearance of my editor, Sanjeevi Perera at Euromoney Books. Thank you, Sanjeevi, for making this publication possible.

To my daughter Adrianne and my son-in-law, Tripp, thank you for your continual encouragement and support and for the inspiration you gave me all the way through to completion.

About the author

LISA GRAY consults with domestic and international families and their advisors on the direct influence of generational perspectives, family dynamics, and governance on wealth management decisions. Lisa has 22 years' experience in the wealth management industry and is the founder and managing member of graymatter Strategies LLC. Based on her experience in working with families of wealth combined with her research and consulting experience through graymatter, she developed the proprietary diagnostic Wealth Optimisation Consulting™ model of service presented in her first book, *The New Family Office: innovative strategies for consulting to the affluent* published by Euromoney Books in 2004. The concept more accurately guides families and their advisors on the journey toward optimality in their relationships as well as in wealth management.

Lisa is certified in a programme designed to guide families in discovering their own solutions to the issues they face, helping families develop pathways that contribute significantly to their long-term success. Her broad-based years of experience offer a singular approach to private family, financial institution, and wealth advisor education and have positioned her as a sought-after media resource for the wealth management industry on family advisory and family office-related matters. She is a regular contributor to *The Journal of Wealth Management*, a member of the CFA Institute's Retained Speaker Program, and a frequent speaker and author on family office and wealth management topics. She teaches courses to advisors in Europe, Asia, and the Middle East for Euromoney Training. Lisa has worked with families of wealth all over the world including Europe, the Middle East, Asia, and Canada as well as in her native America. Her work was referenced significantly by a Wharton Global Family Alliance Report on single family offices published in May 2008. *The New Family Office* topped Euromoney Books' best seller list in May 2010.

Bibliography

'The long way to women's right to vote': http://history-switzerland.geschichte-schweiz.ch/chronology-womens-right-vote-switzerland.html; also 'Women's suffrage: a world chronology of the recognition of women's rights to vote and to stand for election': www.ipu.org/wmn-e/suffrage.htm.

Adler, M.J., *How To Think About The Great Ideas: from the great books of Western Civilization,* (Peru, IL: Open Court, 2000)

Adler, M.J., 'Aristotle's *Ethics*: the theory of happiness II', the Mortimer J. Adler archive: http://radicalacademy.com/adleraristotleethics2.htm.

Aldrich, N.W. Jr., *Old Money: the mythology of wealth in America,* (New York, NY: Allworth Press, 1996).

Alvarez-Holmberg, A., 'Using generational perspectives at work', Media Communications Association International, MN: www.mcai-mn.org/resources/articles_generations_0412.html.

Baker, C., 'Position of women in Chinese history', BellaOnline, the Voice of Women, 2010: www.bellaonline.com/articles/art29973.asp.

Brizendine, L., *The Female Brain,* (New York, NY: Morgan Road Books, 2006): www.morgan-roadbooks.com.

Brockner, J., Siegel, P.A., Daly, J.P., Martin, C., Tyler, T., 'When trust matters: the moderating effect of outcome favorability', *Administrative Science Quarterly,* September 1997: http://findarticles.com/p/articles/mi_m4035/is_n3_v42/ai_20345588/.

Broughton, P.D., 'The rise of Japan's 'Girlie Man' generation', *Timesonline, The Times,* November 5 2009. www.timesonline.co.uk/tol/life_and_style/men/article6903043.ece.

Brown, P.L., 'Growing old together, in a new kind of commune', *The New York Times,* February 27 2006.

Brunel, J.L.P., *Integrated Wealth Management,* 2nd edition, (London: Euromoney Books, 2006).

Chartered Management Institute, 'Victor H. Vroom: motivation and leadership decision making, *Thinkers,* March 1 2002; www.accessmylibrary.com/coms2/summary_0286-25331792_ITM.

Clark, P., *The Chinese Cultural Revolution: a history,* (New York, NY: Cambridge University Press, 2008).

Covey, S.M.R., *The Speed of Trust,* (New York, NY: Simon and Schuster, 2006).

Das, S., Markowitz, H., Scheid, J., Statman, M., 'Portfolio optimization with mental accounts,' *Journal of Financial and Quantitative Analysis,* Vol. 45, No. 2, April 2010.

Deen, T., 'Women: reservations grow over UN Women's Treaty', *World News,* Inter Press Service, March 2010: http://web.archive.org/web/20040423160533/http://www.oneworld.org/ips2/mar98/unwomen.html.

Egerton, J., *Generations: an American family,* 20th anniversary edition (Lexington, KY: The University Press of Kentucky, 2003).

Ehlern, S., 'Family offices in Europe and the United States – a different evolution with common objectives', (Zurich: Ferguson Partners Family Office, private yearbook, Zurich 2008).

Ehlern, S., 'Global private wealth management: an international study on private wealth management and family office services for high net worth individuals', doctoral study (London, Zurich: Ferguson Partners Family Office, 2006–2007).

Ehlern, S., Who needs a family office? *Private Wealth Management*, 2007, pp. 60–3.

Ehlers, M., 'What's up with Gen Y?: Here comes a group that rivals the boomers'. *The News & Observer,* February 5 2006: www.newsobserver.com/690/story/396515.html.

Encyclopedia Britannica, *History and Society: Modernisation,* Encyclopedia Britannica, 2006–2009: www.britannica.com/EBchecked/topic/387301/modernization.

Erikson, T., 'Generational differences between India and the US', *Harvard Business Review* Blog, February 2009.

Fernea, E.W., *'The Family in the Middle East'*, Center for Middle Eastern Studies, The University of Texas at Austin, 1984–2009.

Fiorani, F., *New Illustrated History of World War II: rare and unseen photographs 1939–1945*, (Newton Abbott: David & Charles, 2005): www.amazon.com/New-Illustrated-History-World-War/dp/0715321021/ref=pd_bbs_sr_2/104-7149888-1235964?ie=UTF8&s=books&qid=118887200 0&sr=1-2.

Forsyth, D.R., *Group Dynamics,* 4th international edition*,* (Stamford, CT: Thomson Wadsworth, 2006); Professor, endowed chair in ethical leadership, Jepson School of Leadership Studies, University of Richmond: www.richmond.edu/%7Edforsyth/gd/; www.amazon.com/Group-Dynamics-4th-International-2006/dp/B001T42J32/ref=sr_1_2?s=books&ie=UTF8&qid=1281910 440&sr=1-2.

Glenn, E.N., *Issei, Nisei, War Bride: three generations of Japanese American women*, (Philadelphia, PA: Temple University Press, 1986).

Goodman, D., 'The struggle for women's equality in Latin America,' *Dissident Voice,* March 2009: http://dissidentvoice.org/2009/03/the-struggle-for-womens-equality-in-latin-america/.

Goody, J., *The European Family*, (Malden, MA: Blackwell, 2000).

Gray, L., 'Generational perspectives and their effects on goal-based allocation,' *The Journal of Wealth Management*, Spring, 2006.

Gray, L., *The New Family Office: innovative strategies for consulting to the affluent,* (London: Euromoney Institutional Investor, 2004): www.euromoneybooks.com.

Greenspan, S., 'Fooled by Ponzi (and Madoff): how Bernard Madoff made off with my money', *eSkeptic*, the email newsletter of the Skeptics Society, December 23 2008: www.skeptic.com/eskeptic/08-12-23.

Hardach, S., 'Japan's big spenders flaunt their new wealth,' *The New York Times,* January 6 2008: www.nytimes.com/2008/01/06/business/worldbusiness/06iht-rtrfeature.9035419.html?_r=1&pagewanted=2.

Hauser, B.R., 'The Next Generation and the pursuit of happiness: Part One', *The Journal of Wealth Management,* Fall 2005.

Hauser, B.R., 'A child's "station in life": inheritance rights and expectations,' *Journal of Wealth Management,* Winter 2001.

Hauser, B.R., 'Family governance: using junior boards for the successful continuation of family businesses in the Gulf Region,' *Arab News,* February 2010.

Hausner, L., *Children of Paradise: successful parenting for prosperous families*, (Los Angeles, CA: Tarcher, 1990).

Hausner, L. and Freeman, D.K., *The Legacy Family*, (New York, NY: St. Martin's Press, 2009).

Hicks, K., *Boomers, Xers, and Other Strangers: understanding the generational differences that divide us*, (Wheaton, IL: Tyndale House, 1999).

Howe, N. and Strauss, W., *Generations: the history of America's future, 1584 to 2069*, (New York, NY: Morrow/Quill, 1991): www.lifecourse.com/books.html.

Howe, N. and Strauss, W., 'The new generation gap,' Part I, *The Atlantic Online,* December 1992: www.theatlantic.com/issues/92dec/9212genx.html.

Hughes, J.E. Jr., *Family Wealth: keeping it in the family,* (New York, NY: Bloomberg Press, 2004).

Jaffe, D.T., 'Stewardship in your family enterprise', (Pioneer imprints, 2010), p. 28: www.pioneer-imprints.com.

'Japan 1990 – United States of America 2006: the past as a window on the future, Part 1 of 5': www.gold-eagle.com/editorials_05/joubert031106.html.

Jolivet, M., 'The sirens of Tokyo', *The Courier UNESCO,* July/August 2001: www.unesco.org/courier/2001_07/uk/doss21.htm.

Kanov, J.M., Teaching notes for University of Michigan Business School course, 'OBHRM 501: human behavior and organizations', Class 6, May 19 2003, taught by Jane E. Dutton.

Kearl, M.C., 'Self types and their differences across generations and the life-cycle,' Trinity University, San Antonio, TX, Fall 2010: www.trinity.edu/mKearl/socpsy-6.html.

Kelly, J. and Nadler, S., 'Leading from below', *The Wall Street Journal*, March 3 2007, p. R4.

Lareau, A., *Unequal Childhoods: class, race, and family life*, (Los Angeles, CA: University of California Press, 2003).

Lasch, C., *Revolt of the Elites and the Betrayal of Democracy*, (New York, NY: W.W. Norton, 1996).

Lucas, S.E. and Lansky, D., 'Managing paradox', *Family Business,* Spring 2010, pp. 68–70.

Mannheim, K., 'The problem of generations,' *Psychoanalytic Review,* 57, 1970, pp. 378–404.

Margolis, D.R., 'Women's movements around the world: cross-cultural comparisons', *Gender and Society*, 1993, p. 381: www.jstor.org/stable/189799.

Márquez, H., 'Women's rights laws – where's the enforcement?', *IPS News*, May 2010: http://ipsnews.net/news.asp?idnews=50560.

Mathews, G. and White, B., (2004). *Japan's Changing Generations: are young people creating a new society?* (New York, NY: Routledge, 2004).

McCurry, J., 'Japan's Prime Minister Yukio Hatoyama resigns,' guardian.co.uk, June 2 2010. www.guardian.co.uk/world/2010/jun/02/japan-prime-minister-yukio-hatoyama-resigns.

Minuchin, S. and Fishman, H.C., 'Family therapy techniques,' President and fellows of Harvard College, 1981 and 1996.

Montgomery, H. and Shimizutani, S., 'The effectiveness of bank recapitalization in Japan,' Asian Bank Development Institute, 2005: www.apeaweb.org/confer/hito05/papers/montgomery_shimizutani.pdf.

Mui, Y.Q., 'Women a big force in business, study finds,' *The Washington Post,* October 2009: http://www.washingtonpost.com/wp-dyn/content/article/2009/10/02/AR2009100205317.html.

Niklos, R. 'Commentary: succession planning creates business continuum', *Daily Journal of Commerce,* March 4 2008.

O'Hanlon, L., 'Black hole simulation breaks ground,' *Discovery News,* July 2007.

Ogg, J., 'The Baby Boomer generation and family support: a European perspective', 2006: www.icsw.org/doc/0041_5e_Ogg_Eng_Abstract.doc.

Pearlman, E., (2006). 'Robert I. Sutton: making a case for evidence-based management', *CIO Insight,* Ziff Davis, 6 February 2006: www.cioinsight.com/article2/0,1540,1930244,00.asp.

Pompian, M.M., *Advising Ultra-Affluent Clients and Family Offices*, (Hokoben, NJ: John Wiley & Sons, 2009).

Pompian, M.M., *Behavioral Finance and Wealth Management*, (Hoboken, NJ: John Wiley and Sons, 2006).

Press Release, 'Research reveals affluent women taking control of their wealth,' *Trusts and Estates*, May 2009: http://trustsandestates.com/press_release/affluent-women-taking-wealth.

Roland, A., *In Search of Self in India and Japan*, In: 'A sociological social psychology: self-types and their differences across generations and the life cycle', (Trinity University, Fall 2001): www.trinity.edu/mkearl/socpsy-6.html.

Rubino, J., 'The importance of self esteem in the treatment of drug, alcohol, and other addictions,' Treatment Centers, March 2010: www.treatment-centers.net/self-esteem.html.

Salles, V. and Tuirán, R., *The Family in Latin America: a gender approach*, (New York, NY: Sage Social Science Collections, 1997), p. 151: http://csi.sagepub.com/cgi/content/abstract/45/1/141.

Seltzer, L.F., 'Child entitlement abuse: how parents inadvertently harm their children, Part I,' *Psychology Today*, September 2009: www.psychologytoday.com/blog/evolution-the-self/200909/child-entitlement-abuse-how-parents-inadvertently-harm-their-children.

Sillerman, L.B., 'Generations of women moving history forward,' Women's Voices for Change, March 2007: http://womensvoicesforchange.org/generations-of-women-moving-history-forward.htm.

Spencer, P., 'Shirtsleeves to shirtsleeves in three generations,' *Pennsylvania Fiduciary Litigation,* Spencer Law Firm, July 18 2008.

Statman, M., 'What is behavioral finance', in: Fabozi, F., editor, *The Handbook of Finance*, (Hoboken, NJ: John Wiley & Sons, 2008).

Statman, M. and Weng, J.A., 'Investments across cultures: financial attitudes of Chinese-Americans,' Santa Clara University Research, November 2009: www.scu.edu/business/finance/research/statman_research.cfm.

Stoltz, J., 'Communication key to cross-generational relationships', *The Business Ledger,* September 2008: www.thebusinessledger.com/Home/Archives/CommentaryViewpoints/tabid/86/newsid415/478/Communication-key-to-cross-generational-relationships/Default.aspx.

Strauss, W. and Howe, N., *The Fourth Turning: an American prophecy* (New York, NY: Broadway Books, 1997).

Strauss, W. and Howe, N., *Millennials Rising: the next Great Generation*, (New York, NY: Vintage Books, 2000).

Strogatz, S., 'Change we can live with', *The New York Times*, April 2010.

Strouse, J., *Morgan: American financier*, (New York, NY: Random House, 1999).

Tsutagawa, K., 'Baby Boomers' retirement poses problems', *The Daily Yomiuri,* July 6 2004. www.globalaging.org/pension/world/2004/boomers.htm.

Twist, L., *The Soul of Money*, (New York, NY: W.W. Norton & Co., 2006).

US Library of Congress, 'Traditional family life': http://countrystudies.us/south-korea/38.htm.

Ward, J.L., *Perpetuating the Family Business: 50 lessons learned from long lasting, successful families in business,* (New York, NY: Palgrave Macmillan, 2004).

Williams, R. and Peisser, V., *Preparing Heirs,* (San Francisco, CA: Robert D. Reed, 2003).

Willmington Trust and Campden Research in association with Relative Solutions, 'The New Wealth Paradigm: how affluent women are taking control of their futures', 40 participants between the ages of 40 and 65, minimum net worth of $25 million with at least one child. Fall 2008.

Woronoff, J., (1991). *Japan As – Anything But – Number One*, (Armonk, NY: M.E. Sharpe, 1991).

Yang, S-h., 'A letter from a man of my father's generation', *The Chosun Ilbo,* January 2010.